RELIGIOUS INNOVATION IN AFRICA

*Collected Essays on
New Religious Movements*

RELIGIOUS INNOVATION IN AFRICA

Collected Essays on
New Religious Movements

HAROLD W. TURNER

G.K.HALL&CO.
70 LINCOLN STREET, BOSTON, MASS.

Copyright © 1979 by Harold W. Turner

Library of Congress Cataloging in Publication Data

Turner, Harold W
    Religious innovation in Africa.

    Bibliography: p.
    Includes index.
    1. Africa—Religion—Addresses, essays, lectures.
I. Title.
BL2400.T85   200'.96   78–10215
ISBN 0–8161–8303–1

This publication is printed on permanent/durable acid-free paper
MANUFACTURED IN THE UNITED STATES OF AMERICA

to

ANDREW FINLAY WALLS

who accepted the earliest of these essays
for publication, and has encouraged all
that followed

Contents

INTRODUCTION ix

A. INTRODUCTORY AND GENERAL

   1. New Religious Movements in Primal Societies   3
   2. African Prophet Movements   15
   3. A New Field in the History of Religions   21

B. METHODOLOGICAL AND BIBLIOGRAPHICAL

   4. Problems in the Study of African Independent Churches   35
   5. The Approach to Africa's Religious Movements   49
   6. A Methodology for Modern African Religious Movements   63
   7. A Typology for African Religious Movements   79
   8. The Study of New Religious Movements in Africa, 1968–1975   109

C. HISTORICAL

   9. Pentecostal Movements in Nigeria   121
   10. The Late Sir Isaac Akinyele, Olubadan of Ibadan   129
   11. Prophets and Politics: A Nigerian Test-Case   133
   12. African Religious Movements and Roman Catholicism   147

D. RELIGIOUS CASE STUDIES

   13. Searching and Syncretism: A West African Documentation   159
   14. Pagan Features in West African Independent Churches   165

CONTENTS

15. Patterns of Ministry and Structure Within Independent Churches in Post-Colonial Africa ... 173
16. The Spirituality of Independent African Churches ... 191

E. THEOLOGICAL AND LITURGICAL

17. The Contribution of Studies on Religion in Africa to Western Religious Studies ... 205
18. Monogamy: A Mark of the Church? ... 215
19. A Theology of Water, in Introduction to J. Ade Aina's *Present-Day Prophets* ... 225
20. Profile Through Preaching: The Use of Scripture as the Criterion of a Church ... 231
21. The Litany of an Independent West African Church ... 245

F. MISSIOLOGICAL

22. A Further Dimension for Missions: New Religious Movements in the Primal Societies ... 255
23. The Hidden Power of the Whites: The Secret Religion Withheld from the Primal Peoples ... 271
24. Dynamic Religion in Africa ... 289

G. SOCIO-CULTURAL

25. The Place of Independent Religious Movements in the Modernization of Africa ... 297
26. African Independent Churches and Education ... 317
27. Study Centre for New Religious Movements: A Contribution to Inter-Cultural Understanding and Third World Development ... 331

ADDENDUM
Other Kindred Publications ... 339

INDICES
General Index ... 345
Movements: Their Own Associations and Centres ... 349
Individuals in New Movements ... 353

Introduction

Even in my second year of teaching in Sierra Leone I was still completely ignorant of what are commonly called the new religious movements of Black Africa, and it was more by accident than by understanding that I first became involved in this field in 1957. Since then these movements have engaged my attention in one way or another almost continuously, and have led to concern with similar movements beyond Africa, in the other continents and in Oceania. The subject does in fact represent a world-wide phenomenon among peoples in the primal societies whose own religious traditions have interacted with the more universal religions, and especially with the Christian tradition, to produce an astonishing outburst of religious creativity. For those new to these matters several of the essays here collected will define and explain the field sufficiently, especially those in Section A.

It is hoped that the diversity of these essays, as indicated in the section groupings and in other ways, will reveal some of the many dimensions of these religious movements, for, without setting out to do so, I find I have been exploring them from one angle after another.

In this diversity, however, there remain many limitations, and I am keenly aware of other viewpoints, especially those represented by the social sciences, which I must leave to those trained in other disciplines. There is much to be done in dealing with the historical, social and cultural context, although in the last section I have ventured in these directions. I must remain content with such historical material as I have managed to include, and with my own concentrations upon the more distinctly religious aspects—phenomenological, theological, liturgical and missiological—together with the methodological questions concerned.

Other limitations derive from concentration on the independent church form of Africa's new religious movements; these are in the great majority as against other types of movement and my own work has lain chiefly in this area. Other movements do, however, appear, especially in the discussion of typologies and terminology. Within independent churches the emphasis is upon West Africa, especially Nigeria, and above all upon the particular church to which I owe my discovery of this whole subject—the Church of the Lord (Aladura) which began in Nigeria, spread around West Africa, and is now established in Britain and is a member of the World Council of Churches. I can only hope that extensive bibliographical work has helped to transcend these limitations and provide a basis for the more general thematic and methodological studies.

The absence of an essay dealing with the question of Islamic movements of this kind indicates my own continuing uncertainties as to how the comparatively few Islamic movements that might be included should be interpreted. Those interested are referred to the work of Dr. Humphrey Fisher whose viewpoint comes fairly close to my own.

In a field of study that has been developing so rapidly during the two decades when these essays were written it is inevitable that some of the earlier statements would benefit from revision in the light of the mass of new information available and from developments in my own viewpoint. I have been content with a few changes of a more factual nature, as in statistics; otherwise the later essays proved to contain refinements rather than radical revisions of earlier efforts. For example the discussion of religious and sociological typologies of 1966 (written in 1962) as in essay no. 7, has been refined in the lectures given in 1974 and 1976 to produce the charts in essays no. 1 and no. 5. Similarly the term "pagan" still found in 1965 was replaced by "primal" in the 1970s, although the earlier term has been allowed to stand in some places as not inappropriate to the context, likewise another suspect term, "tribal". The more obvious repetitions of material have been deleted unless this would have destroyed the integrity of the text.

The essays collected here originally appeared in diverse publications in Africa and elsewhere, scattered through some fifteen different journals and in symposia, reports, etc. Access to some of these is now difficult or even impossible for many who are interested in this subject. Other relevant writings not included in this selection are listed separately, and attention is also drawn to my account of the literature of this whole subject in the series entitled *Bibliography of New Religious Movements in Primal Societies*, first to the volume I on Black Africa issued in 1977, and also to the later volumes on North America (1978) and then Asia/the Pacific and Latin America/the Caribbean to follow, all from G. K. Hall and Co. of Boston.

HAROLD W. TURNER

Project for New Religious Movements
in Primal Societies, University of
Aberdeen, Scotland.

A. INTRODUCTORY AND GENERAL

The first essay offers a general survey of new religious movements across the whole world of the primal societies and religions. The range and variety are examined, there is a working religious classification system, a systematic analysis of causes, and a brief evaluation of the significance of these developments. The second essay narrows the focus to the African movements, and the third returns to a more formal definition of the phenomena and its place in religious studies.

1
New Religious Movements in Primal Societies

This was originally a lecture given at the founding conference of the Australian Association for the Study of Religions, Adelaide, in August 1976, and published in V. C. Hayes (ed.), Australian Essays in World Religions. *Adelaide: A.A.S.R. 1977, pp. 38–48. In that context the majority of the movements referred to for illustration came from the Pacific area, but these, when added to the African examples also given, may serve for comparative purposes and to place the African phenomena in the world setting. The diagram has been added, and themes dealt with more fully elsewhere have been deleted.*

We are all familiar, even if in a somewhat vague way, with the great expansion of the Christian religion across the continents and cultures of the world, especially during the last two centuries which have seen the rise of the modern missionary movement. By any token this is a most important development in the overall history of religions and although its systematic and scholarly study has hardly begun, most of us have a general picture of the arrival of missionaries, the building of a mission community, the growth of an indigenous church and the emergence of new autonomous churches where the missionary is either a full member, a fraternal worker, or not needed at all. We have an image of the successful planting of Christianity and of its growth in somewhat new forms in many races and cultures; we also know that this growth has been very uneven, with a massive response as among the New Zealand Maoris and a meagre result as with the Australian aborigines. It would be possible to refine this picture by further study of this fascinating story, and yet to pass over the extensive and allied phenomena that form the subject of this essay. Behind and yet along with the story of missionary expansion, there is another story of a vast range of new religious movements in the same primal societies where Christianity has seen its greatest growth; here is a whole new dimension of the interaction between the primal and the Christian religious traditions that is only now coming over the horizon of mission, of Church and of public awareness.

ORIGINS

Although I have begun by reference to the Christian context it is important to realize that such movements may be found in India, and in south-east Asia; whether similar movements can be identified where Islam has been interacting with the primal religions is at present a moot point. Since the Hindu and Buddhist interactions have been comparatively restricted in geographical extent, the overwhelming proportion of these new religious movements is to be found where Christianity has been the universal religion involved. This brings us back to the massive penetration of the tribal world by the modern missionary movement, the theme with which we began, and in the rest of this discussion I shall restrict the subject to the primal-Christian interaction.

I myself became involved in this field through encountering in West Africa one of its forms, the movements usually known as the African independent churches. When I pushed back the enquiry into the historical origins of the Nigerian aladura movement, I found the most specific sparking point lay in the 1918 world-wide influenza epidemic. This traumatic experience, when neither the white man's medicine nor his churches were of any help, led a group of Nigerian Christians to form their own prayer healing group for protection against the plague — and with some apparent success; from this independent initiative, which continued after the plague had passed, there developed a range of independent African churches with many new and unorthodox features from the viewpoint of missions and the older churches.

A few years later, I was able to examine more seriously some of the "offbeat" religious movements among the Maori people in New Zealand and to find that the largest and best-known of these in the present century, the Ratana Church, stemmed from a similar successful and independent initiative by its founder, Wiremu Ratana, in the same 1918 influenza epidemic. Later again, I was to discover that the largest independent church in Africa, the great Kimbanguist Church of Zaïre and many other countries, also had a founder, Simon Kimbangu, for whom the 1918 epidemic had been a critical point in his experience. In every case, a traumatic situation had led to the formation of a new religious movement drawing on the two different religious traditions available and creating a new amalgam. The more one examined these developments across the world the more it became evident that here was a new and creative religious contribution common to the primal societies in all areas.

DISTINCTIVE FORMS

The forms taken by these movements are so varied and the points of view from which they have been described are so diverse, that it is not surprising to find them described by many different names: thus we have prophet, syncretist, messianic or millennial movements, independent or separatist churches, nativistic or revitalization movements, crisis or deprivation cults, adjustment movements and the overpublicized and little understood cargo cults of Melanesia. While some of these terms are appropriate in particular cases, none is suitable as a generic term and I therefore use the simple expression "new religious movements", adding "in primal societies" when necessary.

The question has been raised as to whether some of the above forms, especially the millennial, revitalization and cargo types, are confined to the interaction situation or may have arisen within primal societies through various stresses in a pre-contact situation. This is a difficult question, for we know so little of the internal developments within primal religions before Western contact occurred, and it is also hard to say just what constitutes contact, which may be very indirect through, for example, the distribution of Western trade goods like steel axes along indigenous trade routes to people who may not see a white man for another fifty years. Apart from the problems, and with full recognition that primal religions have had their own history of development, I suggest there are three features that distinguish these new religious movements from purely internal developments. The first is the fact that primal religions are non-missionary, while a large proportion of the new movements are distinctly missionary in nature and spread across tribal boundaries. The second feature is the presence of a new kind of eschatology; this goes beyond anything enshrined in the traditional mythology or expectations, which usually promise a return to a paradisal past or golden age rather than the advance to a really new order of existence that has never been conceived before. And finally, these movements serve as a form of adjustment to an exceptionally severe and prolonged traumatic experience from which there is no escape, due to the interaction of two societies that are very disparate in power and sophistication.

It is also asked whether there is any difference between these new movements and the many other new developments within the whole history of religions, for were not Christianity and Islam themselves, and most other forms, new when they first appeared? Certainly they were and it has even been suggested that Islam itself might belong to the category I am establishing insofar as it was a movement arising in the interaction of the primal tribal religions of Arabia with the more sophisticated faiths of the Jews and Christians; the answer to this may even have something to do with the lack of such movements in the subsequent primals-Islamic encounter. There is, however, something distinctive about these movements from modern primal societies, even though this is hard to define. I suggest it has something to do with the modern situation in which they have arisen.

WORLD RANGE

However this question may finally be answered, there is no doubt about the extensive appearance of these new movements over the past four centuries when the primal world had to deal with a society with a great disparity of power as compared with their own — think of what gunpowder alone meant as compared with the spears and bows and arrows of the Roman Empire as it advanced over Europe. The earliest recorded movements in modern times appeared in Latin America as the Christian Spaniards and Portuguese advanced among the Indian peoples; a messianism in Guatemala in 1530, a movement in Colombia in 1546, a Paraguayan prophet in 1558, an Indian "church" in Brazil in 1583; and many others, totalling over a hundred right up to the Mama Chi movement among the Guaymi of the mountains of Panama from 1961 and the Rastafarians of Jamaica who have been mounting in influence over the past forty years.

In North America, again over a hundred movements may be identified, including what may be the first, the Narragansett Indian Church which has continued from the 1740s right till the present day, the Yaqui syncretist churches ever since the 1760s, the Handsome Lake religion among the Iroquois since 1800 and still active, the short-lived but dramatic neo-primal movements known as Ghost Dances in the 1860s and late 1880s, the small but persistent Indian Shaker Church, a syncretist movement from the 1880s, many small independent churches among the Seminoles, the Hopis, the Creeks, the Navahos and others and, above all, the massive peyote cult, or Native American Church over the past hundred years across more than fifty tribes. What do North American Christians know of these things? And yet none of it would have happened if the whites and their Christian religion had not come.

Similar movements are much rarer in Europe and Asia, although early this century there was a "Big Candle" movement among the Cheremish, a tribal people in European Russia. There have been some examples among the tribal peoples of India and of south-east Asia in relation not only to the Hindu and Buddhist influences, as we have already noted, but also in relation to the more recent Christian contacts. Indonesia also has examples, but the great development has been in the Philippines with perhaps three hundred or so independent churches or other kinds of new movement. There were notable movements in Polynesia last century and this is still going on more than might appear, for recently in Fiji I came across four most interesting and important current examples that had hardly achieved any mention so far in the literature. Among New Zealand Maoris there have been not only the Ratana Church with over twenty thousand adherents, but perhaps a dozen other movements of some significance and many more minor ones. Melanesia is widely known for its cargo cults, which may be numbered by the hundred and have caught the eye of the TV camera and the popular journalist on account of their (to us) exotic features; but there are other non-cargo movements such as the one still flying the Australian flag from its sacred meeting ground when I visited it recently in the hills of New Britain, or the Christian Fellowship Church of Eto, a former Methodist, in the Solomons since 1959. Of the Australian aborigines there is little to report: the Kurrangara movement late last century, the Worgaia cult from about 1954 and especially the Elcho Island movement since 1957; there have been other incipient developments, a few cargo ideas and some independent pentecostal churches on the eastern seaboard, but perhaps the era of new religious movements in Australia has yet to come.

It is in Black Africa, however, that the most massive growth of these movements is to be found. There were early forms back in the seventeenth century or even before this in what was then the Congo, with Portuguese missions. In the last hundred years, as Black Africa has been moving into the position of the great Christian cultural-geographical area that promises to surpass all others, there has been a vast proliferation of new religious movements of all kinds. Taken together these movements clearly form a most extensive and important sector of the growing Christian community in Africa, insofar as they are to be called Christian and churches, or if not then of the influence of this faith upon the primal religions and societies of Africa. Some of the independent church forms have been admitted into national Christian Councils and others are now members of the World Council of Churches.

A RELIGIOUS TYPOLOGY

At several points I have spoken of different forms of these religious movements and it is now time to look more closely at their range and variety. The following classification was worked out in relation to the African phenomena but for the most part has been found to work reasonably well in all areas. The spectrum of movements runs from those which are nearest to the original primal religion and which seek to revitalize it by reworking it in the light of the Christian influence and perhaps with specific Christian borrowings; these movements I call neo-primal, and here I would include the first three Australian movements already mentioned, many of the Melanesian cargo cults and the Maori Hau Hau cult.

The next form, moving along the spectrum, I designate as syncretist; this is in spite of the fact that all these movements are syncretistic in different ways and is in default of a better term. They are explicitly and consciously syncretist in the sense of rejecting the old primal tradition, not wanting to become Christians in the churches and yet taking their religious content from both these sources. They represent a quite new mix of their own. It is possible that some of the Australian aboriginal pentecostal churches belong in this group; certainly this is the place for many of the Melanesian cargo cults, for the Eto Church of the Solomons, for some of the Fiji movements mentioned and probably for the King movement's Taraio faith and the Pai Marire cult in New Zealand.

Further still along this same spectrum, I find we need a group called "Hebraist". By these I mean movements that have made a radical transference from the primal faith into the world of the Bible, especially into that of the Old Testament, but which reject the Christian Church and usually the New Testament, or else have no christology. They cannot be called Christians or churches and yet they have a prophetic form of religion under one moral god who acts as saviour of his people; their form of religion seems to correspond closely to that of Israel in her classic period, and some of these groups actually call themselves "the Israelites" and believe they are descendants of the ancient Jews and especially of the lost tribes. This is not so surprising when we note what a ready-made model Israel in Egypt, Israel struggling to the promised land, Israel under successive foreign imperial powers, presents to primal societies under the colonial yoke. It is difficult to find an example of this category in Melanesia, unless it be a group known as the "Remnant" which existed in the Solomons from the 1950s to the 1970s, but in Polynesia there were "Israelites" in Tuamoto in the 1870s, and perhaps Ofa Mele Longosai, the Tongan prophetess of the present day, should be so classified. What is striking here is that most of the largest and longest-lasting Maori movements clearly fall into this class, from Papahurihia of the 1830s, through Te Whiti's Parihaka village, Te Kooti's Ringatu cult and Rua's Seven Wells of Jehova cult to the Ratana Church. Why this should be so, and more than anywhere else in the world, is another question, but the facts speak plainly enough.

Finally, there are what may properly be called independent churches, bodies which intend to be Christian, which use the Scriptures, and which often regard themselves as having effected a local reformation of European

A TYPOLOGY BASED ON RELIGIOUS FORM AND CONTENT

NEW RELIGIOUS MOVEMENTS IN BLACK AFRICA

PRIMAL RELIGIONS	Neo-Primal	Syncretist	Hebraist	Independent Churches		MISSIONS & OLDER CHURCHES
				Prophet-Healing; Zionist Aladura, etc.	Ethiopian: "African", Orthodox, etc.	
Internal revivals						Internal revivals

(A simplification as well as a further development of the charts of 1963 and 1967 given in chapter 7. The broken vertical lines are a reminder that the boundaries between the various categories are not clearly defined and that movements may straddle two adjacent forms and also move in the course of time from one category to another.)

Christianity and so have become more Christian than the missions and their connected older churches. There are many cases, and certain respects, in which I am prepared to accept this claim as well founded. In Africa, where this form predominates, they may be described as having been founded in Africa, by Africans, for Africans to worship in African ways and to meet African needs as Africans themselves feel them; the same process of complete indigenization may be identified in the independent churches of other cultural areas. Some of the Australian aborigines' pentecostal churches may properly belong here, as also the Congregation of the Poor and the Daku community in Fiji, the early Paliau movement in the Admiralty Islands, the Anglican Church of Nauru from the 1920s, the early Kukuaik from 1940 in New Guinea and the Pentecost (sic) movement from 1954 in Irian Jaya. Among the Maoris there have been the Maori Evangelical Fellowship since 1959 (although of rather different white-connected origins) and the Absolute Established Maori Church which was formed by secession over matters of religious principle from the Ratana Church in 1941. In Africa this category may be further subdivided into Ethiopian churches, which resemble their parent orthodox churches in most matters, except perhaps in polygamy, and the prophet-healing churches which are variously known as Zionist, aladura, spirit, or spiritual in different countries; these latter are much more African in form and content and their two main emphases are indicated in the phrase that describes them; they have also been the main form of the last fifty years and are still appearing as new prophets arise and, not all of them I fear, entirely genuine.

This spectrum should be regarded as a rough working system and there are always individual movements that are difficult to so classify or that seem to span more than one of these classes. It should also be remembered that these movements are full of the flexibility of youth and may prove very mobile as to form and content, so that what seems to be a syncretist movement in one decade may well have to be reclassified in the next. This has happened to the Kimbanguist Church in Zaïre which looked like a syncretist or even an anti-Christian movement in the fifties and yet was admitted to the World Council of Churches before the sixties were out. On the whole it would seem that the general movement tends to be across the spectrum from the neo-primal form towards the more Christian categories, especially as the Christian Scriptures come to be used more or better understood. Not many of the neo-primal forms show extensive growth or last through long periods of time, although striking exceptions can sometimes be found.

CAUSES

Many different disciplines have attempted to identify the causes of these new religious movements and, naturally, to do so in terms of their own special categories, whether sociological, economic, political, psychological, theological, etc. We can be certain, however, that as in all things human there will be a complex of all such factors at work and with varying degrees of importance in different cases. Since on the face of it at least, these are religious movements, there is a presumption that distinctively religious causes are to be found; but those who hold reductionist positions will of course always convert these into non-religious factors. It is perhaps better to approach the question of causation from another angle and to identify four classes of causes.

There are the situational causes, the kind of encounter and interaction situation wherein two very disparate societies and their religious traditions meet, often in a conquest or colonial relationship. This is a necessary but not a sufficient cause, for there are quite a few "negative instances" where none of these religious movements has arisen. Then there are what I call contributing factors, which may be of all kinds and in varying combinations — psychological stress, social and cultural disintegration under rapid social change, political domination or oppression especially in the harsher colonial forms, economic deprivation — especially the loss of the land sacred to a people as well as necessary for support, and religious and moral conflicts due to the clash of two different world views and sets of values, especially over matters of magic and marriage. There is, however, no necessary correlation between these and the emergence of movements. For instance, Ghana has had one of the highest per capita incomes among the countries of Africa and an early and comparatively peaceful transition from a benevolent colonial regime to independence and yet there has been a tremendous development of these new movements since that event.

Thirdly there are what may be called precipitative factors which, in a situation that is ripe for such development, push things over the edge. These are more accidental and incidental in nature — a personal crisis such as the sudden deaths of the two children of the young woman Gaudencia Aoko who became leader of the Legio Mario independent church in Kenya, the effects of a plague like the 1918 example already mentioned, a sudden economic depression where the price of local commodities like palm oil or copra mysteriously plummets, the disciplining of a mission agent, or, and most importantly, the emergence of a charismatic individual to provide a crystallizing point for an incipient movement that will otherwise never surface into history.

Finally, there are the more intangible enabling factors, features of the two cultures concerned in the interaction that either predispose towards these new developments or discourage their appearance. For instance, if a Melanesian society has a mythology containing the promise of a golden age that will return in the future, this can readily be reworked in the light of Christian teaching about the Second Advent and the hope of the world to come and serve as the basis for a new cargo cult. If, on the other hand, the mythology tells of a golden age that is for ever gone and perhaps also includes stories of the different fortunes of two brothers, one brown and one white, then this society can come to terms with the advent of the Europeans in a realistic way without the emergence of new cults with which to face the future. On the other side of the interaction it appears that the Christian religion has considerable "enabling capacity" as compared with, say, Buddhism. It brings a clear-cut gospel with a rich eschatology and a strong identification in its scriptures with the oppressed and the sick and the poor; it also comes associated with European wealth and power and not with a monk and begging bowl. The extensive association of these new religious movements with the spread of Christianity may therefore be much more than a merely quantitative matter due to the extent of the geographical expansion of this particular faith. It is significant to note that even when local peoples have become disappointed with Christianity for not bringing them social equality with the whites or equal economic and political power, or for not healing all diseases as seemed possible in the Bible and solving all personal problems, even then there has been no rejection of this new faith, but so often a persistent attempt to discover its secrets and secure its powers through their own new religious movements, their own truer forms of the religion of the whites.

EVALUATION

Behind all the different factors at work in the emergence of these phenomena there stands a deep desire for spiritual autonomy and human maturity on the part of the primal societies, a longing to enter into the larger world that has opened up to them and to stand therein on their own feet as men who are recognized and accepted by all other men and who have their own spiritual contribution to make to the human experience. This is the motive that must be seen and valued behind all the crudities and excesses, the misunderstandings and futilities, the heresies and immoralities that may be found in some of these movements. This is the motive that is also at work in the achievements that deserve much more appreciation than has as yet been given them — the contribution to medical care through spiritual healing, the discipline for disoriented peoples when they have a new "place to belong", the new trans-tribal unities and missionary outlook, the authentic indigenization of Christianity in many of the independent church forms and, in general, the great spiritual and mental shake-up that breaks through the confines of the old world view and opens the way for new incentives, new visions of the future, new basic assumptions and values.

These considerations reveal how the primals' new religious movements which seem ignorant or reactionary, may in fact be making a most important contribution to the development and modernizing of their societies. Much more could be said on this, especially with reference to some of their own economic activities, their new model communities and their ethic with its common banning of alcohol and tobacco. On this last point it is clear that what may be tolerable luxuries in affluent societies are economically disastrous in the newly developing areas; one has only to explore the effects of that most tragic Western contribution to Papua New Guinea, South Pacific beer. A cargo cult may be very much astray as to where the future wealth of the nation is to come from, but it is right on the ball if it forbids the use of alcohol.

To the Christian community in all continents these movements present new issues. It is not sufficient to oppose, criticize, deplore or ignore them; they are too extensive and they will not just go away. Nor can the Christian community escape responsibility for their very existence — if the whites and the Christian faith had not come to these peoples there would be none of these movements. They are the offspring of the Christian encounter, illegitimate offspring if you must see it that way, and if the primal society be the mother then the white society as father is now summoned to his responsibilities. While from the academic point of view the new religious movements of the primal societies form what I have called a new field in the study of the history and phenomenology of religions, from the contemporary human viewpoint they raise questions of a much more urgent and active kind.

2
African Prophet Movements

This was my first unsophisticated attempt at a general African survey, and concentrates on the various causal factors at work, with emphasis on the religious and spiritual motives. It was written from Sierra Leone, where new indigenous movements have been less common.

The movement towards political independence over the whole African continent has engaged world-wide attention. Behind this movement there is to be found another continent-wide development that is much less publicised, the religious bodies known as prophet movements, separatist sects, or independent indigenous churches. These movements for cultural integrity and spiritual autonomy have for the most part preceded those aiming at political independence, and their influence may prove to be more profound and to continue long after the political movements have reached their consummation.

Although there are examples of similar religious movements among the Pacific Island peoples and the Indians of the American northwest, in the West Indies and many parts of South America, the most wide-spread development seems to be in Africa. Why this should be so is a question not yet answered. It does not appear to be due to any tradition of secession or of prophet-leaders in the indigenous religions of Africa; Dr Parrinder's book on African traditional religion does not even mention prophets until the epilogue on recent times, and any claims that the prophet is a traditional figure will be found to refer rather to mediums and diviners, who may have certain features such as possession in common with the prophets, but who did not give rise to the kind of movement that has arisen in so many parts of Africa in this century. These are almost all to be found where Western culture and the Christian religion have penetrated, although why there should have been little similar reaction to the impact of Christianity on the peoples of Asia is another question we should try to answer. . . .

All the colours of the religious spectrum are to be found somewhere in these manifold movements in Africa. They range from churches almost indistinguishable from the most westernized products of Christian missions, to cults that are a revival of traditional pagan religions with no more than a few Christian glosses. Indeed, it is impossible to find one term to cover with any accuracy all forms of prophet movement, healing cult, separatist sect, or independent church, and the term prophet movement is used here rather loosely for them all. Some idea of the extent of this development may be gained from the few places where figures are available. In South Africa Bantu groups that are known to the government number some 3,000, embracing perhaps 3 million members. In Zaïre some 400 movements are estimated, and the largest of these, the Kimbanguist Church, has increased from perhaps 100,000 in 1959 to several million claimed in the 1970s after the spread of the Church into a number of adjacent countries. In East Africa there are large numbers in Kenya where the African Brotherhood Church has grown since 1945 to the 60,000 claimed as members in 1970, and the Church of Christ in Africa includes about 75,000. In Liberia there are probably at least 50 distinct bodies, scores in the Ivory Coast, up to 500 in Ghana, and several hundred in Nigeria where the Christ Apostolic Church and the combined Cherubim and Seraphim groups have each some 100,000 members. Even in Malagasy, which is little known, about 20 movements have been traced since 1894. For the whole of Black Africa the estimate made in 1968, even excluding the more non-Christian or neo-traditional forms, suggested that about 7 million people who regard themselves as Christians find their spiritual home in approximately 6,000 movements.

A good deal of discussion has been focussed on the cause of this extensive and still growing movement, and almost every possibility has been canvassed except that of doctrinal dispute which has caused secessions in the churches of the West. In the popular mind polygamy has often been regarded as the main cause of what seems like a breakaway from orthodox Christianity. While many of these groups do allow polygamy, the more one studies them the more it becomes plain that this is not an important factor in itself, unless it was so in the instance reported by Dr. Baëta of Ghana. A group was so dissatisfied with the confused and hypocritical situation in an ostensibly monogamous church that it seceded to found its own church where polygamy could be practised "in decency and order"! I have heard an excellent sermon on monogamy preached at a wedding service in a church that allows polygamy, and it seems that there is a movement towards monogamous practice in some of the polygamous churches; but if and when it succeeds it will not remove the reasons for their existence.

Another explanation has been in terms of economics. It is alleged that just as the smaller sectist bodies of Europe and America have been regarded as a protest by the submerged disinherited classes against their lot in life, so we may look upon African prophet movements as a protest from the ranks of the ordinary African people who have failed to secure a share in the riches being exploited in their own countries by the colonial powers. Compensation is found in the consolations and promises of religion, under their own leaders. In some areas it may be true that this has had a good deal to do with the rise of prophet movements. Dr. Sundkler has shown the connection between Bantu separation and the alienation of their lands in South Africa, while a French sociologist, Balandier, has suggested a correlation between the successive economic crises in the Belgian colony of the Congo and the various outbreaks of prophetism there.

On the whole, however, it would seem that such factors should be regarded as contributary rather than basic causes. There are too many instances where they cannot be applied. Ghana has one of the highest standards of living among African peoples, and there the prophet movements have proliferated during the very period of this prosperity, and have appealed in Ghana, as elsewhere in West Africa, to wealthy individuals.

The economic explanation has been applied mainly to the colonial areas in Africa, and so has been linked to the attempt to explain prophet movements in political terms. African peoples have been frustrated politically through their colonial status, and have turned to one of the few forms of organization open to them, the development of a new religious movement under their own auspices. This has then been used as a training ground for independent leaders and as a form of organization of the masses under cover of religion, in preparation for the time when the fight for political independence comes out into the open. A prophet movement is then, on this view, a form of anti-colonialism and of nationalism, and also assumes a racial aspect as an anti-white movement. This thesis is especially attractive when applied to some areas of Africa, such as the former Belgian Congo, and as an interpretation of the widespread suppression of prophets by colonial governments. In fact quite a harrowing story could be told of the persecution of African prophets over the last fifty years. . . . It is true that in some cases the individuals concerned can be shown to have been engaged in direct political activity, and it would be surprising if this were not so in a society not accustomed to the distinction between the sacred and the secular, between religion and politics. But what is more surprising is the fact that many of the prophets who have run foul of the authorities were really religious leaders without political interests or intentions. This seems to have been true of Prophet Harris, and probably also of Simon Kimbangu, who has subsequently become a political martyr through the doubtful attribution of a political role to him by the Belgian authorities. Latest reports show that he is now regarded as the father of the independence of the Congo, the subject of a statue in Leopoldville, and that he has been reburied in the capital. No one could have been more astonished at this reputation than Kimbangu himself. The reverse process, whereby a political leader is given a religious significance, appears in the report of the Déïma cult in the Ivory Coast, which in some areas deified the then African Deputy Houphouët, until he expressly declined the honour.

There is undoubtedly some truth in the political interpretation, but in varying measure in different areas and only to be discovered by detailed study of the particular instances. It must not be used as a general explanation, for it is by no means adequate to account for this wide-ranging and manifold phenomenon in Africa, and least of all in West Africa where political development has been more rapid and race-relations easier, than in most other areas. The final inadequacy of this interpretation is to be seen in the continuing growth of these prophet movements and the foundation of new ones once the colonial situation has passed. At the same time an intriguing question remains in the background—how far is there some deeper connection between the movements for political independence and for spiritual autonomy? That there is some similar connection between the rise of nationalism and the religious movement known as the Reformation in Europe is generally admitted; but there seems no prospect of ever finally establishing exactly which influenced which and at what points. Probably it will prove equally impossible to reach a final analysis of the African situation in this twentieth century.

In an attempt to probe more deeply into the origin of African prophet movements, it is suggested that they represent a creative response to the breakdown of the old forms of African society by the formation of new groups providing fellowship, security, and some sanctions and guidance for living. The prophet then becomes a substitute for the chief, and his church takes the place of the extended family and clan. There is clearly a great deal in this view, and it is possible to go further and to describe these movements as a cultural reaction of the African peoples in which they are seeking to rediscover themselves and their own kind of life, a way of life to which they can really belong because they have worked it out themselves. This way of life is to be expressed in religious forms of their own, which many members of the prophet movements hope will become the great church which has yet to grow on African soil and be accepted and respected by the peoples of the world.

And so we are led to regard the prophet movements as at bottom spiritual and religious movements. They are not social, economic, or political reactions disguised as religious movements. It would be truer to say that certain social economic and political forces have in varying degree been expressed through some of the prophet movements and that we must recognise the extent to which these latter have had political implications, or been conditioned by the economic situation, or prompted by social changes, and by cultural needs. But they are basically what they seem to be, and what they claim to be, religious movements to be studied by the methods appropriate to the study of religions and to be evaluated in religious terms. Apart from a minority of such movements which are clearly a nativistic reaction and a few which are openly political, the great majority claim to be Christian. Their achievements in this respect may sometimes appear to be minimal, but at other points can be most impressive; their intentions to develop as Christian churches can seldom be dismissed as insincere, even if their understanding of what is implied is often confused. The fact that so many of their members come from the older orthodox or mission churches must not be allowed to suggest that this is a movement away from Christianity. It is certainly a protest, though with remarkably little bitterness, against the older churches, and an evidence of a great spiritual hunger for a satisfaction they have not found or have not recognized in their parent churches. There can be few better methods of discovering the real impact of the older churches on their members than to investigate the individual spiritual histories of former members now in the prophet churches. This can be a chastening experience. It also reveals the way in which the prophet churches perform a salvaging or rescue function in relation to the main body of African church life, preventing dissatisfied members from reverting to paganism by providing a recognizably Christian and easily available alternative spiritual home. That it may be called Christian is best seen when we recognize that many of these movements may be called Pentecostal forms of the Christian church; and that it cannot be regarded as simply a paganizing reversion is evident in the characteristic rejection of all forms of traditional African "medicine" and magic, a rejection that often occurs only after leaving the parent church for the prophet movement.

From the standpoint of Sierra Leone where this was written, it is difficult to recognise the extent or the significance of African prophetism, for in relation to the whole African scene, this country is something of a "negative instance", one of the areas where there has been little development of this kind. The two prophet churches of any consequence are importations, the God is Our Light Church from Ghana, and the Church of the Lord (Aladura) from Nigeria, and neither has made great headway in the Creole community. Whatever attempt is made to explain this different position in Sierra Leone will probably only serve to reinforce the argument above, for it is not so much in its economic or political history as in its religious and Christian history that the Creole community occupies a special position. Here there are three churches that owe their origin not to missions but to their being the churches of the early African settlers, and Christianity in its western forms has been part of Creole society and culture for well over a century and a half. There has been no need here to win self-respect through the foundation of an African church of one's own, no search for a more congenial spiritual home and a place where one can belong. The Creole has had all this from the beginning of his history in Sierra Leone, and from this vantage point has to try to understand the very different prophet movements in so many of the other nations of Africa.

3
A New Field in the History of Religions

This essay derives from a paper delivered at the International Congress for the History of Religions at Stockholm in 1970, and therefore exhibits a more academic and systematic form, with a more precise definition of the movements concerned and of their place in religious history. It aims at full academic recognition of this field of study within religious studies.

In one sense it is a bold suggestion that there is anything new in the history of religions. On the other hand there would be little religious history if there had not been a succession of new developments, new features, new religious experiences, and most of the major religious traditions claim an origin in some new departure. Our present suggestion is that the religious reactions of primal societies to higher cultures, and in particular to encounter with Western-culture and its Christian religion, present a range of phenomena sufficiently distinctive to be designated as a new field of study in the history of religions.

The existence of this field is indicated in the literature of recent decades, since Dr. Katesa Schlosser (1949) surveyed prophets and their movements in the whole African continent. Ten years later Professor Guariglia (1959) extended the study to a world survey of what he called prophet and salvation-seeking movements. Then came another world survey, Professor Lanternari's well-known book on religious movements seeking

Religion: A Journal of Religion and Religions 1 (1), 1971, 15–23.

freedom and salvation among oppressed peoples (1963). In the same period there has been mounting interest among social anthropologists who have attempted their own world classifications and general theory (e.g. Linton 1943, Wallace 1956, and Smith 1959), as also among other social scientists and among historians. Our own bibliographies of 'modern African religious movements' now contain some two thousand items on this area alone (Mitchell and Turner 1966, Turner 1968, 1970).

It seems clear that there is an informal consensus as to the existence of a range of new religious developments with so much in common that they may initially, at least, be regarded as belonging together and constituting a common phenomenon, distinguished by four features.

1. They have appeared in the same historical period, the 'modern' period of Western expansion, and in the same encounter situation where one people and culture have dominated another, usually in the colonial manner.
2. One party to the encounter has been a primal society; the other has most often been Western culture.
3. The reactions by the primal society have taken the form of movements that have been predominantly religious, and even where they have assumed a more political or economic appearance there has usually been a religious dimension also.
4. The religious phenomenology of these movements is remarkably similar across all the culture areas in the five continents principally concerned.

On this basis we may group together Maori churches and cults in New Zealand, prophet movements among Australian aborigines, messianic and cargo cults in Oceania, indigenous movements in the Philippines, Indonesia and South-East Asia, nativistic and syncretist movements among North American Indians, prophets or revivalists among the Eskimo, new religions and Afro-American cults in the Caribbean and South America, and finally the prophet-healing movements and independent churches of sub-Saharan Africa, where the latest estimate (Barrett, 1968) suggests some six thousand distinct groups or movements.

We are well aware of how loose and question-begging these remarks are as a demarcation of a field of data and a consequent area of study. But we suggest that they do in fact mark out an area where scholars from various disciplines have been working to some profit, and that we may usefully proceed on this rough pragmatic basis and see if we can define the field and organize its study with more precision.

It is, of course, a truism that most religious traditions have been 'new religious movements' at some earlier stage of their history—the Jewish, Buddhist, Christian, Islamic and Sikh traditions, among many others, have begun in this way. The phrase does, however, have its value at various creative or innovative points in religious history. Professor Byron Earhart (1969) has attempted a four-point phenomenology for the 'new religions' of Japan, and although it is doubtful if any of these belong to the field we have been marking out, his account serves as a useful statement on new religious developments of any kind. These are regarded as sharing the following features:

1. They presuppose a prior and established 'classical' tradition against which certain movements may be described as 'new.'
2. There is a substantial or even radical break from the classical tradition, usually occurring at an identifiable time and place and rooted in the new religious experience of known leaders; the outcome is recognized by both parties as a new departure that differs from internal reforms and schisms. There may be some retention of the original membership by those in the new movement, but this occurs because the classical and the new movements *are* so different.
3. The classical tradition having become moribund or fossilized, or having ceased to serve men's religious needs in a new situation, the new movement provides a thrust towards renewal or revitalization.
4. The outcome is a significantly new religious phenomenon, with new cultic and social forms, a reforming ethic and distinctive ethos, and a new symbolic system; it is often based on a new or further revelation supplementing, correcting, or superseding the revelation belonging to the classical tradition.

Earhart's phenomenology (which we have developed slightly in our own way) will, of course, cover everything from Montanism of the second Christian century to Mormonism in the nineteenth or the latest Melanesian cargo cult. We suggest that it may be used to provide the basis for a working definition of those particular new religious movements we have demarcated, as follows:

'A historically new religious phenomenon arising in the encounter of a primal society and its religion with one or more of the higher cultures and their major religions, and involving some substantial departure from the classical religious traditions of all the cultures concerned, in order to find renewal through a different religious system.'

This suggests that there may be a new field in the history of religions as specific as any of the fields traditionally recognized at international congresses or in the journals of religious studies, and a field that may no longer be subsumed under the terms primitive or pre-literate religions—terms which we replace by the more accurate, positive and inoffensive word 'primal.' Indeed, it appears that this astonishing world-ranging phenomenon is without previous parallel in human history, and therefore deserves attention in its own right. Whether it finally proves to be such a new field will depend on the answers to a whole range of questions raised by these movements. We shall content ourselves here with outlining some of these questions, together with the provisional answers we are inclined to offer for later detailed examination. It is important, however, to stress the need for an open, empirical approach, for we do not know clearly in advance what we are observing, and we must allow the data to raise new questions, and suggest new categories and terminology. In particular it is important not to impose terms such as sect, syncretism, messianism, pentecostalism, etc., drawn from church or mission history or the history of religions, even while we cautiously use these concepts as leads for our enquiry into the new field.

1. The first question asks whether the *encounter* situation is an essential milieu for such movements. Are they always exogenous, or can essentially similar movements arise internally within a single culture and its religion? This question may conveniently be divided into two:

a. Is there any difference between such movements and the sects and schisms that endlessly arise within the major religious traditions? Do they differ from folk religious movements, as in Southern Italy or in the recent Lou prophet movement in Holland? Or again, should they be regarded as 'derivatives,' such as Sikhism from the Hindu tradition, or the Mormons, Jehovah's Witnesses or Christian Science from the Christian tradition, or the 'new religions' within the Japanese situation? Most of these examples continue to share the cultural background of the classical tradition from which they departed; and although they claim a new revelation associated with the classical traditions, yet they appear to be variations on these traditions, albeit heretical from the classical viewpoints. In spite, therefore, of much phenomenological similarity between these movements within a single major tradition and the movements we are presenting, there may well be something quite different where two disparate cultures and religions are involved, even though we have not yet managed to specify what this is. Mormonism, with its prophets and its polygamy, might appear similar to many an African movement, but there seems to be little congeniality between them when Mormon missionaries endeavour to establish their movement in Nigeria.

b. The second part of this question concerns the possibility of such movements arising within a primal society and religion apart from any special culture contact of the kind we are dealing with. Have there been prophets, messianisms, millennialisms, and radically new religious developments in pre-contact situations? We know there have been creative individuals, saints, reformers, as in other religions. Is it merely our ignorance of the earlier history of the primal religions that hides such movements from us?—for changing history they have had, despite the commonly implied assumptions about the static, unchanging nature of the primal societies. And then are we sure as to what we mean by the prophet figure before we ask whether this has appeared in the primal religions? One of the urgent questions is to ask this of African traditional religions and to see whether the term prophet as used in history of religions is properly applied to diviner, medium, medicine-man or any other figure in African primal religions, or whether the prophetic function is derivative from contact with the Semitic religions.

And then again, how are we to understand the difference between a search for a future paradise in modern millennialisms and messianisms, and the effort to secure the return or revival of some primeval golden age that marks so many primal religions? To which of these two categories do the pre-Christian contact antecedents of the Ghost Dance in North West America, or the early stages of the Koreri cult in Papua, or the wanderings of the Tupi-Guarani in South America, really belong? And even if these movements should appear both to antecede the encounter situation and to resemble our modern developments are they not so few and intermittent that the very proliferation in the modern situation is itself on such a scale as to create what is virtually a new phenomenon?

It is a familiar scientific principle in many disciplines that the scale creates the phenomenon, so that we do not need to say that nothing like this has ever happened before. Obviously the very fact that these are religious developments means that a great deal that is very similar has happened before. The encounter situation, however, seems to provide at least a powerful new stimulus for development on an unprecedented scale, and we suggest that there is also something of a new form and content associated with this sudden increase of scale within the encounter situation of recent centuries. If we can say this much then the question of similar phenomena in the earlier history of primal religions, while important in itself, does not determine the newness or otherwise of the field we are surveying.

2. The next basic question is whether one of the participants must always be a *primal* religion, in encounter with one or more *major* religions? What of the movements that have arisen in the meeting of two of the major religions themselves? We think of those that have emerged from the relationship between the Western-Christian tradition and Hinduism, such as theosophy and similar sophisticated syncretisms, or from the same Western tradition when it produced the Chinese Taiping movement, which has remarkable similarities to the new movements in Africa. In Japan some would relate

Sokagakkai to the Western-Christian encounter, likewise the Ahmadiyya sect in Islam; as for the Christian-Buddhist meeting, there are the millennial movements that arose in Burma during the Western colonial period. Other possible examples where neither party was a primal society might be found in the messianic movements that arose in the earlier penetration of Buddhism into Japan, and the recent I-kuan-tao cult after the Japanese occupation of China.

It is possible that a somewhat similar answer will obtain here: that although there may be similar developments in the encounter of higher cultures and religions, where one of the parties is a primal society an important difference of scale appears as well as major differences of content which are not yet clearly discerned, but which may well be related to the peculiar features of the primal religions themselves.

3. A third question asks whether *any* of the major religions associated with a higher culture, or even *two* major religions, can precipitate or arouse such movements in encounter with a primal religion? It appears that an affirmative answer must be given, for there are examples where the tribal peoples of India have produced these reactions under the influence of Hindu culture (Fuchs, 1965) and the hill-tribals of South East Asia have responded in like manner to contact with Buddhism, or with Buddhism and Western Christianity at the same time.

The case of Islam is more obscure, for where one would expect to find an abundance of such movements in the course of Islamic expansion into Black Africa, similar to those arising from Christian penetration, it is difficult to find a single one that is anything like a parallel example. There have been prophets and movements in plenty, as Dr. Schlosser has made so plain, but these seem better described as sects or reform movements within Islam itself rather than as new or independent religious developments. It is possible that closer study of the Senegalese Murids and other movements in Francophone West Africa would provide examples. The Yoruba people, however, offer a striking test case, for they have been invaded by Islam from the north and Western Christianity from the south during the same period, and have responded to each of these new faiths in approximately equal numbers. While there are numerous and large independent movements with a Christian background, none has developed from the equal engagement with Islam; the Yoruba Bamidele movement described by Dr. A. R. I. Doi (1970) appears as a most un-African reactionary reform movement within Islam.

It may be that north African tribal peoples can provide a few examples, such as the Confrérie d'Ait-Atelli among the Kabyle, and that more have recently occurred in Indonesia among tribal peoples relatively untouched by the earlier presence of Islam for several centuries. If so, then the absence of such movements from Black Africa is all the more puzzling. There is also the intriguing question of whether Islam itself was not just such a new religion arising in the encounter between Arabian tribal society and the higher Mediterranean and Syrian culture associated with Judaism and Christianity.

Even if we recognize that any of the major religions can provoke new religious developments among primal peoples, it remains true that the overwhelming majority have arisen from encounter with Western culture and its Christian religion. Is this due merely to the historical accidents of Western and Christian expansion into the tribal world being so much more extensive than that of any other culture and religion? Or was this very expansion itself in some way derivative from the Christian religion with which it was associated? And, further, is there something in the Christian religion especially provocative of such reactions among tribal peoples? As Dr. W. E. H. Stanner (1965) has put it, '... is it, incredibly, to be supposed that, say, Buddhism in New Guinea would have had effects comparable to those of Christianity?'—including, presumably, the cargo cults.

It has been suggested, (Montgomery, 1969) that we can identify several reasons for this alleged peculiar potentiality of Christianity:

1. Its built-in appeal to the poor and the sick, the defenceless or the oppressed in primal societies, especially in the colonial period. The troubled history of Israel as discovered in the Old Testament has a special fascination for many tribal peoples, who can readily identify themselves with Israel's sufferings as a people without political, economic or military power, and equate their own new prophets with Moses, Elijah or other Old Testament figures. Likewise they can respond to the attitude of Jesus towards the sick and the poor and powerless, and find in him a fellow-sufferer who died at the hands of the foreign authorities who occupied and ruled his country.

2. The fact that it does not remain completely identified with the cultures (in this case, the Western) that it helps to create, but exhibits a tension between itself and all cultures. There is no need to deny that this can happen in other religious traditions also, in order to appreciate the extent to which it has occurred in the Western-Christian colonial expansion. Missions and governments have been too often identified as acting hand-in-glove, overlooking the extent to which even the missionaries of established churches have opposed their own colonial governments—whether it be Roman Catholic priests defending Indians in the Spanish American conquests, or a Bishop Tugwell incurring arrest in Nigeria during his campaign against the legalized traffic in trade gin. In the tribal world the last decade has seen the final separation of Christianity as a religion from its associated

Western governments, and increasingly the Christian mission among primal peoples stands on its own merits, often in opposition to governments and to many features of the steadily invading Western culture. Tribal peoples have sensed this distinction and thus have been encouraged to draw from the Christian tradition for their own movements of renewal and liberation.

3. The special nature and place of eschatology within the biblical tradition have made a basic contribution to the new values and outlook upon time and history necessary before primal peoples can face the Western and modern world and their own problems with hope and confidence. This is exactly what many of their new religious movements enable them to do. As W. E. Mühlmann (1965) has said, it is '... an open question ... whether nativistic movements of really eschatological character can be found outside the historical diffusionist reach (at least by repercussions) of the genuine eschatological religions—Judaism, Christianity and Islam—since the concepts of a saviour and of time-reversal and revolutionary activity seem to be only embedded in the spirit of these religions.'

4. Is there any *particular* Christian tradition more liable to precipitate such movements than other traditions? It is still commonly suggested that Protestant Christianity is of this nature. There is undoubtedly some truth here, supported by Dr. D. B. Barrett's examination (1968) of the extent to which translation of the Scriptures into tribal vernaculars has been a major factor in the appearance of independent movements in Africa. On the other hand, Roman Catholicism has also revealed a capacity to arouse these religious reactions, as witness the earlier history of the European presence in Central and South America, and many areas where Catholicism has been the dominant tradition (Turner, 1969). Nor has Eastern Orthodoxy failed to produce similar effects, within its much more limited geographical and missionary expansion, as is seen in movements reported from Central Asia.

5. Were similar new movements produced during the *earlier* expansion of the Christian faith in association with a higher culture (Graeco-Roman) among the tribal peoples of northern Europe and north Africa? It does not seem possible to discover tribal prophets and messiahs, neo-pagan revivals or independent churches, healing movements and cargo-cults in this period; if they did occur they seem to have left little in the way of record and cannot have been on anything like the scale of modern times.

The chief candidate as an earlier and parallel movement appears to be Montanism, a kind of independent church and prophet movement in second century Phrygia. Per Beskow (1969) has pointed out the many phenomenological similarities with current African movements—a new revelation, prophets and prophetesses, a holy city, etc. In spite, however, of its rural milieu in a Phrygian culture where ancient traditional (primal) religion was still alive, this was no primal society, but a literate and comparatively highly civilized society with a sophisticated religious system, at least in the urban centres, and the heir of the many higher cultures that had advanced and receded over Asia Minor in the previous millennia. Montanism would appear to be a heretical Christian sect rather than a new movement or independent church in the modern sense. And yet to investigate Montanism from the new angle of these modern movements might prove especially fruitful, and reverse the answer here tentatively proposed, for there are undoubtedly many similarities between modern independent churches among primal peoples and second century Christianity in general. As a further example of the possibilities there is the recent suggestion (Fabian, 1969) that the Jamaa movement from within Roman Catholicism in Central Africa represents an African Gnosticism, where the cosmological model of a hierarchy of worlds has been replaced by a social model drawn from the structure and unity of the family. Jamaa, however, is hardly a clear example of a new movement in the sense we have been adopting.

On the assumption that the earlier expansion of Mediterranean culture and Christianity was not marked by our more modern phenomena, or certainly not on the same scale, the further question arises as to why this was so. Among the possible answers, there is the suggestion that Mediterranean culture had already penetrated into the European and north African tribal worlds before it became intimately associated with the Christian religion. Its own religions were basically similar to those of the primal societies, being in fact only more sophisticated forms of this kind of religion, and so had no revolutionary or provocative effect on the tribal religions. Further, even Mediterranean culture, for all its sophistication and technical achievements, was far less removed from tribal cultures than modern scientific, technological, industrial Western culture has been. In modern times this Western culture has been in precipitate encounter with entirely disparate primal cultures, and has arrived along with a quite disparate religion. The combination of these factors then offers some explanation of the efflorescence of these religious movements in modern times and their apparent absence or rarity in the earlier period. If this is so then we can add another phrase to the working definition presented earlier, such as 'arising in modern times,' or more specifically 'arising since (say) 1600 A.D.'—or any other date that seems convenient.

The wide range of questions raised in the course of our attempt to demarcate this new field clearly leads out into many of the social and historical disciplines, into the phenomenology and history of religions, and into the theologies of the major religions. This endeavour also poses new questions in many traditional areas of study; in particular, in the history of Hellenic and Roman imperialism, in the early history of Christianity, and in modern colonial history. At the same time it opens up new demands for comparative sudies; it is clear, for example, that New Zealand cannot understand its own Maori prophets, Ringatu cult and Ratana Church unless it sees these in relation to their counterparts in Africa and the other areas we have mentioned. Such study as we have been advocating has indeed many forms of immediate practical value, especially when it comes to our understanding of the third and developing world; nowhere else can the personal and social dynamic, the inner forces and motivations that make or mar the current attempts at modernizing this world, be more clearly seen than in these spontaneous indigenous spiritual creations of the primal societies that we have labelled so inadequately 'new religious movements.'

Bibliography

Barrett, D. B. 1968. *Schism and Renewal in Africa*. Nairobi: Oxford University Press, *passim*.

Beskow, P. 1969. In P. Beyerhaus and C. F. Hallencreutz (eds). *The Church Crossing Frontiers . . . Essays in Honour of Bengt Sundkler*. Lund: Gleerup, pp. 33–35.

Doi, A. R. I. 1969. 'The Bamidele Movement', *Orita* iii/2: 101–118. See also the ambiguous position of Hamallism in P. Alexandre. 1970. 'A West Islamic movement: Hamallism in French West Africa', in R. I. Rotberg and A. A. Mazrui (eds.). *Protest and Power in Black Africa*. New York: Oxford University Press: 497–512.

Earhart, H. B. 1969. 'The interpretation of the "New Religions" of Japan as new religious movements'. Paper read at annual meeting, American Academy of Religion, Boston; Japanese translation to appear in *Nihon Bukkyo*; also brief discussion in his (1970) *The New Religions of Japan; a Bibliography of Western-Language materials*. Tokyo: Sophia University: 4–10.

Fabian, J. 1969. 'An African Gnosis . . .' *History of Religions* ix/1: 42–58.

Fuchs, S. 1965. *Rebellious Prophets*. London: Asia Publishing House.

Guariglia, G. 1959. *Prophetismus und Heilserwartungs-Bewegungen . . .* Vienna: Berger.

Lanternari, V. 1963. *The Religions of the Oppressed*. New York: Knopf; Italian original, 1960.

Linton, R. 1943, 'Nativistic Movements', *American Anthropologist* xiv/2: 230–240.

Mitchell, R. C., and Turner, H. W. 1966. *A Comprehensive Bibliography of Modern African Religious Movements*. Evanston: Northwestern University Press.

Montgomery, R. L. 1969. 'Domination versus an alternative route of change', *Bulletin, Christian Institute for Ethnic Studies in Asia* iii/3–4: 17.

Mühlmann, W. E. 1965. In *Current Anthropology* vi/4: 452.

Schlosser, K. 1949. *Propheten in Afrika*. Braunschweig: Limbach.

Smith, M. W. 1959. 'Towards a classification of cult movements', *Man* 59, art. 2: 8–12.

Stanner, W. E. H. 1965. In *Current Anthropology* vi/4: 458.

Turner, H. W. 1968. 'Bibliography of Modern African Religious Movements', Supplement I. *Journal of Religion in Africa* i/3: 173–211.

———. 1969. 'African Religious Movements and Roman-Catholicism', in H. J. Greschat and H. Jungraithmayr (eds.). *Wort und Religion: Kalima na Dini.* Stuttgart: Evangelischer Missions Verlag: 255–264.

———. 1970. 'Bibliography of Modern African Religious Movements', Supplement II. *Journal of Religion in Africa.* iii/3: 161–208.

Wallace, A. F. C. 1956. 'Revitalization Movements', *American Anthropologist* xviii/2: 264–281.

B. METHODOLOGICAL AND BIBLIOGRAPHICAL

Essays four, six and seven were written in 1962 as prolegomena to the work that later appeared in 1967 as *African Independent Church*, and together form a systematic exploration of the methodological issues involved; at several points they have been refined, as will be seen in essays one and five. The essays in this section move from the general problems found in the study of any living religion, especially when it differs from one's own, through the questions concerning the academic equipment for the study of *any* religious movement (essay five), and then for studying a *Christian* religious movement (essay six), to the problems of a working language and of ways of grouping and classifying the diverse phenomena (essay seven). The final essay takes a detailed look at the studies which appeared in the decade after these prolegomena were written and notes the disciplines and viewpoints that have been employed.

4
Problems in the Study of African Independent Churches

The main concern in this essay is with the problems peculiar to the study of living religion; it explores the various dimensions of the relationship between a scholar belonging to one culture and one religious allegiance, and those he is studying within another culture and with a very different form of religious life. Although these problems are different from the academic problems examined in the following essays they are of considerable importance as part of a scientific approach appropriate in the case of religious phenomena.

Increasing attention is being paid to the study of that large section of modern religious phenomena in sub-Saharan Africa variously known as prophet movements, syncretist cults, separatist sects, or independent churches. If these modern developments are primarily religious in nature, rather than basically political or cultural reactions to the changing situation in Africa of the past century, and if their religious content is in many cases identifiable as Christian rather than as Islamic or pagan-traditional, then it is essential that they be studied as Christian religious phenomena by means of the appropriate religious and theological disciplines. In this essay an attempt is made to identify the particular problems that arise in such a study, and although many of these will be familiar to all who have engaged in research on the living forms of religion the familiar problems are liable to assume a different complexion when they arise in the African context. This is especially true for the student who seeks to understand these movements as forms of the Christian church, and who therefore comes into fullest contact with the phenomena and reaches the deepest understanding if he himself is a member of some Christian communion, and makes this explicit in his relationship with the group he is investigating. This is one of the implications of the fully scientific theological method, but it raises special problems which must be recognized and dealt with if the scientific quality of the method is to be preserved.

THE PROBLEM OF EVIDENCE IN RELIGION

Religion involves the relationship between human nature at its deepest levels and realities that are intangible, and the chief problem in discovering and understanding religious phenomena is to find a satisfactory indicator of what is really happening in this relationship. Because of the peculiarly intimate connection between the theological and the non-theological factors that enter into its structure religion may be expressed in any aspect of human life and yet be directly observable in none. It may regularly be manifested in certain forms and yet have no full or permanent correlation with any of these, so that the normal signs of religious reality may suddenly prove completely misleading.

Religions, especially in Africa, usually have visible collective and social expressions through which understanding of the underlying religion may be gained. Only if we reduce religion to a function of the social order can we regard the social activities of religion as a full and reliable index of its nature, and then what we are doing by this procedure is discovering more about society itself, and not about religion. Even if we reject this complete correlation of religion with society and expect only a limited manifestation of religion in social forms the greater part of its reality will still escape us. This has been well expressed by Evans-Pritchard in his study of the religion of the Nuer:

> "The role of this religion in the regulation of social life . . . is subsidiary to its role in the regulation of the individual's relations with God, its personal role. The two roles are of different orders and have different functions, and . . . though Nuer religious activity is part of their social life and takes place within it they conceive it as expressing essentially a relation between man and something which lies right outside his society . . ."[1]

This is a useful warning against imagining that personal religion exists in the individualistic West but is absent from the collective societies of

Africa. These societies are often well aware of the personal nature of religion. Horton has shown that the Kalabari of the Niger Delta in West Africa distinguish clearly between real religion and a merely social use of religion, and that religion is used by individuals for individual ends that have no social reference or that may even be anti-social.[2] As Horton then remarks, we cannot define 'the substance 'linen' in terms of its occasional use as a flag.'

The social or public manifestations of religion include traditions, institutions, symbols, rituals, doctrines or beliefs, codes and practices; while all these may indicate something of the religious reality from which they spring, they never set it forth in its fulness, and on occasion they may serve to hide it altogether. Even though these form the context for all personal religious development, 'The religious life of an individual may often be richer and deeper than that of the official religion to which he belongs, notwithstanding the fact that he expresses himself in the framework of the traditional terminology.'[3] It is most important to remember this when studying the newer African religious movements, and to allow for an inner spiritual life more Christian than some of the traditional African practices associated with these movements might suggest, or, of course, more pagan than the external Christian forms they may have adopted.

This warning is especially relevant to our use of an African's verbal account of his own religion. Here the words he uses may represent the conventional Christian beliefs and expressions which he has acquired from the older churches and which have little relation to his own convictions and understanding; or, on the other hand, his use of words, especially if he is not employing his mother tongue, may be so limited that they convey but poorly the rich religious reality of his experience. A further factor that complicates the efforts of the observer to interpret the discussions he has with Africans is the widespread desire to say what is thought to be expected, or what will please the Westerner, and only a greater degree of trust and understanding will remove this obstacle.

Joachim Wach has emphasized the supreme importance of intention in the reality of any religious activity,[4] and of distinguishing the primary or basic religious intentions from those that are secondary or associated. It is especially important for the Western observer to try to reach the basic intent behind activities that may be strange to himself, and not to interpret such things as possession by the Spirit, visions and revelations, prolonged fastings, and holy water in a superficial way, or in terms of the needs of which he himself is conscious in religion. Intentions, like motives, may be extremely complex and mixed, and those most accessible to an observer may not be the most profound or permanent. Secondary intentions in an African religious movement may derive from the historical or cultural situation of the African people in one particular area, and embody a desire to become independent of the whites, to throw off the colonial yoke, or to restore tribal unity or cultural integrity. Behind these may lie a primary intention of the kind that runs through so many of these movements, a deep desire for a dynamic encounter with the Divine, and although at times these may be subordinated to the other less fundamental intentions it remains the profoundest clue to the understanding of the movement. All this must be remembered lest these movements or individuals in them be judged by visible achievements of organization, expression, or conduct that are inadequate signs of their inner religious reality.

All religions, and not least Christianity, ask to be judged in this way, for, 'Since every religion has to do with transcendent reality, it is part of the truth of that religion to be dissatisfied with its extant forms.'[5] More important than the achievements or the external manifestations of African religious movements are the dissatisfactions which they express with themselves, and the nature of their own self-criticisms. These may form a better guide to their real convictions, intentions, and aspirations than any overt aspect of their existence. The kind of dissatisfaction revealed may be significant for our classification of the inner religious dynamic, for the self-criticisms of the Christian will not be identical with those of the pagan. Here again there is the danger of the dissatisfactions which are actually expressed being accommodated to the views of a Western enquirer, so that the regret which is manifested over the small place taken by the sacrament of the Lord's Supper or over the prominence given to dreams, and the tolerance of polygamy, may be far from genuine. And yet again, many who deplore their own lack of good buildings, a trained and educated ministry and stable organization may be more than satisfied with the spiritual superiority of their religion in comparison with the older Christian churches or missions.

All this is to affirm that religious reality is never completely correlated with any of its expressions or manifestations.

> "We are studying, then, something not directly observable. Let us be quite clear about this, and bold. Personally, I believe this to be true finally of all work in the humanities, and believe that we should not be plaintive about it or try somehow to circumvent it. It is our glory that we study not things but qualities of personal living".[6]

We would prefer to describe the basic reality of religion as a personal relationship between the divine and the human, where the observer, whose study is confined to the human end, sees only dimly and in part what is really happening. His ability to learn even this much depends in turn upon his own personal relationship with the religious man and upon the extent to which he can share in the same religious experience. As has been said of the human sciences when at work in Africa, 'An approach making for genuine rapport should be given priority over considerations of technical refinements.'[7] If this is recognized as important for other disciplines it is supremely so for the study of someone else's religion.

Friendship, then, is the only door to an understanding of the inner reality of an African religious movement, and in many cases this will mean that the enquiry becomes to some extent a joint enterprise wherein both parties gain a deeper and a clearer comprehension. In Africa, this is made possible by the open-hearted and uninhibited way in which a stranger will be received once some reason for confidence has been established, and their community of interest has become apparent. The writer has never had any difficulty in explaining that one part of his interest was to prepare a history of the church he was studying, to which the history of the individual with whom he was talking might have quite a contribution to make, and that this would make plain all that God had done for them and enable their grandchildren to learn how it all began. Once there was a sense of partnership in this task, the most intimate personal religious history was often freely available, for many enjoy recounting their own experiences and have a remarkable memory for dates and other factual details. As we have already suggested, verbal accounts of religion have their own limitations, but where a longer friendly relationship has been possible one begins to read between the lines and to sense the true nature of the inner religious reality.

This situation has one very important consequence for the student. All that he finally has to say about the movement he is studying must commend itself to both the parties who have been involved together in the study in this intimate way. Cantwell Smith has emphasized this for the study of religions in general, and we may use his words at this point:

> ". . . no statement about a religion is valid unless it can be acknowledged by that religion's believers . . . (It) must be intelligible and acceptable to those within. In order to be sincere, and of any use, it must also of course be intelligible and acceptable to the outsider who makes it . . . it is the business of comparative religion to construct statements about religions that are intelligible within at least two traditions simultaneously".[8]

We would qualify this by saying that one's work must be intelligible and acceptable to at least some of the more perceptive believers in the movement being studied, and that if these should all reject it then its value is suspect. No doubt this is a counsel of perfection, but in these days of ecumenical activity within the Christian world, and of increasing contact between all the religions of the world, it expresses a very important principle. The fact that in a particular African movement there may be very few such 'perceptive believers' who are able to read an academic statement does not alter the principle, and it is almost certain that there will be members who can do so in the future.

In further qualification of this principle it must be remembered that believers' interpretations of their own religion are not infallible and may be mistaken at major points. A clear example of this in an African religious movement is provided by the so-called Church of the Herero people in South West Africa, upon which Reeh comments that

> 'this paganism, which is based on the animistic, magic understanding of the world, accepted (external) elements of the Christian worship . . . considers itself a Christian church, and applied for recognition by the Government'.[9]

Even here it would be hoped that an account of this situation might be so presented as to commend itself as true to some perceptive Herero.

THE PROBLEMS OF PARTICIPATION

If the chief 'procedure' in the study of an African religious movement consists of this encounter at the personal level and the establishment of a joint enterprise, we should set forth as clearly as possible the issues that arise when the investigator seeks to work on this basis. The joint enterprise cannot be limited to the combined search for information and understanding of which we have already spoken, but must become to some degree a common participation in the life of the movement concerned. Here the most complex and subtle problems confront both the investigator and his friends and hosts. We shall discuss here that which we know—the situation of a Christian Westerner investigating an African movement already provisionally identified as in some sense a Christian church, and desiring to engage in full personal encounter with a view to later theological analysis. The degree to which there can be common participation in religious activities is naturally much higher than if the movement had been tentatively identified as belonging to some non-Christian class. The problems that arise may be conveniently considered in terms of participation, commitment, objectivity, and detachment.

Participation

The investigator feels grateful for being allowed to share in the worship and the social activities of this group so different from that to which he himself belongs, and will set himself to do all that his new friends do, so far as in him lies. This may mean donning a white gown and walking with them in public procession before the curious eyes of other Westerners; removing shoes for prayer or before entering the church, and engaging with simplicity and sincerity in the various 'spiritual exercises'. It should not be hard to clap with the singing, and it is a very stolid Western visitor who can then resist the invitation to dance, to the delight of his hosts and, surprisingly, to his own enjoyment. It may be harder to restrain his curiosity and remain unperturbed when several of the worshippers become possessed by the Spirit and one of them has to be carried outside. It is certainly more difficult to kneel on a concrete floor for ten minutes while some inspired prophet gives one a personal revelation, to take it seriously because it is seriously intended and because the grace of God spurns no channel, and to continue to do so when the inspiration spreads and a succession of others appears with further messages to be received upon one's knees. When the receiving of the offerings may take two and a half hours and the whole service extend to five hours or more, the principle of participation begins to wear thin in the mind of the investigator.

Through all such demands for stamina and adaptability, it must be remembered that one is participating in Christian worship, offering one's own praise and prayers, sharing in the praise and prayers of others, and together with them receiving the divine blessing of forgiveness, enlightenment, and strength. One must also be willing, if called upon, to engage in preaching or the conduct of some part of the service, as two expatriate doctoral candidates, a layman and a woman studying aladura independent churches, are doing in Nigeria as this is written. To be able to participate in these ways is to experience some release from the inhibitions and conventions circumscribing the traditional worship of one's own allegiance, and to enter into new and rewarding possibilities of worship in other modes. The academic enquiry becomes inevitably also a personal discovery.

In the course of sharing not only in the liturgical but in all the activities of the church, one must be prepared to learn from those who are educationally and theologically illiterate, to take them seriously and really listen to them with all the ears of one's being, not merely as a possible source of information for the researcher, but as living men with their own genuine insights into life and their own report to give of the impact of the Divine upon our human existence. There will be much that is distasteful or merely boring, where genuine participation breaks down, but the right attitudes can be sustained if there is sincerity and humility, gratitude and affection. Where there is patronage, condescension, or mere academic exploitation of interesting phenomena, and where one's attempts at accommodation and participation are made in the spirit of the tourist who will try anything quaint once, Africans will sense the situation and there will be no genuine rapport nor any measure of identification. On the other hand the simplest or most halting of genuine efforts to share in the activities of the movement will be greeted with a warm response. It was almost pathetic to hear public thanks expressed to 'This European, who has stepped so low as to take off his shoes and actually dance with us!'

Commitment

It will be evident from the above discussion that the investigator who participates in the life of an African independent church becomes personally involved and cannot avoid accepting various commitments, barring those which in all conscience he may not be able to undertake. This is a common experience in the social sciences when field work is undertaken, and raises the problem of how to withdraw gracefully and in good faith when the particular investigation is completed. This is not so easy for one who investigates a Christian church in the only appropriate and therefore scientific way that we have indicated. Here one is involved with other people and with their expectations and needs, at the deepest level of all, and under a divine constraint. The situation is completely different from that of the entomologist who concludes his study of beetles and decides he will turn to spiders, and it is very different from that of the sociologist who lives a while in a mining village to study its social structure and attitudes, presents his report, and moves to another task.

Where the investigator is a member of a Christian church, and has been sharing in the life of another Christian church, he cannot take his farewells so easily. When the community of interest is so deep, and in the life of both there is the same divine source and sanction, it becomes impossible to avoid a continuing responsibility for the welfare of the church that has been studied, and for the establishment of a firmer bond of connection with the older churches represented by the investigator. His very work will have established some connection, and the African church will look for this to continue and to expand after his immediate work is done. It is of the nature of the Christian faith that those who profess it should reach out to one another in fellowship across whatever racial, cultural, or historical differences there may be between them, and if the body under investigation is in any sense a Christian church, then the Christian investigator believes that God is at work there through the Holy Spirit precisely to this effect. Whatever report the student may prepare itself becomes an instrument of this deep and permanent commitment, and although he himself may not be able to further it by his own presence, he has a responsibility to encourage others in the older churches and in their Christian councils to do so, and to continue the support of his own prayers and interest. There are some signs that African independent churches are becoming a favourite field for doctoral candidates who arrive from overseas for a year's field work and then depart with neither the desire nor the ability to honour the commitments involved in the relations established with the church they have studied. Subsequent investigators then receive a different welcome and may even be deliberately misled. To dabble in this field and then retreat at will can therefore have adverse consequences both for the churches and for later students, and is a serious failure to appreciate the procedures essentially involved in this kind of study, and to foresee the consequences of undertaking it.

Objectivity

It may seem surprising to turn from the demand for commitment to stress the need for objectivity, but it has been well said that 'While these commitments are bound to colour . . . understanding to some extent . . . the illusion of complete non-involvement, with all the deceptions it nourishes, is more detrimental to objectivity than a lively sense of involvement'.[10] In this sphere of study the approach to objectivity depends not on the assumption of a neutral or external position but on a resolute attempt to become aware of all the factors at work in the relationship between the observer and the church with which he is concerned.

When this is recognized the factors that are liable to interfere with one's understanding or corrupt one's judgment may to some extent be allowed for. The disturbing factors to be eliminated may be grouped as those that lie within the observer himself, those that arise from the fact of the observer's presence in the church he is studying, and those that derive from the influence of the church on the observer.

Sufficient has already been said about the right personal attitudes and relationships, but some earnest Christian investigators will still need to be warned lest they approach one of these independent churches 'much as the commander of an invading army investigates enemy territory, and with much the same motivations'.[11] Attitudes that are wrong can be abandoned, but one cannot so readily change one's own denominational allegiance and the various convictions and doctrinal beliefs of one's own religious position. Some of these, when strongly held, may make it difficult to appreciate a totally different position in an African church. For instance one who believes that an ordered ministry with certain forms and successions is essential to the Christian church will find great difficulty in doing justice to an African church which seems indifferent to all these matters. One who emphasizes the sacraments and associates certain sacrificial theories with Holy Communion will be in similar difficulty with churches where there is no celebration of the Communion, or where it is interpreted in a quite different way. Protestants who are strongly anti-Roman will find it hard to give fair consideration to the hypothesis that prophet movements and independent churches are an epiphenomenon of Protestant mission work, especially when this thesis is proposed by Roman Catholic writers. Again, those sections of Western Christianity which have rather despised its pentecostal bodies are most likely to provide students of these African movements where pentecostal features are so prominent.

Other disturbing factors that lie within the observer may be regarded as due to his position as a Westerner rather than as a Christian of a certain denomination. His monogamous tradition will make it difficult for him to acknowledge as Christian a church associated with a polygamous marriage system. He will expect Africans to structure their Christian existence on the pattern of the ecclesiastic models that are significant for Westerners, and he will be confirmed in this by all that he knows of the missions and older churches in Africa with their Gothic churches in the tropics, their parish organizations, schools, seminaries, magazines, and conferences. He will assume 'the idea that a person can be a member of only one religious community . . . a notion which stems directly from confessional Christianity,'[12] and he will be puzzled at Africans who seem to be sincere in their membership of one of the older churches and of a new religious movement at the same time.

At a deeper level the observer will tend to analyse, classify, and interpret African religious existence in terms and forms developed in the West and built into the very structure of his thinking — the rational, critical, conceptualized systems of Western Christian thought which may not be adequate to embrace all Christian existence, and may falsify the understanding of African religious movements if they are imposed. The result may be an impasse where only African-type answers are offered to Western-type questions.[13]

Finally, the Western observer tends to be imprisoned at the point in history where he stands, for this provides the emphasis and viewpoints against which the African movements are interpreted. An excellent example is provided by the two concluding paragraphs of a book published in 1912 and entitled 'Dawn in Darkest Africa.' This lamented a cloud rising across the dawn, for

> ". . . already in several colonies the natives are restive under an inadequate white control and leadership . . . they are breaking away from Christian government and forming themselves into Christian communities in which personal desire is never allowed to conflict with accepted standards of ethics . . . The mission societies are forced to leave the movement almost alone and thus it spreads and will continue to spread, until Central Africa is completely brought under the influence of a form of Christianity which for many years will be a caricature of the religion of Christ. The only hope . . . is that the religious wave . . . will be followed by an ethical wave which will give the 'Light eternal' to the Dark Continent".[14]

This represents the image of these movements in the mind of many Westerners during the colonial period; they were pathological phenomena, no more than a regressive and syncretistic caricature of Christianity with no contribution to the future of Africa. Bastide[15] has traced the changing attitudes to what he calls messianisms from the colonial era through the period of de-colonization from which we are now emerging, and speculates on the views that may appear in the post-colonial period. In the second period the negative views were often replaced by positive appreciation of these religious movements as a genuine adaptive reaction to change, transcending tribalism and preparing for a new social structure, and seeking to weld together the best of the past and the essential features of Christianity. In the period now commencing Bastide suggests that an over-emphasis on development and modern nationhood may lead to another negative evaluation of the same movements.

To make all these influences clear to himself is the most that the investigator can do to reduce the ways in which his own religious, cultural, and historical position may affect his study of an African church.

The disturbance arising from the very fact of the observer's presence may be more briefly dealt with. In the first place the fact that he is not himself an African[16] must have some effect in the present racial climate, and his hosts will be aware to some extent of many of the features of his own outlook which we have just surveyed. The participation of someone like this for the first time in their activities will create new problems for them. They will wonder how to deal with him, what to tell him or not to tell him, and how they may possibly turn his presence and his purpose to their advantage. The more positive their reaction to him, and the more he participates in their activities, the more they will feel encouraged and confirmed in their own peculiar or most controversial features, for has not this educated Westerner, a man of repute in missions and their older churches, allied himself with them? Jacqueline Eberhardt tells of the changes that came over South African religious groups in the course of her contact with them, Zionists commencing with a welcome and ending with suspicion and exclusion from their activities, and the traditional religions passing from initial suspicion to open acceptance. She relates how one's disturbing presence within the group may be turned to advantage if it reveals tensions or problems lying below the surface; without her presence these would not have appeared, but once exposed they exhibit the true nature of the group.[17]

The third source of disturbance is to be found in the influence of the church on the observer himself. The more sympathetic and identified he becomes the more he exposes himself to this influence, until he begins to feel the pull of the body he is studying. This of course is a sign that he is approaching the point of understanding, and, as Dr. Cragg has been reminding us in connection with Islam, this attraction is essential for a real grasp of another's religion. His response to this attraction is likely to focus on that which is new in comparison with his own tradition, especially on that which is complementary to his own or which reveals its defects and limitations. The more sincere and open he is in his participation the more this is likely to occur. The Westerner will perhaps be especially attracted by signs of the miracle-working power of God and the evidence of divine healing or of the presence of the Spirit, and a Presbyterian like the writer will respond to the virtues of fasting and the spontaneity and joy of African worship, neither of which is a feature of his own tradition. As a result one may unconsciously pay greater attention to these phenomena or become an open protagonist of the newly discovered elements. Again the only remedy is to become fully conscious of the situation, and to that extent become objective about these and all the other possible sources of interference.

Detachment

This awareness of all the factors involved in the parties concerned is the major step not only towards objectivity but also towards the relative detachment that is essential in theological evaluation. The theologian has a special kind of commitment to the truth which must be maintained in the midst of his participation in and commitments to the church of his own allegiance, or of his outside investigation. Where the church he is studying is one of the African movements we are considering there will be far less understanding of the critical functions of theology and of the standards of scholarship than he finds in his own church, which is often little enough.[18] Their sheer inability to comprehend critical academic work may afford him some protection, but there is the constant danger that responsible theological criticism in anything he publishes will be mistaken for mere hostility. African churches are capable of considerable self-criticism at some points, and such criticisms may be expressed bluntly to their own members and freely to others. This criticism, however, does not necessarily coincide with that which comes from a theological study, and considerable skill is needed if the investigator is to speak the truth in love and retain the confidence of those about whom he writes.

If this confidence remains unimpaired one's relative detachment may come to be valued by some at least in the African church, and appeal may actually be made for one's comment in matters where they are uncertain. In this way the scholar may be able to show the church to itself, especially by setting forth the biblical teaching and the historical experience of the wider church that are relevant to any issue. Some at least in the independent churches in West Africa have seen their own threatened divisions and their various secessions in a new light when told the history of the Bantu independent movements in South Africa with their fragmentation. This kind of responsible detachment thus leads to proper participation in the life of the church, and commitment to its welfare.[19]

It is clear, therefore, that he who sets out to investigate African independent churches must face considerable personal demands that will test his integrity as a scholar and his genuine participation as a fellow believer, not to mention his sheer physical endurance, as he keeps company with enthusiastic and seemingly tireless worshippers. Only by a resolute attempt to fulfil these requirements and to endure the tensions that arise between them will the profounder study of these wide-ranging African phenomena be advanced.

Notes

1. Evans-Pritchard, E. E., *Nuer Religion*, London, 1956, p. 286; see also pp. 313, 320.
2. Horton, Robin, A Definition of Religion and its Uses, *Journal of the Royal Anthropological Institute*, 90 (2) 1960: 202–3, 218–9.
3. Bavinck, J. H., The Problem of Adaptation and Communication, *International Review of Missions*, 45 (179) July 1956: 307–8.
4. Wach, Joachim, *The Comparative Study of Religions*, New York, 1958: 26 ff.
5. Smith, W. Cantwell, in Eliade and Kitagawa, *The History of Religions*, Chicago, 1959: 50, n. 36.
6. *Idem*, pp. 34–5.
7. See Bieshuvel, S., Methodology in the Study of Attitudes of Africans, *Journal of Social Psychology*, 47, 1958: 169–184.
8. Smith, W. Cantwell, in *op. cit.*, pp. 42, 52; also p. 44 and the whole essay on personal encounter; likewise Eliade, M., *Myths, Dreams and Mysteries*, E. T. London, 1960: 232–3, 244, etc. Note also criticisms of Tempels, P., *Bantu Philosophy*, E. T. Paris, 1959, as being an example of Europeans telling Africans what they really believe.
9. Reeh, Günther, The Half-Opened Door, *International Review of Missions*, 50 (199) July 1961: 293–6.
10. Schwarz, Benjamin, quoted by Kitagawa in Eliade and Kitagawa, *op. cit.*, p. 28.
11. *Ibid*, p. 15.
12. Benz, Ernst, in Eliade and Kitagawa, *op. cit.*, p. 126, and the whole essay.
13. See Kitagawa in *ibid*, p. 22; and especially an essay discussing the same point in terms of Europe and Asia by Jackson, Herbert C., The Forthcoming Role of the Non-Christian Religious Systems as Contributory to Christian Theology, *Occasional Bulletin*, 12 (3) Mar. 1961, Missionary Research Library, New York.
14. Harris, J. H., *Dawn in Darkest Africa*, London, 1912: 287–9.
15. Bastide, R., Messianisme et développement économique et social, *Cahiers internationaux de sociologie*, 31, juillet-déc. 1961: 3–14.
16. In this field we have found only two published studies of any substance by African scholars – Baëta, and Mqotsi and Mkele.
17. Eberhardt, Jacqueline, Messianismes en Afrique du Sud, *Archives de sociologie des religions*, 4, juillet-déc. 1957: 39. For the new role created by the observer within the society studied see Emmet, D., in *Journal of the Royal Anthropological Institute*, 90 (2) 1960: 199.

18. We have discussed this and kindred problems for the theologian in a university in Sawyerr, H. A. E. (ed.), *Christian Theology in Independent Africa,* University College of Sierra Leone, Freetown, 1961: 15–17.
19. Even the non-Christian religions can be assisted by Christian scholarship to know themselves better; see Kraemer, H., Ancient Religions in the Modern World, *Frontier*, 1 (2) 1958: 127, and Smith, W. Cantwell, in Eliade and Kitagawa, *op. cit.,* p. 43.

5
The Approach to Africa's Religious Movements

> *This essay deals with the more academic equipment necessary for the study of these movements—the working definitions and basic terminology, the relevant disciplines and classification systems, and the various methods employed, sociological, comparative and religious (in the sense of phenomenology and history of religions). The diagram has been added in view of further development of the sociological classification from essay seven.*

Our approach to any range of phenomena is both revealed and influenced by the names we bestow upon it. Serious study cannot dismiss the issue with the offhand popular remark, 'What's in a name?' A name may prejudice the issues by saying too much, or fail to delineate the field concerned by being too vague. Only after much detailed study can we secure precision of terminology, but in the early stages it is better to err on the side of looseness and openness than to adopt terms that are too specific and restrictive. On this basis I have come to use the simple and straightforward phrase 'new religious movements' as a general term for the phenomena in Africa embraced by a bewildering variety of names: syncretist sects, prophet cults, Zionists, aladuras, separatist sects, post-christian movements, millennialisms and messianisms, proto-nationalist and

---

African Perspectives (formerly *Kroniek Van Afrika*) no. 2 of 1976 (issued 1977), pp. 13–23.

protest movements, independent, pentecostal or spiritual churches, as well as the great range of special terms coined by anthropologists since Linton's 'nativistic' religions of the 1940s. The term 'religious' needs no explanation for it is the background common to all these terms even where various kinds of mundane implications are also present. The word 'movement' is chosen as being the most comprehensive expression for an ongoing corporate activity that has some distinct identity; any of the alternatives, such as sects, cults or churches is too restrictive. These religious movements are then designated as 'new', but this clearly needs further specification. In Africa both Islam and Christian missions and churches in many areas could also be described as new religions, and within African primal religions themselves there are current examples of 'new religious movements' such as the developments within the Mwari cult among the Shona recently described by M. L. Daneel and others.[1]

This further specification is secured by relating the 'newness' of our movements both to their religious nature and to the historical circumstances in which they emerge. The historical situation is that of interaction between a primal society and a much more powerful and sophisticated society and its religion, in this case the interaction between the African peoples and the Arab-Muslim and Christian-Western societies which have pressed into the black continent.

As to newness in the other sense, of religious form and content, I refer to the fact that these movements cannot be seen merely as developments within either of the two contributing religious traditions involved. On the one hand there is usually some radical difference at certain points from the traditional primal religion of the area, and on the other hand there are differences from the religion of the dominant society, be it Islamic or Christian. The differences are such that these movements are usually disowned by those who adhere either to the continuing African systems, or to the invasive Islamic or Christian systems.

A DEFINITION

The vague phrase 'new religious movements' has now been given both a religious and an historical specification, and on this basis it is possible to refer to 'new religious movements in primal societies in interaction with dominant cultures'.

It will be noticed that while we have been considering a suitable general term for these African movements there is no specific reference to that continent. This has been deliberate in the hope that the terminology chosen will also be available for use in other cultural-geographical areas of the world where substantially similar phenomena may be found. It is highly desirable to possess such a terminology in view of the great importance for Africa and for the other areas of cross-cultural and comparative studies. By contrast mention may be made of certain terms sometimes widely and loosely used beyond their essentially local application; thus Zionist movements should not be used outside southern and central Africa where the term originated and is recognized, and in the reverse direction a term such as cargo cult is better confined to the particular kinds of movement to which it was first applied in Melanesia.

The validity and usefulness of the basic language here proposed will also be seen if we ask whether it is usable by the great variety of disciplines interested in this field. As a general working phrase it would seem to serve the purposes of a common language in a way that is impossible for any of the more specialized and technical terms emanating from these disciplines themselves. It is quite legitimate for, say, the political scientists to examine 'protest' or 'proto-nationalist' movements among 'oppressed' peoples if they use each of these terms in a strict sense. Similarly the social anthropologists may study their 'acculturative', 'nativistic', 'revitalization', 'transformative', etc., movements. But these two languages do not embrace exactly the same phenomena — they merely overlap in some unspecifiable way. Each discipline is then liable to extend its vocabulary to embrace all the phenomena of interest to its fellow disciplines, and the result is the general application of particular technical terms to the whole field we are examining in a way that is confusing and usually quite inaccurate. Thus we hear the whole phenomena being described as 'protest movements' when some of these are not making any particular protest against anybody or anything, but seeking spiritual power in a new religious system for their own very personal and practical purposes of healing or security. And again these same movements may be regarded as 'the religions of the oppressed' (to quote the English title of the best known general world survey[2]) in spite of the fact that there is no necessary connection between social or political oppression and the appearance of many of the independent churches or other new movements in Africa; if there were one would expect a correlation between the degree of oppression and the extent of these movements, with more movements in, say, Portuguese territories in Africa and fewer after the ending of the colonial period. In fact the reverse seems to be the case, with a preponderance of movements in such lightly-ruled areas as Ghana and Nigeria, few in Angola and Mozambique, and a noticeable efflorescence in some areas after political independence had been achieved: Ghana again, and Botswana may be quoted as examples. It would be much better to seek to identify those particular movements among the whole range of new religious phenomena which clearly involve the motive of protest or derive from a situation of oppression, and thus to recognize that these are only two of the vast range of causal factors operative in this sphere.

MESSIANISM AND MILLENNIALISM

The same issue may be further exemplified from the sub-title given to Lanternari's survey mentioned above: 'A study of modern messianic cults'. It has become necessary to deal very firmly with the widespread practice of using the term 'messianic' and its companion term 'millennial' for the general description of our field, and above all to deprecate this practice in the African context. These terms originate in religious history and have specific meanings in religious studies; a millennial movement is dominated by the divinely supported promise of a radical and total change that will amount to a New Age, a New Order of existence to be effected in the time process, be it in the nearer or the more distant future. A messianic movement includes these hopes with the addition of a messiah figure who stands in a special relationship to God as the divine agent of the transformation; it may also be used as roughly equivalent to millennial, and when there is no messiah in the strict sense, but some other charismatic or prophet leader. There are plenty of movements of this kind in history, and the terms should be restricted to these and not extended to describe any sort of new religious or even secular movement, with any kind of promises and expectations, as has been the tendency in the social sciences.[3] Only a movement *dominated* by this particular *radical* New Order to be established by *divine* power should be called millennial, or in the looser use, messianic. If we depart from this specific usage the term is soon reduced almost to a synonym for 'religious', since most religions have their dissatisfactions with the present and their hopes, visions and promises for the future. That it cannot be accepted as a constitutive element of the notion of religion is soon apparent when we discover that religious communities have often been divided between those who warmly espouse millennial interpretations of their religion and those who equally strongly oppose such views from within the same religious tradition.

When we apply these considerations to Africa their importance becomes evident at once. We find that the idea of messiah figures appeared rather tentatively in the first major and certainly the most influential study, in *Bantu Prophets in South Africa* by B. G. M. Sundkler in 1948; there he explored Isaiah Shembe, founder of the ama-Nazaretha church, in terms of a 'Black Christ', a phrase he continued to use for some time; this, of course, meant an African messiah replacing Christ the Christian messiah. In the second edition of 1961 Sundkler added a substantial discussion (pp. 323–337) of the idea of a 'Bantu Messiah', and gave some seven examples, four being Zulu and discussed in some detail, one being Shona, and the other two being non-Zulu South African founders. On this basis he extended his typology from the now familiar Ethiopian and Zionist classes to a third Messianic type. The latter term was taken up rather too readily by many disciplines, and began to be used for movements of any type in Africa as a whole.⁴ Two things had been forgotten: firstly, that Sundkler's study was really confined to the Zulu of Natal and was therefore rather misnamed, and, more importantly, that he himself had emphasized that the messianic group of movements included 'perhaps one per cent of the fifteen hundred Zionist churches'. (p. 323). Since then Sundkler has been steadily qualifying even this modest assertion, and in his latest major work, he is concerned to play down the messianic role and to reinterpret some of his earlier data so that 'the mediating role of the Zulu prophet does not, at least, exclude the Jesus of the New Testament'.⁵ The notion of a mask or *eikon* is now suggested for the role of founders like Shembe, Khambule and others, rather than that of a Black Christ.

What Sundkler asserts of movements among the Zulu is fairly characteristic of Africa as a whole, where messiahs in any strict sense of the term, as Black Christ-substitutes, are very rare. Millennial movements in the same strict sense are also rare; although promise of a radically new divine order may figure in the early history of a new religious movement even these movements tend to settle down to dispensing the more immediate benefits of congenial forms of worship, a new corporate life-style and ethic, healing, and revelations for personal guidance and security. The hopes and promises are pragmatic and present, rather than those of a grandiose millennial future, and where these latter ideas continue, they tend increasingly to be in a minor key.

One of the rather confused applications of the messianic term to African movements occurs in H. Desroche's fascinating *Dieux d'Hommes: Dictionnaire des Messianismes et Millénarismes* (Paris: Mouton, 1969), with its stimulating introductory essay on messianism as understood within the sociology of religion. He has chosen some eighteen African movements or founders as examples, and this number in itself is significantly small in relation to the total of many thousands of distinct new religious movements in Africa. Only two of those originally called messianic by Sundkler (Shembe and Lekganyane) are included, and even these are qualified as being prophetism rather than messianism, like most South African movements (p. 15). Of the sixteen others only three or four could be substantiated as messianic or millennial in any definite sense (Kamwana and the Kitawala movement, Mgijima's Israelites, and Umhlakaza of the Xhosa cattle-killing); many of the rest are clearly not so — especially Harris and Oppong, the present E.J.C.S.K. or Kimbanguist Church, and the Cherubim and Seraphim, who, as the dictionary itself tells us, are concerned with immediate healing and the solution of daily problems (p. 89). It is certainly more than time that we ceased referring to Africa's movements as millennial or messianic, and confined the terms to those few examples where detailed examination substantiates their use. It is an abuse of language to apply these terms to the general exuberance of religion in Black Africa today with its active search for spiritual power, its pride and joy in being African, and its confidence that it has spiritual treasures to give to the whole world, and especially to the whites. These hopes and aspirations are not millennial.

ADJUSTMENT OR CRISIS CULTS

It would be wearisome to pursue in critical fashion the other general terms that have been used of African movements as a whole, or for such phenomena across the whole world, but mention may be made of two of these. Anthropologists have spoken in recent times of 'adjustment movements', a term much favoured with reference to Melanesian phenomena. While this has the virtue of not being too narrow or technical, it is on the other hand probably too wide; as with my own suggestion of 'new', all religious developments can be considered as forms of adjustment to unsatisfactory situations in an attempt to solve these — even the modern Ecumenical movement and the post-Vatican II changes within the Catholic Church may be seen as adjustment movements. But unlike the term 'new' it is rather difficult to provide the further specification that would relate it to the range of phenomena with which we are concerned, as has been possible with the word we have chosen. If this could be done, and perhaps it should be attempted, then it might be the best available alternative.

The other phrase that has gained some currency recently is 'crisis cults', especially under the influence of Weston LaBarre.[6] Again the term is either too wide and loose, for almost all religions in their origins might be so described and much daily religion is concerned with the minor crises of personal life; or else it is too narrow and inaccurate, especially if the term crisis is given a more substantial sense, with the meaning of an occasional major emergency marked by danger and suspense. If the word is extended beyond this, as for instance to designate the whole series of changes, problems and tensions that mark Black Africa through the last seventy or more years, it loses its real value and all life becomes crisis. In its particular meaning it is not the term that one would apply to the situation in which so many of Africa's new religious movements have arisen; since there has been a constant stream of these emerging through the greater part of this century we would have to see African history as one continuing crisis for all the peoples involved if this were the most appropriate term. This would be a rather hysterical view of African affairs and would overlook the fact that many of those among whom such movements have appeared have not been personally or consciously involved in many of the critical events that have occurred.

Our discussion has focussed on the most suitable general term for the African movements as a whole and for use with similar phenomena in other parts of the world. Most of the other terms mentioned still have their value either within the particular discipline concerned, within certain cultural or geographical areas, or for individual movements. It will still be necessary to speak of nativistic or reformative cults, religio-political and proto-nationalist movements or movements of revolt and rebellious prophets, syncretistic or pentecostal cults, zionists or aladura or Apostolics, and independent or African churches, or to use any of the other terms appropriate for the occasion.

PLURALITY OF DISCIPLINES AND CLASSIFICATION SYSTEMS

This is to say that Africa's new religious movements must not be approached with what Weston LaBarre has aptly called the 'tunnel vision' of any one discipline, even that of the religious disciplines to which they might seem primarily to belong. This would, as he says, be to employ 'only one disciplinary "language" to describe a holistic human phenomenon', 'and we must avoid doctrinaire disciplinary reductionism even though we can use only one language in one breath'. Limitation to one approach only, and one set of categories, produces simplistic explanations that 'impoverish the phenomena.'[7] This is well said and of direct application to the African situation. Such complex phenomena require a comprehensive exploration from every possible viewpoint — theological, religious, psychological, sociological, anthropological, cultural, political, economic, geographical, historical, biographical — even physiological and medical, where certain sacramental drugs are used (as *iboga* in the Gabon Bwiti cult) and where healing is such a prominent concern. It is rather pathetic that we should still be at the stage where social anthropologists and historians are not quite sure that they need each other, and where the wider possibilities of a multi-disciplinary approach are still largely unexplored.

A plurality of methods of study carries with it a plurality of systems of classification. Each discipline has the task of ordering a complex mass of data in terms of its own interests and categories, so that there can be no single final system serving all purposes, although each discipline does tend to regard its own system in this way. Insofar, however, as the religious dimension of these movements provides their common basic feature a classification according to religious form and content may be expected to be of interest to all disciplines, especially as to the degree of correlation between this and other classification systems. Over the years my own system for those movements arising from the African primal / Western Christian interaction has developed as follows, in a continuum with four main groups and two sub-classes:

1. Neo-Primal Movements:
These are new forms of traditional or primal African religions, distinct from further developments within the old system and often strongly opposed to it, yet at the same time attempting to revitalize or remodel traditional forms; this is done under the challenge of the Western-Christian encounter and with certain forms or ideas borrowed from this new influence in order to deal with the inadequacies of the old system. As examples there are the early Congo movements associated with Bullamatare (1570s) and Casolla (1630s), Makanna among the Xhosa (1815–19) and their cattle-killing movement (1856–57), the Yakan water cult in Uganda (1880s), in Kenya the cult of Mumbo from 1908 and the Dini ya Misambwa or Cult of Ancestors from the 1930s; in Nigeria the Reformed Ogboni Fraternity from 1914, the Aruosa national religion of Benin from 1945, and the National Church of Nigeria from 1948, which united with Aruosa to form Godianism (the God of Africa) in 1964. These movements have usually been anti-Christian.

2. Syncretist Movements:
Although this term applies in certain senses to all religions, and in other senses to all new religious movements in Africa, it is employed at this point in the spectrum to refer to those movements that are consciously and intentionally syncretist in the sense that they create a new system by borrowing both from the African primal and from the invasive traditions; in this way they intend to be neither traditional nor Christian. Examples are the Antonians of prophetess Beatrice in the Congo kingdom up to 1706, Ntsikana the early 19th. century Xhosa prophet, the Bwiti cult among the Fang of Gabon from the 1890s, Kitawala, the Africanized form of the Watchtower movement in central Africa from about 1907, the Déïma 'church' of the Ivory coast since 1922 and Bodjo Aké (1926–54), the Herero Church in Namibia from 1955, and the Catholic-background Church of the Sacred Heart in Zambia from 1956.

3. Hebraist Movements:
This somewhat unexpected category is required for a small but quite distinctive group of movements that have strongly repudiated traditional practices especially the use of magic, have adopted the biblical tradition in its Old Testament form, but have rejected the New Testament and the distinctive christology of the Christian position. They tend to identify with ancient Israel and to regard themselves as African Jews, following Jewish ways of worship and styles of life. The three main examples are Enoch Mgijima's Israelites in South Africa from 1912, with a remnant still surviving; the Bayudaya (i.e. 'the Jews') of Uganda who emerged in 1923 from a more Christian independent movement and who have developed

contacts with modern world Jewry; and the God's Kingdom Society founded in Nigeria in 1934 by a former member of a Western Hebraist type of movement, Jehovah's Witnesses.

4. Independent Churches:
These represent the Christian end of the spectrum, and since they intend to be Christian and retain the whole Bible and usually some kind of christology they may properly be called churches. Here we retain Sundkler's further division into Ethiopian and Zionist sub-types, especially if we rename the latter by a term usable anywhere in Africa — prophet-healing churches. In theological and liturgical matters, the former usually resemble the parent orthodox churches from which they sprang, but they also reveal certain African cultural forms such as the toleration of polygamy. The latter are much more Africanized at all points, with healing and revelations through a prophet as their main emphases. Ethiopian types are represented by one of the earliest, the United Native African Church in Nigeria (1891–), the Ethiopian Church in South Africa (1892–), the First Ethiopian Church in Rhodesia (1910–), the African Greek Orthodox Church in East Africa (1929–), and the Bagatla Free Church in Botswana (1937–). The prophet-healing type is found in Shembe's Nazarites in Natal (1911–), some of the Harris churches in the Ivory Coast (1915–), in Ghana the Musama Disco Christo (1922–) and the Feden (formerly Eden Revival) Church (1963–), the Cherubim and most aladura churches in Nigeria (1925–), Zion Christian Church in South Africa (1925–) and most other Zionists, the African Apostolic Church in Rhodesia (i.e. the Vapostori, 1932–), African Israel Church Nineveh of Kenya (1942–), the Spiritual Healing Church of Botswana (1952–), Zambia's Lumpa Church of Alice Lenshina (1953–), and the Maria Legio of Kenya (1963).

It is evident from these representative samples that they occur in many different areas of Africa and that the Ethiopian type is the earlier form. It is possible that some independent churches, especially more recent formations, no longer fall easily into either sub-category. It is also possible that the whole category of independent churches will be less serviceable in the future as the older churches derived from missions become more African, and the independents become more orthodox and establish their place in the Christian community as members of national Christian Councils and in other ways. Then they will be better examined as part of the whole Christian history of an area, and be seen over against the remaining sections of the independent spectrum of new movements — Hebraist, syncretist, and neo-primal.

It will be noted that there is no place in this system for a messianic or millennial class, these features, in greater or lesser degree, may occur in any of the four groups I have designated and do not correspond to the degree of approximation to either pole of the continuum, primal or Christian, represented by these four classes.

A CLASSIFICATION FOR THE SOCIOLOGY OF RELIGION

In distinction from this classification in terms of religious form and content briefer mention may be made of the different classification I have come to use in terms of social form or structure, i.e. a classification for the purposes of the sociology of religion. A Westerner naturally approaches these phenomena equipped with the familiar Weber-Troeltsch categories of sect, denomination and church. This system was worked out for the phenomena of Western societies and the Christian religion, and it is soon apparent that these categories obscure rather than clarify the African data. It may also be noted that they are under increasing criticism within the Western-Christian context. My own alternative system has been derived empirically from the forms that seem to be most evident among the great range of new religious movements, and consists of five classes:

1. The initial vague or inchoate movement that gathers round the work of an individual prophet or charismatic figure, or the more compact secession group that separates from the parent body; this may be called the *prophet movement* or foundation group as best suits the individual case, but the former is by far the more common.

2. This movement may consolidate and organize in the familiar forms of a church or denomination with individual local congregations, hierarchy of leaders and a central organization or headquarters. This form could be called an independent church but I prefer a slightly more open term such as *religious society*.

3. The organization may be more tightly knit, the benefits more comprehensive and the control over members more intensive when the initial movement issues in one of the many new 'holy cities' or 'New Jerusalems' that I call a *total community*. Here there is one central headquarters with a great range of activities providing for all the needs of the members — religious, social, economic, health, moral discipline, etc. Congregational branches elsewhere play a very subordinate role and most members will gather at the New Zion for the major festivals and perhaps reside and work there for long periods. As examples we may mention New Tadzewu and Mazano in Ghana, Salem and Aiyetoro in Nigeria, Nkamba in Zaïre, Guta Ra Jehovah in Rhodesia, and Zion City Moriah in South Africa.

4. If the initial movement does not consolidate in the above ways it may pass over into the residual form that may be called a *clientele*, focussed on a

```
                    PROPHET OR FOUNDER
                            ↓
              SECESSION ( OR ) MOVEMENT
                      ╱    ╲
                   A ╱      ╲ D
                    ╱        ╲
          CLIENTELE ○────B────○ RELIGIOUS
                    │╲  C    ╱│  SOCIETY OR
                    │ ╲     ╱ │  DENOMINATION
                    │  ╲   ╱  │
                    │   ╲ ╱   │
                    │    ╳    │
                    │   ╱ ╲   │
                    ○────────○
             ANCILLARY      COMPREHENSIVE
               CULT          COMMUNITY
```

A TYPOLOGY OF SOCIOLOGICAL FORMS

A, B, C, D = the most common developments

Other lines = other possible developments in either direction

(A development from the lower part of the earlier chart of 1967, as used in Chapter 7.)

practitioner (the prophet or healer) but with no member-to-member relationships. This form is more likely to occur in urban areas.

5. The other possible form is what I call an *ancillary cult* where the group ✓ has an independent existence and corporate activities for certain purposes, but where the participants retain an earlier membership in one of the older churches or some other religious movement that provides their basic religious allegiance. This amounts to plural belonging, which is not uncommon in Africa although rare in Western societies.

These five forms seem to cover the various social structures found among Africa's new religious movements. They should not be regarded as distributed along a linear continuum but rather arranged in a circle with the prophet movement at the top. Then the movement's development may be represented by a line drawn to any of the four other forms, or through any one of these towards any of the remaining three. In other words the dynamics in this African field are much more complex than the simple linear transitions in either direction that are suggested in the Western sect-denomination-church continuum; indeed, at some point in its history, a movement might move from any one to any other of the four later forms, and then on again to yet another of these social structures. This mobility is a striking feature of some African movements both in their religious content and their social form; a Zulu movement that might appear messianic in its early stages is found repudiating the term at a later stage,[8] or the Kimbanguism that earlier seemed to exalt Simon Kimbangu to the godhead is later admitted to the orthodox fellowship of the World Council of Churches. Classification of individual movements should therefore be somewhat tentative and open to revision at later stages.

THE IMPORTANCE OF WORLD COMPARATIVE STUDIES

The emphasis in these last remarks has been upon the development of appropriate categories governed by the African phenomena themselves, rather than the use of imported systems that were designed for use in Western societies. This openness to the distinctiveness of African data must not be allowed to suggest that new religious movements of this kind are peculiar to Africa; it may well be that they have much in common with those of other areas where primal societies have been interacting with Western, Islamic, or other sophisticated and powerful societies and their religions. Just as a whale surfacing may look like a fish, and be discovered to be a mammal only when the whole creature has been seen and studied, so with the African movements — their full significance and nature may not appear until they are seen as part of a massive world-wide reaction in primal societies over the last few centuries. Then it is possible that some of the interpretations and explanations developed for the African scene alone will be confirmed or modified or even rejected when examined in the wider world context.

For instance, what of the four-part religious classification system described above? My own applications of this to all the other culture areas where similar movements occur in similar interaction situations suggests that the same system works equally well in all parts of the world. In the two Americas, in the Caribbean, among the tribal cultures of India, in the Philippines and in Indonesia, in Melanesia and in Polynesia, in all these it appears helpful to think in terms of neo-primal, syncretist, Hebraist, and independent church movements. It is especially significant that the Hebraist class, the smallest of these categories, in terms of number of African examples, is also represented in at least six of the above eight culture areas, and with the same paucity of instances except for the New Zealand Maoris, most of whose major movements are of the Hebraist form. This helps to confirm the classification system and suggests that the basic religious dynamics operative in the African movements are the same as those in all other primal societies.

Other similarities can be mentioned only briefly here, such as the very early appearance of neo-primal and syncretist movements in both the Congo and Brazil when they were first under Portuguese influence in the sixteenth century, and in Colombia under the Spanish in the same century. There is also the discovery that none of the Afro-American cults such as Candomblé, Macumba and Umbanda among the littoral population of African descent in Brazil possesses millennial or messianic features; movements of this kind have been conspicuous among the hinterland mestizo population of European background.[9] Then again holy cities or new total communities may be found in Melanesia and Polynesia, in the Philippines, and in Latin America and probably elsewhere also.

On the other hand there are some striking differences, especially in the relative number of movements at the four different points of the spectrum; here Africa is distinguished by the overwhelming preponderance of the independent church form, a feature which it shares although to lesser degree with the Philippines and the Caribbean; in each case there has been a long Christian history or this religion has become the dominant faith. It is also noticeable that there have been sophisticated neo-primal forms in Africa, such as the Nigerian Godianism and the Reformed Ogboni Fraternity where there are highly educated members not commonly found in this type in other cultures.

Comparative study on a world basis is, however, still in its infancy and the few attempts made so far have not been satisfactory,[10] especially in their dealing with the African material. Further progress here awaits clearer definitions of the phenomena to be included and of the methods to be used, and fuller understanding of the nature of individual movements. Exactly the same may be said of the new religious movements in Africa, for in spite of the great amount of literature on this subject[11] there is still much to be done in their serious and systematic study.

Notes

1. See especially M. L. Daneel, *The God of the Matopo Hills*, Mouton, The Hague/Paris, 1970.
2. V. Lanternari, *The Religions of the Oppressed*, Knopf, New York, 1963, English trans. of Italian original *Movimenti Religiosi di Libertà e di Salvezza di Populi Oppressi*, Feltrinelli, Milan, 1960.

3. For millennialism in the wider sense in the history of European expansion and colonialism, especially in the U.S.A. and Latin America, see M. Eliade's essay, 'Paradise and Utopia' in his *The Quest,* Chicago University Press, Chicago and London, 1969, pp. 88 et seq.; but these aspects would not be called 'millennial movements.'
4. For example, E. Benz (ed.), *Messianische Kirchen und Sekten im Heutigen Afrika,* Brill, Leiden, 1965, to which the present writer contributed without using this language.
5. See his *Zulu Zion and Some Swazi Zionists,* Gleerups and Oxford University Press, Lund and London, 1976, p. 310.
6. See his *The Ghost Dance: Origins of Religion,* Doubleday, Garden City, N.Y., 1970, ch. 8; also his Materials for a History of Studies of Crisis Cults: a Bibliographic Essay, *Current Anthropology,* 12(1), 1971, pp. 3–44, and the ensuing ten-page critique by fifteen scholars.
7. LaBarre, *The Ghost Dance,* pp. 293–4; the whole section is important.
8. See Sundkler, op. cit., 1976, p. 309, on Paulo Nzuza.
9. See M. I. Pereira de Queiroz, Messiahs in Brazil, *Past and Present,* 31, 1965, p. 76.
10. The major world surveys of phenomena more or less identical with the field as here defined are: (1) G. Guargiglia, *Prophetismus und Heilserwartungsbewegungen als völkerkundliches und religiongeschichtliches Problem,* Berger, Vienna, 1959. (2) V. Lanternari, op. cit. (3) B. R. Wilson, *Magic and the Millennium. A Sociological Study of Religious Movements of Protest among Tribal and Third-World Peoples,* Heinemann, London, and Harper & Row, New York, 1973. A briefer survey may be found in my article, Tribal Religious Movements, New, *Encyclopaedia Britannica,* 1974 edn., vol. 18, pp. 697–705.
11. See my bibliography *New religious movements in primal societies. Vol. I: Black Africa.* G. K. Hall & Co., Boston, 1977.

6

A Methodology for Modern African Religious Movements

After discussing where the data may be found, the "Is it animal, vegetable or mineral?" type of question is asked in order to identify the phenomena further and choose the most relevant disciplines. [*Since the movements are primarily religious the history and phenomenology of religions are central disciplines; since many movements also claim to be Christian and "church", Christian theological analysis, which recognizes the divine action, is also essential.*] *The factor of divine action, however, is not one alongside others, but in theological understanding is regarded as operating in and through the secular or "nontheological" factors; these must therefore also be studied through the social science and other disciplines.*

LOCATING THE PHENOMENA

The existence of a widespread religious phenomenon in Africa appearing under many names, in corporate manifestations as new groups and in individual form as new prophets, is evidenced in many ways. Even the most casual observer driving through a large African town cannot fail to notice the succession of exotic names on sign boards or to meet a white-robed religious procession, and if he tries to trace the bell-ringing, drumming, and chanting that fill the night air for hours on end the chances are that he will be led to one of these sign boards and to some humble structure filled with tireless worshippers. Occasionally the bizarre behaviour of a prophet or 'sect' provides material for the journalist seeking sensation, or leads to an appearance in the police courts, or even to military action, as in Northern Rhodesia in 1964 against the Lenshina movement. Strange churches apply for membership of Christian councils, and ministers and missionaries are perplexed when some of their members secure spiritual help from a semi-literate prophet, or transfer their allegiance to an unknown church with an outlandish name.

These developments are referred to in a great range of academic work; they appear in the writings of historians of religion such as Groves, Parrinder, Dammann, and Schlosser, of sociologists such as Balandier, political scientists such as Coleman, anthropologists like Gluckman and Holas, and historians such as Shepperson or Ranger. In official government archives or in general historical works we learn of clashes between these religious groups or individual prophets and governments in most areas of Africa, and of their connection with rebellions in Nyasaland, the former Belgian Congo, Liberia, Kenya, and elsewhere.

It is clear that an extensive phenomenon does exist, and that it poses problems to governments, churches, and missions, and important questions to a wide range of disciplines. This is sufficient to establish our starting point, the existence of what we shall call modern African religious movements: by this we refer to the great range of sub-Saharan movements within the last century, which include movements described as nativistic cults, syncretistic and messianic movements, prophet movements, separatist sects, or independent churches.

The next question concerns the incidence and scale of these movements: where are they located and how extensive are they individually and in sum? The answer to these questions involves three exercises — in religious cartography, in religious statistics, and in religious history. These exercises can be completed only on the basis of detailed local surveys, which as yet are far from providing the material needed for the whole African picture. It might seem that further study should be confined to the detailed and the local in order to proceed by logical inductive order to the comprehensive and the general for Africa as a whole. It is better, however, for the wider and the narrower studies to proceed simultaneously, so that the provisional maps and statistics, and the preliminary historical accounts of these movements throughout Africa, may provide fruitful questions for use in local intensive studies. For instance, if the first tentative map of the incidence of such movements were to indicate a preponderance in Protestant rather than in Roman Catholic mission areas, or in areas connected with American missions more than with European missions, or again in older rather than in younger mission fields, attention would have to be paid to the special features of particular Protestant, or American, or older mission areas that might account for this distribution. It is already apparent that most of these movements do occur in areas where Christianity has been well-established for some time. Some such tentative answers are necessary as suggestions or clues if we are to know what we are looking for.

There is one important aspect of African incidence that is often overlooked, the 'negative instances' to which Evans-Pritchard has drawn attention in these terms: 'If a general theory is put forward as an explanation of some phenomenon, it must be shown *in terms of that theory* how we can account for the absence or different nature of the phenomenon in other areas or instances.'[1] We have as an example J. V. Taylor's attempt to account for the paucity of these religious movements in Buganda.[2] The same can be done for those areas of West Africa, Sierra Leone and Liberia, where the few movements of this kind have been imported. The explanation of these and other negative instances such as the predominantly Muslim areas provides valuable clues as to why these movements have proliferated elsewhere.

The negative instance may lie in the absence of a certain variety or type of these religious movements from one particular area, although other forms do occur there. For example the kind of independent church we call prophet-healing seems to be largely absent from the Cameroun Republic, where the 'orthodox' or 'Ethiopian' type has appeared, although there are prophets and healers in Nigeria to the north and in the French-speaking areas to the south.

In like manner it is important to study not only religious movements that have survived but also those now defunct; this is a kind of negative instance in time rather than in space. The story of the failures may have its own contribution to make to our knowledge of this phenomenon, although the documentary material about many of these may be slender or non-existent and it will probably be difficult to capture the history of most of them. The Sect of the Second Adam[3] and the African Universal Church[4] in Ghana are examples, and we ourselves recently found documentary evidence of nearly forty such bodies now defunct in Eastern Nigeria.[5] If we should find that many of these movements are born only to vanish, but that the whole movement reveals permanence and growth in spite of this, then we should have discovered another important aspect of the phenomena.[6]

A world map of religious movements similar to those in Africa would probably show that they have appeared in certain areas, but have been absent from others. This variant incidence prompts a whole range of questions about the underlying factors present in one group and absent or nullified in the other.

Other questions are furnished by the use of the comparative method at the pan-African level. If the first general histories commonly feature a founder who has stressed polygamy, who has been disciplined by a church or mission, or who has set himself up in the style of a traditional chief, special attention would be paid to these matters in intensive local studies. As these increase it becomes possible to apply the comparative method more fully and exactly, always remembering the danger of patternism, of assuming the universal presence of certain features commonly found and failing to recognize major differences and the great variety in African religious movements. For instance, it soon becomes apparent that in spite of the frequency of the prophet-type of founder or leader they cannot all be regarded as prophet movements; nor can they be spoken of in general as messianic movements, as some have done, when there is little trace in West and East Africa of the messianic idea found in South Africa.

It is, however, at the less speculative local level that the comparative method is still more fruitful. A particular religious movement can be examined in relation to local antecedent and contemporary movements of a similar nature, and its beliefs and practices set in comparison with those of the local Christian missions or older churches from which it has emerged.

IDENTIFYING THE PHENOMENA

At an early stage in any study it is necessary to make a preliminary identification of the data as belonging to the sphere of one or more of the recognized disciplines. In the language of the parlour guessing game, we must ask, 'Is it animal, vegetable, or mineral?' If it should be mineral, there will be nothing but confusion if the methods of zoology or botany are applied to it. In the human sciences in particular it is often exceedingly difficult to make this preliminary identification and to decide whether psychology, anthropology, sociology, the science of religion, or theology is the discipline with the greatest relevance.

It is at this point that a good deal of uncertainty is apparent in the study of modern African religious movements, and studies are being made from within so many different disciplines that the communication necessary between workers in any field of study is not taking place as it should. The only major study of these movements in East Africa might be described as sociological and historical.[7] One of the three major studies of these phenomena in any South African area is the work of an anthropologist and theologian.[8] It is hard to see these as the contributions of fellow-workers in the common enterprise of understanding African religious movements, able to discuss their procedures and their evaluations with mutual profit, and it is not altogether surprising that the later of the two makes no mention of the earlier in its bibliography, nor indeed of two other major works on other areas of Africa. When this can occur it is clear that this study is not being as well served as it might be.

A brief survey of the way in which half a dozen disciplines have been endeavouring to give account of the origins and nature of these phenomena in Africa will illustrate the situation further. The political scientist, J. S. Coleman, sees the early secession churches of Nigeria as the forerunners and agents of nationalism, as 'the religious strand of African nationalism',[9] and G. Shepperson, the historian, discusses the early independent churches of British Central Africa in the same context of the history of nationalism.[10] Others have done likewise for the Congo and elsewhere, so that a political explanation of these African movements is sometimes regarded as established, and their importance is judged in political terms. This is the interpretation that is most likely to appear in studies that are heavily dependent on administrative documents in government archives, for it is precisely the political significance, real in some cases and imaginary in others, with which governments, and especially colonial governments, were most concerned. In a recent survey of documents in the Nigerian national archives, local government papers covering the last 50 years were found to include files on no fewer than some 66 different religious bodies, mostly the smaller and more ephemeral independent groups.

Sociologists likewise have studied the same movements, and found them to be manifestations of resentment against colonialism, of racial tension, or of the disturbances due to rapid social change, which have led to new forms of social organization replacing structures of tribe, clan, and family that have disintegrated. From the studies made by anthropologists these movements appear to be due to the contact or clash of cultures, as a reaction towards nativism, as a search for a new African cultural expression, or for messianic fulfilment of African aspirations through a 'Black Messiah'. The psychological approach reveals yet other explanations. These may point to individual prophet-leaders resenting mission discipline, frustrated in their ambitions for leadership, or possessed of abnormal powers suppressed in the traditional churches; or they may deal with a widespread search for security and a 'place to belong' no longer found in traditional African forms nor yet discovered in the churches that have come from the West. Finally, the economist speaks of the relation between these movements and the hunger for land, especially that which has been alienated to Westerners in South Africa and in Kenya, and also traces the correlation between economic depressions or the degree of colonial exploitation and the outbreaks of these religious movements, as in the former Belgian Congo.

It might be imagined that there is little left to learn about a field that has been subject to such a battery of disciplines. While each has contributed important insights and analyses, their very multiplicity and the occasional implication that a particular approach has reached the heart of the matter, suggest some confusion in the identification of the African phenomenon. The 'animal, vegetable, or mineral?' question has not been properly asked and answered, so that a concentration of effort may be made from within the discipline to which the data primarily refer, and a genuine critical conversation occur between the work of one student and that of another.

Reflection on the diverse explanations and analyses offered us suggests one of two conclusions. On the one hand it is possible that we are really confronted by a series of different movements, in one area fundamentally economic, in another psychological, in a third a political reaction and in a fourth a cultural development, and in some instances a combination of one or more of these. It is difficult to accept this conclusion when we observe the similarities in movements from so many different situations and areas in Africa. On the other hand, if we are dealing with an African-wide phenomenon possessing certain basic common features then none of the six disciplines we have mentioned has managed to identify it. In each case it can be shown that there are particular African movements, and individual members in many such movements, where the factors we have surveyed are absent, only minimally present, or else not peculiar to the last century when these movements have developed.

Some illustration of these exceptions must be given. The explanation in terms of economic stress fails in Ghana, where these movements have proliferated in a country with one of the highest standards of living in Africa and have attracted some wealthy and socially prominent members; likewise the land hunger factor is absent from West Africa as a whole. There is no political explanation for those bodies in Nigeria and elsewhere which were far less interested in politics than the older churches and missions before independence, and which continue in their indifference after independence has been achieved. The explanation in terms of colonialism fails for Liberia, for the negative instances in colonial areas, and for former colonial areas where new movements continue to arise. Nor is it sufficient to speak of recent social stress and disturbance in a continent where we see the clash and movements of peoples, wars and conquests, slaving and migrations, through the far reaches of its history. An account in terms of racialism runs into difficulties when it comes to Liberia, to the individuals who transfer from the independent all-African church of their birth to one of the new prophet-healing churches, and to movements which desire to extend to Europe and incorporate white members, as some have recently done. Psychological explanations are difficult to apply to the large number of normal, stable, well-adjusted individuals in these movements, or to those bodies which have no dynamic founder or leader, such as the God is our Light Church in Sierra Leone and Ghana. Thus each discipline is confronted by negative instances which exceed its capacity for explanation, and suggest that identification in terms of that discipline is inadequate.

A more basic identification results from recognition of these African movements as fundamentally a religious phenomenon. Allowing for the existence of border-line situations such as the political movement masking its activities by a religious exterior, and for the lunatic and charlatan fringe that attends many religions, we can subsume the great majority of these movements under the categories of religion. They exhibit some sense of a revelation of the numinous or the divine, and some response in worship or praise, in prayer, trust, or obedience; they seek some religious blessing of power or illumination for the human situation; they are rightly called African religious movements. To deny them facilities for worship, or to ridicule their convictions about their relationship with the divine realm, would be to strike at the core of their existence. As Joachim Wach has expressed it, '... religious bodies are not, certainly not primarily, associations for the fostering of any material or even ideal purpose, though such notions do play a part, but . . . they desire to be worshipping groups and should be understood and interpreted with this intention so long as it is not disproved.'[11]

At this point we may comment on the difficulty of having this identification accepted and of securing recognition of the religious category as *sui generis*. The positivist assumptions of the nineteenth century are still alive in the later twentieth century, endeavouring to reduce the religious dimension to a manifestation or product of something else, especially of culture, of society, or of human psychology. Fortunately some of the strongest protests against this reductionism, which is a kind of academic piracy, have come from within the offending disciplines themselves. Mention should be made of the Oxford group of social anthropologists whose studies of African religions avoid these 'naturalist prejudices', and we may quote Evans-Pritchard's own repudiation of this fallacy in the introduction to his study of the religion of the Nuer:

> So strong has been the rationalist influence in anthropology that religious practices are often discussed under the general heading of ritual together with a medley of rites of quite different kind, all having in common only that the writer regards them as irrational; while religious thought tends to be inserted in a general discussion of values. Here the view is taken that religion is a subject of study *sui generis*, just as are language or law.[12]

Eliade has developed this axiom with admirable clarity when he says that

> a religious phenomenon will only be recognized as such if it is grasped at its own level, that is to say, if it is studied *as* something religious. To try to grasp the essence of such a phenomenon by means of physiology, psychology, sociology, economics, linguistics, art or any other study is false; it misses the one unique and irreducible element in it — the element of the sacred.[13]

The proper study of religion in Africa therefore requires its own special disciplines, and it is the almost total neglect of these in the growing number of African Studies programmes that leads us to emphasize this point in our discussion of methodology, in the hope that justice may yet be done to the manifold religious phenomena, both traditional and modern, of the African continent. In explanation of this academic blindness we may refer to the suggestion of a writer complaining of the same failure in historical studies of the early Christian centuries:

> Today religion . . . is not with the majority of people a dominant issue and does not arouse major passions. Nationalism and socialism are, on the other hand, powerful forces . . . Modern historians . . . argue that mere religious . . . dissension cannot have generated such violent and enduring animosity as that evidenced by the Donatists, Arians, or Mono-physites, and that the real moving force behind these movements must have been national or class feeling.[14]

Exactly the same assumptions seem to operate in many studies of these modern African religious movements where the explanation of their origin, vigour, and growth is sought in non-religious factors, which may be more significant in the personal experience of the scholars concerned.

An example of this is found in a recent comment on Katesa Schlosser's pioneering work on African prophets,[15] where she classifies them according to the provenance of their predominant religious ideas as pagan, Christian, or Muslim. Of this procedure Worsley says: 'This seems to me at best only a preliminary classification; more importantly the movements need to be classified in terms of social process and not merely fitted into pigeon holes. This African material therefore still awaits an adequate sociological analysis.'[16] There can be no objection to the last statement, but the rejection of religious classification of religious material as unimportant, and the assertion of sociological interpretation of religious movements as more important, merely declares the author's evaluation of the religious dimension. The initial evaluation of the data is therefore of the utmost importance for its correct identification, and a wrong decision at this point will affect all subsequent study.

CHOOSING RELEVANT DISCIPLINES, I: RELIGIONSWISSENSCHAFT

The application to Africa of the two main disciplines contained within the science of religion has scarcely begun. There is an increasing volume of general surveys and individual descriptions of traditional and modern religious movements made from within various disciplines, but there has as yet been little application of the phenomenology of religion to provide a scientific identification and typology of their religious features, and a framework within which comparisons can be made and generalizations substantiated. A case in point is the controversial question as to whether the prophet-type of religious leader occurs in traditional religions in Africa, or emerges only subsequent to the impact of the Semitic religions of Christianity and Islam in which the prophet is a central and characteristic figure. The question is of the utmost importance in the understanding of many of the modern developments, but will not be settled by any number of scholars from different disciplines using the term in different and ill-defined senses. It is the task of the phenomenology of religion to provide the tools with which this and similar issues may be resolved.

The sister-discipline, the history of religions, is also rarely visible in African studies, and is not represented in official mission histories or biographies, and very little in the more academic works on Islam or Christianity. As for the modern religious movements we have in mind in this discussion, there is no single history providing a full examination of the religious development of a particular group, although Andersson's work on Kimbanguism perhaps comes nearest to what is desired. Nor can these movements be placed in their full historical religious context when no attempt has yet been made to write the history of a single traditional religion; contrary to common assumption these have had their individual historical development, which is not covered by accounts of their more recent declines, changes, or revivals written from the viewpoint of social anthropology. Despite the formidable difficulties this is an urgent task, and if intelligible accounts can be given of the religion of pre-historic man in Europe it should not be impossible to discover the religious history of historic men in Africa.*

Even now, however, it is possible to trace various connections between the modern movements and the traditional religious life of Africa. Thus it can be shown to what extent modern baptismal and water rituals may be developments from ancient purification rites, or religious ecstasy from traditional spirit-possession, revelations from the diviners' arts, and exalted prophet leaders from traditional sacral kings or chiefs. But even if the first step be taken correctly and these African movements be recognized as religious, it is possible to err in the next step by failing to recognize the distinctions between pagan, Christian, and Muslim that Schlosser was making. A full typology for modern African religious movements has been attempted below, but we may insist here on the importance of the distinction between

---

* The complaints of these two paragraphs were written in 1962, and have been answered to some extent by numerous historical works that have since appeared. These are noted in the bibliographical essay at the end of this section, but represent "ordinary" historical study of the more recent past rather than a full-scale approach in the technical "history of religions" sense. See especially the works of T. O. Ranger and associates, of Haliburton, Sundkler's *Zulu Zion*, and for phenomenology H.-J. Greschat on West African prophets.

primal religions and Christian movements, for phenomenological and historical disciplines adequate for the study of the former are insufficient for the description, analysis, and interpretation of Christian religious phenomena. For this task further highly developed disciplines are available and must be employed. While the general science of religion may explain some aspects of these movements in terms of traditional African religious practices and ideas, it finds more difficulty in dealing with the widespread dramatic burning of fetishes and rejection of traditional magic and 'medicines', and the new reliance on faith in and prayer to the one God of the Christian Scriptures that is found in so many modern movements. These new features indicate a further dimension derived from the Christian religious tradition, and reveal the relevance of the Christian theological disciplines in the full study of these phenomena.

In point of fact the great majority of modern religious movements in Africa claim to be Christian. They must, of course, be taken individually and each treated in detail, and here the writer can only report with confidence on the particular movement of this kind with which he is best acquainted. This acquaintance began when he came across a group of white-clad Africans engaged in what seemed to be religious devotions at the seaside. This casual contact led to attendance at a Sunday morning service in their Freetown church. Here the initial identification as a religious group was confirmed, for this was plainly a genuine act of corporate worship. Further, it bore many of the signs of being Christian worship in the layout of the building, the conduct of the worshippers, and the content of the service, so that one was compelled to take the second step and identify the group provisionally as part of a Christian movement, and in fact as some kind of Christian church. It was not a pagan temple or shrine, nor was it a mosque; on the face of it one could only call it a church in spite of the many features, such as dancing and the recounting of visions, new to the visitor's ecclesiastical experience. This then became the initial tentative identification of one particular movement.

CHOOSING RELEVANT DISCIPLINES, II: THEOLOGICAL

On the basis of a provisional identification it is possible to select the methods of study appropriate to this kind of material, and we turn to consider the theological method necessary for the study of a Christian church. If the initial identification is correct, this method will prove rewarding and thereby confirm the correctness of the starting point. If, on the other hand, this movement should prove to possess no more than a superficial and misleading veneer of Christian forms, then the study by Christian theological methods will peter out and so reveal the false step taken in the initial classification. This is exactly the procedure and the risk taken in all scientific studies. Likewise the care taken to choose the right initial 'value-premises'[17] is part of a properly scientific method, for which no special apology should be needed when these value-premises prove to be those of the Christian religion.

There is a further sense, however, in which not only those movements provisionally classed as Christian but all modern African religious movements are susceptible to study by the theological method. Even those movements which we classify as neo-primal or as Hebraist have some essential relation to the Christian religion, for they have appeared in areas where Christian missions and churches have had a considerable and disturbing influence. One form of this influence has been to provoke a reaction which may seek to revitalize one of the traditional religions of Africa but can do so only with the assistance of some elements or inspiration borrowed from the Christian religion, by virtue of which the new movement assumes a neo-primal form. Beyerhaus, who takes a very sceptical view of the Christian nature of many of the South African movements, envisages their giving rise to 'A new African religion . . . which according to its nature and content would be purely heathen. Christian missions would have rendered one service to this new religion: They will have acted as a catalyst by having made African animism self-conscious and having shown to it how a faith can and must be developed into an organization in order to become a competitive religion.'[18] In this sense all modern African religious movements are post-Christian phenomena, by way of reaction positive or negative, but never entirely negative, to the impact of the Christian faith, and Christian theological methods are therefore relevant to the study of the whole field.

When the historical development and distinctive features of modern movements in Africa are set in the context of the history of Christianity, and examined in the categories and terms developed for the interpretation of the latter, interesting comparisons arise with earlier syncretisms, revivals, or separations, and charismatic or messianic figures, as well as with such particular phenomena as glossolalia, healings, holy water, and religious dancing. These comparisons will not necessarily coincide with those which might be made by an anthropologist or sociologist with historical interests, such as the common comparison with the 'sects' in Western Christian history. While this may have value within sociological terms of reference, it must be pointed out that 'sect' is not a category with any generally accepted theological definition, as opposed to 'church', and the theological historian of any form of the Christian religion would be well advised to avoid the term. He will probably find that there is only limited value in comparisons with medieval groups or with 'sect' development in submerged classes in the West, and that these comparisons may even prove misleading when applied to modern African movements, which do not fall neatly into classifications established for Western phenomena and by the secular disciplines.

More enlightening analogies may well exist between second-century Christianity in the Mediterranean world and post-Christian religious movements in Africa, and a book such as Campbell N. Moody's *The Mind of the Early Converts* (London, 1920), may open up such questions as why these African and modern Chinese interpretations of Christianity both closely resemble that of the second century A.D. and yet only in Africa has there been such a range of independent prophets and movements. These comparisons and questions arise only in the course of theological examination of the phenomena.

This examination requires theological concepts even for systematic descriptive work, but still more for analysis and interpretation. In illustration we may refer to our own attempts to make a liturgical and doctrinal analysis of the liturgical and other texts of a West African independent church by detailed comparison with their background in the Anglican Book of Common Prayer, and with Christian liturgical and doctrinal history in general.[19] Similarly we have attempted to use the results of biblical and doctrinal studies in an analysis and interpretation of 8,000 biblical texts chosen as a basis for preaching in the same aladura church;[20] this study may well be developed by use of computer methods to examine the relation between much larger numbers of texts (which are available in some parts of Africa) and other significant factors such as historical period, ethnic affiliation, professional training, etc., in which the human sciences may also be interested.

Having identified our subject matter and set forth the need for theological methods, we must now hasten to recognize the essential contributions of the disciplines we may seem to have rejected, lest we be accused of a mammoth act of academic piracy in reverse, and indeed of a new kind of reductionism whereby the complexities of corporate human existence are attributed to the operation of only one factor, the divine initiative that lies behind all Christian phenomena. The dangers of the one-factor analysis and of the attempt to avoid it by the method of 'the balanced view' have been pointed out in recent studies of the methods of the social sciences[21] with which we are in full agreement. Theology, however, has its own internal grounds for rejection of all single-factor analyses even of Christian phenomena themselves, and it is important for other disciplines to realise that they do not have to assert their relevance in the face of a threatened theological monopoly.

The theological premise is that the central and constant factor at work in all Christian phenomena is the action of God towards the world through Jesus Christ and in the Holy Spirit. The theological understanding of this action is that it does not occur as a divine 'bolt from the blue' and in isolation from all the other causal factors at work in history. It recognizes that the religious experience to which this divine action gives rise, 'without fail occurs in a concrete situation; that is, in a temporal, spatial, historical, sociological, cultural, psychological, and — last but not least — religious context.'[22] It is because factors from every aspect of the whole context of any event are operative in that event that no analysis in terms of one factor only can ever be satisfactory. In all this, theological method agrees with the methods of the human sciences. Its interpretation, however, of the exact relation between the divine action and these manifold contextual factors gives it a much stronger reason for recognizing their importance. The action of God is not merely one factor working alongside many others in the total situation, and therefore to be recognized in any complete view. On the contrary the divine action is much more intimately related to each and all the 'non-theological' factors because it occurs only and always in them and through them, never apart from them, and never merely alongside them in an external or competing relationship. This has been aptly described as the 'mediated immediacy' of the divine presence and action,[23] and if it is a true picture of the nature of God's action in history it explains why analysis of events into constituent causes will never reveal one factor, standing alongside others, to be labelled 'the divine force'. The relation of the divine to the other factors must be described as instrumental and mystical rather than associational and observable. At the same time the instrumental relationship never destroys the distinctive nature of the 'secular' factors which retain their own proper autonomy, force, and importance.

On this theological ground, then, the factors studied by the human sciences, and possibly even by some of the natural sciences, are all relevant to our understanding of modern African religious movements. Tillich, in discussing the parallel relationship of theological to secular language, has said that 'every significant theological term cuts through several levels of meaning, and that all of them contribute to the theological meaning'.[24] In the same way it is essential to the theological method that the methods of the other disciplines should also make their contributions to this study. This principle has been openly acknowledged in recent times in connection with the study of the forms and divisions of the Christian church in the West, where it is common to speak of the non-theological factors at work, and in like manner, it must be acknowledged in the study of African religious movements.

Where other disciplines have not yet made their contributions to the study of these movements it may be necessary for the theologian to attempt to make good the deficiency, in an amateur tribute to their necessity. Fifty years ago there was the astonishing work of prophet Harris in the Ivory Coast and western Ghana, which gave rise to the largest religious mass movement of the century in West Africa. There have been some tentative studies from the theological side but a surprising neglect on the part of the human sciences; fortunately, scholars in a number of disciplines are seeking to remedy part of this defect. Similarly, there has been no history of the widespread aladura prophet movement in Nigeria, so that our own study had to begin with a working history in default of the contribution of the trained historian. In this way too many writers from the theological side have been deflected from their own proper study of African religious movements into the work of other disciplines for which they are ill-equipped. In studying the theological factor in these movements, we are examining the central constitutive by virtue of which they may all be regarded as forming a single connected African phenomenon and called 'churches', since this is a theological term. The other factors with which the different human sciences are concerned may be present in varying degrees and combinations, and the contributions of these disciplines will vary accordingly from one prophet, independent church, etc., to another. Economics may have considerable light to throw upon one movement but very little illumination to offer for another; theological study should be enlightening in varying degrees for them all, and be able to welcome the results of all studies by the human sciences.

Notes

1. E. E. Evans-Pritchard, in introduction to R. Hertz, *Death and the Right Hand* (London, E. T., 1960), p. 22.
2. J. V. Taylor, *The Growth of the Church in Buganda* (London, 1958), pp. 97–99.
3. G. Stoevesandt, "The Sect of the Second Adam", *Africa*, VII (October 1934), pp. 479–492.
4. C. G. Baëta, *Prophetism in Ghana* (London, 1962), p. 5.
5. H. W. Turner, "Independent religious groups in Eastern Nigeria," *West African Religion* 5, Feb. 1966, pp. 7–18; *idem* 6, Aug. 1966, pp. 10–15.
6. See further in R. Bastide, "Le messianisme raté", *Archives de Sociologie des Religions,* V (1958), pp. 31–37.
7. F. B. Welbourn, *East African Rebels* (London, 1961).
8. B. A. Pauw, *Religion in a Tswana Chiefdom* (London, 1960).
9. James S. Coleman, *Nigeria, Background to Nationalism* (Berkeley, 1958), p. 175.
10. G. Shepperson, "The Politics of African Church Separatist Movements in British Central Africa 1892–1916", *Africa,* XXIV (July, 1954), pp. 233–246; "External Factors in the Development of African Nationalism, with Particular Reference to British Central Africa", *Phylon,* XXII (1961), pp. 207–225; and with T. Price, *Independent African . . .* (Edinburgh, 1958). Shepperson has also contributed to the discussion of methodology: see his "Religion in British Central Africa" in *Religion in Africa* (Proceedings of Seminar, Centre of African Studies, Edinburgh, 1964), pp. 47–51, where he warns against excessive emphasis of the political aspect; and also his "The Comparative Study of Millenarian Movements" in S. L. Thrupp (ed.), *Millenial Dreams in Action* (The Hague, 1962), pp. 44–52.
11. J. Wach, *Types of Religious Experience, Christian and Non-Christian* (London, 1951), p. 203; see also his *The Comparative Study of Religions* (New York, 1958), p. 34.

12. E. E. Evans-Pritchard, *Nuer Religion* (London, 1956), p. viii. See also *op. cit.*, p. 17, and J. Daniélou in Eliade and Kitagawa, *The History of Religions* (Chicago, 1959), p. 81.
13. M. Eliade, *Patterns in Comparative Religion* (New York, 1963), p. xiii.
14. A. H. M. Jones, in *Journal of Theological Studies,* N.S. X (October 1959), p. 295. For a similar complaint concerning the neglect of the religious factor in the *Cambridge Modern History* account of the Reformation, see B. Hall, *idem*, XI (April 1960), pp. 110ff.
15. Katesa Schlosser, *Propheten in Afrika* (Braunschweig, 1949).
16. P. M. Worsley, *The Trumpet Shall Sound* (London, 1957), p. 222.
17. E.g., see G. Myrdal, *Value in Social Theory* (London, 1958), especially pp. 128–9, 134, 155, 260–2.
18. P. Beyerhaus, "What is our Answer to Sects?" *Ministry* (Morija, Basutoland), I (July, 1961), p. 12.
19. H. W. Turner, "The Litany of an Independent African Church", *Sierra Leone Bulletin of Religion,* I (December, 1959), pp. 48–55 (also in *Practical Anthropology,* VII, November-December 1960, pp. 256–262); "The Catechism of an Independent West African Church", *Sierra Leone Bulletin of Religion,* II (December 1960), pp. 45–57, also as International Missionary Council, London, *Occasional Paper,* I, 9 (1961).
20. H. W. Turner, *Profile Through Preaching* (London, 1965).
21. G. Myrdal, *op. cit.*, pp. 11, 131, 235.
22. J. Wach, *The Comparative Study of Religions* (New York, 1958), p. 54.
23. John Baillie, *Our Knowledge of God* (London, 1939), pp. 178–198.
24. P. Tillich, *Systematic Theology* (London, 1953), II, p. 62.

7
A Typology for African Religious Movements

> *This is a longer attempt at an exhaustive discussion of terminology and at the development of systems of classification applicable to Africa. Later development of the three-class religious classification to four will be found in essay one, and of the four-class sociological typology to five in essay five.*

INTRODUCTION

One cannot proceed far in the study of the wide-ranging and manifold phenomena found in the modern religious life of Africa without some system of classification. Various writers have developed typologies and terminologies for use in the study of phenomena in a particular area, and some of these systems, particularly that of Sundkler's pioneer work in South Africa, have been given a much wider reference, even to Africa as a whole, in default of general agreement on a system that has been properly established for this wider use. The number of local or regional studies is now reaching the point where it becomes important to find a common framework and language, not only for comparative purposes, but also in order to distinguish the essential features of these religious developments.

The attempt to establish a typology at this early stage is dangerous for two reasons. On the one hand there is the danger that all new fields of study must incur; the initial system can be no more than a hypothesis depending for its confirmation or correction upon its success in clarifying and analysing the phenomena to which it is applied. If it is seriously incorrect it may serve to obscure and distort our understanding, and even if substantially correct it tends to overlook the complexities of the field, and to be satisfied with applying a single label to examples that in reality are complex to the point of containing features that the system regards as incompatible. In such a field as this it is probably wiser to think of a typology of tendencies and emphases rather than of individual religious bodies or movements.

On the other hand there is the further danger that the very concept of a typology, whether used by African or by other scholars, is a Western mode of thought, and the terms used to elaborate it may have been refined in the West and retain a connotation that is primarily Western. In the sphere of religion, the most subtle and profound of all areas of intellectual exploration, we may easily impose an irrelevant Western framework on a new and very different African form of religious life, which awaits a much more extensive, intimate and understanding study than it has yet received.

POSSIBLE CATEGORIES:
THE NEED FOR AN AFRICAN TYPOLOGY

We shall endeavour to bear these warnings in mind as we examine the various terms offered us by those disciplines that have essayed studies in the field of religious movements whether in Western countries or in other parts of the world. For instance there are the categories of psychology as it endeavours to type religious founders or leaders, or even whole groups.[1] Here we should attempt to classify African religious developments according to whether the dominant feature was intellectual (rationalist, doctrinal), or activist (ritualistic, sacramentarian, social reforming), or emotional (enthusiastic, ecstatic, revivalist), and there are some who feel satisfied when the last of these categories is applied to the African movements. Whatever truth there may be in this, no one with much experience will accept this as characteristic of all the newer religious life of Africa, or as offering any very important and penetrating insight into even the most ecstatic groups of African worshippers. In like manner there are many other categories which lie in the borderlands of psychology, anthropology, and sociology, and are capable of intelligible use in an African connection, but which leave the knowledgeable observer with the conviction that the religious heart of the matter has not yet been reached. We may with some truth classify these movements and their leaders as individualistic, communal, or authoritarian, as conservative and traditionalist, or as radical, reformative, and protesting; or yet again we might embark upon the deeper waters of psycho-analytic terminology without reaching a satisfactory end to our search.

Anthropology has probably done more work in this African field, and among similar new religious movements in other parts of the world, than any other discipline, and notable attempts have been made to secure a system of classification that will have world-wide validity.[2] From these we may secure the following terms and categories: cults or prophet movements that are revitalistic, nativistic or perpetuative, vitalistic, syncretist, eschatological, millenarian, messianic, or 'cargo-cult'. Many of these terms are penetrating and accurate when used by the anthropologist in his study of changes in a culture, and especially of those changes which result from the contact between an indigeneous and an invasive culture such as has been occurring in Africa on such an unprecedented scale in the last hundred years. Some of these categories clearly have a religious origin or religious reference, and there are three in particular—prophet and messianic movements, and syncretism—that we shall have to use and examine in their religious connotation.

The categories of sociology of religion would seem in principle to be even more useful, but in fact very little help can be found from this quarter. The range of terms referring to the different kinds of religious community is very wide. We may speak of groups or movements, of communities, brotherhoods, societies, fellowships, associations, or followings, of cults, schisms, and various kinds of sects, of denominations and communions, and of various kinds of churches—gathered, established national, ecumenical, universal, schismatic, etc. Almost all the study in this field has been concerned with Europe or North America, and that fact alone should make us careful in attempting to apply it to Africa. Many of the terms here listed are not yet defined by sociology, and those that have won general acceptance as terms in a system of classification are proving increasingly unsatisfactory when subjected to theological examination. We refer to the well-known scale of forms that derives from the work of Weber and Troeltsch, and that runs from cult through sect and denomination to church, as a developmental series. Current theological examination of the term 'church' moves increasingly towards a christological definition, and as a corollary every religious group which is Christian insofar as it is related to Christ is also thereby in some sense 'church'. This means that the church is not one among other alternative forms of Christian group, and a reappraisal has to be made of the familiar sect-church typology.[3] In these circumstances the most relevant section of the sociology of religion is unable to be of any firm assistance. Further reasons for avoiding use of the term 'sect' will be given at a later point, so that we are able to use only the most general terms such as 'movement' and 'church'.

Those who have accepted the description of certain Christian groups as 'sects' have made many attempts to reach a satisfactory classification of their various forms and emphases.[4] The frequent use of the same term as a general description of the newer African forms of religion suggests that such classifications may be useful in this sphere also. It will be sufficient here to mention only the terms used, without discussing their various combinations in the different systems of classification. These terms attempt to indicate the dominant religious emphasis or interest in the different groups, which are described as adventist, eschatological (chiliast, millennial, or messianic), holiness, perfectionist, or pietist, mystical, esoteric, or gnostic, antinomian, pentecostal (illuminist, charismatic, or enthusiastic). Very few terms in this catalogue commend themselves as appropriate for use in Africa, and few will be found in the index of works on the African religious movements with which we are concerned. These do not take predominantly adventist, holiness, or mystical forms, but we shall have to take account of the messianic element where it occurs, and to consider the term 'pentecostal'.

This latter term would seem to offer a real point of connexion between some of the forms of religious life in the West and many of those in Africa, which share the associated ideas of illuminist, charismatic, enthusiastic and ecstatic. In both there is an emphasis upon direct revelation through the Holy Spirit, the second baptism of the Spirit, and behind this upon believers' baptism. In this sense many African movements are pentecostal. The term has, however, other concepts always associated with it in the West when we refer to a pentecostal group or church. The clearest characterization of this type is probably that contained in a Pastoral Letter of the Dutch Reformed Church on the church and the pentecostal groups in the Netherlands.[5] This distinguishes eight basic marks of the pentecostal type, which may be reduced to four as follows: Believers' baptism and second baptism of the Spirit, millennial adventism, holiness as to ethos, and congregationalism as to polity. The second and third of these, in the senses in which they apply in Western Pentecostalism, are rare in African movements, and their polities may be of any kind. When so many important concomitants of Western pentecostalism are absent from African groups which stress the revelations of the Spirit, it would be only confusing to attempt to classify these latter as 'pentecostal'. We shall, however, retain the word as an adjective to refer to that stress on the presence and revelation of the Spirit which they share with the Western pentecostal churches.

For the purposes of a strictly religious typology, rather than an anthropological one, the light thrown from the West upon the African field is indeed meagre. Welbourn has sought to place his discussion of several independent churches in East Africa in the context of the whole of Christian history, and indeed of human history;[6] at many points such as the causes of schism, and the forms of worship, this is a fruitful undertaking, although somewhat premature until we know a good deal more about Christian existence in Africa. Our typology, however, cannot be found ready-made, and the only safe course is to proceed to construct an African typology based on the ways in which the phenomena tend to be grouped. This may have two results: it is possible that we shall then find a similarity at certain points with some of the types and classifications of the West, and because we are now more confident that such a similarity is based on the facts rather than on Western presuppositions, we may be able to subsume the African and the Western religious forms under more universal categories. We may also find that an African typology casts new light upon phenomena outside Africa and so, as Welbourn recognizes, 'help towards the understanding of the development of religious sects in Europe and America'.[7]

Only the most general phrase can include the whole range of phenomena we have in view, and we suggest for this purpose 'modern African religious movements'. By 'modern' we mean within the period covering approximately a century, during which the invasion of western missions, commerce and colonialism has occurred, and within this period the present century in particular; by 'African' we refer to the continent south of the Sahara; by 'religious' we include the traditional religions of Africa, Christianity, and mixed forms syncretizing the pagan and the Christian, together with Islam, although such movements in the Muslim areas of Sub-Saharan Africa are either not indigenous or else very few by comparison, and we shall not have occasion to take them into our account.[8] The term 'movements' is sufficiently general to cover churches, secession-groups, prophet movements, healing homes, cults, shrines, and religious communities of all kinds. Besides the corporate connotation there is the advantage that the word has no restricted usage, yet carries dynamic overtones appropriate to phenomena that are involved in the great cultural, social, and religious changes under way in Africa. We may agree with the sociologist's statement that 'intention to change the pattern of human relations and social institutions is the essential characteristic of a social movement',[9] and may recognize something of this intention to alter human life in the religious movements we are to examine.

NEO-PRIMAL AND HEBRAIST RELIGIOUS MOVEMENTS

Within this genus of modern African religious movements we shall distinguish three main species for our purposes, ignoring Islamic movements for the reasons given, and also those non-African communities that practise Asian religions. Our species are neo-primal, Hebraist and Christian. We say 'neo-primal' because we are not concerned with African traditional religions as such, but only with those new forms that have appeared as part of the reaction to the great changes occurring in African life in our period. Those who have felt the disturbing effects of contact with Western culture and religion, and have seen their own sanctions and unity being undermined, have sometimes sought to develop new forms of the old religions. These have been classified in the anthropological terminology already noted as revivalistic (deliberate return to the old), nativistic (purging foreign intrusive elements under the influence of race-consciousness, nationalism, or in the interests of tribal unification), vitalistic (borrowing selected elements from the intrusive religion but remaining essentially traditional), or syncretistic (incorporating selected elements from both traditional and intrusive religions in a new synthesis that remains non-Christian). It will be sufficient for us to illustrate these categories by reference to some examples; all of these are clearly neo-primal, but information about some of them is insufficient to enable us to classify them further with confidence. Very few are entirely revivalistic, but two specified by Beecher,[10] the People of God and the Cult of the Ancestral Spirits in Kenya, were so described, and in Nigeria it is reported that 'The Ancient Religious Societies of African Descendants' Association' has been registered under the Companies Ordinance, and aims at restoring the traditional religion by co-ordinating its traditions, training priests, and establishing places of worship.[11] Most of the neo-primal movements seem to be vitalistic, incorporating borrowed Christian elements without altering their original basis; some of these movements are also nativistic, seeking to eliminate all foreign features under the influence of some kind of Africanism, even while they imitate Western Christian Churches in their organization, hymn-books, catechisms, etc. The National Church of Nigeria,[12] now called Godianism, reveals both these features, and in varying degrees other Nigerian neo-primal movements such as the Aruosa religion founded in Benin in the nineteen-forties,[13] the 'Church of Orunmila' of the last twenty years,[14] and the Adulawo movement,[15] are of the same kind. In other parts of Africa we may mention the Herero Church of 1956 in South-West Africa,[16] which incorporates Christian rites in a continuing animistic and magical view of the world; the Church of the Ancestors which started in 1959 in southern Malawi;[17] the Déïma cult founded by prophetess Marie Lalou in 1942 in the Ivory Coast;[18] and the Bwiti cult of the Gabon and Spanish Guinea areas over the greater part of this century.[19] Some of these, such as the Déïma cult which rejects all idolatry, might be better classed as syncretistic in view of such a major departure from traditional religion, but none could be called Christian.

Hebraist may seem a strange term for one of the main species of African religious movements, although Judaistic has been used in other discussions. [We use it to refer to those movements that have made a radical break-through in favour of faith in the one God they find in the Old Testament, but which have not reached a Christian position.] There are two distinct religious forms found in the Old Testament period: the earlier classical religion of Israel, and the later Judaism, and because we feel each of these is represented in African movements we are compelled to reject the loose use of 'Judaistic' to include them both. 'Hebraist' is used in default of any other inclusive term, although we realize that it can also be understood to include the category of Christian, and we choose this unusual adjectival form to distinguish these African movements from those properly called Hebraic. We shall employ it to cover two sub-species, for which we can find no better terms than 'Israelitish' and 'Judaistic' movements, and we shall retain the adjectival form in order to avoid having to speak of an African Judaism, which would suggest a community properly called 'Black Jews', such as exists in southern India. Here we mean no more than those African movements that are sufficiently similar to the religions of Israel and of the Jews to be called Israelitish and Judaistic, and that are better designated by these terms than by any others.

Israelitish African movements are those which reject idolatry and magic, and now feel that the one God of the Scriptures is loving and helpful and speaks to the community through its founder or successor prophets, commanding faith in himself alone, together with various moral reforms. This is such a radical departure from primal religion that it comes as a gospel of joy, a great message of deliverance comparable to that which Muhammad brought to the peoples of the Arabian peninsula, indeed as a kerygma. Many of the prophet movements, especially in their earlier forms, seem to belong to this class, and we may mention the kind of religious group found after the work of prophet Harris in West Africa.[20] It is important to distinguish this type from the Judaistic, since the latter term has overtones of criticism and rejection when used by Christians. It should be clear that from a Christian point of view an Israelitish African movement is a remarkable achievement, analogous to the earlier and authentic form of the people of God in the Old Testament period, and capable of travelling a similar path towards a Judaism or a fuller Christian faith.

African movements of the Judaistic type share in what we have described as the radical breakthrough, but introduce important emphases lacking in the other class. They may be less joyous, like the Turban people of Kenya[21] who preach repentance in face of the imminent wrath of the Spirit, and make ready to endure the persecutions that descend upon the people of God. There may be more emphasis upon laws, rituals, and taboos, upon baptisms, and purifications and festivals; a sense of exclusiveness may appear in hostility to the white race and in messianic expectations focussed upon a 'Black Messiah' who will see justice done at last to the suffering African people of God; finally, direct revelation through prophets may have ceased. The shift in emphasis here is that which occurred in the later history of the people of Israel, and it may occur during the development of a single African movement. One of the clearest examples of this Judaistic type is the God's Kingdom Society[22] founded in Nigeria in 1934. Although Jesus Christ is retained as a mediator, the society is unitarian, replaces the Lord's Supper by the Feast of Tabernacles, and follows the Old Testament rather than the New; it insists upon a rigid prescribed form of righteousness, and judges offenders severely with excommunication; those who remain as faithful members of the society will enter God's kingdom when it shortly appears upon earth. This is an African version of Jehovah's Witnesses to which the founder once belonged. Welbourn[23] has described the Judaistic features of the Bamalaki, or Society of the One Almighty God, in Uganda, and even of an explicitly Judaizing section within the society, while the Nomia and Israel movements mentioned by Beecher in Kenya[24] would seem to be of a similar type. The Church of Christ of James Limba,[25] which is widely established in South Africa, and other more messianic groups may be classified in the same way.

TWO KINDS OF CHURCH

Now that we have identified the neo-primal and the Hebraist species we may turn to the third species, modern African Christian movements. By common consent the forms of Christian life in Africa are divided into two broad groups. There are first the missions and the churches that have developed from modern missionary work, together with the churches of white settlers and administrators. Many of these are linked together in regional Christian councils; they range through most of the familiar names in the ecclesiastical spectrum of the West, Anglican, Baptist, Congregational, Lutheran, Methodist, Presbyterian, Roman Catholic, Salvation Army, and many others less well-known which have commenced work in more recent times, together with the large and small interdenominational societies such as the Sudan Interior Mission or the Worldwide Evangelization Crusade. These are normally included in some such phrase as the 'missions and churches', with the emphasis shifting rapidly from the former to the latter term. Anticipating the conclusion of this process we shall refer to all these groups as 'the churches', and as 'group A' until we find the best designation.

The other main group includes the whole range of modern religious movements that are recognizably Christian in some sense, or to such a degree that they cannot be classified as neo-primal or Hebraist. Although they occur almost entirely in the same areas as the churches, these two groups have little or nothing to do with each other, and the second is often called 'the separatists' or 'the independents' by those within the churches, or more fully, 'the separatist or independent sects'; others attempt to extend the term 'prophet movements', or even less justifiably, 'messianic movements', to cover all the forms found in this broad group. Here we reach the first major problem, for there is urgent need of an agreed and satisfactory term for this sub-species of African Christian movements, which in the meantime we shall call 'group B'.

It is our conviction that the distinction that undoubtedly does exist between these two broad groups cannot be described in theological or religious terms, but only in historical and perhaps sociological terms. Those who have drawn the distinction in terms of church and African sect have intended that the word 'sect' should have a theological rather than a sociological connotation, and that it should contain an implied adverse theological judgment. We have already commented on the unsatisfactory nature of the church-sect distinction within the context of the sociology of religion; it is even more unsatisfactory when the attempt is made to use the distinction in a theological context, for although a generation of sociologists has been able to work with a recognized meaning for the term 'sect', it has never received a precise theological definition. The increasing volume of theological study of the doctrine of the church is unlikely to produce results that will support the familiar sociological distinction, for bodies that have regarded themselves as churches are beginning to realize that they have often acted as sects, and what they have called sects may have important marks of the church in their life, and may act as churches more than some of the churches do. In this situation it is impossible to accept a theological or religious distinction between 'churches' and 'sects' in Africa. Even if this were not so, it would still be unwise to try to use a term that almost no Christian group will accept when applied to itself, and which is always used of others in a somewhat derogatory sense.[26] It is exactly at this point of how others regard them, that many of these Christian movements in Africa are most sensitive.

The great majority of this second group call themselves churches, as is evident in Sundkler's twenty-page list of names in South Africa,[27] and most of them want to be so recognized by the other churches. While this in itself does not decide the issue, it is an important part of the evidence for an initial tentative classification, for it reveals something about their intentions. Whether the achievement or the actual religious life of the group that claims to be a church substantiates the claim can be decided only by detailed investigation. In the initial classification we may be guided by some such criterion as that adopted in 1961 by the World Council of Churches, whereby bodies applying for membership are accepted as Christian churches if they acknowledge 'Our Lord Jesus Christ as God and Saviour, according to the Scriptures', and are admitted to membership if they are prepared 'to fulfil together their common calling to the glory of one God, Father, Son, and Holy Spirit'. By this criterion we may immediately exclude from the species 'church' those groups which have some other view of Jesus Christ, such as the God's Kingdom Society already mentioned, and those which do not accept the Scriptures, at least in intention, as regulative of their life, such as the National Church of Nigeria. This exclusion from the church category does not mean that they can still be placed in some other Christian category, such as 'sect', for if this other category is recognisably Christian it is because it has the attitude to Jesus Christ and to the Scriptures that indicate a church. If it lacks these two features then it must be classified as Hebraist or neo-primal.

In adopting this position we are in effect broadening the term church, and at the same time giving the benefit of the doubt to a large number of African Christian movements which in our present ignorance we should not unchurch. In view of prevailing uncertainties this is the only approach that is both Christian and scientific, and to attempt to evade this procedure by the erection of another category of 'sects', or of 'groups that are outside the church but inside Christendom',[28] a category that is imprecise and controversial, will confuse rather than assist our typology. We should make it clear that we are not here discussing the admission of any of the churches in group B to membership of Christian councils, but merely attributing to them the term 'church' along with many other churches such as the Roman Catholic which are outside these councils.

Some have attempted compromises such as 'sect-church'; in a similar way the World Council of Churches organized its 1962 consultation on 'African independent church movements.'[29] We respect the intention of these double terms, but would regard their adoption as more confusing than enlightening.

There are, however, other phenomena in this field where the term movement may rightly be used. Within or alongside the Christian churches, which can provide for the whole religious life of all the members of a community, there are movements such as the Y.M.C.A., various Christian student organizations, interdenominational guilds of divine healing, societies, orders and many other groups with a limited interest, function, or appeal. Something of the same occurs in Africa with specialized groups such as the healing homes of Nigeria (insofar as some may be Christian), the spiritual societies to which church members also belong in Ghana, and the women's prayer bands of Sierra Leone.[30] Many of these would not claim to be churches, any more than would their western counterparts, so that we need another term to secure their inclusion. These are not central to our purpose in constructing this typology, and we are satisfied for the present to call them simply 'movements', and to specify them as 'subsidiary' or 'secondary', as offshoots from the whole group of churches, but not a sub-species.

TERMINOLOGY: INDEPENDENT CHURCHES

If groups A and B are both called churches, we shall require some other term to denote each class. There is an increasing tendency to retain the adjectives 'separatist', 'independent', 'indigenous', etc., that were formerly applied to African sects, and to apply them to the churches in group B. It will be necessary to examine these qualifying terms individually. Some would speak of the 'prophet churches', but this suggestion is readily dismissed since there have been prophets such as Sampson Oppong in Ghana, and Joseph Babalola in Nigeria, who cannot be held to have founded churches, and there are churches in this second class, such as the Ethiopian churches of South Africa and the so-called African churches of Nigeria, which have never been part of any prophet movement.

The term 'native churches' may be dismissed with equal speed, for although some Bantu churches use it in their own titles, the history of its use by non-Africans is so offensive, and its meaning so indefinite, that it is useless for our purposes. It might be said that all Christian churches in Africa aim to become native to their own areas and peoples. The kindred term 'indigenous' might seem to have more possibility of use. In much mission literature it has come to refer to the self-propagating, self-supporting, self-governing church that missions aim to produce, but in a penetrating article[31] W. A. Smalley has shown that when these concepts are interpreted in a Western way the result may be far from a truly indigenous church. Eugene A. Nida[32] has attempted to refine the term further by distinguishing four kinds of churches—mission-directed, national-front (mission-directed behind the scenes), indigenized (retaining funds and influence from abroad), and fully indigenous. The last term is meant to indicate churches that have grown entirely from local leadership and funds, although they often owe much to the mission or church from which they broke away or which they imitate. This certainly applies to all the churches in our group B, but is equally applicable to other African churches, such as the West African Methodist Church, and others in Sierra Leone, Liberia, and elsewhere, and might be regarded as the legitimate goal of many mission-founded churches, especially those with a congregational polity. If we were to stress the cultural aspect of indigenization, it would still be true that many churches in group A would welcome this description. The essential feature of churches in group B cannot be described by the term 'indigenous'.

Another possibility is to speak, as some have done, of the 'syncretist' churches. The word has already been used in its strict sense for one of the forms of neo-primal movements, where a new eclectic religion is derived from both Christian and primal sources, and remains non-Christian. If this is what is meant, then it would be impossible to speak of a syncretist *church,* for church is a Christian category, and any syncretism at a fundamental religious level could produce only a new kind of primal religion, or at best a Hebraist form. There are, however, other uses of the term to refer to a religion that has borrowed elements from other religions and cultures, and has so transposed them in the process that its own basic features have remained intact and merely been given new modes of expression.[33]

This might be termed a cultural rather than a truly religious syncretism, and will be found to have occurred very widely in the history of religions and above all in Christianity. In this sense all Christian churches are syncretistic, and the more indigenous an African church becomes the more syncretistic it will be. We need a new appraisal of syncretism of this kind so that the term is given a clear positive meaning,[34] and as this is done it will become quite clear that it cannot be used to demarcate churches in our group B. There is of course always the danger of cultural syncretism passing over into religious syncretism, through a failure to transform and reinterpret indigenous African elements, and if there has been a substantial failure of this kind in any particular case, then the answer is not to call it a syncretist church but to re-classify it as a non-Christian group. The phrase 'syncretist church' must remain either a contradiction in terms, or else a term of approval; any intermediate usage represents a confusion of thought.

In West Africa churches in group B often speak of themselves as 'spiritual' churches. This derives from their emphasis on the presence and power of the Holy spirit, and their search for spiritual power in religion. The term 'spiritual', however, is too readily confused with the similar word 'spiritualist', and in its Western usage this has a non-Christian connotation, as many West Africans discover to their surprise and confusion when they visit Europe or America. Further, the term could apply only to those pentecostalist churches in group B which we shall later classify as prophet-healing churches, and it is used as a general term by Baëta in his study of Ghana churches (albeit with reservations) only because all the groups he surveys happen to be of this prophet-healing or spiritual type. There are many churches in our group B which are not 'spiritual' in this special sense.

We must now examine the common practice of referring to group B churches as 'separatist', and here we are faced with a formidable list of scholars who have adopted this term. It was used by Linnington in a report of 1924, and appears in some of the latest substantial treatments such as those of Pauw and Baëta.[35] Pauw has chosen it in preference to the main alternative, 'independent', in spite of the fact that it is also used for 'European churches which are separatist in nature'. If we examine the term in its European and Western provenance we find that it has three quite distinct senses, although there have been individual churches which could be described as separatist in all of these senses. 'Separatist' may refer to separation from the world, as with some pietist and holiness churches; it may mean the independent form of church polity known as congregationalism; or again it may indicate the dissenters who separated themselves from the Anglican establishment in England in the seventeenth century. No one using the term 'separatist' for the African churches of group B would suggest that holiness or congregationalism was meant. The third sense, of dissenting, would be better confined to an unhappy period of English church history; for if it is extended for use elsewhere it retains something of derogatory meaning and is akin to the word 'sect'. When churches in group A refer to the others as separatist there is a suggestion of satisfaction with themselves as the only point of reference. For this reason Welbourn has recently rejected the term, and also pointed out that the independent African Greek Orthodox Church is no longer 'separated' now that it has accepted the authority of the Patriarchate of Alexandria.[36] 'Separatist' is also inaccurate as a description of new churches formed not by secession but by a gradual development from the work of some individual prophet. The fact that such a new church develops in separation from those in group A is more incidental to its history and less constitutive of its nature than the term 'separatist' would suggest. It is even more inaccurate for the increasing number of churches in group B which want to end their separation from those in group A, especially by being admitted to Christian councils. In making applications for membership they do not intend to surrender the distinctive features that belong to them as a class, and therefore we must find a better term to describe this class.

We are now left with the main alternative adjective, 'independent', which Pauw rightly points out means congregationalist in polity in its original Western usage, and in Africa indicates that independence from mission support and control which all churches seek as they mature. In spite of this we intend to employ it in preference to 'separatist', and for two reasons. The first is that it avoids the further meanings attached to 'separatist' in the West, and at the same time is a much more positive term. This is because it is free from some of the derogatory overtones of 'separatist', and in Africa is surrounded at present by a certain glory through its use to describe the vast movement of the African peoples towards political freedom, a movement not unconnected at some points with the influence of the independent churches, as we now describe our group B. The second reason is that although the word 'independent' applies in a sense to all churches that are free from outside control, those in our group A are properly called 'autonomous' rather than independent, and emphasize their continuing fellowship with the parent church or mission and with the Church universal. This gives us a certain freedom to attach the term more specifically to the churches in the other group, for whom independence is a more conscious and vital concern.

We realize that it is not as precise a term as one could wish to denote class B, but at least it is devoid of offence, and free from the confusions and the more patent inaccuracies associated with the other terms we have surveyed. Although Sundkler had used 'separatism' in an earlier article, in the first edition of *Bantu Prophets in South Africa* (1948) he restricted this to secession churches and spoke more generally of the 'independent' churches; he has, however, returned to the use of 'separatist' in the extra chapter on recent developments added to the 1961 edition; on the other hand, some have chosen the word independent,[37] and it is hoped that greater clarity in our understanding of the typology of modern African Christian movements will lead to greater confidence in its use. In expansion of the particular meaning we would wish the word to possess in our typology we may define an independent African church as one which has been founded in Africa, by Africans, and primarily for Africans; a three-fold description that is intended in a factual and historical sense, and not as a slogan.

In describing a church as founded by Africans, neither we nor the church concerned would overlook the fact that no man can 'found' a church except insofar as he is called and empowered by the Holy Spirit. To have been founded in Africa indicates in this context that it is not a remote development from a church rooted in some other land or people. That it is primarily for Africans should be understood not in a negative or racially exclusive sense (for, although some independent churches do accept a racial basis, others specifically reject it), but in a positive sense of designed for and adapted to the nature of African life and its needs. In this sense such a church is parallel to the 'chaplaincy' churches that were planted in African colonies primarily to meet the needs of Europeans in government or commercial service in a congenial and effective way.

Independent churches of this three-fold nature usually reveal some major discontinuity with the Christianity of the West in their origin or development. While some of them may trace their origins in part to an initiative from such Western Christian bodies as Faith Tabernacle, or may have retained a tenuous connection with a Western church such as the African Methodist Episcopal Church of the United States, the major factors in their development remain African, and for the greater part of their history they have existed without effective fellowship with the wider Christian world. In this further sense they have led an independent existence. In summary phrase they may be described as 'independent churches of African origin', more briefly as 'independent African churches', or simply as 'independent churches'.

TERMINOLOGY: OLDER CHURCHES

Now that we have arrived at a positive and reasonably accurate term for the churches in group B we must seek a similar term for those in group A. This cannot be a simple antonym such as 'dependent', nor a negative such as 'non-independent' or 'non-separatist'. Pauw[38] falls back on this latter expression, but to speak of separatists and non-separatists is very close to a tautology, and negative terms are undesirable in a system of classification. By these terms Pauw means 'connected or not connected with Europeans', and this comes close to our own distinction in point of fact; but more satisfactory terms are required, and a wider reference to the churches of the Western world rather than to Europeans alone.

Some have spoken of mission churches,[39] and while this is intelligible it is not quite accurate, for there are churches brought not by missions but by settlers, both black and white; nor is it acceptable to the maturing churches of Africa to be labelled permanently in this way. The term 'regular churches' has been used,[40] but this is too vague, and its implications for the independent churches are too negative. Others have used the expression 'traditional churches',[41] and this would seem more acceptable because it does indicate that the distinction depends on whether a church lies within or outside the Christian traditions of the West. Unfortunately it does not indicate the precise ways in which the independent churches lie outside this tradition, and would mask the fact that many of them are firmly planted in this Western tradition with respect to their polity, or their doctrine or worship. Then again, some churches of Western origin and affiliation would be unhappy about the conventional and formal suggestions they would find in the term; others would feel that the word 'traditional' when used of religion in Africa inevitably suggests the indigenous primal religions.

One writer has spoken of 'the non-historical groups in Latin America and elsewhere',[42] and this would suggest the term 'historical' churches, which is that chosen by Baëta.[43] This is clearly the best term encountered up to this point, for it indicates those churches in Africa whose history shows a direct connexion with the Christian community of the West, either through their origin or through later intimate association. In this way they share in the history and traditions of Western Christianity. We have seen that the independent churches, on the other hand, lack any substantial historical continuity with the 'historical' churches, although there is of course a deeper continuity of another kind through their founders or through the Scriptures and many other elements they have retained, and by virtue of which they can be called Christian churches. Behind this again we may find a still deeper and different continuity through the repetition in the independent churches of aspects of Christian history from other times and places. When all this has been recognized it is still true to say that there has been a major break of an historical kind between the independent and the 'historical' churches.

Baëta also suggests several secondary characteristics associated with this distinction. The 'historical' churches are mostly older, larger, and more firmly established, as against the independent churches which are usually of more recent origin, and exhibit 'certain special features which make them stand apart from the main stream of Christianity'. If these features were religious or theological, and could be specified succinctly, then we should have a more satisfactory criterion for distinguishing the two groups of churches; unfortunately this is not possible, and there are no signs at present that increasing knowledge of the independent churches will lead us in this direction. One of the other secondary characteristics, however, deserves further attention—the fact that the historical churches are mostly *older* than the independent churches. In our opinion this is sufficiently correlated with the group denoted 'historical' to serve as an alternative term. In addition to conveying something of the flavour of the historical, it also points to an important feature of the relationship between the two groups of churches as a whole. Some of the independent churches may be older than some of the historical churches, but they are always younger than the first churches in the general area in which they have arisen, and from which their founders have sprung. The independent churches as a whole are always a later reaction to the planting of Christianity in some part of Africa, and in that sense derivative from it. It is always the historical churches which have opened up new areas of any size, and in this way they are always the older churches.

The term is simpler than the word 'historical', is accurate at the vital historical point, and is acceptable to both groups and offensive to none. We suggest it as the best term for all the churches in our group A, with the reminder that the other group cannot thereby be designated by the correlative term 'younger'; this is an insufficient description of their relation to the older churches, and would lead to confusion with the distinction between 'older' and 'younger' churches in the ecumenical context, where *all* the churches in Africa are among the younger churches. In our strictly African context we distinguish among these between the 'older' and the 'independent' churches. The fact that these older churches have given rise to another generation of churches of a different type suggests that it will not be possible for the ecumenical world to continue indefinitely to describe them as among the 'younger' churches. It should be emphasized that our two categories of 'older' and 'independent' churches are distinguished on historical and not on theological grounds, and in the present state of knowledge about the independent churches this is certainly the more objective basis for a typology.

THE TWO TYPES OF INDEPENDENT CHURCH

We may classify the independent churches into two groups according to whether they were formed by secession, or through the work of a prophet and the movement to which he gave rise. Those that are clearly secession independent churches usually have a definite point of departure and are immediately organized and functioning as a church. Those which derive from prophet movements may have a vaguer point of origin, and a more gradual development before emerging into organized churches, and when they do so they are more likely to include among their members those who have been drawn straight from the primal religious tradition. The earliest independent churches, called 'Ethiopian' in South Africa and 'African' in Nigeria, are secession churches; the Kimbanguist churches of the Congo and the Harris churches of the Ivory Coast are prophet movement churches; the Lumpa church of Zambia, and some of the churches which derive from Garrick Braid in East Nigeria, share the features of both groups, being definite secessions through the work of a prophet. These again are historical distinctions which it is useful to have clarified for some purposes.

Further classification of the independent churches can, however, be made according to their different religious features or content, and therefore on a theological basis, and to this important task we now turn. We shall understand the religious nature of the independent churches best at the level of their sub-types, and through the endeavour to find the appropriate terms to denote these, and at this more intimate level it is especially important to seek for a terminology acceptable to the members of these ✓ churches themselves.

Many who have worked in this field have already formulated their own types and adopted their own names for these, and our task is to examine these categories established in different areas to see if there is any correlation between them, with a view to suggesting a typology for the whole of Africa. The terms used by eight different scholars may be set out in tabular form as follows:

South Africa (Zulu) Sundkler (1948, 1961b)	Ethiopian	Zionist
South Africa (Tswana) Pauw (1960)	No special emphases (i.e. orthodox)	Sabbatarian, pentecostal (healing-pentecostal?)
East Africa Beecher (1953)	Separatist Churches (i.e. orthodox?)	Pentecostal, Heretical
W. Africa, Nigeria Parrinder (1953)	Orthodox	Prayer-Healing or Aladura
W. Africa, Ivory Coast Deschamps (1954)	Independent Churches	Prophet Movements
W. Africa, Ghana Acquah (1956)	Orthodox	Prayer-Healing

| World Survey Köbben (1960) | Bantu, anti-European Yoruba, religious independence | Healing, Prophecy, Ecstasy |

In this table we have confined ourselves to forms that are in some major sense Christian, and not included the further non-Christian categories such as syncretistic, neo-primal, etc., that some of these writers also distinguish. We have also excluded other writers such as Schlosser and Eberhardt who have repeated the formulation of Sundkler in South Africa.

THE ETHIOPIAN TYPE

It will be immediately apparent that there is extensive correlation between the classes described in the different parts of Africa. Those in the left-hand column have no special religious features to mark them off from the orthodoxy of the older churches, but exist through a common desire for spiritual independence. In order to characterize this group more precisely we shall adopt the scheme used by Molland in his recent comparative symbolics[44] and describe these churches in terms of their four basic aspects of doctrine, polity, worship, and ethos. All churches possess these four aspects, but one in particular is usually emphasized as the starting point and focus for the others, and is the heart of the organism. On this basis the left-hand group in our table may be described as fairly orthodox in doctrine and worship. In polity there is much imitation of the forms of church organization found in the West, provided spiritual independence is maintained in any contact with other churches. This is the basic emphasis and is revealed chiefly in the ethos of these churches. Here it may appear in the practice of polygamy as an assertion of freedom for Africa's traditional pattern as against that of the West; or it may be represented by strong race-antipathy towards the whites, or be expressed in the form of nationalist or pan-Africanist ideas. It is the emphasis on spiritual independence for Africans that is the chief distinguishing mark of this group of churches, which Sundkler has named 'Ethiopian', following the use of this African word by churches of this type from their first appearance in South Africa. We agree that it is an admirable term, with an ancient African origin, capable of a positive rather than a negative interpretation, acceptable to African Christians themselves, and free from any misleading Western associations. As Sundkler points out, it seeks to find the promise and the actual beginnings of an African church in the Scriptures, especially in Psalm 68 : 31 and Acts 8 : 26–39, and no quarrel can be taken with this. The kingdom of Ethiopia, with its ancient Christian church, has become a symbol for the wider independent Christian church which it is hoped will yet arise throughout the African continent.

THE PROPHET-HEALING TYPE

Turning now to the churches in the right-hand column, we find that only Pauw's sabbatarian group seems to lack a parallel in the other areas. When we examine his descriptions[45] of his two groups, sabbatarian and pentecostal, we find that both feature ritual taboos, believers' baptism by immersion, and divine healing, and that he recognizes the extent to which these two groups are similar over against the churches he classifies as being without any special emphases, and therefore, presumably, as orthodox. If Pauw's three classes can therefore be subsumed under two, as orthodox and healing-pentecostal, we find that the churches in his area reflect the same distinctions as those found elsewhere. Various writers have attempted to specify the main characteristics of the churches in this second class with which they have been concerned. Sundkler[46] describes the Zionist churches as syncretistic Bantu movements, where healing, speaking with tongues, purification rites and taboos are the main expressions of their faith. If by 'syncretistic' he means a basic religious syncretism, then such movements are not churches and are outside the Christian species; we understand his later addition of a Messianic type, which is possibly not Christian, to cover this kind of Zionism, and that there are other Zionist churches where the syncretism is more cultural. Eberhardt[47] has attempted a more detailed characterization, in terms of nine features in Zionist churches: believers' baptism by immersion, healing through prayer, revelatory messages through prophets and tongues which have to be interpreted, sabbatarianism, African traditional elements in worship, concern to find land and establish a holy city, seasonal festivals incorporating traditional African occasions, prohibitions of alcohol, tobacco, medicines and certain other things, and polygamy. Debrunner[48] has described these movements in Ghana as founded and ruled by prophets, with prophecies, tongues, and much emotion in their services, interested in baptism and the development of their own rites, sometimes stressing the second baptism of the Spirit or tolerating polygamy, and strongly emphasizing faith healing. A missionary with long experience of the Nigerian aladura groups describes them as exuberant in worship through tongues, revelations from the beyond, trance and frenzy, as stressing prayer, self-sacrifice, and freewill offerings, as rejecting charms and ju-ju, and often western medicine also, as loving white uniforms and tolerating polygamy.[49] These descriptions are obviously of very similar churches, but are unsystematic, and we shall attempt to present their characteristic features in terms of Molland's four-point system.

On this basis we find the most important and distinctive emphasis lies in the realm of belief—we do not call it doctrine, for it is seldom formulated explicitly and systematically, but we shall nevertheless describe it with the use of our own theological terms. These churches have made the same fundamental breakthrough that we attributed to the Hebraist movements in their rejection of all deities but the one supreme God of love and power, and their abandoning all magical practices. From this point they have gone on to stress two aspects of the totality of Christian belief. The first is pneumatological, for the Godhead is envisaged as present and powerful through the Holy Spirit, who reveals the will of God and the destiny of the individual, guides through dangers, and fills men with new powers of prophecy, utterance, prayer and healing. The prophet has these charismata in a special degree, but many others may share in them both through his ministry and by their own experience of the Spirit. It is this emphasis which lies behind the concern for the second baptism of the Spirit, and the value put on dreams, visions, the gift of tongues and various signs of possession by the Spirit. In the West it is associated with the pentecostal type of church. We are fully aware that many of these phenomena may have been common in the traditional religions of Africa, and may be prominent in some of the neo-primal religious movements. Here we are concerned with their manifestations as signs of the pneumatological emphasis of those African movements which reveal this pentecostal type of Christianity.

The second basic emphasis in the realm of belief may be called soteriological. Those who have rejected both the spirits and deities of the traditional pantheon, and the medicine-man with his magical powers and techniques, have turned to the Christian God for their salvation when in trouble, and for their protection from the host of evil forces that surround them. Salvation has been interpreted in an extremely practical and this-worldly fashion, it may lack emphasis upon salvation from the guilt and power of sin and upon Christ's atonement, but there is commonly some reference to the mediation of Christ, and however defective or limited it may be in Western eyes, it is difficult to say that this has nothing to do with Christian salvation. A full discussion of this complex question must await a later detailed treatment; here we merely point out that this is the way in which large numbers of Christians in these churches most urgently feel the need of salvation, and that on the human side the requirements are faith in God alone and an earnest approach to him in prayer. By the grace of God the faithful are then delivered from the fear and power of witches and magicians, from childlessness, from sickness, from slavery to alcohol, and from many other evils. The rituals, the fastings, the holy water and all the other practices that may be associated with this deliverance, are subordinate to this basic soteriological belief. Their elevation to a primary position, and their interpretation as new forms of the old magic in some particular group, may be such that it can no longer be classed as Christian, but this is another issue and must not be allowed to obscure the basic characteristics of the type we are examining.

The other three aspects of this type of church may be dealt with more speedily. The polity may follow any of the forms with which we are familiar in the West, although hierarchical features are common and congregational polities rare. In addition there may be a strong emphasis upon the communal life, and in some instances the establishment of model villages or holy cities. Where there is a prophet founder or leader the church may be organized around him in a way that reflects the traditional organization of the community round the chief or king. In brief, the polities of this group may be described as a creative eclecticism, incorporating elements both from the traditional past and from the Western churches.

A similar description applies to the worship, where there is much evidence of what we have called cultural syncretism, in the use of dancing, drumming, and clapping, of symbols, ritual avoidances, festivals and rites, some of which are reinterpreted or given a new mandate through the Scriptures. Believers' baptism by immersion is stressed, and the sacrament of the Lord's Supper is sometimes omitted and seldom emphasized. Western liturgical forms, prayers, hymns, symbols and church architecture are freely borrowed, and the use of Scripture is prominent as a basis for the biblical mythology within which the church attempts to set its whole life.

The ethos of these churches has much in common with that of some of the holiness and pentecostal groups of the West, with a morality often legalist and rigorist, stressing the necessity of tithing, fasting, sabbath-keeping, observing the hours of prayer, and avoiding alcohol and tobacco. Some of this derives from a biblical literalism, and some from traditional codes of morality. There is also an emphasis upon fellowship within the community, showing kindness and avoiding malice, and giving the church a good name before the world; even when the world persecutes the Christian he must be ready to endure through the grace of his master who suffered before him. The traditional African ethos is revealed most clearly in those churches which exhibit polygamy, although this is usually tolerated rather than encouraged; some are monogamous, and so polygamy is not the universal and important characteristic of these churches which some have thought.

It must be remembered that we are here constructing what is to some extent an ideal type, with a range of characteristics within which many of the features that mark any one church will be found to fall. Another way of expressing it is to say that we have described a common tendency among independent churches, whereby many of them exhibit a large proportion of the features we have mentioned and so may be grouped together as one class or type, to which we must now give a name. There are, fortunately, two terms popular in Africa among these churches themselves. The first is 'Zionist', which originates in South Africa and has been adopted by Sundkler and others. The second is found in West Africa, the Yoruba term 'aladura'. This is formed by the combination of the word *adura* meaning prayer, with the prefix *oni* referring to the owner or practitioner of anything; when the prefix is transformed according to the rules of the language the resultant term means 'one who prays'. 'Aladura' is now the common term for churches of this type that have emerged in Western Nigeria in the last forty years; it is welcomed by these churches themselves and some use it in their official name; it has also been used by Parrinder and some others in the West African context. It is clear, however, that 'Zionist' is too deeply entrenched in South African usage to be replaced by another term such as 'aladura'; likewise it is inconceivable that the latter could be replaced by 'Zionist' in West Africa. In these circumstances we may adopt the compromise accepted at the World Council of Churches consultation at Mindolo in 1962, and speak of 'Zionist or Aladura' churches, or else seek another term, such as Baëta's 'spiritual'. We have noted one objection to this, and it would also be most unfortunate in its implications for other churches; a more objective and specific term is required.

If we recall the two 'marks' of these churches to be found in their central beliefs about revelation from the Spirit through prophets and a practical salvation in which healing is prominent, we are led to suggest 'prophet-healing' as the most accurate and satisfactory descriptive phrase suitable for general adoption. It is similar to the term 'prayer-healing' which some have used, but which refers only to the salvation-interest of these churches and neglects the possibly more important emphasis on revelation and the Spirit. 'Prophet-healing' is equally cumbrous, but does indicate both basic emphases, and can include those churches in this class where the healing concern is minimal or even absent. For instance, the healing interest seems to have been absent from the earlier independent churches in Kenya, and the prophets there did not operate as healers; likewise Harris in West Africa performed few healings and in an incidental way. On the other hand it is reported that the healing interest is appearing in more recent developments in Kenya, and we may regard the words 'prophet' and 'healing' in our phrase as indicating the two poles between which the emphasis within this group of churches moves. In default of any satisfactory single term we may describe them as the 'prophet-healing' churches, or as 'aladura' churches when speaking within the West African context, and as 'Zionist' churches when the reference is to South Africa.

In his study of churches in East Africa Welbourn has said that he does not find the distinction we have now named 'Ethiopian' and 'prophet-healing' to be helpful. In view of the types distinguished by Beecher in Kenya, which seem to be congruous with our distinctions, we wonder if Welbourn's difficulty is with the terminology, rather than with the types or classes themselves. It would seem to us that the churches he has described exhibit many of the features we have been discussing, although it may be that they are less 'true to type' or more mixed in form than those in other regions of Africa. It must be remembered that any all-Africa typology will not be equally useful in all areas, but will serve its purpose if it calls attention to any widespread traits.

The prophet-healing churches seem to have appeared later than the Ethiopian, most of which were formed in the later part of the last century or the first two decades of this century. In West Africa the dividing line falls fairly clearly about 1920, and we suspect that this is fairly representative of Africa as a whole. This observation is supported by Pauw's remarks[50] that 'there is a greater tendency within Separatism toward Sabbatarianism and Pentecostalism, than within non-Separatism, and that this tendency is relatively recent,' although in the area he studied the oldest prophet-healing type is as late as 1932. This means that the initiative has now passed to the type which stresses particular beliefs in the realms of pneumatology and soteriology rather than spiritual independence of the whites, and the attempt to understand the independent churches must increasingly be made at these deeper religious levels.

THE SUB-TYPES, AND MESSIANISM

As a contribution towards this we shall explore the possibility of carrying this typology a stage further, and distinguishing the groups or tendencies that may be found within the categories of Ethiopian and prophet-healing. Sundkler has already indicated[51] that the Ethiopian churches exhibit a 'wide scale of difference running from a right wing comprising Churches which in their structure and outlook are 'carbon copies' of their parent Mission Churches, to a left wing where Zionist tendencies loom large.' This corresponds to the distinction which Molland[52] draws throughout Christendom between right and left wings according to the attitude adopted towards tradition. Webster, in studying the Nigerian Ethiopian or African churches, tentatively suggested 'high church' and 'low church' for the two groups he finds among them,[53] but the Western usage of these terms is not very satisfactory, and their African use is less so. We have suggested that the terms 'ecclesiastical' and 'evangelical' might be considered; the former for churches which are more Western and traditional in their liturgy, more clerical in their polity, and which emphasize monogamy; the latter for those which are more revivalist in their worship, give greater place to laymen and to missionary extension, and which allow polygamy. These latter, like Sundkler's churches of the left, would appear closer to the prophet-healing type. While these proposals can be made in the West African situation where they arose, we should need many more intimate studies of Ethiopian churches elsewhere in Africa before we could discuss their wider application.

Something of the same division may be made between right and left wing churches of the prophet-healing type, at least so far as West Africa again is concerned. Some lay greater stress upon the soteriological element in their beliefs, faith healing is prominent, and an attempt is made to limit the manifestations of the Spirit to certain forms or specified occasions, or even to private spiritual exercises. The large aladura church known as the Christ Apostolic Church is an example, and as this seems to bring it nearer to the older churches as well as to the Ethiopian churches, we would call this a right wing church. Others, such as some of the Cherubim and Seraphim Societies, make the revelations of the Spirit their primary concern, and divine healing of secondary importance; there will seldom be a service without messages, visions and someone being at least partly possessed by the Spirit, while healings may be confined to special healing services or to private pastoral ministration by the prophet. Both groups are pentecostal, but for one the chief gift of the Spirit is healing, for the other prophecy. It is difficult to find satisfactory terms to denote these two emphases, the soteriological and pneumatological, and we suggest with some diffidence that they might be called 'therapeutic' and 'revelatory'. R. C. Mitchell[54] has suggested 'apostolic' and 'spiritual', taking his lead from local terms associated with prominent churches of each type, but while this would be intelligible in Nigeria it would be confusing elsewhere.

Baëta has not attempted to classify the 'spiritual' or prophet-healing groups he has surveyed in Ghana, but they will be found to fall readily into the two sub-divisions we have proposed. Of the five groups to which he devotes most attention, three are clearly of the therapeutic class: the Church of the Twelve Apostles, the Musama Disco Christo Church, and the Etodome Prayer-Healing Group all proclaim healing as their main concern. The other two, the Saviour Church and the Apostolic Revelation Society, do not regard healing as a primary activity, and even divine healing may be a long and slow process; the first of these derives from the work of prophet Harris, the second is led by prophet Wovenu, and both emphasize preaching and moral and communal reform. They may be regarded as very sober and non-ecstatic examples of the prophetic or revelatory class.

Alongside these two classes of prophet-healing church there stands a third distinct type, the messianic, which shares in the emphases on revelation and on salvation, but which exalts the founding prophet or leader into the position of a messiah. The Mindolo consultation of 1962 described as messianic those groups 'which, centred around a dominant personality, claim for him special powers involving a form of identification with Christ. It should be noted that when this identification becomes substitution, the group has . . . moved outside the sphere of the Christian Church.' The classification of these groups presents some difficulties, for although the messianic concept is ultimately of biblical origin,[55] and these groups usually lay great stress upon the Bible and desire to be known as Christian, some

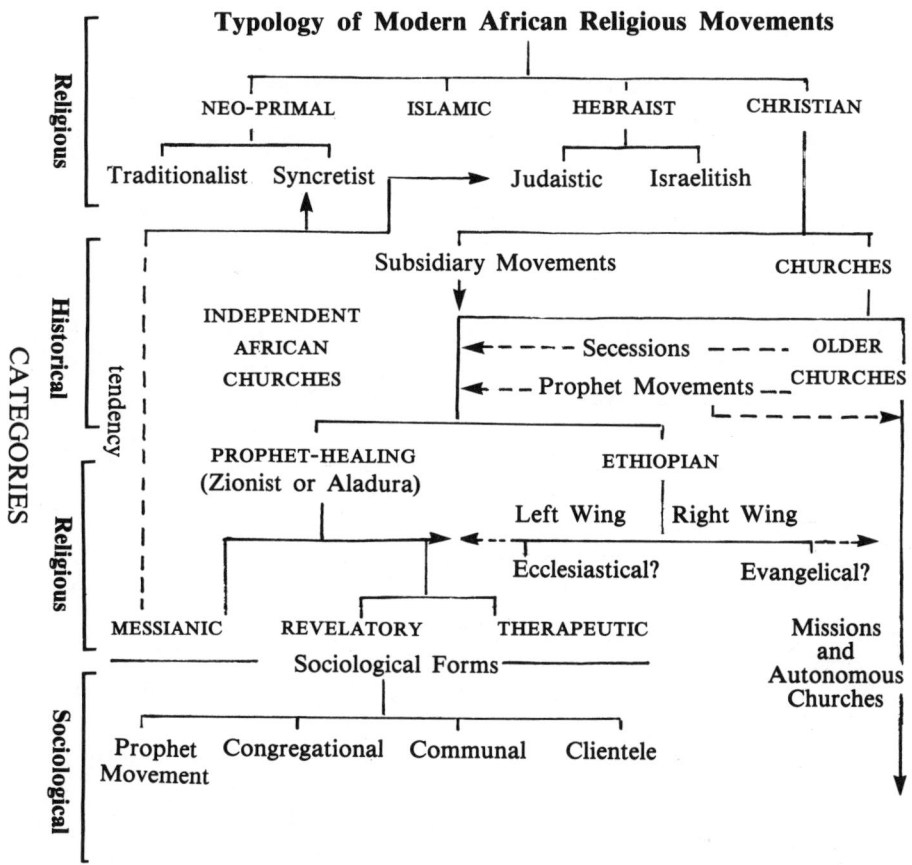

(This chart is a modified version of that contributed by the author to *African Independent Church Movements,* ed. V. E. W. Hayward, London, 1963. For later refinements see the charts in chapters 1 and 5 above.)

of them have so far replaced the Christian centre, which is Christ, with another centre of African origin that they can no longer be properly regarded as Christian. In that case they have moved over into the Judaistic or syncretist categories, for messianism in Africa is not confined to Christian groups; it may appear in neo-primal or Hebraist movements, in Islam, or even in secular form in political movements such as Nkrumahism in Ghana. Within the Christian category it is not widespread, for it seems to be almost entirely absent from East and West African independent churches, and to be confined to those in Central or South Africa. Even in the South, where it is commonest, Sundkler asserts that there are no more than about ten to fifteen such groups among the very large number of Bantu independents. It is then a great mistake to use it as a general term for independent churches or for modern African religious movements, as some writers have done.[56]

SOCIOLOGICAL DISTINCTIONS

Our subdivision of prophet-healing churches has been based on religious categories, but it is also possible to make a sociological classification according to the types of corporate existence which occur among them, and these may be briefly mentioned. There is first of all the more inchoate and unorganized prophet movement, which influences a large number of people in varying degrees without necessarily offering them any new or alternative religious community, and which depends only on the influence of the charismatic leader, as this waxes or wanes. This is commonly the initial form of modern religious movements in Africa, and it has usually led to the formation of the familiar pattern of church life in local congregations linked together in some wider district or national organization. This may be called the congregational type. A third type is found where new villages have been founded and a Christian communal life has developed,[57] as at New Mazano and at Tadzewu in Ghana, at the remarkable Aiyetoro village in Nigeria, at the 'village of Mary' of the Children of the Sacred Heart in Zambia, and at the holy cities of some of the messianic Zionist churches of South Africa, which are described by Eberhardt as 'total' societies of a theocratic-charismatic nature. Yet a fourth type may be called the 'clientele' form that consists of patients attached to a practitioner renowned for his healing powers, and sharing in the religious exercises and teaching that are part of the treatment. They may attend periodically at his centre, or live for shorter or longer periods in his 'healing home', or at a small village such as the 'Bethesda' kind of community in the South African reserves described by Sundkler.[58] There does not seem to be any special correlation between these four sociological types and the three types of religious emphasis found in the prophet-healing churches, except in the last example, the clientele form, which is clearly associated with the therapeutic emphasis. Otherwise the range of beliefs which we have designated as prophet-healing may be expressed through any of these social forms.

PURE AND MIXED TYPES

This concludes our attempt to establish a working typology for these African religious phenomena. It may well be that it will be found to apply more readily in West Africa, with which we are more familiar, and where the independent churches may prove to be 'purer' types because their origin and development have been determined very largely by religious factors. They have been freer from the problems of racial conflict, economic exploitation, political repression, and land hunger, and have advanced towards independence faster than most other parts of Africa, where the operation of these factors has often profoundly affected the history of the independent churches. The more complex situation elsewhere, especially in South Africa, may have produced more 'mixed' types which seem to belong to more than one of the classes of our typology. For instance, there are churches among the coloured people of South Africa which fit both the Ethiopian and prophet-healing categories; there are pentecostal churches which are Ethiopian because similar in pattern to older and Western-connected pentecostal churches, but Zionist in their peculiar emphasis on the Spirit; and there are Ethiopian churches which reflect the pattern of no single Western parent church, but exhibit a new African combination of various features all drawn from the older churches.[59] Any typology, however, will be found to apply in varying degrees to different regions in such a vast area as Africa, and yet may still serve to exhibit the extent to which there are common features in the manifold phenomena of these modern African religious movements.

Notes

1. Clark, E. T., *The Small Sects in America*, New York, 1949, 21 f., and references there to McComas, H. C., *The Psychology of Religious Sects*, New York, 1912, chs. 6–7.
2. See Smith, Marian W., Towards a classification of cult movements, *Man*, 59, art. 2, 1959, 8–12, surveying the main contributions from 1943 to 1958. For world surveys see Köbben, R. J. F., Prophetic movements as an expression of social protest, *International Archives of Ethnography*, 49 (1), 1960, 117–164, and especially Guariglia, G., *Prophetismus und Heilserwartungsbewegungen als völkerkundliches und religionsgeschichtliches Problem*, Vienna, 1959; for Africa see Fernandez, James W., African religious movements—types and dynamics, *Journal of Modern African Studies*, 2 (4), 1964, 531–49.
3. Indications of this in Bainton, R. H., The sectarian theory of the Church, *Christendom*, 11 (3), 1946, 382–7; Littell, F. H., Church and Sect, *Ecumenical Review*, 6 (2), 1954, 262–76; Schweizer, E., et al., *Die Einheit der Kirche und Sekten*, Zollikon, 1957.
4. For example, Clark, *op. cit., passim*; Wach, J., *Sociology of Religion*, London, 1947, ch. 5; Wilson, B. R., An analysis of sect development, *American Sociological Review*, 24 (1), 1959, 3–15; Friedmann, R., The concept of the Anabaptists, *Church History*, 9 (4), 1940, 341 ff.; and especially the summary in the latter of Kuhn, J., *Toleranz und Offenbarung*, 1923.
5. *De Kerk en de Pinkstergroepen*, Den Haag, 1960.
6. Welbourn, F. B., *East African Rebels*, London, 1961, 165, 168 f.
7. *Ibid.*, p. 183.
8. But see Schlosser, K., *Propheten in Afrika*, Braunchsweig, 1949. The Ismailia and Ahmadiyya movements are influential in our area but not indigenous.
9. Voget, F. W., in *Man*, 59, art. 25, 1959.
10. Beecher, L. J., African Separatist Churches in Kenya, *World Dominion*

31 (1) 1953, 5–12; see also Kenyatta, J., *Facing Mount Kenya*, London, 1961, 273–9.
11. *Daily Times,* Lagos, 6.3.62; and private paper prepared by P. B. Blanshard Jr., Dec. 1961.
12. Coleman, J. S., *Nigeria: background to nationalism,* Berkeley, 1958, pp. 302 f.; Parrinder, E. G., *Religion in an African city,* London, 1953, 10, 128, 186 f. Abundant literature may be available from 219 Cameron Road, Aba, E. Nigeria.
13. Church of England in West Africa: *Report of Proceedings,* 3rd session, 9th synod, Diocese of Lagos, 1946, 50 f., 54 f., 78; also its own literature. Aruosa, or the National Church of the Edo, has now amalgamated with Godianism.
14. Idowu, E. B., *Olódùmarè: God in Yoruba belief,* London, 1962, 214f.
15. Personal communication from the Rev. T. A. Adejunmobi, 1962.
16. Reeh, G., The half-opened door, *International Review of Missions,* 50 (199), July 1961, 293–6.
17. Wishlade, R. L., Chiefship and politics in the Melanje District of Southern Nyasaland, *Africa,* 3 (1), 1961, 44 f.
18. Holas, B., "Bref aperçu sur les principaux cultes syncrétiques de la Basse Côte d'Ivoire," *Africa,* 24 (1), 1954, 58–60; see also his *Le Séparatisme religieux en Afrique noire,* Paris, 1965.
19. Balandier, G., *Sociologie actuelle de l'Afrique noire,* Paris, 1955, 219–32; Thompson, V., and Adloff, R., *The emerging states of French Equatorial Africa,* Stanford, 1960, 313, 349, 555 note 27; De Veciana Vilaldach, A., *La Secta Bwiti en la Guinea Española,* Madrid, 1958.
20. Groves, C. P., *The Planting of Christianity in Africa,* London, vol. 4, 1958, 45–6, 124; Platt, W. J., *An African prophet,* London, 1934, *passim.*
21. Kamenyi, J., *Prophets (Aroti): Turban people—Andu a Iremba,* Nairobi, 1960—an African student's research report, for which I am indebted to the Christian Council of Kenya.
22. There are only a few journalistic articles on this Society, but its own publications may be available from the headquarters, P.O. Box 90, Warri, Nigeria.
23. *Op. cit.,* 45, 50 f.
24. *Op. cit.*
25. Mkotsi, L., and Mkele, N., A separatist Church: Ibandla lika-Krestu, *African Studies,* 5 (2), 1946, 106–25.
26. See *The old and the new in the Church,* London, 1961, p. 64, for the need of a better typology, excluding the term 'sect.' Similarly Molland, E., *Christendom,* London, 1959, 5.
27. Sundkler, B. G. M., *Bantu prophets in South Africa,* London, 2nd. ed. 1961, Appendix B, 354–74.
28. A classification suggested by Boerwinckel, F., *Kerk en Secte,* 's Gravenhage, 1956.
29. 'Church movement' has also been used by Lea, A., *The native separatist church movement in South Africa,* Cape Town, 1926; Loram, C. T., The separatist church movement, *International Review of Missions,* 25 (59), 1926, 476–82; and Kitagawa, D., *African independent church movements in Nyanza Province, Kenya,* Nairobi, 1961 (a report to the Christian Council of Kenya).
30. See Ndanema, I. M., The Martha Davies Confidential Benevolent Association,

Sierra Leone Bulletin of Religion, 3 (2), 1961, 64–67; Baëta, C. G., *Prophetism in Ghana*, London, 1962, ch. 6, for a similar group; Busia, K. A., *Report on a social survey of Sekondi-Takoradi*, London, 1950, for the socio-religious burial societies of Sekondi-Takoradi. Others include a prayer group in Lomé, Republic of Togo, reported to have grown in eight years to 2,000 members, including Protestants and Roman Catholics. Women's societies in S. Africa similar to those in Sierra Leone are the subject of Brandel-Syrier, M., *Black woman in search of God*, London, 1962.

31. Smalley, W. A., Cultural implications of an indigenous church, *Practical Anthropology*, 5 (2), 1958, 51–65; these features are no longer used to define the term 'indigenous' by many writers on the younger churches.
32. Nida, E. A. The indigenous churches in Latin America, *Practical Anthropology* 8 (3), 1961, 97–105.
33. On such transposition, see Van der Leeuw, G., *Religion in essence and manifestation*, London, 1938, 610 f.
34. This usage is called for in a report of the World Council of Churches, Division of Studies, Christian encounter with men of other religions, *Bulletin,* 7 (1), 1961, 9.
35. Pauw, B. A., *Religion in a Tswana chiefdom*, London, 1960, 42; Baëta, C. G., Conflict in Mission: Historical and separatist churches, in G. H. Anderson (ed.), *The Theology of the Christian mission,* New York, 1961, 290. Others using 'separatist' include Dlepu in 1925, Loram, *op. cit.*, Lea, *op. cit.*, Shepherd in 1927, Mqotsi and Mkele, *op. cit.,* Beecher, *op. cit.*, Parrinder, *op. cit.,* Shepperson in 1954, Dougall in 1956, Groves, *op. cit.*, Vilakazi in 1959, Eberhardt in 1960, Köbben, *op. cit.,* Taylor and Lehmann in 1961.
36. *Op. cit.*, 3–4.
37. Welbourn, *op. cit.,* Kitagawa, *op. cit.,* Deschamps in 1954, Parrinder at various times, and the World Council of Churches Consultation on African Independent Church Movements, Mindolo, 1962, Shepperson in 1963, and Van Wyck in 1964.
38. *Op. cit.*, 3–4.
39. E.g., Parrinder, E. G., Indigenous churches in Nigeria, *West African Review*, 31 (394), 1960, 87; Delano, I. O., *One Church for Nigeria,* London, 1945, *passim*, and as convenient common usage.
40. E.g., Raaflaab, F., in *Evangelisches Missionsmagazin* (Basel), 3, 1961, 114.
41. E.g., Kale, S. I., and Hogan, H., *Christian responsibility in an independent Nigeria*, Lagos, 1961, 86, 102.
42. Dudley, R. A., in *Ecumenical Review,* 13 (3), 1961, 380.
43. *Op. cit.*, 2.
44. Molland, E., *Christendom,* London, 1955, 6.
45. *Op. cit.*, 43–6.
46. *Op. cit.*, 2nd edn., 1961, 54 f.
47. Eberhardt, J., Messianismes en Afrique du Sud, *Archives de Sociologie des Religions*, 4, 1957, 31–56, and Christianity and African separatist churches, *Occasional Papers*, (International Missionary Council, London) 1 (4), 1960.
48. Debrunner, H., *Witchcraft in Ghana*, Kumasi, 1959, 151.
49. The Rev. W. J. Mellor in a private communication, 1962.
50. *Op. cit.*, 61.
51. *Op. cit.*, 54.
52. *Op. cit.*, 4.

53. In personal discussion, but these must not be taken as his final terms.
54. In a paper read at University College, Ibadan, 1962, and in personal discussion.
55. Balandier, G., *Sociologie actuelle de l'Afrique noire,* Paris, 1955, 447, and *Afrique ambiguë,* Paris, 1957, 237, asserts that messianism is not found in traditional African mythologies; similarly Eberhardt, *op. cit.,* 1957, 45–7.
56. E.g., the French-speaking scholars who use 'messianismes et syncrétismes' as a general term for African independent religious movements. On messianic groups see especially Sundkler, Bantu Messiah and white Christ, *Frontier,* 3 (1), 1960, 16–21; Eberhardt, *op. cit.,* 1957, and many articles in *Archives de Sociologie des Religions,* 1957–1958, on the world incidence, especially that by Pereira de Queiroz in 1958 pointing out that messianism is absent from Brazilian negro religions.
57. See Baëta, C. G., *Prophetism in Ghana,* London, 1962, 60–4, and ch. 5; also Anon, Aiyetoro, *Nigeria Magazine,* 55, 1957, 356–86; Duckworth, E. H., A visit to the Apostles and town of Aiyetoro, *Nigeria Magazine,* 36, 1951, 386–440; Eberhardt, *op. cit.,* 1957.
58. *Op. cit.,* 1961, 151–6.
59. Information from S. African members of the Mindolo Consultation, 1962.

8

The Study of New Religious Movements in Africa, 1968-1975

This survey of the most significant work subsequent to the above methodological essays reveals that some of the lacunae noted there are being filled, and that the religious dimension is receiving more adequate attention and reductionism is less prevalent. Likewise the theological importance of African independent churches is recognized. The historians have also been hard at work, and the question of new religious movements of a similar kind but in the Islamic context is also being discussed.

The choice of such a short span for this survey is dictated by the abundance of published work in a field of such size and variety, and of such popularity among so many disciplines, as the new religious movements among the peoples of sub-Saharan Africa. A more comprehensive study would have had to reach back at least to 1948, to the pioneering work of Bengt Sundkler, *Bantu Prophets in South Africa* (rev. edn 1961), that is probably the best known publication on the subject; this outline may be allowed to commence with the other work that is becoming as well known as Sundkler's, D. B. Barrett's *Schism and Renewal in Africa* (1968), which marks the first attempt at a continent-wide study of the phenomena and a comprehensive theoretical interpretation. Each of these is in fact more limited than is generally realized: Sundkler's book primarily to the Zulu, and Barrett's to movements that are professedly Christian. Barrett's book,

---

Religion: Journal of Religion and Religions 6 (1), 1976, pp. 88-98.

however, does provide a landmark for the start of this bibliographical journey.

It would be well to take first a quick glance at the world scene where single works attempting an overall study and interpretation of similar phenomena in primal societies might have something to contribute to work in the African sector. Here the results are disappointing for none shows any special interest or competence in African studies. W. La Barre's 'Materials for a History of Studies of Crisis Cults', *Current Anthropology* 12 (1), 1971, is an ambitious attempt to employ a single category for almost all religious movements (the more one succeeds here the less meaningful it becomes!) and is valuable for bibliography and for the stress on a multidisciplinary approach and on many-factored explanations. He seems, however, indifferent to the religious disciplines and especially hostile to the 'theological empyrean', and to ignore Barrett and other major African studies and the whole sector of independent churches; nor is there any adequate African critique among the fifteen comments published with the essay.

V. Lanternari, whose *Religions of the Oppressed* (Eng. trans. 1963) has become the most used world survey, provides a useful review of terminology, typologies, and the various disciplinary viewpoints in his 'Nativistic and Socio-religious Movements: a Reconsideration', *Comparative Studies in Society and History* 16 (4), 1974; but there is little specific reference or relevance to Africa. In Bryan Wilson's massive *Magic and the Millennium* (1973) our continent does receive much more adequate attention. This book might replace Lanternari's as a student text as it is factually more accurate in its summaries of African movements; on the other hand it operates within an elaborate sevenfold typology much of which either doesn't apply to Africa or else ill consorts with the phenomena. As for the title, the less said the better, for most of the African movements are opposed to magic and not especially interested in the millennium.

A totally different and quite modest world survey comes from a Dutch anthropologist-missiologist in the American Seventh Day Adventist seminary. G. Oosterwal's *Modern Messianic Movements* (1973) is published by the Mennonite Church (!) whose mission board has unsurpassed experience of African independent churches; Oosterwal himself has long field experience, but not in Africa. Here the subject is placed firmly within religious categories, with clear critical analyses of causal explanations, terminologies and typologies; despite his use of the term 'messianic' this is the best introductory work, with a holistic approach in which theology provides the 'creative centre', and where African material can be quite at home. At this point mention may be made of my own survey article in the *Encyclopaedia Britannica* (new 1974 edn) entitled 'Tribal Religious Movements, New'; this has something in common with Oosterwal and combines a theoretical analysis with an historical survey—but again the African section is necessarily limited. The same applies to an earlier theoretical article, 'A New Field in the History of Religions', that appeared in the first issue of this journal in 1971. Other theoretical articles with an African reference are J. D. Y. Peel's 'Understanding Alien Belief Systems', *British Journal of Sociology* 20 (1), 1969, and J. W. Fernandez' 'Contemporary African Religion: confluents of enquiry', in G. M. Carter and A. Paden (eds), *Expanding Horizons in African Studies* (1969)—an anthropological viewpoint.

Turning now to the African scene itself we find several new developments in these recent years; for instance, organized Christian bodies are taking these movements seriously and contributing to their study. Chief among these has been the American Mennonite Church which has produced for its own purposes a large number of surveys and reports covering some six areas in Africa, and two published missiological works by their pioneering team, Edwin and Irene Weaver: *The Uyo Story* (1970) on eastern Nigeria, and *From Kuku Hill* (1975) on Ghana. These are primary missiological sources and not to be ignored by academics because of their apparent simplicity. The World Council of Churches has commissioned studies of several independent churches by *their own members* and published them in the *Ecumenical Review* 19 (1), 1967 and 24 (2) 1973; this is a new genre of variable quality, since accounts that are idealized need substantial interpretation. Also from the W.C.C. there is an issue of *Risk* 7 (3), 1971, which serves, apart from its unfortunate editorial, as a good introduction, with brief studies, excellent photographs, and a useful Who's Who of independent church leaders.

One of the most striking developments is the work now being done by Roman Catholic scholars in a field they once regarded as an undesirable Protestant offshoot but which is now discovered to be much more involved with Catholicism than they had imagined. Fr René Bureau, the French anthropologist, has brought his long researches to the publication stage. *Le prophète Harris et la religion harriste* has appeared as a monograph in *Annales de l'Université d'Abidjan* Série F, tome 3, 1971; at the same university the Institut d'Ethno-Sociologie has since published two mimeo volumes: *Essai sur le Bwiti fang*, and *Lexique du Bwiti fang*. These cover the main movements in the Ivory Coast and the Cameroun. In Zambia the White Fathers have been studying the Lumpa movement of Alice Lenshina; this was pioneered by Louis Oger back in 1960 with a substantial mimeo publication including primary materials, and it has been followed by Jean Calmettes in 1970 with an English translation of his Paris thesis: *The Lumpa Church I: Genesis and Development 1953–1964*, again a substantial mimeo publication.

In Tanzania the Maryknoll Fathers commissioned a French sociologist of religion to study the independents in their vicinity; this issued in the first major study of movements in a Catholic area, first in French and inaccessibly in Zaïre, and then in English as *Basic Community in the African Churches* (1973), by Marie-France Perrin Jassy. It is highly commended as a model of problem-orientated research with conclusions already being applied by the mission. Fr Peter Dirven's substantial doctoral study of the largest breakaway movement from a Catholic milieu, the Maria Legio in Kenya, awaits publication but his work is outlined in a number of articles such as 'A Protest and a Challenge' in the *African Ecclesiastical Review* 12 (2), 1970. The leading Catholic missiologist in Africa, Fr Adrian Hastings, also pays careful attention to these phenomena in a manner that was most unlikely even a decade ago. My own attempt to open up the question of 'African Religious Movements and Roman Catholicism' appeared in H.-J. Greschat and H. Jungraithmayr (eds), *Wort und Religion* in 1969, but already needs revision and extension.

All these developments coincide with a certain change of emphasis from socio-economic-political factors towards the religious nature and dynamic of these movements. This has been assisted by the fact that the passing of the colonial era in Africa around the year 1960 has not brought a decline in this field but if anything an even greater effervescence than before. The attitudes towards the religious dimension have also become more positive; thus the independent churches are being interpreted as authentically African forms of Christianity and even as a new African reformation of the Christian faith. This reformation has been compared to the 16th century 'radical reformation' in its emphasis on the Scriptures, on community, and on the rediscovery of the power in the original Christian forms. The terms 'Schism and Renewal' in the title of Barrett's book could apply equally well to both the main Protestant and the left-wing sections of the European Reformation; similar interpretations will be found in J. D. Y. Peel's sociological study, *Aladura: A Religious Movement Among the Yoruba* (1968), where the guiding forces were earnest élites rather than semi-literate peasants as is sometimes imagined.

Another Western category currently being applied to some of the African movements is that of pentecostalism, and notably by W. J. Hollenweger as in his *The Pentecostals* (1972) for the South African scene, and in various articles on Kimbanguism. D. Williams and T. D. Verryn did the same in their *Pentecostalism: A Research Report* (n.d.—1972?) from within South Africa; likewise my own 'Pentecostal Movements in Nigeria', *Orita* 6 (1), 1972, which appeared earlier in a German symposium edited by Hollenweger, *Die Pfingstkirchen* (1971). Much greater care is needed at this point, for the African movements have distinctive dimensions of their own that may be masked by Western categories. This danger is especially evident when terms which apply well enough to certain movements are used as general categories for all. Here the chief offenders are 'messianic' and 'millennial' which appear in so many titles of articles and books dealing with all parts of the world, and which are particularly distorting when applied to much of the African phenomena.

More positive attitudes are found not only in studies of the religious dimension but also in understanding the secular effects of Africa's new movements. These are reflected in the titles of two of my attempts in this direction: 'The Place of Independent Religious Movements in the Modernization of Africa', *Journal of Religion in Africa* 2 (1), 1969, and 'African Independent Churches and Education', *Journal of Modern African Studies,* July 1975; the former stands in need of revision, but the latter seeks to correct the common image of illiterate religious enthusiasts.

A rather different but still positive approach is found in A. R. Sprunger's paper, 'The Contribution of the African Independent Churches...', in H.-J. Becken (ed.), *Relevant Theology for Africa* published in Durban in 1973. In one sense this is part of the new concern with Black Theology which is particularly strong in South Africa; in another sense it represents a recognition that these bodies deserve serious theological consideration in their own right. An attempt to push this idea still further was made in my essay on 'The Contribution of Studies on Religion in Africa to Western Religious Studies', in M. E. Glasswell and E. Fashole-Luke (eds), *New Testament Christianity for Africa and the World* (1974); most of the examples were taken from the new movements. Scholars entombed in Western culture have much to learn from Africa.

A more systematic phenomenological approach is represented by H.-J. Greschat's *Westafrikanische Propheten: Morphologie einer religiösen Spezialisierung* (1974); this studies the call experiences of some fifteen prophets and establishes a typology of four basic forms. Perhaps H.-J. Becken's thematic work can be included here: *Theologie der Heilung: das Heilen in den afrikanischen unabhängigen Kirchen* (1972); a brief account occurs in *Credo* 18 (2), 1971 in English. In another direction again there are David Dalby's articles on West African indigenous scripts which include new scripts from religious movements, in *African Language Studies* vols 9 and 10, 1968 and 1969.

As is to be expected, movements of a neo-primal or more syncretistic nature and therefore at the traditional end of the spectrum have been studied by anthropologists more than others, and their work appears in several symposia. Thus Colson, Field, Lee, Middleton, Southall and Welbourn have essays in J. H. M. Beattie and J. Middleton (eds), *Spirit Mediumship and Society in Africa* (1969), and in R. I. Rotberg and A. A. Mazrui (eds) *Protest and Power in Black Africa* (1970) there are major essays by Elizabeth Hopkins on the Nyabingi cult in Uganda and by Audrey Wipper on the Gusii rebels and their cult of Mumbo in Kenya. B. M. Du Toit has written on 'Emakhehleni—a Revivalistic Cult', in *Communications from the African Studies Center University of Florida* 1 (1), 1970. The Yakan water cult in Uganda has received substantial treatments in Anne King's article in *Azania* 5, 1970, and by Middleton in his essay on 'Prophets and Rainmakers' in T. O. Beidelman (ed.), *The Translation of Culture* (1971). From the Malagasy Republic, ill-represented in the literature and easily overlooked, there comes a study which includes accounts of the *tromba* possession cult: G. Althabe's *Oppression et libération dans l'imaginaire* published in Paris in 1969.

The historians have also been at work with increasing industry at this end of the spectrum. We may mention a substantial article by Jan Vansina on 'Les mouvements religieux Kuba (Kasai) à l'époque coloniale', in *Etudes d'Histoire Africaine* 2, 1971, a study of witchcraft eradication movements. The chief influence in this field has been the school of younger historians associated with T. O. Ranger at Dar es Salaam and at Los Angeles, and the symposia which Ranger has helped to assemble. The first of these, *The Historical Study of African Religion* (1972) is mainly concerned with the addition of historical depth to the study of primal religions in east and central Africa but provides valuable background to prophets and protest movements which are also included. Since then he has co-edited *Themes in the Christian History of Central Africa* (1975) which has more material directly on our subject, including a major essay on The Mwana Lesa Movement of 1925, by Ranger himself. An earlier symposium, *Aspects of Central African History* (1968), contained reliable and handy summaries of new religious movements of all kinds in Zaïre, Zambia, Malawi and Rhodesia. Much of this historical work opens up the question of the relation between indigenous and foreign influences in the emergence and development of our new religious movements, and of whether the term prophet is rightly used of individual figures in African primal religions. The issue is complex and will require an extended religio-historical investigation.

In almost all the works referred to above it is the Christian religion that has been the invasion influence in the history of new movements; it must not be forgotten, however, that Islam may have had a similar effect in its own areas of strength. I say 'may' to indicate that the issue seems to be still wide open; and even if it is decided that there are in fact *new independent* and *African* movements from an Islamic milieu then the question arises as to why they are so few in comparison with the thousands of movements with a Christian background. Among recent contributions to this problem we note the following: P. Alexandre, 'A West African Islamic Movement: Hamallism', in the Rotberg and Mazrui symposium already mentioned; H. J. Fisher, 'Independency and Islam: the Nigerian Aladuras and some Muslim Comparisons', *Journal of African History* 11 (2), 1970; M. Quechon, 'Réflexions sur certains aspects du syncrétisme dans l'Islam ouest-africain', *Cahiers d'Etudes Africaines* 11 (2), 1971—using Lanternari's theories; and D. B. Cruise O'Brien, *The Mourides of Senegal*

(1971), and various articles on the same theme. Most of these works include comparisons with African movements set in a Christian context.

Within the confines of this essay there remains time for no more than a hasty journey across the continent, noting in passing some of the most significant works not already mentioned. In effect we shall be confined to the countries of substantial Christian influence, commencing with Sierra Leone which has nothing to report. Liberia is little better, although W. Korte's 'Note on Independent Churches in Liberia', *Liberian Studies Journal* 4 (1), 1971 makes a start until the results of his extensive research can be published. Any work on prophet W. W. Harris, of course, is likely to cover his earlier and later years in Liberia, while concentrating on his astonishing influence on the Ivory Coast. In addition to Bureau's work already mentioned there is G. M. Haliburton's painstakingly researched historical work, *The Prophet Harris* (1971) and also an abbreviated edition; note also the critique by J. Pritchard entitled 'The Prophet Harris', *Journal of Religion in Africa* 5 (1), 1973. At the other end of the spectrum there is the Déima cult which is the subject of two massive volumes by J. Girard, under the general title *Déima*, published in 1973-4 from Grenoble; the second volume contains documentary texts and is a valuable primary source.

The abundance of movements in Ghana might have produced more major studies than seem to have appeared. We can mention J. W. Fernandez, 'Rededication and Prophetism in Ghana', *Cahiers d'Etudes Africaines* 10 (2), 1970; this amounts to a small monograph on the Apostolic Revelation Society. There is a full report of one other independent church, set in the context of a general Ghana survey: D. M. Beckmann's *Eden Revival* published in 1973 and under somewhat different auspices in 1974; Beckmann was an American Lutheran divinity student who lived with the founder and worked for the church. A series of shorter articles on individual churches and a directory of 'spiritual churches' in Ghana has come from K. A. Opoku and appeared in the *Research Review* of the University of Ghana as follows: 5 (1), 1968, 6 (1), 1969, and 7 (1), 1970.

A somewhat similar complaint might be made of Nigeria where there has been no further major study since J. D. Y. Peel's *Aladura* already mentioned. This covers the Christ Apostolic Church and the Cherubim and Seraphim societies from the point of view of a non-reductionist sociology of religion. R. C. Mitchell's major work on the Aladura has yet to appear, but a foretaste is offered in his essay 'Religious Protest and Social Change', in the Rotberg and Mazrui symposium. There have been many essays and several dissertations on the Holy Apostles Community at Aiyetoro; from a recent dissertation two important contributions have emerged to give a more up-to-date picture of this now changing utopia: S. R. Barrett's 'Crisis and Change', in E. B. Harvey (ed.), *Perspectives on Modernization* (1972), and his own *Two Villages on Stilts* (1974). Finally we should mention

E. A. Ayandele's *A Visionary of the African Church: Mojola Agbebi* published in Nairobi in 1971, as a short account of an outstanding Nigerian independent churchman.

In Gabon we are indebted to the industry of S. Swiderski of Ottawa who has produced at least ten articles in French, German or Polish since 1969 on 'syncretistic cults', especially on Bwiti among the Fang. The more accessible essays may be found in *Anthropos* 65, 1970, and 66, 1971 (in French), or in *Anthropologica* (Ottawa) 15 (1), 1973, where he has a major article, 'Notes biographiques sur les fondateurs et les guides spirituel des sectes syncrétiques'. Otherwise there seems to be only another contribution on the Bwiti from J. W. Fernandez, 'The Affirmation of Things Past: Ayong and Bwiti', in the same symposium of Rotberg and Mazrui.

Materials from Zaïre, as expected, are abundant, and the emphasis has been increasingly on source documents and bibliographies of the major movements. Thus T. Filesi has given us *Nazionalismo e religioni nel Congo all' inizio del 1700* (1972) and the same material on prophetess Béatrice from early missionary sources in two issues of *Africa* (Rome): 26 (3), 1971 and 26 (4), 1972. There is also a long account in his *San Salvador. Cronache dei re del Congo* (1974), and another by E. Dos Santos under the alternative terminology, 'O Antonianismo', in *Studia* (Lisbon) 30–31, 1970. Béatrice has even become the subject of a three-act opera, *Béatrice du Congo* by B. Dadié, published in Paris in 1970.

Simon Kimbangu has also been honoured with a five-act play by Elébé Lisembe, *Simon Kimbangu ou le messie noir* (1972). The English translation of Marie-Louise Martin's major work is now available: *Kimbangu: An African Prophet and his Church* (1975). Interest in Kimbangu is indicated by the fact that there are some six hundred items in A. Geuns' 'Bibliographie commentée du Prophétisme Kongo', *Les Cahiers du CEDAF*, 7, 1973, Série 5: Bibliographie. In the same publication, 9–10, 1972, Série 4: Religion, D. Feci has a critical study of the early source materials, 'Vie cachée et vie publique de Simon Kimbangu'. Early missionary documents on Kimbangu are examined by E. Libert in *Etudes d'Histoire Africaine* 2, 1971, while Cecilia Irvine gives a masterly blow-by-blow account of the earliest period and the documentation for it in *Journal of Religion in Africa* 6 (1), 1974. Other important works can merely be listed: P. Raymaekers' primary sources in *Archives de Sociologie des Religions* 16 (1), 1971; A. Ryckmans' *Les Mouvements prophétiques Kongo en 1958* (1970); an even more comprehensive work by M. Sinda, *Le Messianisme congolais et ses incidences politiques* (1972); Mwene-Batende's 'Le Phénomène de dissidence', *Les Cahiers du CEDAF* 6, 1971, Série 4: Religion, on the major secession from the Kimbanguist church; J. M. Janzen and W. MacGaffey, *An Anthology of Kongo Religion* (1974) provide primary texts and discuss the effects of literacy on the religious functions of language. In another direction J. Fabian's *Jamaa: a Charismatic Movement in Katanga* (1971) has a biographical sketch of Placide Tempels and an unusual (for an anthropologist) account of a most unusual movement. The other Francophone areas can offer only E. Andersson's *Churches at the Grassroots: a Study in Congo-Brazzaville* (1968).

For Uganda there seems to be little more than A. Oded's 'The Bayudaya . . . an African Jewish community', *Journal of Religion in Africa* 6 (2), 1975. In Kenya the *Kenya Churches Handbook* (1973), edited by D. B. Barrett et al., has five articles and much photographic and classified information on independent churches. Jocelyn Murray has a substantial account of 'The Kikuyu Spirit Churches' in *Journal of Religion in Africa* 5 (3), 1973, and J. Anderson's *The Struggle for the School* (1970) deals with the independent church-cum-schools movements from the 1920s. For more neo-primal movements G. S. Were has 'Dini ya Msambwa Revisited' in B. A. Ogot's collection, *Politics and Nationalism in Colonial Kenya* (1972). For Tanzania there is only T. O. Ranger's survey, *The African Churches of Tanzania* (n.d.–1970?), apart from the extensive work on the Maji Maji by G. C. K. Gwassa, J. Iliffe, O. B. Mapunda and others: see, for example, Gwassa and Iliffe (eds), *Records of the Maji Maji Rising. Part One* (1968).

The Watch Tower movements in central Africa continue to attract research. A former Belgian administrator, J. E. Gérard, provides a substantial study in *Les Fondements syncrétiques du Kitawala* (1969); shorter essays have appeared from A. Welo in *Problèmes Sociaux Zaïrois* 96–97, 1972, from J. M. Assimeng in the *Journal of Modern African Studies* 8 (1), 1970, and from J. S. W. Cross on an outstanding leader in C. Allen and R. W. Johnson (eds), *African Perspectives* (1970). The famous Lumpa church is dealt with in A. D. Roberts' long essay in the Rotberg and Mazrui symposium, and new material for this movement appears in L. Charlton's *Spark in the Stubble. Colin Morris of Zambia* (1969).

In Malawi the early leaders of independency are being studied for the second time round. Rotberg himself, in his symposium with Mazrui, reconsiders Chilembwe; others doing this are R. K. Tangri in *African Historical Studies* 4 (2), 1971, and J. and I. Linden in the *Journal of African History* 12 (4), 1971. Joseph Booth and Charles Domingo receive further examination by K. P. Lohrentz in the same journal, 12 (3), 1971. In Rhodesia the research scene is dominated by M. L. Daneel's massive work. Two of his projected four volumes have now appeared: under the general title of *Old and New in Southern Shona Independent Churches* (1971, 1974); there is also his small *Zionism and Faith Healing in Rhodesia* (1970). Otherwise we have M. W. Murphree's *Christianity and the Shona* (1969), Sr Mary Aquina's 'Zionists in Rhodesia', *Africa* 39 (2), 1969, and T. O. Ranger's *The African Voice in Southern Rhodesia* (1970).

Nothing has come from Mozambique but from Angola there are substantial studies. A. Margarido provides a major survey in *Rivista Storica Italiana* 80 (3), 1968 and a still more detailed study comes from E. Dos Santos in his *Religões de Angola* (1969), the second half. An important symposium edited by R. H. Chilcote, *Protest and Resistance in Angola and Brazil* (1972) contains an essay by Chilcote that is valuable for classification and for bibliography, and another by A. Margarido on the Tokoist church; the latter is also studied by A. Da Silva Rêgo in the *Luso-Brazilian Review* 7 (2), 1970.

The more southern part of Africa deserves a review of its own, but a self-denying selection must include the following. For Botswana there seems to be only a brief article by S. Grant in *Botswana Notes and Records* 3, 1971; in Lesotho G. M. Haliburton's work has not yet appeared as this is written; in Southwest Africa or Namibia there is at last a major study, T. Sundermeier's *Wir aber suchten Gemeinschaft* (1973), and an African viewpoint in E. Kandovazu's *Die Oruuano-Beweging* (also in a Herero version) (1968). G. C. Oostuizen's *Post-Christianity in Africa* (1968) and several subsequent articles maintain his critique of African independency, especially as over against H.-J. Becken's interpretations in his many articles. J. H. Van Wyck has published *Separatisme en inheemse kerkbeweging onder die Bantoue van Sothogroep* (1973); W. K. Hancock's *Smuts. The Fields of Force 1919–1950* (1968) gives a detailed account of the Bulhoek incident in ch. 5; and the Order of Ethiopia has been studied by T. D. Verryn in his *History of the Order of Ethiopia* (1973), and by Beryl Wright in the *Sociological Yearbook of Religion in Britain*, 5, 1972. Two articles should be noted in *African Studies* 33 (2), 1974 on Zionists in Durban and Soweto (Johannesburg) by J. P. Kiernan and M. E. West, also the latter's major publication, *Bishops and Prophets in a Black City* (1975).

The veteran in the South African field, B. G. M. Sundkler, is still in action with reinforcements of the new interpretation he adopted in his 1961 revised edition and renewed emphasis on the limited application of the term 'messianism'; this may be seen in his 'Messies Bantou?' in C. J. Bleeker et al. (eds), *Ex Orbe Religionum* (1972). More important, however, is his new work based on extensive field and documentary research concerning movements among both the Zulu and the Swazi, entitled *Zulu Zion and some Swazi Zionists* (1976); in my opinion its greater depth and detail give it a more permanent value than the earlier work which did so much to open up this whole field for us all.

N.B. Only the barest bibliographical details could be given in this survey. If readers in search of any items cannot trace them further in the bibliographical reference sources available to them full information can be obtained from the author.

C. HISTORICAL

The essays in this section show something of the variety of historical questions that arise—questions concerning the relation of these movements to Pentecostal Protestantism, to Roman Catholicism, to colonial governments, and the place of the outstanding individual, be he prophet or not, in the historical process. The only detailed historical treatment of a particular movement will be found in volume one of *African Independent Church* (on the Church of the Lord [Aladura] and allied movements in West Africa), but essays fifteen and twenty-six are also historical in a more thematic way.

9
Pentecostal Movements in Nigeria

The first of these three Nigerian historical studies was written by request for inclusion in a symposium on world Pentecostalism, and therefore used this term of necessity. The word is used in the light of the warnings expressed briefly in this essay and more fully in essay seven. It should be noted that the essay also includes many Western groups properly called Pentecostal, along with the African movements that I prefer to call "prophet-healing".

The first pentecostal forms of Christianity in Nigeria appeared rather more than fifty years ago, in the form of spontaneous and independent prophetic or 'spiritual' movements in communities where non-pentecostal missions had already planted churches. It was not till 1932 that a Western pentecostal church established mission work, so that the first developments were peculiarly African in form and local in origin. Like their Western counterparts, they were both revivals within and then reactions from older African churches which had no special pentecostal emphasis.

Nigerian pentecostalism does not usually share in certain features

---

* This is a slightly revised form of the section on Nigeria, pp. 115–124, in Walter J. Hollenweger (ed.), *Die Pfingstkirchen: Selbstdarstellungen, Dokumente, Kommentare* (Kirchen der Welt, VII), Stuttgart: Evangelisches Verlagswerk, 1971; we offer thanks to the publishers for permission to print the original English text.

Orita 6 (1), 1972, pp. 39–47.

commonly found in the West; its policy may take any form and is not necessarily of the congregationalist type, there is little real interest in millennial adventism, or in stress upon personal holiness. It does, however, stress believers' baptism by immersion, the importance of prayer, and above all the presence and power of the Holy Spirit made evident in charismatic gifts and visible signs and results. These spiritual gifts are often regarded as due to the "second baptism of the Spirit" and include faith healing, prophecy (dreams, visions, predictions), and ecstatic motor phenomena (trances, speaking in tongues and various forms of possession by the Spirit). This pneumatological emphasis and the demand for visible manifestations of the power of the Spirit clearly identify its central features with those of Western pentecostalism.

The first movement with these emphases arose among the Ijaw people in the Niger Delta area of Nigeria late in 1915 through the activities of Garrick Braid, who was already known for his spiritual power in prayer and healing as a member of the Anglican and all-African Niger Delta Pastorate Church. The actual beginnings of the movement are obscure, but the social situation in the area is clear enough—an Anglican church with many second-generation Christians and not in the best of spiritual health, Eastern Nigeria caught up in the first World War and especially in the long-drawn out campaign fought by Nigerian troops against the neighbouring German colony of the Cameroon, and the consequent disruption of trade aggravating the great social changes already beginning to overtake the Delta communities. In this situation it apparently took no more than reports of an alleged healing through the prayers of Braid to create great public excitement and the gathering of crowds to him.

Once Braid found himself the centre of a popular movement he assumed the position of leader of what he felt was a great revival and reform. He encouraged regular church attendance and Sabbath-keeping, attacked the notorious gin trade and enjoined total abstinence, forbade the common resort to litigation that was so ruinous financially and socially, and encouraged the destruction of traditional shrines and idols and of all fetish-medicines and charms. In these activities he certainly stood in the historic prophet tradition, but they were not necessarily pentecostal in nature. This feature appears rather in the healings and the prophecies that attested his special charisma to his followers.

His own method of healing seems to have been through faith consequent upon his prayers and imposition of hands, and such was his reputation as a man of spiritual power that many sought healing through drinking or anointing themselves with the water in which he had washed. His prophecies included reference to the British colonial power, to avoidance of imported European articles and government medical services, and to a better future for the African; these activities were regarded as seditious and a variety of charges brought against him by the government led to his imprisonment—in our opinion, unjustly.[1] There is no evidence of ecstatic behaviour on Braid's part, although this assuredly appeared among his followers; his reputation as a man raised up in the power of the Holy Spirit rested upon his healings and the boldness of his utterances against traditional religion and possibly against the colonial power.

The Anglican authorities welcomed the movement in its early months as a great revival, but attacked it strongly when it led to mass baptism without preparation and to excesses such as those indicated above; in the end it led to an overhaul of the Anglican church in the Delta area, after it had lost half its members in some districts to the new Christ Army Churches that grew out of Braid's work, and continued after his death in 1918. These churches were among the first independent churches of the prophet-healing type in Africa.

Other "spiritual" churches emerged from the next identifiable movement in the east of Nigeria, the Spirit Movement of 1927 among the Ibibio and Efik people in the Uyo Division near the Cross River, where three non-pentecostal missions had been at work during the previous two decades—the United Free Church of Scotland, the Primitive Methodist Church from England, and the Qua Iboe Mission, an undenominational group from Northern Ireland.

The movement began without warning or any evident cause, although there was tension between government and people over new taxes, a census and the establishment of forest reserves. It appears to have been strongest in the area of the Qua Iboe mission where the Rev. J. W. Westgarth was working. He was strongly evangelical and revivalist, but although he had seen the effects of the 1904 Welsh pentecostal revival when a student he had not encouraged similar features himself. He was astonished when members of his village churches began holding spontaneous meetings, confessing their sins, making restitution, effecting reconciliations, abandoning native magical practices and tobacco and alcohol, and displaying many of the ecstatic phenomena associated with a pentecostal revival—tongues, shaking, dancing, visions, and emotional displays of joy. He treated it as a revival from the Holy Spirit and sought to both encourage and yet control and advise the movement. Strangely enough there is no evidence of healings and little of prophesyings, the two features basic to most African movements of this kind.

Government reports of the time show a different side of the movement, for it undoubtedly got out of hand, and groups of women or of younger people roamed the countryside extorting confessions, torturing those who refused, attacking traditional shrines and sacred objects, and defying the chiefs and elders. One report recognized that although at first it resembled a European pentecostal movement, in the end, as a result of "half-tutored natives reading revivalist pamphlets followed by occultist literature it ended in an African witch-hunt".[2] Many were arrested and a number executed for murder.

Similar but less extreme forms of the Spirit Movement appeared at intervals and equally mysteriously over the next dozen years. One of the most striking phenomena has been the emergence from this movement of a small independent church that still exists, known at first as the Messifident Holy Spiritual Church, and now as the Obere Okaime Church. The new words in these titles are not African, but belong to a language claimed to have been revealed by the Spirit, along with a special script; "Messifident" is interpreted as "messiah" and "Obere Okaime" as "church healing without charge". Schools using the new language and script were actually set up until government and popular opposition closed them, and literature is still available in the Spirit-language and writing. As the second name indicates, healing later became a function of the church which now conforms to the common revelatory-therapeutic type, along with the hundred or more small "spiritual" churches that have proliferated in the eastern Nigerian States in the last fifty years.

A few of these are branches of similar prophet-healing churches that have developed in the same period among the Yoruba in western Nigeria, and that are referred to collectively as the *aladura* (i.e. praying) churches. These again emerged from a non-pentecostal background, usually that of the Anglican Church, and gathered round a charismatic leader who was noted for his power in prayer or gifts of healing or prophesying. For a while the new group would continue within the parent church, but within a few years its rejection of infant baptism and of Western medicine and its insistence on ecstatic forms of worship would lead to its separation.

One such group which appeared in 1925 around two charismatic figures, Moses Orimolade Tunolase and Christianah Abiodun Akinsowon, developed into the Cherubim and Seraphim Society which has now splintered into ten or more major and other minor sections; most incorporate the original name in part of their title, and some have spread to Ghana. When the Anglican connection was broken in 1928 the synod expressed appreciation of the reliance on faith and prayer instead of on charms and fetishes, but described their dreams and visions as "replacing superstition with superstition" and deprecated the "dangerous excesses" of "weird movements of the Seraphim type".

In the same year, 1925, a young Anglican school teacher called Oshitelu began having intense visionary experiences, coupled with a sense of call. After breaking with the Church in 1926 he spent three years in spiritual preparation through prayer and fasting, and recorded in his journals many revelations from the Spirit in English and in Yoruba, and sometimes in a strange new script; he too received new spiritual words, but these did not form a language, and are still used as words of power in the Church of the Lord (Aladura) that he founded in 1930. He resembled other aladura in his judgments on idolatry and native medicines and charms, his reliance on healing through prayer, fasting and holy water, his gift of prophecy and encouragement of ecstatic signs of the presence of the Spirit. His church never became large—perhaps five or six thousand members at any one time—but it has been strongly missionary and has spread to Ghana, Liberia, Sierra Leone, and in 1964 began a branch among West Africans in London, where several other aladura churches now meet and maintain their own more "spiritual" forms of worship.

The largest product of the aladura movement is the Christ Apostolic Church, a well-organized body of about one hundred thousand members. Its origins may be traced to the world-wide influenza epidemic of 1918, when a group of Anglican Christians began meeting for prayer in protection against the plague. By 1922 it had broken from the Anglican Church, for reasons such as those mentioned above, and within a few years there was a loose association of several similar groups ranging from Lagos to Ilesha, about one hundred and fifty miles inland. Almost all used the name Faith Tabernacle, which they had borrowed from an evangelical church, Faith Tabernacle of Philadelphia, U.S.A. This Church, founded in 1897, had long circulated its monthly journal, *The Sword of the Spirit*, together with tracts and the sermons of its pastor, in many parts of Nigeria, and although it never sent missionaries it has had considerable influence on Nigerians who were looking for more spiritual power in their Christian experience. The Philadelphia church emphasized prayer, healing and holiness, but rejected ecstatic phenomena as unbiblical, and under its influence the Nigerian Faith Tabernacle church also discouraged visions, dreams and possession phenomena, which were regular features of the other aladura groups.

In 1925 the Philadelphia congregation split and one section formed the First Century Gospel Church which also circulated sermons and its journal, the *First Century Gospel*, in Nigeria. As a result some Nigerian groups have adopted this name and entered into a loose affiliation with this American church.

By 1928 the Nigerian Faith Tabernacle Church was beginning to query the Philadelphian restriction of the manifestations of the spirit, and was earnestly seeking revival and fuller power. Some of its members had a brief association with the Faith and Truth Temple, a similar church in Toronto, which sent a party of seven missionaries to West Africa in 1928. Five died soon after reaching Lagos and the remaining two, Mr and Mrs C. R. Myers, worked with the Faith Tabernacle leaders until Mrs Myers died in childbirth. The fact that this occurred in a hospital suggested to the Nigerians a lack of reliance on faith alone, and was one factor in their breaking from Myers.

The revival they sought was to come through the most famous and charismatic prophet figure in the aladura movement, Joseph Babalola, an Anglican public works employee who had received a call in 1928 and became an itinerant preacher proclaiming judgment and repentance, destruction of idols, and healing through prayer. Late in 1929 he was accepted by Faith Tabernacle leaders and baptized by immersion, and in July 1930 he became the centre of mass healings and a pentecostal type of revival that soon stretched from Abeokuta almost to the Niger River, and for a time was identified with Oshitelu's movement. Rejection of traditional medicines, magic and idols was widespread and the new spiritual healing was the central feature. Pagans as well as mission members flocked to Babalola and other leaders and Faith Tabernacle churches spread widely; the missions had mixed feelings about these competitors, and the government was anxious about the social disturbance involved. The new churches met increasing opposition, and once again looked for help from a Western pentecostal church.

Again the contact had been established through literature, this time from the British Apostolic Church, a product of the Welsh pentecostal revival. Three British leaders were invited to Nigeria in 1931, recognized that a great revival was under way, and reached an agreement with the Faith Tabernacle leaders that they would all work together, and that the British would send missionaries to help. The name Apostolic Church was soon adopted, and in this form the movement secured recognition by the government and missions, spread and consolidated.

Tensions between Nigerians and British arose when it was found that some missionaries used quinine, although on all other points the British church was fully pentecostal, stressing healing, prophecy, and the ecstatic gifts, and so matching their Nigerian colleagues. Further tensions appeared when the latter found their church being turned into a mission of the British Church under the authority of its missionaries, and the ablest leaders gradually broke away about 1939 and formed their own Christ Apostolic Church; one of these leaders became the traditional Olubadan of Ibadan, was knighted by the Queen of England as Sir Isaac Akinyele, and died in 1964 as president of this independent church. The smaller continuing Apostolic Church has also grown, spreading into the eastern areas of Nigeria where it had a thousand assemblies in 1965, and also to Ghana.

Other pentecostal literature also circulates widely in Nigeria. The Apostolic Faith of Portland, Oregon, issues its journal of the same name in five main Nigerian languages and sends blessed healing cloths across the Atlantic; the Christ Faith Mission of Los Angeles also sends handkerchiefs and its *Herald of Hope,* and has a number of churches using this name and affiliated with it, and also sends an occasional American missionary; the World Christian Crusade contributes its *Herald of His Coming* in Yoruba, Hausa, and English, and works through a former missionary of the British Apostolic Church in loose association with a number of Nigerian churches. *Faith Tabernacle* and *The Voice of Faith* are similar journals, and in many of these periodicals it is common to see testimonies from Nigerians. Since 1953 American revivalists from Latter Rain and Global Frontier groups have been working in Nigeria and using radio sessions, but without the response received by earlier pentecostalists.

There have, however, been several other American pentecostal missions that have arrived in the eastern areas at the invitation of a Nigerian prophet-healing church that may already have taken the American name. World Wide Missions Incorporated has had some rather ill-starred work, but the Church of God (Cleveland, Tennessee, founded 1886 and 1909) arrived in 1952 and now has several thousand members. The most successful has been the Assemblies of God, which commenced work in 1939, at the invitation of the leader of a revival that broke out in Ibibio country, largely due to the influence of its *Pentecostal Evangel*, which had also been circulating for some years. By 1961 they had about 20,000 believers and were growing more rapidly than most other churches, a success that may be connected with its being a fully pentecostal church.

The indigenous pentecostal prophet-healing churches welcome the general designation of "spiritual" churches, and claim to have received the power of the Holy Spirit to meet all human needs. This often implies a new direct revelation through dreams, visions, and ecstatic experiences, or through the charisma of a prophet, with little or no relation to the revelation in Jesus Christ; in fact Christ's person and work of atonement mean little in many of these churches, and he is little more than another powerful teacher, healer and prophet. The pentecostal features may readily pass over into forms of traditional divination that continue the *babalawo* or diviner-healer tradition, or into commercialized healing-homes where prayer, fasting and holy water are merely new forms of the old magic.

On the other hand there are many signs of the development of controls over pentecostal phenomena: it is seen that the spirits must be tested to see if they are of Christ, and certain leaders are recognized as gifted in discernment; rules are made to control the excessive demand for revelations or their unchecked recital in public worship; biblical and other tests are provided to distinguish the true from the false prophets; and ecstatic behaviour decreases in the more sophisticated congregations. The demand for miraculous healing is also modified by greater willingness to use scientific medical services, although many leaders of the Christ Apostolic Church still refuse to compromise on this point. The main hope for the future of these churches lies in their widespread reverence for the Bible and the desire to be a biblical church, even though present facilities for understanding the Scriptures, and especially for training a ministry capable of this, are woefully inadequate. It is all the more remarkable that the spirit-empowered prophet-leader has in many cases led large numbers of nominal Christians and some others to make a sharp break from magical practices or reliance upon the ancestral and other spirits, in order to trust completely the one God of the Scriptures and His Holy Spirit. It would appear that it takes a pentecostal form of the Christian faith to effect this fundamental change for large numbers of Africans in areas where Christianity has entered upon the second or third generation of its history.

Notes

1. See H. W. Turner, Prophets and politics: a Nigerian test case, *Bulletin, Society for African Church History* 2, (1) 1965, pp. 97–118.
2. National Archives, Enugu: SCE 1/85/869, Annual Report, Calabar Province, 1927, para. 17.

Bibliography

Adams, R. F. G. "A new African language and script", *Africa* 17 (1), Jan. 1947, pp. 24–34 (as revealed in the Spirit Movement).

Grimley, J. B. & Robinson, G. E. *Church Growth in Central and Southern Nigeria,* Grand Rapids, Michigan: (1966), pp. 299–316 (prophetism) and 346–8 (Assemblies of God).

Mitchell, R. C. & Turner, H. W. *A Comprehensive Bibliography of Modern African Religious Movements,* Evanston, Illinois: 1967, items 259–64, 401–2, and the section on Nigeria, pp. 39–55.

Omoyajowo, J. A. "The Cherubim and Seraphim Movement—a study in interaction", *Orita* 4, (2) (December 1970), pp. 124–39.

Turnbull, T. N. *What God Hath Wrought: a Short History of the Apostolic Church,* Bradford, England: 1959, pp. 71–87.

Turner, H. W. *African Independent Church,* 2 vols. Oxford: 1967 (On the Church of the Lord (Aladura); especially Vol. 2, ch. 12, Pentecostal Revelation, and ch. 22, Holy Words.)

Westgarth, J. W. *The Holy Spirit and the Primitive Mind* London: Victory Press, 1946 (a sympathetic first-hand account of the Spirit Movement).

10
The Late Sir Isaac Akinyele, Olubadan of Ibadan

This item was written as an obituary notice for one of the great modern Nigerians who, although not himself a prophet or a charismatic, was a founding member and later head of the largest prophet-healing church in Nigeria. I was privileged to have an interview with him three years before his death. The item will serve to counter the popular impression that these movements concern only the unsophisticated, and to show that they can appeal to some of the most outstanding individuals in African societies.

Oba Sir Isaac Babalola Akinyeye, K.B.E., the Olubadan of Ibadan and Minister without Portfolio in the Government of Western Nigeria, died on 26 May 1964 at Oke Alafara, Ibadan (his birthplace). This obituary seeks only to draw attention to a remarkable figure in the history of Nigeria, whose full-scale biography should now be undertaken, and to offer some indication of his place in Nigerian religious history.

He was born on 26 April 1882 at Oke Alafara, and grew up in St. Peter's (Anglican) church and school, Aremo, Ibadan. Later, from 1898 to 1901, he attended the Church Missionary Society grammar school in Lagos. In 1903 he began his career in the public service as a clerk in the Ibadan Native Administration, rising to court clerk, and acting treasurer

---

West African Religion no. 4, July 1965, pp. 1–4.

in 1919. P. A. Talbot had Akinyele's help in the census work of the early 1920's, and acknowledges his debt to his assistant (mis-spelt Akinele) in the massive *The Peoples of Southern Nigeria* (1926).

In the Anglican Church Akinyele served as a Synodsman for St. Peter's from 1915 to 1925, and was usually a member of the Diocesan Board between 1917 and 1926. Here he was associated with J. B. Shadare, another member of both Synod and Board (Diocese of Western Equatorial Africa and later of Lagos) during much the same period. Shadare represented St. Saviour's, Ijebu-Ode, and was the moving spirit in the foundation of the first aladura-type church in the West, the Precious Stone Church, in the years 1920 to 1922. Both men must also have been either involved in, or at least aware of, the synod's ecclesiastical court during 1917–18 which enquired into the activities of the Rev. S. S. Macarthy in the Garrick Braid prophet movement of the Niger Delta area in the years 1915–16. This establishes some connection between the first prophet-healing movements in East and West Nigeria.

Akinyele followed Shadare into the Precious Stone Church in January 1925; early in the 1920's this became known as Faith Tabernacle through association with a group of the same name in Philadelphia, U.S.A., which sent its religious literature to Nigeria. In one of these magazines, *First Century Gospel*, 1 (11), Dec. 1926, p. 6, there appears a letter sent by "I.B.A." from Ibadan, describing an annually recurring sickness on which he had spent money for medicines in vain, but which ceased after he had meditated upon some tree branches on his farm in the form of a cross. It is known that Akinyele never took medicines of any kind from that time onwards—he was 82 when he died.

Another former member of St. Saviour's, Ijebu-Ode, who had joined the Precious Stone Church, J. Ade Aina, found himself lonely in Ibadan in 1924, and through addresses provided from Philadelphia sought out Akinyele and some others and formed an Ibadan branch of Faith Tabernacle in 1925. Akinyele and Aina served as pastors, and there were two small congregations when a great religious revival broke out during a Faith Tabernacle conference at Ilesha in 1930. This began through the charismatic healing powers of Joseph Babalola, now to become the most famous prophet in Western Nigeria, and the Faith Tabernacle began to spread in Yorubaland. There was a temporary alliance in the second half of 1930 with Josiah O. Oshitelu and the newly-founded Church of the Lord, but this came to grief in January 1931 on the issue of the use of mysterious "holy words" of power in the latter Church. Records have survived of an all-night meeting at Akinyele's house, in which the question was thrashed out; Akinyele himself had asked for God's guidance, and reported: "In a dream I heard these words: 'Incline thine heart to keep this law. These names can bring no forgiveness, salvation, or benefit of any kind to anybody . . .' as we were promised everything in the name of Christ, all other names should be left aside". Although Akinyele did not possess the charismatic powers of Oshitelu, or of Babalola and others in Faith Tabernacle, there is no doubt that as one of the leaders he gave stability to the new church and helped preserve an evangelical outlook, and that his house was one of the main centres of activity.

The greatly enlarged Faith Tabernacle Church made contact with the British Apostolic Church, whose literature had reached Nigeria, and received a visit from three British leaders late in 1931. Although the details of the next few years are not at all clear, it seems that a working relation was established, the African Church became called the Apostolic Church, missionaries were received, and difficulties between Government and the churches that had sprung up after the revival were resolved, for the Apostolic Church was now "recognized" and under "competent management". Increasingly this meant European management, and Akinyele, Babalola, and others of the original Faith Tabernacle Church were uneasy at this turn of events. Their intended "association" with the British Church had virtually become, in their eyes, absorption. There were also differences on other matters. The African leaders were less rigid in debarring polygamists from the Church, and were disillusioned to find British missionaries of a church which believed in divine healing resorting to the use of quinine, vaccination, etc. Akinyele in particular remained adamant on the rejection of all medicines for he asserted it was impossible for Africans to use these without associating them with magic and traditional religious ideas.

In consequence of these strains a process of separation from the Apostolic Church, which began about 1938, led to the formation of the Christ Apostolic Church by 1941. Its early support came from the Ibadan and Ijebu areas, but it has since grown into the largest and best organized of the independent churches which have emerged from the aladura movement, with nearly a hundred thousand members, and branches in Ghana. For some seven years before his death Akinyele was the 'chairman, head, and Father' of the Church he had done so much to found and develop. It is noteworthy that an elder brother, A. B. Akinyele, became bishop of the Anglican diocese of Ibadan.

Isaac Akinyele was the author of a history of Ibadan and Oshogbo, and of many religious publications, of which Ibadan University library possesses some fourteen belonging to the last decade of his life. An earlier publication, *Bi Ati Se Jewo Ese Tokantokan* ("How to Confess Sins Wholeheartedly"), about 1941, seeks to answer the question why prayer and fasting in his church no longer produce spiritual life. There is an impediment in the form of unrecognized or unconfessed sins, and the booklet proceeds to suggest how these sins both of omission and commission may be discovered and dealt with. The whole effect is that of a man who knew the human condition well, and who possessed a profoundly spiritual and evangelical Christian mind with an unusual ascetic emphasis.

Along with such an active church life Akinyele had a distinguished public career. He became an Ibadan councillor in 1930, an assessor in the Ibadan Native-Court in 1936, and later its chief judge. Queen Elizabeth conferred a Knighthood upon him, and in 1961 he was persuaded to accept office as Minister of State without portfolio in the Government of the Western Region.

He was equally distinguished as a traditional leader. In 1935 he was installed as a chief, the Ikolaba of Ibadan, and became Balogun, or Commander-in-Chief in 1953, to be followed two years later by election to the supreme office of Olubadan, the Oba or King of what was then described as the largest all-African city in sub-Saharan Africa. Most of its inhabitants follow the Muslim or traditional religions, and Christians were estimated to be no more than twenty per cent. When chosen as Balogun he at first refused the office, since the installation was attended by non-Christian ceremonies and sacrifices. When the request was pressed he agreed, but on condition that his installation should be freed from these traditional rites. That one who was so publicly identified with what many regarded as an off-beat Christian Church without pedigree should have become a respected traditional civic figure provides a commentary on the status of such independent churches in Nigeria, and on the possibilities of Christian leadership in a mixed community.

Along with his devotion to his own Christ Apostolic Church Akinyele possessed a catholicity of outlook, and in 1959 visited Europe in connection with the Moral Re-Armament Movement. It is all the more regrettable, therefore, that the passing of a man of this calibre should have been marred by a dispute over the place of his burial between the Church of his earlier years, and the Church over which he presided at the time of his death, and that neither group attended the burial service of the other Church. He lies buried, not in the vault with his wife in the Christ Apostolic cemetery, where it is said he had expressed the desire to lie, but in St. Peter's churchyard, Aremo, near where he was born.

11
Prophets and Politics: A Nigerian Test-Case

In contrast to the co-existence of (independent) Church and (colonial and independent) State exhibited in the person of Sir Isaac Akinyele in the above essay, we now observe the clash between the first known Nigerian prophet and an exceptionally able and anthropologically competent colonial administrator, who completely misunderstood the movement. The detailed story is set in the framework of similar clashes between prophets and colonial governments right across Black Africa. It is hoped to present a full book-length study of prophet Braid at a later date.

The term "prophet movement" is one of the more comprehensive of the many phrases used to describe modern African religious movements, for it may be applied within each of the four main groups which we have elsewhere distinguished as neo-primal, Islamic, Hebraist and Christian; it is in the last of these groups that its main limitation occurs, for it aptly designates the independent churches of the last forty to fifty years that stress revelations and healing, but seldom applies to the earlier "Ethiopian" or "African" independents from the 1880's to the 1920's.

We use the terms "prophet movement" and "prophet" in a fairly comprehensive sense, and are here concerned with one aspect only—the clashes of prophets and similar religious leaders with government authorities, that form a striking feature of the history of these movements. Over thirty years ago a writer described prophet risings as one of the two main forms of "revolt in Africa",[1] and evidence that might be used to support such a judgment has continued to accumulate. African prophets, therefore, would appear to be faithful representatives of the prophet figure in the history of religions, and especially of Biblical religion, in so far as they have come into conflict with the ruling powers, and suffered for their actions and convictions.

It may be useful to make a brief survey of the reported instances of these clashes, which may be traced to some of the earliest records of African reactions to Western contacts and Western Christianity. At the end of the seventeenth century there was prophetess Béatrice in the Bakongo under the rule of Pedro IV; her superficially Christianized nativist movement led to her being burnt alive in 1706.[2] Early in the nineteenth century, Makana, one of a line of Xhosa prophets, was conquered and imprisoned about 1819, but was drowned while attempting to escape.[3] The twentieth century opens with another South African incident, the various imprisonments and the final deportation of an evangelist named Johannes, who preached "Africa for the Black Man".[4]

From this point there is a steadily mounting roll of prophetic and similar movements that have been in various kinds of trouble. The Epikilipikili movement of 1904 in South Kasai in the Belgian Congo exemplified the belief that has appeared from time to time to the effect that supernatural powers invoked by a leader have rendered his followers immune to the bullets of the whites, with the inevitable tragic result.[5] In Nyasaland, Elliott Kamwana who became leader of a millennial nativistic movement under the influence of Watch Tower ideas was deported in 1909; a few years later the same ideas contributed to the rising of 1915 in the Shiré highlands, in consequence of which John Chilembwe's nationalistic church was banned.[6]

At the same time the Grebo prophet Harris from Liberia was deported by the French from the Ivory Coast after having set on foot the largest mass movement in the religious history of West Africa,[7] and Garrick Braid, the "Second Elijah", was imprisoned in Eastern Nigeria. In 1921 the followers of Enoch Mgijima in his "Israelites" community in South Africa held the same beliefs, and met the same fate at Bulhoek, as the Epikilipikili people in the Congo.[8] In the same year Simon Kimbangu was sentenced to death within a few months of becoming a prophet in the Belgian Congo, and although sentence was commuted to life imprisonment (he died in prison thirty years later) various movements and prophets who traced their origins or their inspiration to Kimbangu plagued the Belgian authorities right up till the eve of independence; there was André Matswa of the Amicale movement who was first arrested in 1930 and finally exiled to

Tchad in 1940, where he died in prison two years later; he was followed by Simon Mpadi who tried to unite all the Kimbanguist elements in a "Church of the Blacks" between 1936 and 1941, and was several times arrested; and in 1956 we learn of forty-six "leaders of subversive sects" being arrested in the Leopoldville area alone.[9]

In the Sudan, Arianhdit, one of the two Dinka prophets of recent times, was exiled by the British administration in 1922;[10] a few years later the same fate befell two leaders of the Society of the One Almighty God in Uganda, when Mugema and Malaki were deported to the Northern Province after a fracas over the enforcement of health regulations, and there the latter died through a hunger strike.[11] In Kenya this succession was maintained by the Arathi (prophets or seers) of the Wata wa Mngu (People of God), three of whom were shot in a clash and others of whom suffered arrest or the closure of their shrines.[12] The Nuer, neighbours of the Dinka, had two of their prophet leaders imprisoned, one banished and one shot.[13]

The Watch Tower ideology which figured in the early part of the century in Central Africa continued to haunt the colonial authorities; the most notorious example of its influence was probably Tomo Nyengwa of the Kitawala, who called himself "Mwana Lesa" and was finally hunted from the Belgian Congo and hanged in Northern Rhodesia in 1926.[14] In Southern Rhodesia Matthew Zwimba, founder of the Church of the White Bird, was imprisoned for the second time in the early 1920's, after unsuccessful attempts to suppress his church; about the same time, Dingiswayo, the leader of the Christian Catholic Apostolic Church in Zion, was deported for sedition.[15]

Similar events were occurring in the same decade in West Africa. The Cameroun pastor who founded the Native Baptist Church in 1926 was imprisoned, ostensibly for political reasons, and in nearby Ibibioland in Eastern Nigeria many of the prophets and prophetesses thrown up by the Spirit Movement of 1927 and the following years were persecuted and imprisoned by both local native and colonial administrations. The Yoruba prophet, J. O. Oshitelu, founder of the Church of the Lord (Aladura), was under suspicion and interrogation in 1931 but escaped more drastic action; his famous contemporary, Joseph Babalola, was less fortunate, for he served six months in prison after allegedly calling someone a witch— there is some evidence that the authorities were far more concerned about the political implications of the extensive aladura movement in a time of economic depression and tax riots, and were determined to do something to halt the movement. In the 1930's the founder of the Judaistic God's Kingdom Society, Gideon Urhobo, was twice imprisoned on charges such as public preaching without a permit and insulting Roman Catholics.[16]

And so the story continues into more recent years, with Reuben Spartas, the founder of the African Orthodox Church in Uganda sentenced to six years' imprisonment in 1949 for implication in political disturbances, but released after serving three years;[17] and Emilio in the Northern Province of what is now Zambia: in 1960 his Church of the Sacred Heart of Jesus was declared illegal, his followers were dispersed, and he himself was arrested for medical observation. But Emilio was one of the lucky ones, for before charges deriving from refusal to pay taxes or to observe traditional morality could be brought, he escaped and vanished.

Even in such a catalogue as this we have still said nothing of the complex question of Mau Mau in Kenya in the early 1950's, or of little known movements such as Simon Toko's "Red Star" movement in North Angola and the Congo, or of the latter's Tonsism and Dieudonné movements in the last two decades. It awaits only the enterprising journalist to pursue enquiries further and collect the stories into one volume to complete the damning indictment.

But who does it damn? Many among orthodox Christians in the churches will straightway answer that it is the false, the semi-pagan or the heretical prophets who are thus brought to judgment. A good deal of public opinion in Africa, and we suspect an increasing volume of academic opinion everywhere, would be ready to lay the condemnation upon the governments concerned, which in any case were almost all colonial governments. Unfortunately for the latter verdict, there was the widely publicized and violent clash in 1964 between the new government of Northern Rhodesia on the eve of becoming Zambia, and, if you please, a lady, the prophetess Alice Mulenga and her Lumpa Church. This church had been in alliance with Dr. Kaunda and his United National Independence Party, for many of the party leaders, including Kaunda, were Bemba, like most of the church members; this alliance had strengthened the party in its civil disobedience campaigns in 1959 and 1961. But in 1962 Alice Lenshina, as she is known, broke from the party and early in 1964 declared armed resistance to the U.N.I.P., which was now the government. The ensuing major military operation ended "with 40 villages burned, 588 persons dead, the prophetess in prison, and Kenneth Kaunda's government deeply embarrassed".[18] When we hear that the Chunya people among the Safwa of Tanzania began their Religion of Jehovah and Michael in 1963 in protest against the ruling political party, the Tanganyika African National Union,[19] and when we remember that long ago the prophet Harris had been imprisoned in the independent state of Liberia before ever he was deported by the French administration of the Ivory Coast, we realize that any generalization about colonial or white oppression and prophetic or religious revolt fails to account for all the facts.

There is, for instance, the rather striking fact that the areas where white oppression and the proliferation of independent religious movements with prophet leaders have been greatest—in South Africa, for instance—appear comparatively little in this catalogue of conflict.

It must also be recognized that in many of the other cases we have quoted there was great provocation on the part of the prophets and their like, and, further, that there must have been extensive but unreported discussions by colonial administrators that issued in a decision *not* to take any drastic action against troublesome religious movements. In the one such instance to which we have already referred, that of Oshitelu in Western Nigeria in 1931, the full account of top-level discussions reveals both the alarm of the authorities and the mixture of caution and tolerance that issued in a decision to bring no charge against Oshitelu. In the event the government fears were unnecessary and the church that has since developed through four West African countries has proved a-political through most of its career.

On the other hand, there were prophetic type leaders who were engaged in direct political activity, as is only to be expected in a society where the separation between religion and politics is a relatively new idea. Then again, prophets and movements that were primarily religious in complexion have on occasion been forced into more political terms; there is a widespread agreement that this mistake was made concerning Kimbangu in the Congo, and some at least of the subsequent movements that have claimed him as a founder. A still further complication appears when we learn that some have received their call to be prophets during their imprisonment on non-religious charges; Sampson Oppong's first impressions were received while serving a sentence in the Ivory Coast and after his release began the movement that stirred Western Ghana, especially in the Ashanti country, in the 1920's; and Harris received his prophetic call while in prison in his own Liberia on a political charge.

Generalizations, therefore, about Africa's prophet movements and their relation to politics must be exceedingly suspect, just as so many other current generalizations about modern African religious movements can be exposed as premature and superficial. Only patient examination of individual cases, one by one, in a way that has not yet been widely attempted and reported, can tell us what really did happen. Much of the essential information lies in government archives, to which access has not grown easier in many parts of Africa in the last few years.

One of the first steps in a fuller examination of the relation of prophets to politics is to analyse and reconsider some of the court trials. This has been attempted for the Mau Mau movement, which we do not include in this survey, and Jules Chomé, a Belgian lawyer who defended Congolese political leaders after the 1959 riots, has essayed a professional critique of the trial of Simon Kimbangu in 1921.[20] Chomé differs sharply from the Belgian priest, Van Wing, who was satisfied that all the rules of law had been observed, and asserts that the trial was a legal scandal; the following year another book on Kimbangu took a critical attitude to Chomé's conclusions,[21] and so the debate continues.

As a test-case in another area we now propose to examine the trials of the first outstanding prophet in Nigeria, Garrick Sokari Braid, who was a public figure in the eastern section of the Niger Delta for only three years before his death in 1918, and who spent nearly half of that period in custody; his movement split the Niger Delta Pastorate of the Anglican Church when it first appeared late in 1915, and has left behind various groups known as Christ Army Churches that continue till this day. This particular instance is of special value for a number of reasons. The situation was complicated neither by white settlers, land hunger, government oppression, nor the presence of white missionaries. The Niger Delta Pastorate was a virtually autonomous section of the widespread Diocese of Western Equatorial Africa, that had broken from all association with the Church Missionary Society in 1892, immediately after the death of Bishop Crowther, and had continued within the Anglican communion under the semi-episcopal leadership of Crowther's son; it had thus been an all-African church for nearly a quarter of a century before the prophet movement appeared, although its ministry consisted largely of "native foreigners" from Yorubaland and Sierra Leone.

The British colonial administration of the area was manned by some outstanding officers during the period of the Braid troubles. The resident or commissioner of the Owerri Province, J. C. Maxwell, who held Scottish degrees of M.A. and M.D., had some twenty years' West African experience, and in the course of a distinguished career became Governor of Northern Rhodesia, and received membership in two orders of knighthood. The district commissioner, Degema division, which included Braid's home area at Bakana, was Percy Amaury Talbot, then nearly forty, with about a dozen years' experience in West Africa, and already marked out by Lugard for promotion. By 1915 Talbot and his wife had each published a substantial book on the culture of the people among whom they lived, and Talbot followed this up with four other works, including the standard *The Peoples of Southern Nigeria* in four volumes; in 1962, seventeen years after his death, it was his data which formed the basis for the volume which appeared over the names of Talbot and Mulhall, *The Physical Anthropology of Southern Nigeria*. Talbot was thus an outstanding combination of administrator and scholar, who was honoured with a doctorate of science by his own university, Oxford, for his anthropological work. This was the man who had to deal with Braid the prophet and who conducted three of the four trials that Braid had to face in 1916.

The other district officer who was concerned with the fate of Braid was Elphinstone Dayrell, who relieved Talbot during the middle part of the year, and conducted the first of the prophet's trials. Dayrell was in his early forties, with considerable and varied African experience, and he too was something of an anthropologist, a Fellow of the Royal Anthropological Institute, and already author of a book on southern Nigerian culture. It seems quite clear, therefore, that Braid was in no sense the victim of blimpish or inexperienced young officers, but was dealing with the colonial administration at its best and most enlightened.

Of Braid himself it is harder to make an estimate at present, except to say that he began with the support of most of the clergy of the Niger Delta Pastorate; these were themselves a remarkable group of men, mostly Sierra Leoneans, and in writing and speech, dress and manner, were conventional orthodox Anglicans of a choice late Victorian vintage, led by the already patriarchal figure of Archdeacon Crowther, and supervised by the even more venerable assistant bishop, James Johnson. Braid had revealed charismatic powers as early as 1909 and had given considerable pastoral assistance for some six years in his home parish before springing into wider fame at the end of 1915. At first he had the support of the leading clergy in the area, who felt that revival had come to the church, and even Bishop Johnson was most favourably impressed on his first experience of the movement. The story of the breach between Braid and the Pastorate church must be told elsewhere, but sufficient has been said to indicate that it was no stranger, no lunatic or passing charlatan, who suddenly appeared in the Delta, but a well-known son of the church which at first hoped for great things from him.

It is with the conflict between this prophet and the colonial administration that we are here concerned. As always, many historical and contemporary factors affected the situation, but the most conspicuous of these was the fact that the First World War was in progress, and that Nigerian troops had been involved in a difficult campaign in the neighbouring German territory of the Kamerun from the outbreak of the war until February 1916. Colonial powers in Africa were very sensitive to local unrest during the war period, as is clear in the deportation of Harris from the Ivory Coast in 1915. The resident of the Owerri Province, however, regarded himself as fortunate in his district officer at Degema, and in his annual report for 1915 commented on the very satisfactory shape in which he had kept the division through his energy, tact and firmness in coping with lawlessness.

This then was the situation when the Braid movement appeared with its crowds and its excitements towards the end of Talbot's tour of duty from 1914 to March 1916. From the beginning there seems to have been a complete failure of understanding between Talbot and the prophet movement, and he early made up his mind that it was to be suppressed. He had apparently heard something of similar religious movements in South Africa, and shared the common European interpretation of these, for in his "handing over notes" to Dayrell, the acting district officer in March 1916, Talbot wrote at length on Braid and the movement: it was "essentially one of Ethiopianism, of blacks against whites, and to a certain extent against all authority . . . sedition . . . still is being preached throughout the Division, while the leader . . . was for a long time too cunning to put himself within reach of the law, fortunately enough evidence has now been collected to warrant his arrest on a charge of demanding money with menaces. . . . The principal results of the movement have been, first a seditious feeling against the government, secondly a great loss to trade" [this had already been brought about by the effects of the war in 1914], "and thirdly a large increase in the death-rate due to excitement and the filthy observances enacted". The habit of giving the sick Braid's bath-water to drink certainly merited this description.

Braid was arrested by Talbot, and bequeathed to his successor, Dayrell, for trial. The prophet must have been expecting this, for on arrest he presented two petitions, one to Talbot himself, and one to "the Governor of Nigeria"; the latter was duly transmitted to Lagos. In both petitions he defended himself as a prophet called by God and maligned by the Niger Delta Pastorate Church and Bishop Johnson, and the one to the "District Commissioner" in true prophetic manner warned him as the local court authority to dispense justice and not to interfere with the manifest work of God; if not, "then know that the power will be taken from you". This may be sailing close to the wind in a colonial situation, but in the religious context in which it was placed it is not clearly seditious.

Dayrell deserves admiration for the thorough job he must have made of the trial—nine whole days of it. The charges had expanded from the original obtaining of money by threats and false pretences, to include behaviour likely to cause a breach of the peace, and wilfully damaging jujus. On the last count, certainly the most specific and undeniable, Braid was acquitted; on the other two charges he received six months' hard labour on the first, and three months on the second charge, to run concurrently.

In examining the full account of these nine days, almost fifty years later, one tries to keep an open mind and to remember both that there was a war on and that prophets are tricky characters for authorities both in Church and State at any time. And yet, if we concentrate on the more definite charge of demanding money under threats and on false pretences, the evidence seems inadequate to support a conviction. We say this in the light of experience of prophets in later Nigerian movements, where the whole situation so easily eludes the understanding of expatriates from other cultures. The threats Braid undoubtedly uttered are quite capable of interpretation as typical prophetic judgments, not so much on refusing to pay money, as on failure to respond to the new order that he represented, a new era marked by the destruction of traditional religious objects, the jujus as they are called, and a turning to the God of the Scriptures who would bring health, peace and prosperity. The money collected by Braid's agents was interpreted in Biblical terms by Braid's pastor, the Reverend M. A. Kemmer, as a modern form of sacrifice to God, and was to be devoted half to the Niger Delta Pastorate and half to communal use as capital for trading purposes and so for greater prosperity. And as for the charge of false pretences, can this stand if the prophet himself sincerely believes in his own election and powers, is widely accepted in the same terms, and has some undoubted cures to his credit? We conclude that the verdict was unjust in so far as it was reached without taking the whole situation into account, and the punishment of six months' hard labour was excessive. That this is not merely the opinion of one who can afford to sympathize with turbulent prophets from a safe distance of half a century is indicated by the fact that the Supreme Court judge who reviewed the verdicts on Braid's appeal quashed the second conviction and reduced the first sentence by half.

This first clash with the law may possibly have provoked a more definitely anti-government and anti-white attitude in the prophet himself. He was released on bail on 8 May, while his appeal was being determined in Calabar, and according to evidence given against him at his next trials, Braid had been out on bail only two days when he delivered much more seditious speeches in his home town of Bakana. In these he was alleged to have claimed to be king of the world, before whom the King of England would come and kneel. He would take the chain the white men had put on the necks of the black men, and would put it on the necks of the whites, and the black men would be able to do everything that the white men could do. In any case the war was a judgment of God upon the English, and he was praying for the Germans to kill off all the English; no one must pray for the English to win, or buy their imported goods, especially rice, guns, tobacco and alcohol—these had all been poisoned by the whites.

Such utterances from an influential colonial subject in the middle of a life and death military struggle might well invite administrative attention. The puzzle is, if this is what he was saying only fourteen miles from the divisional headquarters at Degema, why was Braid left at liberty for another five months? The fact that he was out on bail to the tune of £350 surely only made it worse. One begins to wonder whether the explanation lies in the supreme forbearance of an officer who had already sentenced Braid so severely, or in the accuracy of the later reports, as they appear in the crop of trials that faced Braid in November. Support for the latter explanation is provided by Dayrell's report in his handing over notes when Talbot returned from leave in mid-September; Braid was out on bail, but had kept quiet and given no trouble.

However this may be, Talbot now took over, despite widespread reports that Braid had prayed for his destruction, and that the Germans had captured him and his wives during his journey to England. It was with difficulty that some were able to believe it was the same man. Early in October the result of Braid's appeal was announced, and he returned to prison to serve the balance of the reduced sentence. By mid-November Talbot was ready with eight further charges against the prophet. But he prefaced these by seven criminal cases in six weeks against a total of eighty-four followers of Braid. The charges were mostly for riot, assault or unlawful assembly; three cases ended in dismissal or a mere binding over to keep the peace; the others resulted in sentences of from six to twelve months' hard labour, most of which the higher authorities (this time the Lieutenant-Governor) later halved.

Talbot then spent the second half of November dealing with Braid himself. The first group of charges concerned receiving stolen property, to wit 3,200 manillas, the metal bracelets traditionally used as a medium of exchange. These had allegedly come from shrines raided or destroyed by one of his agents, Don John Pedro, who had been given six months' hard labour just nine days previously. However correct the facts probably were, larceny and receiving seem rather subtle and refined descriptions of the basic conflict between the old and the new religions. The categories of statute law and of religious faith were in different worlds. And once again six months' hard labour was the voice of the law.

The next group of charges, twelve days later, concerned Braid's alleged seditious utterances and incitements against the British on his second day out on bail, now over six months back. We have already described these statements and the problem they raise. Braid's lawyer called no witnesses for the defence and relied on a straight denial by Garrick, who claimed, as any prophet would, that he had only preached the word of God; in addition the lawyer raised a few legal technicalities. The prosecution witnesses had been unanimous and the verdict was inevitable, another six months' hard labour.

This trial had occupied 27 and 30 November. In between there was room for yet another trial, on 28 and 29 November, concerning utterances still further back, early in January at Abonnema. When we realize that Abonnema was only about five hundred yards across the water from the divisional headquarters, from which Talbot had not yet gone on leave, we wonder why such dangerous words had not been brought to book until nearly eleven months later. And when we read the evidence of the witnesses for the prosecution, our uneasiness increases. It shows a remarkable verbal identity through the two trials and all the witnesses; of the nine main witnesses there were four from the House of Yellow, and two of these were to bring a civil claim against Braid within the next two months; the same two, husband and wife, had been leading witnesses for the prosecution at the first trial in March. If the authorities were on the alert for sedition in the prophet movement, as they were, and if Braid had uttered these wildly subversive remarks in a public meeting just across the river from headquarters in January, and had been heard to do so by two people who had testified against him in charges of breach of the peace during the nine-day examination in March, then it seems remarkable that they had to wait to the end of November to tell their story of sedition. Once again the defence either knew the truth of the charges or else realized that the cards were stacked against them; no witnesses were called. Braid gave a long and complicated Biblical interpretation of what he had said, a few legal technicalities were introduced, as it seems, *pro forma,* and another six months was added to the prophet's score.

In the event he seems to have served twelve months; there was no bail, no reduction of sentence beyond treating two of the terms as concurrent.

We have not disguised our dissatisfaction with the fairness of these trials, and with the interpretation put upon Braid's public statements. While Talbot was clearly an outstanding officer, the energy and firmness with which he was credited do not easily keep company with depth of understanding, in spite of the fact that he was a pioneer in attempting to describe the culture and religion of the peoples among whom he served. If our suggestions are correct, then he simply failed to understand the Braid movement at all.

We might be more hesitant in arriving at this judgment were it not for the evidence of similar misunderstandings in the same quarters of other prophet movements, and we have quoted Oshitelu as a case in point. There is also the extent to which the local court judgments, in these cases and also in others we might have quoted in the same division in 1916, were quashed or the sentences reduced. But even more significant is the quite different attitude adopted by the two Residents of the Owerri Province in this period. In his annual report for 1915, Dr. J. C. Maxwell referred at length to what he called "an entirely novel set of circumstances . . . a religious revival"; he noted that there had been "practically no sale of trade spirits locally since he [Braid] began his crusade", and that some cures were "probably genuine". "The movement is of considerable interest, and while care must be taken to prevent it causing serious breaches of the peace it might . . . lead to distinctly beneficial results; for it was in no way political".

In the following year he commented that in 1916 the nearest approach to unrest had arisen from the rumour that British rule was coming to an end, "but the return of the troops from the Cameroons scotched this". This helps to explain the firmness that Talbot felt was necessary, but also suggests that the unrest had no particular connexion with the Braid movement. Dr. Maxwell again gave this considerable space, as "the most interesting and important movement" of the year. "The leader," he continued, "was an ignorant and illiterate man, who, as might have been expected, got into trouble ... the difficulties that have arisen have been mainly with the existing religious organisations" [the side of the 1916 story that requires a separate telling elsewhere]. "Some officers took a serious view of the political importance of the new movement. At present the political significance is not great, although it would be wrong to say it has none. The new body professes loyalty to the Government" [one would never guess this from the court record books]. "At the same time one of its avowed objects is the creation of a Native Church in which there shall be no 'exotic' influence, to quote one of the leaders of the movement. ... A body showing this jealousy might very readily become a centre for disaffection."

In contrast to these calm and, as events proved, more balanced and accurate observations by the Resident, the energetic Talbot wrote his handing over notes to his successor in Degema at the end of January 1917: "If my recommendations as to Garrick Braid and the Bakana chiefs are carried out, the outward manifestations of hostility to Government should cease and the seditious element in the movement be eliminated." He then went on to refer to the anti-government spirit displayed in the court cases of the previous November. Evidently the machinery of the colonial administration ensured that a copy of the handing over notes from one office to another at the local level reached the Resident, for only two weeks later the acting-Resident, E. D. Simpson, was adding his own sarcastic and sceptical comments in the margins of Talbot's notes.

It is of course arguable that Talbot's firmness had drawn the sting of the Braid movement or turned it into less subversive directions. But the contrast between the attitude of the administration at the local and the central offices is most striking and lends support to our interpretation of the political side of the 1916 events. Only eighteen months later the District Officer at Bonny, which had been a centre of the movement somewhat outside the troubles we have surveyed, was able to report: "I do not attach any political importance to their hobby of setting up new churches and religions." One can appreciate this as the almost inevitable attitude of a government official in face of the effervescence of religious movements in the Eastern Region in the past forty to fifty years. And yet it is remarkable to trace how closely government did watch these new developments, not only in time of war, or of economic stress, but as a regular exercise through this whole period, and how comprehensive their information has been. On the whole they have managed to avoid an open clash with the prophets and their movements, as they avoided it with Oshitelu. It is almost certain that they were wrong in the more drastic treatment of Garrick Braid.

Notes

1. L. A. Cook: Revolt in Africa, *Journal of Negro History*, 18 (4). Oct. 1933. 396–413.
2. P. Decraene: Les incidences politiques des religions syncrétiques et des mouvements messianiques en Afrique Noire, *Afrique contemporaine*, 17, jan.–fév. 20, 1965, and references there given.
3. W. M. Macmillan: *Bantu, Boer, and Briton*, 2nd ed. Oxford, 1963. 51, 80, 341.
4. B. G. M. Sundkler: *Bantu Prophets in South Africa*, 2nd ed. London, 1969. 68–9.
5. Decraene: *op. cit.*, 20.
6. G. Shepperson: The Politics of African Church Separatist Movements in British Central Africa 1892–1916, *Africa*, 24 (3), July 1954, 233–46; G. Shepperson and T. Price: *Independent African: John Chilembwe*. Edinburgh, 1958.
7. W. J. Platt: *An African Prophet*. London, 1934.
8. Sundkler: *op. cit.*, 72–3.
9. E. Andersson: *Messianic Popular Movements in the Lower Congo*. London, 1958. J. van Wing: Le Kimbanguisme vu part un témoin, *Zaïre*, 12 (6), 1958, 563–618.
10. G. Lienhardt: *Divinity and Experience*. London, 1961. 76f.
11. F. B. Welbourn: *East African Rebels*. London, 1961. 43.
12. J. Kenyatta: *Facing Mount Kenya*, new ed. London, 1961. 273–9.
13. E. E. Evans-Pritchard: *Nuer Religion*. London, 1956. 305.
14. L. H. Gann: *A History of Northern Rhodesia*. London, 1964. 231–6.
15. T. O. Ranger: *The Rise of Independency in Southern Rhodesia*, unpublished lecture given at Salisbury, typescript, n.d.
16. Gideon M. Urhobo: *Eighteen Years' Kingdom Service*, Warri, Nigeria, n.d. [1951].
17. Welbourn: *op. cit.*, 27.
18. R. C. Mitchell: Africa's Prophet Movements, *The Christian Century*, 18 November 1964. 1427.
19. D. B. Barrett: *Reaction to Mission: An Analysis of Independent Church Movements Across Two Hundred African Tribes*, unpublished Ph.D. dissertation, Columbia University, 1965. 154.
20. Jules Chomé: *La passion de Simon Kimbangu*. Brussels, 1959.
21. G.-A. Gilis: *Kimbangu*. Brussels, 1960.

NOTE.—Where no reference is given information has been derived from personal communications, or from archives that are not willing to be identified. The material on the Braid trials comes from the relevant district and provincial court record books and reports in the Nigerian National archives at Enugu.

12
African Religious Movements and Roman Catholicism

The Pentecostal forms of Christianity examined in essay nine were necessarily Protestant, for the neo-Pentecostal movement had not yet surfaced within Catholicism. This essay opens up the question of the relation of Catholicism in Africa to the rise of new religious movements, in comparison to the more obvious relationship with Protestantism. The exploration is no more than preliminary, on the basis of evidence available by the 1960s. Later evidence confirms the conclusions, but the question now needs study at deeper levels where the whole styles of Catholic and of Protestant missions in relation to African cultures can be examined and compared. Reference may also be made to the Catholic influences clearly evident in the next essay.

There has been a widespread thesis which alleges that modern African religious movements, especially in their independent church forms, are the inevitable offspring of Protestant missions and churches and therefore absent or rare in Roman Catholic areas. When presented by Roman Catholic

---

H.-J. Greschat and H. Jungraithmayr (eds.), *Wort und Religion: Kalima na Dini* (Festscrift, E. Dammann). Stuttgart: Evangelischer Missionsverlag 1969, pp. 255–264.

writers this is an extension of the traditional Roman Catholic thesis of the fissiparous nature of Protestantism. Even in its original application in Europe the unity of Lutheranism and the number of schisms from Rome suggest that it could be questioned; but even if it might be substantiated there, as a Western-originated thesis it must be examined critically when transferred to the African continent, or to other cultural areas.

The author of one of the two major world surveys of new religious movements, Dom Guariglia of Milan, takes the view that there are hardly any prophetic-salvation movements (as he calls them) where Christianity has spread in its Catholic form, since this presents a complete and effective salvation so satisfying for the ethnic peoples that they have no need of other movements.[1] Professor Lanternari, the author of the other comprehensive survey, writing as neither Protestant nor Catholic, points out the extent to which Roman Catholic areas have in fact produced new movements — in both the Americas, in South Vietnam, the Philippines and New Guinea, and in Oceania.[2]

In Africa, however, the issue hardly arose during the first phase of independent movements, when the more orthodox Ethiopian type of churches developed in South Africa and western Nigeria between 1880 and about 1920, for the Roman Catholic Church was not then strongly established in these areas. It was with the advent of prophet Harris in West Africa in 1913, and Simon Kimbangu in the then Belgian Congo in 1921, both areas with considerable Catholic mission work, that the thesis of Protestant responsibility was developed, for Harris was of Protestant Episcopal background and Kimbangu a Baptist catechist, and both had an extensive and disturbing effect on Catholic members. An acrimonious controversy appeared in the Belgian journal *Congo*,[3] the charges brought against the Protestants by an anonymous Catholic contributor being answered vigorously by Henri Anet. In the following year another Catholic writer repeated the thesis and applied it to other movements in Africa: Harris, he claimed, was a Protestant catechist, Malaki in Uganda an Anglican agent, Kausapala in Angola had been trained by Calvinist Boers, Chilembwe in Nyasaland had been educated by United States Protestants, and in the Congo Kimbangu had followed his Protestant teachers in his attitude to the Bible, in seeking a rapprochement with Catholics, and in being anti-Belgian, and it was a Protestant judge who had signed his reprieve from the death sentence! Catholicism suppresses these movements, while Protestantism encourages them; in fact, prophetism *is* Protestantism.[4] A Belgian newspaper even suggested that Protestant missionaries had "invented" Kimbanguism as a means of stirring up a Protestant revival.[5]

This theory of the new African movements was widely accepted in French and Belgian administrative circles, and continued to appear in Catholic discussions, as at the Museum Lessianum symposium[6] and in a work by Fr. Adrian Hastings.[7] It has also been used by Protestant and other scholars, although often in a less absolute form; thus Hodgkin asserts that "though Catholic missions have bred their own separatist churches and leaders it is natural that Protestantism should be the more fruitful source of new protest movements".[8] Similarly Lanternari recognizes that while the Protestant theory is an oversimplification it remains true that Protestantism is a "favouring factor".[9] Even a recent inclination to dispense with this thesis because "The significant variables in the missionary influence ... are to be found not in the missionaries' allegiance to Protestantism or Roman Catholicism, but in their modes of preaching and in general mission policies" and in their ideologies, could well lead back to the same thesis.[10] There is still need, therefore, for more detailed examination of the relation of Africa's religious movements to these two great Christian traditions, and it is to be hoped that the new ecumenical climate will facilitate more accurate results than were possible when the question began as a controversy over forty years ago.

A first survey of sub-saharan Africa for the incidence of independency in relation to Roman Catholicism suggests that there may be an inverse relationship. Thus one finds a very large proportion of Catholics in Uganda and few religious movements, while in South Africa with its vast range of independent churches the proportion of Catholics in the population is one of the lowest south of the Sahara. Those who regard religious and political independency in Africa as closely connected will find a parallel result in Coleman's demonstration in 1954 of the inverse relation between the degree of overt nationalism and the proportion of Catholics in the population in six African territories.[11] Coleman, however, recognized that many other factors were at work and that some of these, such as the strength of Islam, had nothing to do with the nature of the dominant Christian tradition; nor has the subsequent achievement of independence been entirely correlated with previous nationalist movements. On the other hand there are striking exceptions in the incidence of independent churches, which are exceedingly numerous in areas with large Catholic populations such as Congo (Kinshasa) and eastern Nigeria.

The position in South Africa requires separate comment. It is true that there appears to be very little connection between Catholicism and religious independency. A well-informed African scholar could remember only one individual who claimed to have broken from the Catholic Church,[12] and H.-J. Becken's survey of a sample of fifty independent churches failed to reveal one with Catholic origins.[13] In explanation of the special South African situation Fr. J. P. Kiernan points out that the Roman Catholic Church has never been allied with the Protestant ruling power, either British or Afrikaans, and has if anything been out of favour with the political authorities. It has therefore not been tempted to engage in politics, and has been more readily identified with the African peoples in their problems and their oppression. It has in fact suffered for taking the part of Africans and so wears an "aura of martyrdom" and has gained the continuing allegiance of its African members.[14] Its position has therefore been the reverse of that in the former French and Belgian colonies, where independency has flourished.

The most comprehensive examination of the relation of the Catholic-Protestant factor to independent churches, if not to all new religious movements, occurs in the course of D. B. Barrett's study of the incidence of independency in some 850 African tribes, of which 290 had independent movements.[15] Of these 290 tribes thirteen percent of those under Catholic colonial powers had independent churches, compared to twentynine percent of those under Protestant regimes. Similarly, the tribe having most independents and scoring highest on Barrett's "scale of religious strain", which measures the likelihood of an independent movement, was the Zulu, which had twelve percent of Catholics. On the other hand, Barrett also found a high correlation between the incidence of independency and the presence of more than twenty percent of Roman Catholics in the tribal unit. He was forced to conclude that although most secessions occurred from Protestant missions, the presence of Catholicism was still a powerful background factor. The Lumpa Church of Alice Lenshina in Zambia, for example, was formed by secession from a Protestant mission but drew perhaps half of the members it had secured some years later from the Catholic community.

It is plain, therefore, that the question is exceedingly complicated, and that any simple thesis is almost certain to be wrong. Let us turn to a survey of the evidence, first examining those movements where the origin or background is known to have been Roman Catholic.

SECESSION MOVEMENTS FROM CATHOLICISM

We may select six examples of whole movements that have emanated from the Roman Catholic Church, including one of the earliest known movements of this kind in Africa, the Antoniens in the Lower Congo at the end of the seventeenth century. This was founded by a prophetess Béatrice who claimed to be a reincarnation of St. Antony and sought to africanize the Christianity established in the Kongo kingdom by the Portuguese. Although she managed to convert members of the court she was burnt alive in 1706.[16]

The first such movement of which we are aware in modern Africa is the Holy Face Catholic Church in and around Uyo, eastern Nigeria. This began as the Holy Face Society, one of the many devotional associations introduced by missionaries in different parts of Africa, and in this case ultimately derived from the Confraternity of the Holy Face founded at

Tours in France in the later nineteenth century. After having functioned as a prayer society ancillary to the regular services of the Church there was (according to the present members) a change of missionaries and in 1944 the withdrawal of approval for the society. Its then leader, Benedict Julius, unsuccessfully sought the rehabilitation of the society, which continued its activities and developed into an independent church. This body now functions as a member of the United Independent Churches Fellowship that has sprung from the reconciling work of American Mennonite missionaries around Uyo since 1959; it retains a few externals such as the crucifix and the rosary, but otherwise differs little from the churches of Protestant background associated with it.[17]

In Zambia there was a striking development of a Catholic Church (or Children) of the Sacred Heart which began about 1954 as a pious and temperance society based on devotion to the Sacred Heart of Jesus. The founder was a former seminarist who had become a zealous Catholic teacher in Lusaka, by name Emilio Mulolani. As a visionary he claimed an authority independent of that of the Church, and sought to establish his League of the Sacred Heart and preach in his own way until the inevitable clash with the hierarchy led to the condemnation of both himself and his society in 1956. Emilio was then presented as an African prophet sent to free Catholics from white rule and began to set up his own churches, for which he secured government recognition in 1958. Encouraged by his visions of the Virgin Mary and St. Thérèse de Lisieux he founded a new village for his followers, and embarked on new forms of communal behaviour that were offensive to traditional opinion and brought Emilio and his members into conflict with the native courts. In 1960 the government proscribed the church, and after continued disobedience Emilio and others were arrested and the new village closed down. He himself, however, escaped, and nothing further is known of him. Emilio was an educated and sincere but unbalanced African, who gave a new mystical interpretation to Catholic teaching and moved in a perfectionist and antinomian direction that neither the Christian nor the traditional community could tolerate.[18]

A quite different kind of neo-pagan movement emerging from time to time since the nineteen twenties among Catholic missions in the Lower Congo has been reported by Igor Kopytoff, who witnessed what he calls the Holy Water movement among the Suku and other peoples in 1958–9.[19] It had begun a few years before when an African Catholic priest had been only too successful in demands for the destruction of traditional "fetishes"; these had been burnt in large quantities and replaced by reliance upon the holy water that he had offered in place of sacrifices, traditional ritual and divination. This syncretist "revitalization" movement stands at the other end of the scale from the independent church type, and produced no leaders above the village level, so that it finally disappeared as its predecessors had done. It stands, however, as a reminder that the whole range of religious movements in Africa is capable of appearance within a Catholic milieu.

In Kenya there have been two independent churches founded by leaders and members drawn from Catholic missions among the Luo people. The first derived from Mariam Ragot, a prophetess who began to oppose the Church of Rome and Europeans about 1952. Her movement was proscribed in 1954 and she and her husband were in trouble with the authorities until derestricted in 1960. Since then the prophetess and her adherents have continued without further trouble in South Nyanza.[20]

Not to be confused with the above "Religion of Mary" is the Maria Legio or Legio Maria founded by a Catholic catechist named Simeo Ondeto after an experience of translation to heaven. By the end of 1963 it emerged as a large public movement with an estimated 90,000 adherents. After 1964, when Ondeto was imprisoned for holding an illegal meeting, and there was a lengthy debate in the House of Representatives on the loyalty and morality of the movement, the public leadership seems to have passed to a young married woman, Gaudencia Aoko, born in 1943. The movement became anti-Roman Catholic, although retaining a hierarchical organization and using Latin, rosaries, crucifixes, vestments and rituals similar to those in the Catholic mission; otherwise it resembled the usual prophet-healing churches with pentecostal features. A small secession from the Maria Legio members in Tanzania in 1963 continued as the African Catholic Legio and followed the Roman Catholic practices as closely as possible.[21]

It is plain that the Roman Catholic devotional societies or pious associations have contributed something to the origins or the shape of several of these movements, whether it be the societies of the Holy Face, the Sacred Heart, or the Legion of Mary. The latter was first introduced from Ireland into eastern Nigeria in 1933 and into East Africa in 1936, and has proved remarkably successful as a lay movement with an extensive hierarchical organization, stressing vernacular prayers and the use of the rosary, and encouraging devotion both to the Holy Spirit and to the Virgin Mary who distributes the Spirit's gifts. It is possible that Mary here plays the part of the traditional ancestral intermediaries, and that other features of the Legion and similar movements help to provide both a defence against secession and a model for the movements that do depart.[22]

There have been other prophetic developments and independent movements within a Catholic milieu that have not been reported. For instance in our own experience there was an Ibo prophetess called Veronica at Nsukka, eastern Nigeria, who claimed a vision in 1963 and asserted that she had been chosen to be the African counterpart of St. Teresa, and had also been given stigmata. She gathered a group of disciples, but unfortunately in 1964 the Catholic chapel at the university was robbed of various liturgical articles with which the group celebrated mass in a hut, and the incipient movement ended in the courts.[23] And as this is written there comes a report of Catholic authorities in East Africa "having trouble with a large movement of blood-red becassocked lay Catholics led by a zealous prophet". There may well be further developments of this kind in the future, especially from some of the lay devotional associations, or a movement such as the Jamaa founded in Katanga by Fr. Tempels late in the nineteen forties and apparently developing its own synthesis of Western and African values in considerable independence.[24] A similar semi-independent development occurred in Congo (Brazza) in 1964, when a pious Catholic, Victor Malanda, established his Croix-Koma or Crucifixion Movement as an anti-witchcraft and magic, reforming and renewal movement in its own right, and somewhat impatient of official Church attitudes.[25]

FOUNDERS WITH CATHOLIC BACKGROUND

The connection of Catholicism with independency is also to be found in the individual leaders or founders who owe their Christian training or background to a Catholic mission or upbringing. In Nigeria the co-founder of the well-known Cherubim and Seraphim societies, Christiana Abiodun Akinsowon, had been a pupil in a Catholic school, and Gideon Urhobo was a Roman Catholic member before departing for the Jehovah's Witnesses and then founding his own God's Kingdom Society. The Nomiya Luo Mission in Kenya was established by John Owalo, an ex-seminarian. In both the Congo Republics the Catholic Church has been strongly established and has also contributed leaders for the independents. André Matswa, founder of the Amicale movement, had been reared as a Roman Catholic and possibly been a catechist. Nganga Emmanuel, who founded a movement within the Matswanist and Kimbanguist tradition near Brazzaville, had been educated by Catholic missionaries and served for eight years as head catechist of his village. Simon Zépherin Lassy who formed a prayer-healing church in 1953 was another product of Catholic schooling, albeit with later Salvation Army training. The Kwilu rebellion of 1964 in Congo (Kinshasa) was primarily a political movement, but had traditional religious overtones that enable one to speak of Mulélisme, after Pierre Mulele, the former Catholic seminarian who led the revolt. The Kimbanguist Church in the Congo had as its secretary-general in 1966 Lucien Luntadila who had received a Catholic education and testimonials, but who repudiated his Catholic baptism on joining the Kimbanguists. In the Central African Republic a former Catholic priest, Boganda, established the Movement for the Social Development of Black Africa with religious as well as political features. Fuller investigation would produce other leaders springing from a Catholic milieu, and if comparisons were made between all these movements and those derived from Protestant backgrounds it would probably be found that essentially similar prophet-healing movements had resulted in most cases, and that differences were confined to externals and to details in rituals and vestments.

MOVEMENTS OF PROTESTANT ORIGIN WITH EX-CATHOLIC MEMBERS

A recent Catholic writer has recognized that "conversions away from the Church are already a rapidly growing phenomenon";[26] he was speaking of transference to "Islam, the Pentecostals, and the separatist churches". The latter have often received most of their members from the older churches and missions, and a good proportion of these has come from Catholic quarters. Our own study of the Church of the Lord (Aladura) in West Africa[27] showed that of 277 members some thirteen percent had originally been Roman Catholics, and this bears some relationship to the relative strength of Catholicism in the main areas concerned. In the Ivory Coast from the beginning of the Harris movement Catholic missionaries were alarmed at the inroads on their flocks, and a recent study of one particular Harris church revealed that ninety percent were Catholic converts, and that all six literates on the governing council of twentyfive were also recent converts.[28] The Kimbanguist movement affected both Catholic and Protestant missions and hospitals, and it was this effect that was partly responsible for the bitter Catholic opposition to the movement. The Kitawala movement in Central Africa also appealed to both Roman and Protestant malcontents in large numbers, and at a later date the Lumpa Church was reported to have received 3,400 Catholics in 1955–6 in the Diocese of Abercorn, and perhaps half its membership over its whole history. Similarly in East Africa the Bamalaki from 1914, the African Orthodox Church about 1929, and now the Maria Legio have drawn large numbers from the Catholic community. With the probable exception of South Africa there is no reason to believe that this transfer of Catholic members is confined to those movements here surveyed that happen to have been reported, for one of the marks of the prophet-healing churches is the way their appeal to Africans in terms of their own felt needs transcends the differences between Christians that have originated outside the continent.

CONCLUSIONS

It is clear that the facts do not support the thesis that independency is a purely Protestant phenomenon to which the Roman Catholic Church has been immune. At the same time it is also apparent that the number of group secessions from the Catholic Church is strictly limited in comparison with the extensive movements from Protestant churches, and that the major movement from Catholicism has been in terms of individuals, and has therefore tended to be less obvious. The reasons for this difference in the *way* Catholicism has contributed to independency lie beyond the scope of this essay, which is confined to a historical survey of the facts. It may be said, however, that the common assertions that independency is due to Protestant individualism, and its distribution of the Scriptures for the half-educated to interpret for themselves, or that Catholicism has been protected by its colourful rituals and more cohesive structure, will almost certainly be found to be quite as inadequate as the thesis we have here examined. The modest results of our present study, which show that no clear line can be drawn between these two traditions to mark the incidence of independency, may also be allowed to suggest that the explanations of these movements and of their appeal to Catholic and to Protestant will likewise not follow the lines usually proposed. As in all things human, and certainly in all things African, the realities of the situation are liable to be far more complex than the ideas with which we seek to understand them.

Notes

1. See his remarks in Museum Lessianum, *Devant les sectes non-chrétiennes* (Louvain, 1962), p. 26. R. Bastide has made similar claims for messianic movements in general.
2. *The Religions of the Oppressed* (New York, 1965), pp. xiii, 218, etc. See also P. Worsley, *The Trumpet Shall Sound* (London, 1957), pp. 105, 119, 191.
3. See "À propos du Kibangisme", *Congo* (Brussels), 5, 2 (1924), pp. 380–8, 771–3.
4. A. Brou, "Afrique – Le Prophétisme protestant", *Études* (Paris), 184, 24 (1925), pp. 730–47.
5. *L'Avenir colonial belge* in 1921; see E. Andersson, *Messianic Popular Movements in the Lower Congo* (London, 1958), p. 243, n 1.
6. *Op. cit.*, e.g. pp. 128, 159–60.
7. *Church and Mission in Modern Africa* (London, 1967), pp. 144, 234.
8. T. Hodgkin, *Nationalism and Colonial Africa* (London, 1956), p. 103.
9. *Op. cit.*, p. xii.
10. See S. L. Thrupp (ed.), *Millennial Dreams in Action* (The Hague, 1962), p. 19, reporting a Chicago symposium.
11. J. S. Coleman, "Nationalism in Colonial Africa", *American Political Science Review*, 48, 2, (1954), pp. 416–7.
12. D. L. Makhatini, in *Our Approach to the Independent Church Movements in South Africa* (Mapumulo, Natal, 1966), p. 130.
13. In a letter dated 5 May 1967.
14. In a statement of 31 August 1967, kindly prepared for me at the request of the Rev. H.-J. Becken.
15. See his *Schism and Renewal in Africa* (Nairobi, 1968).

16. For summary account see Andersson, *op. cit.*, pp. 244–5.
17. Information received personally; no published accounts or confirmation of this version.
18. See H.-C. Chery, "Les Sectes en Rhodésie du Nord", *Parole et Mission* (Paris), 2, 7 (1959), pp. 585–9; L. Oger, "L'Église du Sacré Coeur (Zambia)", *Notes et Documents* (Rome, White Fathers), 51 (nov. 1964), pp. 421–30; also information received from Prof. H. Griffiths, a former administrative officer in the area.
19. See his classifications of religious movements in M. E. Spiro (ed.), *Symposium on New Approaches to the Study of Religion* (Seattle, Wash., 1964), pp. 77–8.
20. See A. Wipper, *The cult of Mumbo* (Kampala, E. African Inst. of Social Research, 1966), p. 7.
21. The basic sources are: Kenya Government, *House of Representatives Debates Official Reports* 3, 1 (1964), columns 512–6, 773–82; Anon., "Splinter sects", *Reporter* (Nairobi), 17 July 1964, pp. 17–19; D. N. Kimilu, "The Separatist Churches", *Dini na Mila* (Kampala), 2, 2–3 (1967), pp. 13, 15–16; an unpublished report to the Maryknoll Fathers Mission, Tanzania, by Marie F. Perrin-Jassy, Dec. 1966. [See P. J. Dirven's thesis and articles from 1970].
22. See further J. Nagle, "The Legion comes to West Africa", *African Ecclesiastical Review* (Musaka, Uganda), 1, 1 (1959), pp. 59–64; *idem* (on East Africa), 1 (2), (1959), pp. 130–50; A. de Beukelaar, "La Légion de Marie et la formation religieuse", in *Formation religieuse en Afrique Noire* (Brussels, Lumen Vitae, 1956), pp. 336–42; *idem*, on other religious societies.
23. A local report by B. I. C. Ijomah appeared in *Eagle* (Onitsha), May 1964, pp. 16–17, illus.
24. See J. Fabian, "Dreams and charisma . . . in the Jamaa-Movement (Congo)", *Anthropos*, 61, 3–6 (1966), p. 545; W. De Craemer, *Analyse Sociologique de la Jamaa* (Kinshasa, Centre des Recherches Sociologiques, 1966(?)). Mimeo.
25. See J. F. Vincent, "Le Mouvement Croix-Koma: une nouvelle forme de la lutte contre le sorcellerie en pays kongo", *Cahiers d'Études africaines*, 6, 4 (1966), pp. 527–64.
26. A. Hastings, *op. cit.*, p. 185.
27. *African Independent Church* (Oxford, 1967), vol. II, p. 10; see also vol. I, pp. 94, 106, 123, 128, 195, and vol. II, pp. 83, 340, 351.
28. E. Amos-Djoro, "Les Églises harristes et le nationalisme ivoirien", *Le Mois en Afrique* (Paris), 5 (mai 1966), pp. 34, 43.

D. RELIGIOUS CASE STUDIES

The first study, of one individual's private spiritual search, is complemented by the general survey of religious features in the following essay on West Africa. The third and fourth essays are general surveys for Black Africa as a whole, firstly of the more external matters, and secondly of the more internal spiritual dimensions of independent Christianity.

13
Searching and Syncretism: A West African Documentation

As this incident occurred twenty years ago we may now identify the individual as a member of the Church of the Lord (Aladura) in Ghana. The story reveals the earnestness as well as the confusions that may exist in the minds of African Christians in both the older and the independent churches. This confusion is not necessarily due to the Western nature of imported Christianity, nor is it always removed by the African nature of the independent churches.

The following evidence is offered as a contribution to the discussion of the nature of the culture-contacts which are occurring in West Africa and as a vivid example of the eclectic nature of much African spiritual searching and of its syncretistic results. The details were discovered quite incidentally while the writer was staying in an African house in a strange town. The individual concerned, an alert and literate young man of about thirty, was a typical product of a mission primary school, now engaged in commerce as a clerk. His 'ex-wife' was no longer living with him in the two comfortable rooms which he occupied in the corner of a good concrete compound, but his quarters were well furnished and neatly kept. There is no reason to believe that his story as here documented is entirely

International Review of Missions no. 194, vol. 49, 1960, pp. 189–194; reprinted in *Practical Anthropology* 8 (3), 1961, pp. 106–110.

exceptional; in so far as it may be a somewhat extreme example it serves the better to reveal a state of affairs that in varying degrees is widespread among African Christians.

His own account of his church affiliations was simple and increasingly common in West Africa. Primary education at a mission school had led to communicant membership of the largest mission-founded church in his country. He had left this church some four years ago and joined one of the independent African churches and was now treasurer of its branch in his town. His own explanation of the change was that in his previous church he had smoked and drunk alcohol excessively and had not been taught to use the Bible aright. In particular he had never learnt the right use of individual psalms. The prayers and teaching of his new church had led him to abandon smoking and drinking and to understand the Bible.

Memberships. The fact of his literacy was proclaimed by a framed primary school leaving-certificate on the wall of the sitting-room. The rest of the evidence here presented may be regarded as a commentary on the results of literacy. In the first place it had enabled him to answer advertisements from oversea sources, and some of the results were to be seen in the other framed certificates in the sitting-room. One of these announced that he was a 'Life Member and Fellow of the Creative Prayer Fellowship (London)'. Its neighbour intimated that he was enrolled in the list of 'Benefactors of the Holy Land' and entitled to all the 'spiritual benefits granted to them in this life and after death by the Holy See'. This was 'Given at the Commissariat of the Holy Land, Franciscan Monastery, Washington, D.C.'. A third framed certificate was that of a subscribing member of 'The Indo-African Welfare Service, Bombay', and therefore he had access to their 'services spiritual, medical, educational, and commercial, free of any consultative charges'. There were books in this room, school texts or books on commercial practice, and magazines, but none of a religious complexion.

Literature. Beside the bed in the bedroom there was a small table with a pile of literature that may be classified as follows:
A. Christian.
    1. General: Three Bibles (A.V.); Frank N. D. Buchman, *Remaking the World* (Moral Rearmament).
    2. Roman Catholic: Fr Keller, *Careers that Changed the World* (Careers guidance); Catholic Truth Society, *A Simple Catholic Directory*, and *Marrying a Catholic*; The Franciscan Monastery, Washington, D.C., *The Crusader's Almanac*; Liverpool Metropolitan Cathedral, *Receipt* for five shillings for the Lady Chapel Fund, together with a promise to pray for the donor.
    3. Protestant: John Foster, *Beginning from Jerusalem*, and James Martin, *Did Jesus Rise from the Dead?* (both World Christian Books); Immanuel College, Ibadan, Nigeria, *Leisure Hours* (Interdenominational

periodical); *Search Me O God* (Methodist); H. S. Bender, *Early History and Law* (Old Testament studies, Mennonite, USA); J. L. Stauffer, *Studies in the Book of Daniel* (Mennonite, USA); P. Erb, *The Alpha and the Omega* (Mennonite, USA); J. C. Wenger, *Can a Thinking Man be a Christian?* (Evangelical, USA).

4. African Independent: *The Church of the Lord Hymn Book* (Nigerian).

B. Muslim.

The Qur'an (in English and Arabic, published by the Ahmadiyya sect); *The Teachings of Islam*.

C. Miscellaneous Religious.

From Paradise Lost to Paradise Regained (Watchtower Tract and Bible Society of New York); A. Gardner, *Vital Magnetic Healing* (Theosophical Research Centre, London); *Practical Healing* (Spiritual healing, England); G. A. Selig, *Secrets of the Psalms,* a Fragment of Practical Kabala with extracts from other Kabalistic Writings as translated by the Author (USA, Occult); *Albertus Magnus: Egyptian Secrets, or White and Black Art for Man and Beasts* (USA, Occult); Yogi Ramacharaka, *A Series of Lessons in Raja Yoga* (Yogi Publication Society, London); V. R. Radar, *The Beggar and the Star* (Religious Poem).

D. Non-Religious.

A Challenge to Kwame Nkrumah (political); a paper-back thriller.

One extract from these books may be allowed in order to understand the significance of the remark about having learnt the right use of individual psalms. *Secrets of the Psalms* prescribed the following treatment for a boil in the left ear; Ps. 119:169–176 should be pronounced 'in a low and conjuring voice over onion water or juice, and let one drop run into the ear, when you will experience instant relief'. Verses 153–160 would have the same effect if used in the same way for a boil in the right ear. Although the owner of this useful book had connected his discovery of 'the right use of individual psalms' with his membership in the independent African church, he had been a member before securing this book, and such teaching is not typical of his new church.

Cult Objects. In one corner of the bedroom, shielded from the rest of the room by a folding screen, there was a shrine embodying the following objects set out on a small wooden table: two crucifixes, a framed colour print of Jesus of the Sacred Heart such as is found all over West Africa, a plaster figure of St Anthony holding a child in his arms, a tallow candle burning, an electric lamp of a special type with a small cross glowing inside it, a bottle of water, an open Bible, a court summons in connexion with a civil action for damages for the alleged seduction of the schoolgirl sister of the plaintiff and a letter of petition to St Anthony praying for help in winning the court case and thus showing the power of God. The shrine was neat and clean, like the rest of the premises. The only other object in the room that suggested a connexion with the above was a box of contraceptives on the dresser.

COMMENTS

1. The literature was not the gradual accumulation of the years, but all seemed to have been purchased within the previous eighteen months. The change of membership to another church had either not satisfied this young African or had perhaps actually stimulated him in the search for spiritual enlightenment and security, through the somewhat eclectic nature of the body he had joined. Taking account of the effort involved in the correspondence that is implied at various points, and of the expenditure represented in memberships, literature and shrine, there is vivid evidence here of the spiritual hunger and active searching to be found in many of his generation in Africa, and that this search continues even where there is comparatively settled spiritual allegiance.

2. The range of the search, from the occult to the orthodox, and from the Orient to the Occident and the New World, and the variety of the material gathered, indicate the tolerant and open attitude of most younger Africans with some education towards all cultures, religions, institutions and ideas. As many paths in the African bush converge on the one village, so now do the roads of the whole world join their commerce in this great continent. The African's eclectic attitude to so many and varied cultural sources means that the new culture emerging in Africa will be a hybrid world that no single contributor will be able to claim as its own offspring or be ready to welcome with any acclaim. The African of the future promises to be neither African, Asian, European, nor American.

3. The three membership certificates indicate simultaneous participation, even if only incipiently, in three mutually incompatible religious groups; likewise the theologies and practices represented in the literature, the shrine and the court case include many incompatible elements—Christian and Muslim; Roman Catholic and Protestant; orthodox and heretical, gnostic or occult; oriental, western and traditional African. The shrine represented his own personal cult over and above his two successive church memberships. Any such shrine, and all its objects except the Bible and possibly the illuminated cross, would have been opposed by his first church. The candle and holy water were probably derived from his African independent church, where they are always present in its church worship and commonly found in the homes of its members. The Roman Catholic picture and figures had probably been added not through any familiarity with their use in that church or with prayers to the saints, but rather because they lent a vivid and attractive Christian content to a shrine with its deepest roots

laid among the traditional African shrines still common in his surroundings. It is impossible not to feel the close connexion between the traditional cult of the ancestors to whom the prayers of the troubled were addressed and this private shrine of a man in distress, with its prayer, not to the Jesus represented thrice, but to the more human figure of St Anthony. What Dr Margaret Mead has called this 'ferment of half-abandoned old and half-understood new' is sheer mental and moral confusion to the western mind, as also to the mind of the Africa that is passing. It is impossible for either to see how there can be any synthesis of elements diverse to the point of multiple contradiction. At the same time we can expect that Africa will so transmute these resources gathered from the wide world that some synthesis beyond our present imaginings will ultimately emerge.

4. One aspect of this comprehension of incompatibles is the not uncommon practice of 'plural belonging', exhibited in the case before us in rather muted form. This man was a member of only one religious group in his own town and had not retained a foothold in his earlier church, as many other members of this independent African church have done. At the same time, however, he had developed a membership, albeit a tenuous one in the circumstances, in a number of other groups from which spiritual help or personal prestige might be obtained. Outwardly there was no suggestion of dissatisfaction with his local church, to which he seemed quite devoted as an active member, nor was there any indication of mere insincerity. It is quite possible that hidden 'plural allegiances' are more common than is realized among loyal members of various West African churches.

5. This record of the religious literature in one man's room sounds a warning to the publishers and distributors of religious material when they compile their statistics and estimate their influence. To have sold a book is not to have penetrated, much less to have won, the mind of the customer. No matter how carefully and clearly written the book may be, its ultimate effect must be quite unpredictable if we reckon with the strange and even hostile company it will be keeping. The sober orthodoxy of the writers of 'World Christian Books' will be jostled on the shelves by black magic and yoga. It was also observed that the two churches of this man's earlier allegiance and later adoption had together supplied probably no more than five items, excluding the Bibles, of the twenty-three religious publications by his bedside. On the other hand, such evidence of the voracious spiritual and literary appetite of a young African cannot but encourage the distributors of religious literature in their efforts.

6. Lastly, one may be allowed to speculate upon the contents of these two rooms in an African house. Was it merely incidental or was there something of a parable in the fact that the general educational and technical books were all in the outer room, while in the inner room there was so much evidence of a searching among the things of the spirit? It is not so

hard to follow what is happening in the outer rooms of African life, where westerners may come and go fairly freely. It is on the rarer occasions when they are invited to the inner room that they begin to see the tumult of the African soul and their own contributions to that tumult.

14

Pagan Features in
West African Independent Churches

I am surprised that I was using the rather derogatory term "pagan" as late as 1965. It has been allowed to remain (and in a few instances in other essays) instead of being replaced by the term "primal", which would not be quite equivalent in this context; and after all "pagan" has a quite appropriate historical meaning. The essay was written quickly while on field work, and for a particular audience rather than for publication; it serves as a popular overall description and evaluation of the better kind of independent church. Some of the details (such as the small attention given to ancestral spirits) will not apply in some other parts of Africa.

Within the last fifty years there has been a widespread independent and indigenous religious development in most of the areas of Africa south of the Sahara where Christian missions have been establishing churches. The extent and variety of these religious groups presents a bewildering phenomenon to church leaders and missionaries, and they have often been lumped together under derogatory labels such as "separatists" or "sects" and dismissed as unfortunate reversions to traditional paganisms or as dangerous syncretisms of pagan and Christian elements.

It is true that there is a great range of belief and practice in these indigenous groups. In West Africa, to which the following remarks primarily apply, we can identify "healing homes" which are often both commercial and pagan in nature, eccentric or charlatan prophets who exploit a personal following, occult and spiritualist groups mixing African and imported forms of paganism, Judaistic bodies which are African forms of Jehovah's Witnesses, revivals of the worship of traditional gods, and a wide range of prophet-healing groups claiming to be spiritual Christian churches. These latter are Christian at least in intention and the increasing willingness to describe them as independent African Christian churches is to be welcomed. How far they are also Christian in practice and to what extent they represent an uneasy syncretism with traditional pagan elements is the question to which this article is addressed.

Any evaluation of the independent churches must begin by recognizing certain ways in which many of them have made a radical departure from pagan worship, for we shall probably exaggerate whatever pagan features do undoubtedly exist, unless we see these latter against the basically Christian nature of most independent churches.

Their main achievement seems to consist of a radical breakthrough, from pagan idolatry and worship of a number of divinities, to worship of the one true, living, loving, and all-powerful God of the Christian Scriptures. This is the African equivalent of the rejection of paganism and idolatry made by Israel in the earlier Old Testament period and is fundamental to all other development. The history of Israel shows that the battle for rejection of idolatry and the recognition of the one and only God lasted some six hundred or more years, from the Exodus to the Babylonian Exile. It is widely recognized that this battle has not yet been won in the older churches in West Africa, even where they are now in their second century of existence. We are satisfied that there has been a more complete breakthrough, in some of the independent churches of *aladura* or prophet-healing type, for a much higher proportion of members.

This is more than the kind of breakaway from past beliefs strikingly manifest in the destruction of fetish objects and medicines, but not necessarily accompanied by conversion to a Christian confidence. In many of the prophet-healing churches there is a most impressive and convincing breakthrough into dependence on faith in and prayer to the one living God of the Bible and this provides the basis for their healing practices.

FAITH HEALING REPLACES MAGIC

These practices represent a rejection of traditional methods of healing involving native practitioners, with magic and idolatry intermingled in the treatments. The great majority of members make no use of magicopagan treatments. In place of these there is the innocuous use of holy water, oil, or sand as a physical agent for the divine healing power, together with fasting as a spiritual discipline, and all set in a context of prayer. Most of this treatment can find biblical support, and the appropriate texts are commonly quoted.

At the same time there is the danger that the holy water, etc., can become a new magical power acting apart from God, and that the sacramental use of wine and bread in the Lord's Supper and of water in Christian baptism will be replaced by a different sacramental use of water and these other elements in new rites of African devising. Some in these churches undoubtedly fall into these dangers and so drift back towards paganism, but we must remember that a magical interpretation of the Christian sacraments is a constant menace in Christian history and is not peculiar to these new churches.

As another Christian achievement, we may mention the collective and active nature of worship in the independent churches and the signs of Christian joy in these people of God. Unlike so much of the worship in the older churches, there is a minimum of passive listening to a minister and of watching him do most things for the congregation. There is a total response in voice and action, through clapping, dancing, choruses, ejaculations, individual spontaneous prayers, and public thanksgivings. A warm community life undergirds this active corporate worship, and there is a great emphasis on the need for loving one another — perhaps all the greater because of the tensions and quarrels that do occur.

As a Christian achievement, this presents a striking contrast to pagan worship, which is essentially individual; in the main, individuals bring their own problems, sacrifices, petitions, or thank offerings to the priest at the shrine of the god. It is true that pagan worship has its communal occasions, its festivals for the whole community, but it does not demand the regular assembly of the people of the god. This is why pagan shrines and temples do not provide a house of meeting for a whole congregation — but only a shrine for the god and a place for the priests. On occasion large groups of worshippers can gather round in the open, but they are not essential for the regular service of the god.

Christian worship, on the other hand, is congregational, the regular assembly of God's holy people, and this aspect of Christian worship is often more evident in these independent churches than in some of the older churches.

Not unconnected with the corporate nature of these fellowships is the considerable degree of pastoral care which many of them offer their members. This again is a distinctively Christian feature that is not characteristic of paganism, where the individual goes to the shrine or to the priest, but is not sought out by the latter under the impulse of a gospel of love and fellowship. Some African prophets are assiduous in proclamation of their message and in bringing the spiritual power of their church (as they would put it) to individuals in need. In this they are assisted by the fact that they often minister to fairly small groups, and live among their members with very much the same style of life. This is a notable Christian achievement when compared with the widely acknowledged lack of a pastoral ministry in the older churches, which is an important factor in the drift of their spiritually needy members towards the independent groups.

At the same time there is another kind of ministry found among the independents, that of the "practitioner" who is consulted by "clients" in need of personal help and who sometimes operates on a semicommercial basis. Even this ministry has pastoral possibilities, for large numbers do go to these leaders with spiritual reputations, but it is obviously more impersonal and open to abuse, and is a development that leads in a pagan rather than in a clearly Christian direction.

PAGAN TENDENCIES

After this brief recognition of some of the Christian achievements which exceed those of the older churches in West Africa, we are in a better position to comment on certain pagan tendencies characteristic of many independent churches.

All over Africa independent churches have adopted adult baptism by immersion, even though infant baptism by affusion is the normal practice in most of the older churches from which their leaders and members have taken their departure. This almost universal change deserves a study it has not yet received. Here we are concerned only with its relation to paganism, and at first sight the change seems to reduce the possibility of a magical interpretation which so easily attaches to infant baptism. Unfortunately there are some signs that adult baptism is used as an effective ritual for the treatment of personal problems, such as sickness, and so "rebaptism" can occur as often as necessary. This amounts to a transference of baptism to the realms of magic and of pagan purification rites, where it is regarded as efficacious for particular human needs and detached from all Christian significance.

Adult baptism is also used as a rite of admission into a particular independent group, rather than as the sign and means of incorporation into the one people of God under the one Christ as head. Therefore those who transfer from one independent group to another, sometimes many times, are found being rebaptized on each occasion in order to become members. It is then no longer the Christian sacrament, but an entry ceremony for a religious society. Most older churches — both Roman Catholic and Protestant — do not rebaptize those who transfer from one church to another, but the reason for this has not been appreciated by the independent churches.

The Lord's Supper or Eucharist is usually neglected among the independents. Some have discarded it altogether, others celebrate it very infrequently and without understanding or as a special rite for an inner circle of more sanctified members. All these practices can be paralleled in the older churches, and there is a pagan implication in some of them. There is, however, no very open and specific paganizing of this sacrament in the independent churches, probably because the death of Christ and the atonement figure very little in the life and thought of most of them. The stress is more likely to be on the resurrection and on the life of joy and power awaiting the faithful, and these themes have not been discovered in the Lord's Supper.

There is no doubt that these churches, which welcome the description "spiritual churches," rest upon their claims to have received the power of the Holy Spirit to meet human needs. This in itself may help the older churches to realize their poverty at this point. It is, however, plain that dealings with the Spirit are not sufficiently related to and tested by the Christ of the Scriptures, and that too often what is implied is a new direct revelation from God through the "spirit" by means of dreams and visions, ecstasy and possession, or through men of special charismatic spiritual powers who are regarded as powerful prophets.

Christian history, however, and the modern Pentecostal churches in many parts of the world, should teach us not to dismiss these phenomena as necessarily pagan. If set in a context of Christian teaching in a stable Christian community, they can serve to illumine and release men for a more effective and Spirit-filled Christian life. On the other hand, if divorced from the Christ of the Scriptures, they can readily assume pagan forms.

It is possible for these experiences to become the vehicle for other spirits, evil and lying spirits which degrade men, destroying character and responsibility instead of developing the strength and beauty of Christ which the Holy Spirit of God seeks to create. This may be evident in an alleged revelation bidding the taking of another man's wife or encouraging a semi-literate man of limited talents in his unrealistic ambitions of personal advancement to power and greatness.

Others may seek these spirit-revelations for the pagan purpose of divination, for information extracted from the spirit-world to serve our human purposes. Here consultation of prophets has degenerated to the level of fortune-telling, often semi-commercialized and quite divorced from a pastoral context within which it could be redeemed.

Emphasis on the Spirit means, therefore, that many of the independent churches are in a dangerous position, especially among their illiterate members who cannot read the Scriptures. While they sometimes exhibit the power of the Holy Spirit vividly applied to the human situation in conversions, healings, and other examples of faith, they also demonstrate how readily the spirit of paganism can infiltrate into their Christian intentions and practices.

OCCULTISM

One example of this is so widespread as to merit special mention. In many churches a secondary or subordinate cult of angels is to be found. A hierarchy of named angels is approached for help through prayers and the use of candles, much as candles might be lit for the saints who are invoked in some forms of Latin Christianity. Sometimes the names of the angels and their associated signs are drawn from imported occult literature, such as the *Sixth and Seventh Books of Moses,* and an elaborate ritual from similar sources is employed. While these practices may commence with the idea of guardian angels found in the Scriptures, they quickly assume a form and an importance that is akin to pagan cults of spirits or divinities.

The occult element in the above practices is also seen in the use of mystic words of power revealed by the spirit or in the appearance of wholly new scripts and "spirit-languages," of which there are several examples in West African independent churches. All of these are misguided but impressive attempts to secure a more effective and powerful revelation than has been given us in Jesus Christ as witnessed to in the Scriptures.

At the same time, if one probes deeply enough, it is possible to discover many signs that independents themselves are aware of the dangers of an undisciplined spiritual church. Those longer established, or with better leaders, tend to recognize that the spirits must be tested, and may name certain prophets among them as specially gifted in distinguishing the spirits. Rules are made to prevent members from demanding revelations from prophets at any time or recounting their own unchecked revelations, their dreams and visions, in the midst of public worship. Sometimes moral and biblical rules for distinguishing true prophets from false are provided, and the exposure of false prophets has occurred on some occasions.

The people of Israel and the members of the early Christian church have already trod this path, and it is most moving to see biblical history being repeated in Africa. Many of these churches are endeavoring to fulfill their intention of being truly Christian and are doing so not through pressures and demands for orthodoxy from the older churches but under what we must recognize as the authentic leading of the Holy Spirit of God in their midst. Indeed, this capacity for self-criticism and internal reformation is one of the essential marks of a genuine Christian church, and it is not lacking in some of the West African churches we are considering. The growth of various means of testing and controlling pneumatic phenomena is far more significant than the excesses which continue to dominate the image of the independents in the minds of the older churches.

Despite the highly evangelical language often used in these churches, especially in gospel hymns and choruses borrowed from Western sources, there is little understanding of an evangelical gospel based on the work of Christ for our salvation. This is, of course, a continually repeated situation in Christian history and infects the older churches also to a large extent. Among the independents it tends to appear in certain characteristic forms, such as reliance on a routine of prayers, fastings, food, and other taboos, rituals connected with thanksgiving after childbirth, recital of specific psalms for particular needs, water purification rites, etc. Some of these practices pass over, as we have noted above, into the realm of magic. All of them are capable of interpretation in a pagan way, and the greater the emphasis placed on such practices the greater the danger of their being regarded in themselves as the effective means of salvation and of spiritual power. The impressive spiritual disciplines of these churches are thus liable to be of an ambiguous nature when subjected to close inspection. For example, the almost universal rejection of tobacco may be due to the belief that the smell of smoke drives away the benevolent angels — a sentiment that could be harmless enough but which is scarcely calculated to strengthen an evangelical faith.

In general we may describe the outlook of the independent churches as moralistic and legalistic in its understanding of Christianity. This would probably be confirmed by an analysis of their use of the Scriptures in their preaching. In one case it was clearly shown that the favorite books were Proverbs and Ecclesiastes in the Old Testament and the Epistle of James in the New Testament. These books are especially open to a moralistic, legalistic use divorced from the gospel. On the other hand, and despite the pagan tendencies of all emphasis on human effort and righteousness, it would be wrong to label this outlook as no more than paganism. It is still a moralistic, unevangelical form — not of paganism or of Islam or of any other religion — but of Christianity, and in spite of various pagan elements these are still properly called Christian churches.

CONCLUSION

Some writers have emphasized the survival of pagan features from African traditional religions in the life and worship of these independent churches, especially in the practice of divination through revelations, in ecstatic worship and spirit possession, and in purification procedures. It is true that externally Christianized forms of such fundamentally pagan practices can be discovered and that this amounts to a religious syncretism that is always at the expense of the Christian element in the mixed form.

It is our conviction, however, that this syncretistic element, like the messianic outlook in African independents, has been much exaggerated. This is partly due to the fact that investigators assumed that these independent groups must be a mixture of traditional African and Christian religious elements, and so found what they set out to discover.

We are much more impressed by the sharp break from African animism and polytheism, and from reliance on traditional magic and medicine, as well as by the small attention given to ancestral spirits. The distinctive and characteristic phenomenon in these independent churches is the prophet-leader. Both the prophet and his revelations of warning and divine judgment are cast much more in an Old Testament mold than in any to be found in African traditional religion, and most investigators (but by no means all) agree that prophecy as found in these movements is at bottom a post-Christian development which would not have occurred without the biblical model and stimulus.

These radical departures from the traditional religions of Africa are so fundamental to the independent church movement that they probably explain why many of the pagan tendencies which do exist in these churches are not specifically African. Our remarks above have suggested that they are very often similar to the distortions and corrosions of genuine Christianity that have occurred throughout Christian history and that will probably continue to do so, not only in Asia and Africa but also in Europe and the Americas.

A striking example of this has already been alluded to — the importation of Western and Asian occultism, spiritualism, and literature of the "new thought" kind, into West Africa. This may present a threat to the independent and to the older churches that is just as serious as the survival of African religious practices in syncretistic guise. Indeed, rank-and-file members of the older churches, who have not made the radical breakthrough found in many independents, may be even less able to resist this imported paganism, which benefits from the prestige of the West or of the ancient civilizations of Asia.

The whole question of pagan features in the life of the independent churches in Africa is, therefore, not nearly so simple as many have assumed, and the dangers and defects of this kind are neither to be derived entirely from African religions, nor located solely in the independent churches.

15

Patterns of Ministry and Structure Within Independent Churches in Post-Colonial Africa

The next two essays were written as papers presented in 1974 in the series of Seminars on Christianity in Post-Colonial Africa held at the School of Oriental and African Studies in London and elsewhere, and supported by the Leverhulme Trust. They are concerned with contemporary and recent events since the ending of the colonial era in much of Black Africa around the year 1960 and therefore lack the qualities that might come from a greater depth of perspective. The first essay concentrates on the more external matters; its use of the five-part sociological typology should be read along with the more systematic presentation in essay five.

I. INTRODUCTION

We may venture a general statement to the effect that there seems to have been no decline in the appearance of new movements nor reduction in the growth of existing movements since the ending of the colonial situation and the accompanying weakening of the missionary presence. Indeed, it might well be that the greatest growth has been in Ghana, where political independence first arrived in Black Africa, and where current estimates

---

In E. Fashole-Luke, R. Gray, A. Hastings and G. O. S. Tasie (eds), *Christianity in Independent Africa*. London: R. Collings Ltd., 1978, pp. 44–59.

speak of some five hundred different bodies. This could be contrasted with South Africa (despite the fact that this is by no means a typical colonial situation) where some falling off in the membership of the Bantu independent churches has recently been reported. We are therefore warned against oversimple theories of a direct relationship between colonial oppression (or missionary control) and the rise of independent churches; likewise whatever we may discover by way of new developments or significant changes in the post-colonial period is not necessarily due to political independence. Much of it may well have occurred in any case.

It must also be remembered that political and religious colonialism (a term that is unfair to missions but perhaps allowable in this context) are not identical. In the formal sense of church government or independence, autonomy as over against the Western Christian parent body both antedated and post-dated political independence in different areas; in the more substantial senses of influence and inheritance religious colonialism may be said to continue little abated, and may even be found in countries such as Liberia and Ethiopia which have been outside the colonial situation in the usual sense.

Armed with these cautions against simplistic explanations we may proceed to an analysis of the relationships of independent churches with other bodies and with one another, and of their membership structures, sociological forms, and leadership patterns.

II. EXTERNAL RELATIONSHIPS

A. Relationships with the Older Churches

1. Formal:

In the sixties a distinct change in the attitude of the older to the independent churches began to emerge, with sympathetic enquiry replacing hostility or indifference. The kinds of article on independent churches that appeared in the *Nigerian Christian,* the (then) *Congo Mission News* and in East African religious journals at the end of the decade would have been inconceivable ten years earlier. This change has been matched by an increasing ecumenical interest on the part of the independents, who were usually the more generous of the two parties in their earlier attitudes. Even the Harris churches of the Ivory Coast who had little love for their older churches were reported to be more ecumenically minded. Independent churches which had their applications for membership in national Christian councils rejected at the start of the decade were members of the same Council a few years later. They are now to be found in the national councils in Sierra Leone, Ghana, Nigeria, Zambia, Kenya, South Africa and other countries, and this means a very great deal to them. Some, such as the African Brotherhood Church of Kenya, are now also members of the All-African Conference of Churches, and the admission of the Eglise de Jésus-Christ par le Prophète Simon Kimbangu to the World Council of Churches in 1969–70 has been much publicized. Several have been welcomed into the International Council of Christian Churches; these include the Eglise Chrétienne Evangélique d'Afrique of Zaïre, and the Eglise Reformée Indépendante de Madagascar, but membership in this smaller rival body to the W.C.C. is probably less stable.

2. More Informal:

a. There has often been an informal and unstructured relationship of inter-dependence between the older and the independent churches, whereby they performed different services for each other's members. Those from the older churches often sought the services of a prophet or healer among the independents, and usually somewhat secretly, while the independents used church or mission schools for the education of their children, church bookshops and journals for their literature, and even retained a second membership in order to secure a proper church burial or for other specific services. These mutual services have probably increased rather than declined in the last dozen years, except where the older churches have lost their schools to the state or the independents have started their own.

b. Other somewhat loose relationships have taken the form of affiliation with or sponsorship by an older Christian body from overseas. It might be thought that with independence this would give way to similar relationships with older churches within Africa, but there is very little sign of this as yet, apart from the tentative use of theological and bible colleges for training ministers. In recent years the independents in the Central African Republic known as the Comité Baptiste invited Swiss missionaries to assist them, the Kimbanguist EJCSK has had help from European Moravians and Reformed, and American Mennonites, the Christ Apostolic Church of Ghana has had "fellowship agreements" with two different American bodies within three years, and a group of Cherubim and Seraphim in Nigeria have sought substantial aid from the Greek Orthodox Church in Athens. The American Mennonite Church Mission Board located in Elkhart, Indiana, has had more experience of this kind of relationship than any other body. After answering a call for sponsorship from an independent leader in eastern Nigeria in 1959 it helped local independent churches to form their own association, with a Bible school; from 1970 [to 1976] it helped the Church of the Lord (Aladura) to establish its own theological seminary near Lagos by providing the main teacher; in the same period it has been the chief agent in assisting Ghana independents to establish a co-operative Good News Training Institute for preparing leaders at various levels; other sponsorship discussions have been held in Dahomey and the Ivory Coast, and explorations towards similar relationships have recently been made in Swaziland and Botswana. Canadian Baptists have also had a team of four married missionaries working fraternally within the body known as the African Christian Churches and Schools in Kenya since 1970.

A somewhat different kind of relationship occurs through the increasing attendance of African independent leaders at international gatherings; thus Yeboa-Kurie of Ghana's Eden Revival [later Feden] Church and others visited the World Pentecostal Assembly in Texas in 1970, and independent leaders are now likely to be present at some World Council of Churches meetings.

3. The effects of these ecumenical and other contacts on the independents, whether formal or informal, are somewhat mixed. The benefits of recognition by the world Christian community, of a wider experience and broader outlook, are sufficiently obvious. Less obvious is the reinforcement of the existing tendency to model themselves on the older churches and in their most Western forms, to place their own financial independence at risk after seeing the relative affluence of Western Christians, and to become ecumenical tourist curiosities or showpieces – soon every Western church visitor to Africa will want the "experience" of worshipping in an independent church, preferably of the more exotic kind. Financial assistance is probably the most dangerous of all forms of help; already it has initiated a project in Ghana at a level the independents cannot easily maintain, and in South Africa it has been a major factor in splitting the African Independent Churches Association.

B. Relationships Between the Independent Churches

The surface view presents a picture of constant division and secession, of a hopelessly fissiparous mass of smallish churches unable to organize effectively for life in modern Africa. There is plenty of truth in this, in spite of the contrary evidence of the amalgamation of distinct bodies or the subsequent return of secessionists. Both processes have been at work throughout the history of African independency. In the post-colonial period there seem to be more frequent and more serious attempts to establish what H.-J. Becken has called "summit organizations", associations that represent the independents' own ecumenism parallel to that of the older churches. Eastern Nigeria has already been mentioned; there have been several such associations in Ghana, including that which Yeboa-Kurie attempted, and the Ghana Evangelical Fellowship of four apostolic-type churches in the seventies; in Zaïre some twenty-eight independent churches were gathered into an association around Luluabourg in 1965; in Kenya there have been associations of Spirit churches in the western area, and the *Kenya Christian Handbook* lists no fewer than fourteen attempts to form an all-Kenya association. South Africa has seen several such developments, especially the African Independent Churches Association that worked with the Christian Institute for Southern Africa for some years, and the Assembly of Sionist Apostolic Churches that affiliated with the Christian Council in 1966. Since 1972 Dr. Marthinus Daneel has been assisting with the establishment of a standing association among the southern Shona independent churches, and by 1974 the possibility of a relationship with the Christian Council of Rhodesia had arisen. In 1972 the Botswana Association of Inter-Spiritual Churches had some twenty members.

This persistent attempt to form associations stems from several sources: the increasingly ecumenical climate in general, the desire for Christian recognition that a single small church cannot achieve on its own, and the practical problems of developing a strong influential church able to make itself visible in the life of the new nations. Here also the effects are liable to be ambivalent. The very attempts at greater unity can provide new divisions, leading to two rival associations as has happened in Ghana and South Africa, or divisions within one of the denominations concerned over the question of membership itself, or of some policy of the new association, as has been happening in Rhodesia. It is probable, however, that the effort at co-operation will continue and increase, even though it is weakened by the continuing divisiveness at other points.

III. MEMBERSHIP STRUCTURE

A. The Membership Spectrum: Tribal — National — International

1. Tribal:

It is plain that many independent churches begin within one tribal people. The question is whether their membership expands beyond this limit, and whether there are secessions by tribal groups from trans-tribal churches. Some churches have shown considerable growth without expanding into other tribes. Thus the African Brotherhood Church numbers perhaps 60,000 but these are almost all Akamba in Kenya despite the desire of the church to include other peoples. Similarly the Maria Legio Church of perhaps 50,000 is open to all and the leaders are quick to declare its inter-tribal nature, but in fact it is very largely confined to the Nilotic Luo in Western Kenya who are unpopular with the surrounding Bantu peoples.

These are two examples of churches that are not inherently tribal in their convictions but are limited by factors they have been unable to overcome. Most churches showing considerable expansion have achieved this by drawing other tribes into their membership. Divisions or tensions within a church then often have a tribal basis, but actual secessions on this basis do not seem to be as numerous as one might expect. In general it would appear that there is no necessary inherent connection between independency and tribal peoples in the sense of tribalism, and that these churches are not inclined to foment the latter as some politicians have done.

2. National:

Many independent churches aspire to a national scope and influence, even if remaining substantially tribal in membership. Political independence has almost certainly encouraged this, just as at an earlier stage some independents were influential in nationalist movements. Occasionally since national independence politicians and independents have tried to use each other for their own ends, but this has seldom lasted, and the striking thing is the widespread spiritual independence among these churches as over against politics. The desire for national influence is that of a free agent able to embrace all the peoples within the nation and to offer them a Christian church suited to national needs and culture. There does not seem to be any case of a single independent church becoming the dominant church embracing most of the Christians in the nation; the Kimbanguist Church might have had such thoughts at one stage in the early sixties, but deliberately rejected this possibility. Most independents, while coveting a national extension, or even after achieving this, seem content with a situation of religious pluralism.

3. International:

Even more striking and more significant is the extent to which churches which began in a particular tribe have extended beyond national boundaries and achieved an international structure. This has occurred even where they may have remained predominantly within the tribe of origin in their own country. Thus the Church of the Lord (Aladura) began among the Yoruba of Nigeria and has spread into other areas of Nigeria mainly among migrant Yoruba, without any great response from eastern or northern peoples; yet in Ghana it has substantial expansion among Fante, Ga and Ashanti, in Liberia it includes many Bassa and Americo-Liberians and others, in Sierra Leone its membership is Creole and Mende, with a sprinkling of other tribes, and it has also a foothold in Togo and branches in London and New York, where members may be of any West African or even other peoples. Here is a comparatively small and ill-endowed church with a remarkable dynamic, that has always seen itself in international terms. The Christ Apostolic Church and the Cherubim and Seraphim of Nigeria have also expanded into other countries, likewise a number of East African independents. Those in South Africa that have extended into Central Africa have seldom maintained any structural unity with their base churches but have produced autonomous churches similar in nature. The Kimbanguist Church of Zaïre claims branches in some ten Central African countries, while the Vapostori of Rhodesian origin are reported to be established also in Zaïre, Congo, Malawi and Mozambique.

The last example suggests that this international expansion can occur irrespective of whether the areas concerned are in a colonial or a post-colonial situation, and in fact much of the expansion outlined above, except that of the Kimbanguists and the Vapostori, had occurred before political independence. It would be difficult to support any statement about international expansion increasing in a post-colonial area, although it is certainly continuing. We should also note signs of new strains felt by such international churches due to the formation of independent nations, strains that were probably less evident in the colonial period. The advent of independence in Ghana saw increasing restiveness among Church of the Lord members at being under Nigerian authority, and this has led to a series of more or less overt rebellions in the Ghana branches, which have sufficient strength to match that of the church in Nigeria. Likewise there has been tension within the African Methodist Episcopal Church (if we can regard this as virtually an independent church) in Central Africa where Zambia, Malawi and Rhodesia each wanted to have the residence of the bishop they share located in their own country.

It may well be that we are observing the decline of a pan-Africanism nourished within a common colonial situation and the emergence of new and stronger national loyalties. It remains to be seen whether any independent church can maintain and develop a strong international organization over a period of time and in face of the shifting patterns of tension between the new nations. At most we can observe a missionary zeal and an intention to transcend the limits of tribe and nation that appear authentically Christian.

B. The Membership Spectrum: Other Aspects

1. Socio-Economic Class:

P. J. Dirven has reported that the members of the post-colonial Maria Legio in Kenya are drawn from the "liminal individuals" in society — the poor, the sick, the insecure and the disaffected. This corresponds to the popular image of the independents, if extended to include illiterates, unemployed, and the lowest socio-economic classes in general. It is well known that something similar obtained in the appeal of the Christian missions in their earlier stages, unless the initial response came from the traditional rulers as in Uganda, or the elites in other areas. And M. L. Daneel has reported that 40% of the members of all churches among the Southern Shona, both older and independent, came from the lowest classes.

Daneel has also shown that, contrary to the suggestion of Sister Mary Aquina, there is no correlation between membership in an independent church and low degree of education. We shall return to the question of education at a later point, but may comment here on the extent to which educated people, with a corresponding higher social status, are to be found among the independents of West Africa, which is probably ahead of other areas in this respect. On a visit in 1973 to the Celestial Church of Christ in Ibadan I found myself in conversation before and after the service with four people — the first two worked in the administrative offices of the University of Ibadan, the third was a lecturer there, and the fourth (who earlier had been observed leading a Bible class in his white robe and bare feet) proved to be the Deputy Vice-Chancellor of the University. Some might say this merely illustrates the proverbial saying about birds of a feather; in fact it indicates the social range to be found in the independents, or that is potentially present. My own impression is that churches may commence with an appeal to the more liminal members of society, although exceptions are to be found, as in the early Faith Tabernacle forms of the Nigerian aladura movement. As firmer structures are established these churches appeal increasingly to members of any social class, and this in spite of the prestige, equipment and trained ministry possessed by the older churches. This process is probably accentuated in the post-colonial situation for several reasons — the decreasing reliance on the educational and medical services of the older churches as these are replaced by public services, the increasingly inadequate level of their ministry without the compensating charismatic powers of the independents, and the more conscious emphasis on African cultural forms in religious matters.

2. *Rural or Urban Locale:*

It would also be difficult to demonstrate whether the independents were predominantly rural or urban in their membership, for some are one and some the other and some combine the two. If there is an increase in urban membership this is because that is where the population is flowing and where the independents are able to offer a ministry relevant to urban problems; they are not left behind as suitable only for rustics. If their strength is still in the countryside it is for the same reason — that is where the people are, as with the southern Shona studied by Daneel. Some churches retain a rural base and headquarters, but have more sophisticated leaders and members in the towns where they deal with government offices. This obtains perhaps more in South Africa where migrant workers in the cities maintain their own rural roots. Sometimes the wealthier city congregations contribute through central funds for the financial support of the poorer rural branches, as with the A.M.E. Church in Zambia. Where there are "holy cities" these will almost of necessity be in a rural area. In one case at least, the Church of the Lord in Nigeria, the headquarters established by the founder in a small bush town in the thirties was shifted in the late sixties to the Lagos metropolitan area; the necessary justification was established by comparing Nazareth to Jerusalem. Whether this is the forerunner of a general trend it is too soon to say.

3. Other Variables:

Evidence is also lacking when it comes to other questions such as whether membership is becoming more stable or continues to reveal the great fluidity whereby members pass from one independent church to another; where there is a constant succession of new bodies, as in Ghana, it would appear that there is still considerable fluidity. The sources of recruitment are not likely to exclude the existing independent churches, but what proportions come from primal religions, the older churches or other independents has been little studied. Similar ignorance prevails about any difference in the appeal to and retention of men as against women in the membership; the common image features a predominance of women, and this is probably usually the case. At the same time one can find congregations very much the reverse, and Daneel has shown that his southern Shona churches have a distinctly greater appeal to men than have the older churches or missions.

IV. FORMS OF SOCIAL ORGANIZATION, LEADERSHIP AND AUTHORITY

A. A Western Spectrum

If we adopt the familiar Western spectrum of sect, denomination and church then the basic questions will be where the African independents start and which way they tend to move along the continuum. In general it might be said that the Ethiopian type of independent body commences and remains as a denomination, but that the prophet-healing type more often starts as a sect and frequently develops into the direction of a denomination. This process is usually associated with increasing size, greater ecumenical interest, the desire for recognition on public occasions, more members from the upper socio-economic classes or involved in public life, a concern for their own social and economic development, for education and a better trained ministry, and for similar development in society at large. In their own self-understanding they have no desire to be a "sect" in the Western sense, but possess the intention of being the real Church of God, reformed as against Western mission Christianity, and with a message and mission to the whole world. This confident and open attitude is strikingly apparent in so many of these bodies.

On the other hand, there are some though perhaps less frequent signs of a movement in the opposite direction, towards a more typically sect form. This has been observed in Zaïre and the Congo Republic where some of those who trace an inheritance from Simon Kimbangu have dissociated themselves from the main Kimbanguist Church, turned their backs on politics or concern with medical or educational services, and retired into their own world of spiritual healing and power sought through an elaboration of ritual. These developments are to be found in the Mayumbe and other groups that broke with the EJCSK Kimbanguists at the beginning of the sixties, and in the Churches of the Holy Spirit described by Janzen and by MacGaffey. Bastide has also discussed this possibility inherent in what he calls messianic movements; these may further modernization under a colonial regime by strengthening the demand for independence, and then in the post-colonial situation come into conflict with the new African regime and withdraw into a more rigid and sectist position of separation from the world. In view, however, of the overwhelming concern for development in so much of ex-colonial Africa this second tendency would seem to be much less common.

B. An African Spectrum

The Western sect-church spectrum probably oversimplifies or distorts the African phenomena like so many other Western categories and analyses. Our own replacement consists of five categories derived descriptively from the wide range of phenomena; prophet movement (more inchoate primary form), church (organized in congregations like the older churches), community (with comprehensive activities in a new village or holy city), clientele (individuals dealing with a practitioner but not themselves a continuing community), and ancillary cult (alongside other forms, for special benefits or purposes). If these are arranged in a circle, rather than as a linear continuum, then we can depict the variety of developments that occur, from almost any one form across the circle to almost any other form. [For a fuller account see essay 5.]

A comprehensive examination of the tendencies since the colonial period ended cannot be attempted here, but some observations may be made. Firstly, there do not seem to be many new large-scale prophet movements since 1960, with the exception of the Maria Legio under Simeon Ondeto and Gaudencia Aoko from 1963 in Kenya; there have, however, been plenty of minor ones which have either faded out or quickly condensed into a small church. Nor do there seem to have been many new communities of the "holy city" or New Jerusalem kind; the fourteen notable examples in our list were all founded by 1959, and the communal villages of the utopian Kingdom movement in Ghana are too small and recent to form a substantial exception, but almost certainly there are others as yet unreported. The famous Aiyetoro community in Nigeria in the mid-sixties repudiated the idea of daughter communities but in the early seventies there were a number of these along the lagoons. It may be that in the freer atmosphere of independent nations there is less reason to withdraw into communities of this kind, less persecution, and a greater involvement in expanding national services and activities. If so then we can expect a profound change in the ethos of these communities, or they may become places of pilgrimage and commemoration set over against administrative headquarters with associated services located in more urban or metropolitan settings; the Aiyetoro community, for example, has a headquarters for its commercial enterprises in Lagos.

Apart from these two observations it is difficult to make any other general statements about social forms since independence. The mission model of congregations organized in a denomination is widely followed, and increasingly so as independent groups become larger and more stable, like the Christ Apostolic Church in West Africa or the African Brotherhood Church in Kenya. It is possible that the main new initiatives occurred in the colonial period and that these independent churches have begun a process of consolidation and of re-alignment of existing bodies which is replacing the continuing emergence of new ones. This of course does not apply to those areas where independency has not yet occurred or is still small in scale.

V. INTERNAL STRUCTURES OF LEADERSHIP AND AUTHORITY

The range of forms here may be thought of in terms of the letter Y and of three main types, charismatic, organizational and ritualistic, placed one at each of the terminal points; then any one form can be examined in terms of its relationship to the other two.

A. The Charismatic Form

The charismatic form is represented more especially by the prophet-healing churches, and by the earlier stages of their development. In the light of what was said above about new prophet movements it is not surprising if we find this form of leadership in decline, and observe the paucity of major new charismatic figures in the sixties. Who should be added to Ondeto and Aoko already mentioned? Josué Edjro, the Ivory Coast healer who attracts mass pilgrimages, has remained within the Methodist Church and so represents no more than a clientele or clinic form. One can perhaps observe a loss of influence on the part of earlier figures such as Reuben Spartas, Alice Lenshina, and Christianah Akinsowon of the Cherubim and Seraphim. Gaudencia Aoko has already lost her charismatic appeal and by 1973 belonged to no church; Simeon Ondeto remained the Spiritual Head of the Maria Legio but the future seemed to lie with its Cardinal Mumbo, the practical business man who dealt with the government authorities. Prophet Wovenu of the Apostolic Revelation Society in Ghana presents the rare combination of high charisma with great organizing ability, and shows no loss of influence.

B. The Organizational Form

The organizational form seems to replace the charismatic, in good Weberian manner, as these movements become more "routinized". Charismatics are less needed and less valued once the initial impetus has been given and a tradition established. Educated organizers are required, on the model of bureaucrats, professional and business men in independent Africa. It has been suggested by Janzen that independent governments are not so suspicious as were the colonial powers of a strong centralised organization, and may even encourage this development in the interests of order, stability, and ease of dealing with the church; charismatic prophets and secular rulers have never comported well together. It is not surprising therefore to find the sixties marked by such organizational leaders as Joseph Diangienda of the EJCSK, Adeleke Adejobi of the Church of the Lord (Aladura), Yeboa-Kurie of Eden Revival (later Feden) Church, and in East Africa Bishop Ajuoga of the Church of Christ in Africa.

C. The Ritualistic Form

The ritualistic form seems to provide an alternative to the bureaucratic organizational type when the charisma declines or is superseded. If power is not found in the spiritual qualities of the gifted leader, or in the strengths of a larger and probably hierarchical organization, then it is sought through the elaboration of ritual regarded as operative in itself, or perhaps by the dispersal of charisma across a wide section of the members who can become possessed by the Spirit within the ritualistic framework. Some of the Cherubim and Seraphim societies in Nigeria should perhaps be classified in this way, for they have lost the originating charisma and have never achieved a strong central and unified organization. The clearest example seems to be that of the Churches of the Holy Spirit in the lower Zaïre region which share the Kimbanguist tradition but have turned away from all the new developments that have strengthened the EJCSK. They have experimented with commerce and then rejected this, they now possess no paid ministry — every male member is a potential prophet, for the structure is egalitarian rather than hierarchic, and elaborate rituals form the main activity. Especially in the local cultural context this is potentially a return to magic. When we examine the organizational types we find that the EJCSK has a restricted and controlled use of rituals and resembles a Baptist church, that the "best organized church in Kenya", the African Brotherhood Church, has very simple worship forms, likewise the strongest and largest of the Nigerian independents, the Christ Apostolic Church; in all of these "pentecostal" phenomena are strictly controlled.

D. Another Dimension of the Charismatic/Organizational Alternatives

Another dimension of the charismatic/organizational alternatives may be mentioned. It is seen in the tension between what may be called the charisma of age and wisdom, expressed in a gerontocracy so characteristic of traditional Africa, and the organizational demands of the more modern youth — the young men of some education who want schools and a national organization for their church. J. D. Y. Peel regards the Cherubim and Seraphim as, on the whole, representing the first position, and the Christ Apostolic Church the second, although even here Yoruba cultural influence led to the re-establishment of some degree of gerontocracy in the sixties with the ageing of the leaders who had controlled the church over its first forty years. Marie-France Perrin Jassy in her study of the Luo independents noted that all responsible posts were held by men aged 25–45, and the old men were simply members; the new religion had so completely replaced the ancestor cult with its ritual roles for the elders that their very position in society had been undermined. The degree of this tension between the old and the young, and its outcome, will of course vary across the different cultures, but we may hazard the opinion that the voice of youth has been more influential since independence.

E. Sources of Revelation

A further dimension of the internal structure of authority and leadership is found in the sources of revelation that are recognized. The first form is often the vision, dream, or death-resurrection trance of the founder. He may later deposit the revelation so received in a book of rules and rituals that is not capable of further development after his death, and so becomes a canonical authority that guides the organizational men who replace him.

This happened with Johane Maranke's "New Revelation", the book of his visions accepted by the Vapostori since his death in 1963. In default of this the leaders in the hierarchy may claim their own revelations as the basis for their decisions, even if not notably charismatic, or simply proceed under their own wisdom. A different source of authority appears where there is emphasis upon prayer and Bible study by all members, for this is liable to produce a critique of decisions by the hierarchy. The same result occurs where there is regular group discussion, as with most matters in the East African Revival movement, and at this stage the system has become democratic rather than hierarchical. Our own limited experience suggests that there is an overall tendency among African independents to develop the kinds of criteria for revelation manifest in the last two forms, where biblical study and reasoned discussion provide a new critique both of revelations and of leadership. This is not incompatible in the African mind with continuing respect for leaders and for authority, although it has also been responsible for some secessions.

F. The Structural Relationship to Traditional Patterns

The structural relationship to traditional patterns should also be examined. No one has set out more fully the various ways in which these independent churches represent a radically new form as over against traditional culture than Perrin Jassy. She observes that here is a private and voluntary group, not coterminous with the whole community, replacing the blood ties of lineage and clan by a spiritual basis of association, introducing a more fluid system in place of fixed roles and status, and providing new roles for youth and for women and a measure of equality for everyone, together with a potential universality that transcends the boundaries of clan or tribe, collective forms of religious expression that were unknown in traditional religious practice, and centralized organization in an acephalous society. While she was describing the contrast for the Luo many of her features apply in varying degrees elsewhere.

In spite of the extent to which a church is a new institutional form it is remarkable that so many independents still reflect the patterns of their tribal society. Sundkler made much of this point in relation to the Zulu, and it is evident elsewhere, as in two of the bodies already mentioned: the African Brotherhood Church which has a hierarchical structure and system of councils very like that of its own Akamba society, and, in contrast, the Holy Spirit Churches in Zaïre which continue the more egalitarian and loosely structured pattern of their own traditional people. In spite of this the latter maintain a sense of communality with similar churches beyond their own cultural areas, so that the traditional and the innovative (i.e. this degree of trans-tribal universality) are not necessarily incompatible.

The problem of succession to leadership upon the death of the founder presents a particular instance of the relationship between old and new forms. Succession from father to eldest son (sometimes disputed by another son) has not been uncommon, as with Isaiah Shembe to his son J. G. Shembe in 1935, and Jehu-Appiah to Matapoly Moses Jehu-Appiah in 1948 in the Musama Disco Christo Church; in the Kimbanguist Church it was Joseph Diangienda, the youngest child, who was chosen by Simon Kimbangu to succeed him, when only three years old. Likewise when E. B. Lekganyane died in 1966 he left instructions for his thirteen year old son to succeed him in Zion Christian Church, as he himself had succeeded his father in 1949. Other examples are Johane Maranke followed by his son Abel in the Vapostori in 1963, and Gideon Urhobo by Emmanuel in the Nigerian God's Kingdom Society late in the 1950s; in this case the succession failed because this Judaistic movement rejected the son who had transferred to a Christian position while being educated in Britain. Oshitelu of the Church of the Lord would have liked his son to follow him but the son felt unsuitable and avoided the issue by leaving the church, so that Oshitelu chose his ablest organiser, Adejobi, who became primate in 1966. It is probable that family succession is becoming less common as churches become larger and therefore have more senior leaders to provide candidates for the headship, and as the access to better education which the son of the head of church has more than other children opens up a wider range of occupations and so undermines the hopes of his father.

VI. LEADERSHIP TRAINING AND EDUCATION

Ethiopian types of independent church displayed a substantial concern for education from the beginning and have maintained this along with the growth of demand for education in the community at large. They have sometimes used the facilities of the older churches for ministerial training but have remained weak at this point; even the A.M.E. Church in Zambia, in spite of its American connections, is still without provision for training a ministry, and its leaders are only self-trained. The prophet-healing types of independent have been more African in orientation, and therefore less involved with education, which has usually meant westernization at the same time. Some have been hostile to education and, as with their opposite numbers in Western society, have depended on the resources of the Spirit.

All churches, however, have shared in the increasing African concern for education in the post-colonial era, and there has been a significant increase in the quantity and quality of ministerial training. More young people have been sent to Bible schools abroad, and even Adejobi himself, while second in the leadership of the Church of the Lord, spent 1961–63 at the Glasgow Bible Training Institute. Others have begun the possibly more difficult practice of sending men for training to the institutions of missions or older churches within Africa; thus eastern and western independents in Nigeria have used the Mennonite Bible school at Ilorin, and the Holy Spirit Church in Kenya sent its first student to St. Paul's College, Limuru, in 1970, and has since sent others to the Friends' Bible School; the African Christian Churches and Schools in Kenya has used the Lutheran college at Makumira in Tanzania, and Epworth College in Rhodesia and other colleges have also been used.

The West African-wide Church of the Lord (Aladura) may serve as representative of the general tendencies. In the first thirty years from its foundation in 1930 there were no educational activities apart from a sketchy training for its ministers, carried on in three countries in the form of the traditional apprenticeship system. In the sixties it had begun a primary school in Monrovia, and was the recognized religion in a few Ghana private schools owned by members of the Church. In the present decade it has launched out with a secondary boarding school and a theological seminary near Lagos, and warmly supports the grammar school being established in memory of the founder in Oshitelu's home town, Ogere.

The principal tutor in the seminary has been provided by the Mennonite Church Missions Board, assisted by the Theological Education Fund of the World Council of Churches. Similar assistance has been given in other training programmes — to the EJCSK in its large seminary operating at very respectable level at N'Kamba, to the African Independent Churches Association's own seminary by the Christian Institute for Southern Africa and others, to the southern Shona churches by M. L. Daneel, to Ghana churches by the Mennonites and others in the Good News Institute already mentioned, and to some other programmes. This is undoubtedly one of the most significant developments since independence, and is almost certain to expand, however mixed its blessings will eventually prove to be.

The motive behind the increasing concern with general education and the establishment by independents of their own schools deserves some comment. Among the complex reasons we find

1. A sense of discrimination — real or imagined — against their own children in mission or church schools, or fear of their children being won over to the faith of the other church; this situation changes with the increasing take-over of education by the new governments.

2. There is also an expectation of financial help for the work of the church to be derived from school fees or government assistance; this also vanishes with state education.

3. In addition there is a declining reliance on their own spiritual dynamic

and an over-estimation of education as the key to everything, together with a

4. genuine concern for the religious dimensions of education. Finally we note

5. the influence of missions and older churches in suggesting that schools belong to the proper model of a Christian church; the prestige and status accorded in the community to "proper" churches on this model exercise a powerful influence on the independents.

The saddest feature of this concern with independent church schools is the failure to realize that the day of the church school is rapidly passing in much of Africa, and the imitation of a model that is increasingly archaic in the more developed areas of the new nations. It is difficult to blame bodies less experienced in such matters when even the older churches often fight a rearguard action against a development they should be welcoming as a sign of the success of their own pioneering of education. It would be equally unfortunate if the new developments in ministerial training were to imitate models that have been only too Western, but some at least of the Western sponsors involved are keenly aware that their own patterns are unsuitable.

In all the other areas, such as polity, where Western patterns and structures have been adopted by the independents, it is usually found that while the terminology may remain unchanged a considerable degree of Africanization has occurred in substance and in actual operation; to this extent, whatever be the new developments in the post-colonial era, these independent churches are remaining true to their most common designation, as both African and independent.

16

The Spirituality of Independent African Churches

> *This general account of the more "spiritual" dimensions of the new movements might be compared with the detailed study of one individual spiritual search in essay thirteen. It is here published for the first time.*

INTRODUCTION

In examining the spirituality of independent churches in Africa we are dealing with one of the most elusive dimensions of religion, and employing a term that combines a descriptive reference with normative overtones that introduce the question of "real" or "true" spirituality. This normative component is inevitably conditioned by one's own religious tradition and culture, although we may take courage from a considerable similarity across the world's religious traditions – a "genuine" saint is likely to be identified as such in many different religious settings. Yet we must constantly remember that African spirituality is not bound to western forms but has its own shapes and content, and not least in the independent churches.

We shall not find ourselves dealing with some of the more obvious forms of Western spirituality such as pietistic or holiness movements, the "imitation of Christ", religious orders with vows of poverty, chastity and obedience, spiritual directors and retreats, devotional exercises, solemn eucharists or Quaker meetings. We shall be in the world of prophets and revelations, visions and dreams, healing and miracles, fasting and struggling in frequent prayer, tongues, trances and other manifestations of the presence of the Holy Spirit in power. The dimensions will be pneumatological and pragmatic rather than Christological and reflective. All this of course occurs in the West also, but there it is peripheral rather than central as in so many of the independent churches.

SELF-UNDERSTANDING IN THE INDEPENDENT CHURCHES

Many of these churches regard themselves as having discovered true Christianity in its spiritual power in contrast with the less effective religion of the older churches. This is apparent in many of the generic names they give themselves ("spiritual" or "prayer" churches in West Africa, "churches of the spirit" in Rhodesia or South Africa and in many other areas) and also in their own individual designations which often expound the claim to be the "true" or "original" or "divine" or "biblical" church that has the authentic spiritual power (e.g. The True Apostolic Faith, The Divine Church of the Lord). Likewise it is characteristic to claim to have been spiritually founded by God calling their first prophet in dream or vision, or even through death and resurrection, and empowering the founder to establish this new church according to a model divinely given. Others may discover the only too human factors at work in the appearance of a new independent church, but for the members it is important to belong to no mere man-made institution. In theological terms, of course, this conviction is essential if a body is to be regarded as indeed part of the authentic Christian church, and we may interpret it here as a sign of a genuine spirituality.

Allied with this view of their origins is the desire for their own African saints, so that we have St. Simon Kimbangu for some, and Saint Oshitelu or St. Joseph Babalola for others. Only a very insensitive Westerner will smile at this, for, unlike some Western saints, these men certainly existed, and unlike some others they have made a major contribution to the expression of the Gospel in their own times and culture. This practice, however, raises the question as to whether these churches themselves produce the saintly figure among their members, fitted to join the roll of saints and martyrs that the older African churches undoubtedly possess. The answer to this is not very clear, and it must be remembered that such figures would be more likely to go unrecorded in this context, and also that the history of the independents is shorter. On the other hand one can think of possible candidates such as Prophet Doh of Etodome in Ghana, with his extreme simplicity and humility, and the late Sir Isaac Akinyele of Ibadan, whose biography must surely be a spiritual inspiration when it receives the attention it deserves.

Even more important is the claim by so many independents that they operate only by spiritual means, presumably in contrast to reliance on education or organization and similar "unspiritual means" in the older churches. Spiritual means refers above all to the power of the Holy Spirit made available through the prophets, rituals and disciplines of the church, and through dreams and visions. The human contribution consists of abundant prayer, either privately or within frequent services, together with fasting and various avoidances or tabus, again interpreted as spiritual means. Explicit forms of possession by the Holy Spirit are not as central as might be expected; some churches make it essential, or actively seek it as a sign of divine power or blessing, others welcome this but do not promote it, many merely tolerate it, and most try to control these pentecostal manifestations. Prayer and fasting may of course become new forms of magic, spiritual rituals guaranteed to produce results, but this is the inevitable distortion of practices that are central to the religious life in so many independent churches, and that do testify to a widespread spirituality among ordinary members.

UNSPIRITUAL FORMS

Behind the wide generalizations of the above paragraphs there lies a spectrum of various kinds of movements and churches ranging from idealist and utopian groups to highly materialistic examples. We need do no more than mention the lunatic and charlatan fringe of fraudulent healers, deluded messiahs, petty despots claiming divinity, and dealers in imported magic and occultism who are sometimes hard to distinguish at first sight from the more authentic forms. More significant is the Eglise de la Foi founded in the 1960s in Zaïre, a kind of African cargo cult for the bourgeoisie. This group claimed upwards of 10,000 adherents recruited from the elite whose skills have enabled them to inherit the positions and material benefits vacated by the Belgians. These benefits come from God through proper performance of the orthodox Catholic rituals formerly kept for themselves by the white priests, but now revealed to the founder of this "church". Its members can therefore retain and expand their prosperity, and they should witness to their faith by living as successful wealthy people without moral scruples; in this way their "spiritual" needs will have been met incidentally. Such an aberration must not be confused with the strongly pragmatic and this-worldly concerns of the independent churches, but must be interpreted as evidence of the deep insecurity of a bourgeoisie that fears the submerged masses whom its exploits, that lacks effective control over the economic fate of the country, and that fails to understand the real nature of the industrial processes that produce the goods they enjoy; it therefore turns to this new "Christian" form of ritual magic.[1] If this group is fortunately an exception it nevertheless reveals something of the social situation in which the more recent independent churches have arisen.

Among the latter there are also painful examples of what we are calling here "unspirituality". The Independent Churches Association in South Africa which began so well has also suffered division through disputes over funds, and was the scene of constant struggles for status, power and financial perquisites throughout its short history; much of this can be explained by the poverty and frustrations of its member ministers, but the spiritual possibilities of this development have been submerged in its very unspiritual history.[2] A more recent and somewhat equivalent association in another country narrowly escaped disaster in its early stages when appointments for its theological teaching work were about to be decided on the basis of desire for the salaries, prestige and kinship loyalties without any reference to the qualifications required; happily the crisis was overcome. Similar factors have been prominent in the succession struggles when a founder dies.

HIGHLY SPIRITUAL FORMS

At the other end of the spectrum we may place the highly idealistic and utopian groups that appear occasionally. Among the latest of these is the "Kingdom" formed in 1967 when 130 members of the Apostolic Church in the Ashanti region of Ghana broke away to form a community of love and brotherhood, uncontaminated by modern life and awaiting the return of Christ. They built a new village on a remote site, operated a single purse, established their own school and focussed their lives on hard work and worship. Although they disintegrated after seventeen months this was not the end, for a remnant began again in another remote area but with outside advice and in a more realistic manner.[3] Other closed groups excluding the impure and the unbelievers have been reported in the 1960s in Zaïre — that of Bisoki at Kinshasa, and another at Fayala near Fatundu in Kwilu; the latter refused to pay taxes and was destroyed by government.

The most famous and remarkable of all these utopian forms has been the Holy Apostles' Community at Aiyetoro in Nigeria, with total communal organization of family, work and money, and a belief in immortality having been achieved. This goes back to 1947 but in the later sixties reports indicate the erosion of the communal principle, decline of the initial spiritual impulse (probably connected with the lack of adequate sources of renewal, such as effective use of the Bible), and the emergence of the usual human weaknesses. Even if this should now prove to be another "failed Utopia", Aiyetoro and other similar groups provide a striking testimony to the capacity for radical spiritual convictions and the courage and energy to put them to the test of practice. This is in keeping with the less dramatic but still radical forms of Christianity that many of the independent churches claim to exhibit.

SPIRITUALITY IN A THIS-WORLDLY AND PRAGMATIC FRAMEWORK

In the middle of the spectrum lie the great majority of independent churches whose concerns seem predominantly this-worldly and pragmatic. To this their names so often testify: The Bible Success Society, the Miracle Temple, the Practical Church of John 14:6, the Divine Healing Church — to take examples from Ghana alone. In one such church twentyfour letters reporting answered prayers were published in its reports over a period of two years; analysis revealed the following subjects of the prayers: healing—12, childbearing—4, court cases—4, examinations—2, lost property—1, reinstatement in work—1. The head of the church interpreted all these as signs of God's deliverance from the powers of darkness.[5] Westerners are inclined to be cynical about a religion of this kind. They should, however, remember that in Christian history both refinement of spirituality and popular "raw" belief in miracles and healings have often gone hand in hand, and that each has its place. Beyond this, and more positively still, they should realize that African spirituality concerns the whole man, and therefore the healing of his sicknesses and the prosperity of his family and affairs. And again, spiritual healing is never solely spiritual, by faith and prayer, but always socio-psychological through confession and the presence of the community, as well as physical through imposition of hands, or a rod of authority, and the use of fasting and holy oils or water. Much of this wholeness has been lost in Western spirituality and is now being painfully sought once more. As Simon Barrington-Ward pointed out in a paper on Isoko spirit possession cults, what was being sought in the new Christian forms of these was divine power for a more satisfying and truly human life, and this was similar to a world-wide Christian search in our own time.

African integration of the Gospel with the most practical of everyday concerns stands in contrast with another feature of the contemporary Western Christian world — the dichotomy that has arisen between an emphasis on evangelism and a concentration upon social reform and aid and development in the Third World. It may be that this same dichotomy will be found among some of the Western-related older churches in Africa, but it is certainly not apparent in the independents, and for reasons we have already indicated. It is therefore not surprising that the wholeness of social action and spiritual emphasis should be apparent in a recent striking development in Nigeria. Monday Uzoechi had some training at an Assemblies of God Bible College and later became an independent preacher; then access of healing power and a call from God turned him into a prophet, "Prophet Demonday", with a special ministry to the insane to be found in the streets and motor parks and slums of the cities. He gathered these together, cast out their evil spirits, clothed, fed and housed them as best he could, imposed a rule of life and tried to teach them a trade, sometimes with assistance from "The Good Samaritan International Movement" (an aladura church), and finally with help from local authorities who had been shamed into action. Thus was a serious social problem tackled with spiritual means and practical methods, even if the final result must remain small amid Nigeria's millions.[6]

As a final example we may report the story told us by a Western missionary who has had more to do with independent churches than most others. He was travelling in the small hours of the morning by car, returning with members of one of these churches from a major, and exhausting, festival. As always there had been a prayer before starting. The driver was falling asleep with fatigue but would not hand over and finally lost control, so that the car turned a complete circle but finished up back on the road and still drivable. After this miraculous escape the journey was completed when they arrived back at the church in the capital city at 4 am. The white man belongs to a Christian tradition strongly marked by piety and is himself a notably "spiritual" man. He had no doubt made his own private thanksgivings in the latter part of the journey, but the young men travelling with him were somewhat shocked when he prepared simply to thank them and set off for his own residence. He had to remove his shoes and join them for a short, corporate thanksgiving service in the Church itself, feeling very much the unspiritual Westerner in the eyes of his African companions.

THE MORAL DIMENSION
IN INDEPENDENTS' SPIRITUALITY

The emphasis on success in practical matters must not be allowed to obscure the remarkable capacity to endure failure and suffering among many independent churches. Some of them began in the context of revolt against colonial conditions and were involved in conflict with governments and in subsequent repression. It might be thought that such sufferings would cease with the ending of the colonial era, but this has not been so. There have still been conflicts with local communities and in some cases with the new all-African governments themselves. The clash between Alice Lenshina's Lumpa Church and the new government of even such a peaceful man as Kenneth Kaunda in 1964, and in subsequent years, is the most dramatic illustration, but there have been others as in Zaïre when Kimbanguists who reject dancing were forced to engage in "authentic" dances, and in several countries where Watch Tower adherents have been suppressed or expelled. It is a common-place for independent churches to teach their members to expect and to endure persecution and suffering, and as an example we may quote from the fifth hymn of the Shembe or Nazarite Church hymnal:

1. You who wish to live in the flock of Jesus,
   remember the hardships of the road which goes towards home.
2. The path is small, and it defeats the cowards;
   also the gate is small, it is entered by (His) power.
3. The birds have nests, they stay well;
   but Jesus has no place where he can stay.
4. Those who wish to follow him should repent first of all; . . . .
5. They should take up the cross on their shoulders;
   they should die for the promise which they were promised.

There can be no doubt as to the biblical origins and Christian spirituality of these injunctions, which could be parallelled in other independent churches right across Africa.

The ethic taught in these churches almost always includes the rejection of the use of alcohol and tobacco, sometimes also of kola nuts, and even of dancing. Some might think that other matters such as corruption and sexual promiscuity especially in the great cities were of more urgent import, and others point out the literalism and legalism that mark the codes of most of these churches, not excepting such a highly spiritual movement as the Revival among the older churches in East Africa.

Before this is criticized as an unspiritual and legalistic ethic we must reflect on the development needs of poor countries and ask whether capital-intensive industries such as cigarette factories and breweries, producing luxury consumer goods, do other than hinder development; the basis for judgment on these matters is not the same in Africa as in Europe, as far as economics is concerned. One would also need to examine the many case histories reporting escape from the alcohol and tobacco habits among members of independent churches.

At a deeper level still one should ask whether an ethic that is rigorous at such points may not be making a contribution to the development of an ascetic tradition within African Christianity. It seems to me that this has not been entirely absent from African cultures and religions, but that it has been clearly overshadowed by the model of the "big man" who exhibits vitality, power, wealth and success. This tradition may have had its own rationale in the past, and is still to be found at work in the heads of many of the independent churches where the members may be happy to share vicariously in the prestige and affluence of their leader. In 1973 on two successive days I was driven home to my lodgings after visits to two independent churches in the leader's Mercedes-Benz! Under modernizing conditions and especially in the post-colonial era this model for a successful man is manifest particularly in politicians and the new elites, with their conspicuous consumption style of life, and is clearly building up to a major social problem. One can appreciate the relative absence of an indigenous ascetic tradition if one looks to the great Asian cultures and religions where the image of the ideal man so often takes the form of the ascetic or holy man who has abandoned the material and even the social world in search of a purer spirituality; one can also recall the importance of the ascetic tradition within the Christian Scriptures and Christian history.

If there is any truth in this analysis then the contribution of the independent churches with a rigorous ethic and a simpler style of life may be of major importance in the history of African Christianity as well as in the economic development of their countries. The influence of the independents is not confined to the few particulars we have mentioned for there are other manifestations of the same outlook or life style. One of these is the widespread use of fasting as a spiritual discipline. Another is the humility or egalitarianism exhibited by some leaders. We recall seeing a small barefooted man in a white prayer gown conducting a Bible class within the Celestial Church of Christ in Nigeria, and discovering on later introduction to him that he was the deputy vice-chancellor of a great African university. The founder and head of the Brotherhood of the Cross and Star in the eastern states of Nigeria was seen sitting on the floor in front of the congregation and in the simplest of clothing. Prophet Doh, the founder of the White Cross Society of Ghana, will come to meet a visiting delegation of Europeans barefooted and clad in Khaki shorts and shirt. The spiritual head of the Kimbanguist Church dresses and lives in simplicity, and the church members divest themselves of jewelry, watches, purses, shoes, and objects of value in some of their services of worship. In some of the older churches we have known, exactly the reverse process seems to operate when attending public worship!

THE EFFECTS OF INSTITUTIONAL DEVELOPMENT

It is well known that the original spiritual impulse leading to the establishment of a new religious group is liable to suffer from the effects of the institutionalizing that is almost inevitable over a period of time. On the face of it the older African independent churches often seem to have maintained their early spiritual power even while they have been developing institutional structures and various controls over the raw religious behaviour of their members. In many ways this is a highly competitive field, with new competitors added weekly in some countries, so that a church that has lost its spiritual dynamic may not long retain its members against the attractions of a new healer or a more powerful prophet. The competition here is in the terms of spiritual power as understood and applied in Africa.

There are, however, some signs of dissatisfaction with the progressive institutionalizing that occurs, and it is enlightening to find this occurring in a movement that has more emphasis on the things of the spirit than most others. and that has avoided becoming a separate institution. The East African Revival Fellowship or Balokole, has on the whole remained an informal, unstructured, more spontaneous fellowship, group-led, without headquarters, officials, ministers, memberships or the usual paperwork. In the 1960s, however, increasing size (20,000 at a regional convention in 1964 and 30,000 in 1970) together with increasing finances have produced the inevitable problems and forced the establishment of more adequate organizations. One result has been the formation of a new movement within Revival variously called "The Resurrection" or the "Re-awakened ones" who oppose these developments because of their deadening effect on the spiritual life, and who have begun to hold their own meetings.[7] A somewhat similar issue occurred in Zaïre in the 1960s when the Churches of the Holy Spirit and the Mayumbe groups separated from the main section of Kimbanguists over the appearance of institutional activities such as schools, dispensaries, agricultural schemes and a professional ministry.

It seems therefore safe to suggest that members of the independent churches are alert to the dangers of institutionalization and are prepared to act in the interests of the spiritual life as they understand it. We can be sure that the permanent need for spiritual renewal in the life of any church is not being forgotten in this part of African Christianity.

TWO CONCRETE EXAMPLES

We may conclude with two specific examples of spirituality among members of independent churches, one reporting an inner conflict and the other an outward and visible attitude of worship. The first is a childless woman's story. Mrs. C. was a member of an independent church but its ministry had not removed the burden of her barrenness. She had befriended another woman who was unhappy in her marriage and who finally had a child by another man. Mrs. C. admired the child and stood by the woman. She loved her own husband who was very kind to her, and was on the point of suggesting, according to much local practice, that he should seek a child for her by another woman. Then her uncle came to break the news to her that her husband had already done so, surreptitiously, and that her friend was the woman and this was the child! In shock and anger at being deceived by both husband and friend she reports her feelings:

"I was nodding from my head to my toes . . . my heart was beating, something was telling me — fall on the ground! run! run in the street! shout! Then the spirit within me said, 'Now you have to show your Christianity'. My uncle said, 'Keep steady; this is your tempting hour . . . don't allow Satan to worry you . . . compose yourself . . . it is your Cross.' All my uncle was saying I couldn't hear; I was just listening to this temptation. My uncle said my husband was afraid to approach me and had asked him to speak to me. He said: 'If really you are a Christian, it is now you should show your Christianity.' Then ah! Satan busy oh! Satan wicked oh! Satan said, Run in the street! Shout! Jump! Then my uncle said, 'Remember, you used to pray to God to give you the child. Perhaps if he had given you, you would have died, having the child. He has given it another way. This child is yours.'

Then the love for the child came in me. I felt at that moment to take the child. But, you know, I was not in good mind for the mother. I could not take the child and hate the mother . . . For days, for nights, I couldn't sleep. I said nothing to my husband immediately. He couldn't sleep. He did not eat. I said nothing. After a few days Satan left.

Then one morning the Spirit of God came to me and said, 'Don't punish this man. Whatever you want to say to the man, say it. Then I thought over everything, and I said: 'As I have told your uncle after the child is weaned, if the mother gives me, by the grace of God I will take the child.' He said, 'Is that so!' Then I had peace of mind. When the child was eighteen months the woman gave me the child. He's quite a big boy now, he's twelve. So I am thankful to God for what I have gained in the Church of. . . . I haven't much, but the little I have I thank God, and that is the grace."

The second illustration comes from a weeknight revival meeting in one of the independent churches in a shoddy building in the back streets of Ibadan. In one of the front rows stood a young man of perhaps twenty, relaxed because absorbed and quite unselfconscious, singing the choruses lustily but not unpleasantly. His whole body matched the song in quiet movements that occasionally assumed the more specific actions of a dance, and his rapt gaze reached, it appeared, beyond the tumult of sound and press of humanity about him to the spiritual world where he now belonged. Here was wholeness and sincerity of worship, manifest before our eyes — an African voice and body expressing in its own way the fulness of an African heart for the blessings he had received.[8]

Probably all who have shared to any extent in the life of African independent churches could offer similar examples of their spirituality, whether drawn from the earlier phases of these movements or from their later developments under the vastly different conditions of the post-colonial era.

Notes

1. G. Bernard, La Contestation et les églises nationales au Congo, *Canadian Journal of African Studies* 5 (2), 1971, pp. 150–2.
2. M. E. West, Independence and unity: problems of co-operation between African independent church leaders in Soweto, *African Studies* 33 (2), 1974, pp. 121–9.

3. K. A. Opoku, Kingdom: a religious community, *Research Review* (Legon), 6 (1), 1969, pp. 66–9.
4. Bernard, *op. cit.*, p. 155.
5. K. A. Opoku, Letters to a Spiritual Father, *Research Review* (Legon), 7 (1), 1970, pp. 15–32.
6. S. U. Erivwo, The Holy Ghost Devotees and Demonday's Ministry: an evaluation, *West African Religion* (Nsukka), No. 15, March 1974, pp. 19–31.
7. G. K. Mambo, The Revival Fellowship (Brethren) in Kenya, in D. B. Barrett *et al.*, (eds.) *Kenya Churches Handbook*, 1973, pp. 115–6.
8. We have related this elsewhere: see our *African Independent Church*, 1967, vol. 2, p. 120.

E. THEOLOGICAL AND LITURGICAL

The extensive range of theological questions posed in a new way by these African religious movements is surveyed in the first essay in this group. Then follow four detailed studies which exemplify the sort of work that emerges in this new context with its new problems. The areas of theological study covered include Christian ethics (essay eighteen), systematic theology (essays eighteen and nineteen especially), biblical studies (essays nineteen and twenty), and liturgics (essay twentyone).

17

The Contribution of Studies on Religion in Africa to Western Religious Studies

This essay is concerned with the reverse effects of African studies, especially of the new religious movements, upon Western religious studies. It was written for the Festschrift offered to one of the most distinguished of all African theological scholars, who successfully embraced both worlds and under whom I had the privilege of serving for seven years. Some of the issues raised are explored further in other essays; methodology in essays five and six; monogamy and criteria of the Church in eighteen; ecumenism in fifteen; the use of Scripture in twenty; and missiology and ecumenics in twentytwo.

All study of African Christianity is potentially fruitful for Western scholars, but it is in the area of the independent Churches and new movements that certain issues appear more sharply defined and Western methods falter more visibly when faced with such unfamiliar phenomena.

After some general considerations, partly methodological, I shall survey some of the benefits from these African studies for the familiar Western fields of biblical studies, church history, missiology and ecumenics,

---

In M. E. Glasswell and E. W. F. Luke (eds.), *New Testament Christianity for Africa and the World* (Essays in honour of Harry Sawyerr). London: S.P.C.K., 1974, pp. 169–178.

systematic theology and Christian ethics, and the history and phenomenology of religion.

The scholar used to Western facilities and the procedures that derive from these soon finds himself under various limitations in Africa. There are, firstly, limited library resources; indeed many of the familiar tools, especially in the historical field, are entirely absent. This means that one has to search out the primary source materials, to locate, collect, classify. bind, and deposit in archives the kind of documentary materials that are taken for granted in Western countries, and also to collect the oral tradition that new recording and storing devices make so much easier. This exercise provides a new feeling for the importance of such primary sources and a new eye for what can be turned to account as a source of information and understanding—indeed for the very idea of what constitutes data in any field.

This same limitation of resources coupled with the difficulty of communications within the African continent encourages concentration on study of what is at hand in living concrete form, the local religious forms. The abundance and variety of these provide a rich and fascinating field of study for a wide range of religious disciplines.

Upon return to a Western milieu one immediately notices the almost entire absence of equivalent serious local and contemporary studies, and the failure to collect the documentary and oral data for these. Where would one find a collection of the invaluable if voluminous weekly literary productions of the Christian religion in a Western country at the parish or congregational level, or even of the domestic periodicals of the various denominations? Yet this is a grass-roots index of what is going on, and ought to be a major resource for the academic articles in the learned journals. The main exceptions seem to be studies of the more exotic or minority groups, and usually by the sociologists of religion, to whom we appear to have consigned what is local and contemporary. A more comprehensive view of the full range of relevant data can have a profound effect on the whole nature of a subject-discipline. In this sense our Western studies of Christianity remain distorted in so far as they take little account of Christian forms in non-Western cultures and of local and contemporary forms in all cultures.

BIBLICAL STUDIES

When we turn to the biblical field we discover that many portions of the Scriptures that we tend to pass over or ignore are taken seriously by African Christians. For example, there is the attention given to dreams, both in the Bible and in traditional religion in Africa. In the Bible dreams are recorded as a means of revelation at many critical junctures and for many prominent figures. There is, however, exceedingly little theological discussion of dreams in Western studies, for we tend to relegate them to the realm of the pathological, or to gloss over them in Scripture exegesis as merely a cultural or literary form, or as belonging to a primitive stage of religious experience.

Are the biblical and the African worlds merely primitive, as compared with ourselves? Or is it rather that the Bible is indeed a 'book for all cultures', and that in its ceasing to speak to our culture at this point we learn more about ourselves than we do about our Scriptures? Perhaps what we lack at this point is suggested by the intriguing advice of a leader in an independent African Church to his members when he exhorted them 'to learn to dream like a Christian'.

However this may be these Churches certainly reveal some of the ways in which our own scriptural study is culture-bound. They also contribute to discussions of the canon of Scripture itself, and in at least two ways. Firstly, they may make a different evaluation and use of certain books as compared with Western evaluations. We recall Luther's judgement on James as an 'epistle of straw' and place that against the fact that both independent and older African Churches which I have investigated on this point all make a greater use of James than of most other parts of the New Testament, and certainly greater use than we make of it. Further, the one independent Church I have studied on this point made use of the whole Bible in its preaching; in comparison I think it would be easy to find many sections of Western Christianity where large areas of the Scriptures have never been used in preaching.

When it comes to the differential use of Scripture, which exists in all sections of the Christian Church, it is interesting to discover that something of a common pattern probably runs through both the West and Africa. My limited inquiries in both areas indicate, for instance, that Gen. 1–11 is used much more than Gen. 12–50, and more than most of the rest of the Old Testament; that John's Gospel rivals that of Matthew in usage, with Mark used least of the four; and that the Acts of the Apostles is used very little. If something of a common pattern in the differential use of Scripture extends even to such apparently 'way out' sections of the Church as the African independents (in spite of their own special quirks at some points) we have new evidence of the way the Bible actually functions across the Christian world, and the exciting possibility of being able to establish the broad lineaments of a world Christian norm for the differential use of Scripture.

CHRISTIAN HISTORY

How the historian of the Christian centuries must wish he could get behind the scanty or enigmatic documents and supply the missing evidence by stepping into a house-church in the second century, following an Irish missionary to Europe, talking to a medieval sectary, seeing for himself what the Anabaptists were really like or what happened to vast crowds of simple folk when Wesley preached in the open fields.

In the non-Western areas of the Christian world, if he stops to look, he can often find living forms that come very close to a recapitulation of parts of the biblical and Christian centuries. Especially in the multitudinous African phenomena he will find many parallels to the earlier stages in the history of the people of God. Some movements have made a radical breakthrough from tribal religion and all magical practices in favour of faith in the one God they find in the Old Testament, but have not reached a Christian position. They may even specifically reject it, and actually call themselves by Old Testament names, as with Enoch Mgijima's Israelites in South Africa, and the Abayudaya or People of Judah in eastern Uganda today.

The Jerusalem community of the New Testament period is recreated before us in the first stages of other African movements, where we find pentecostal phenomena, communal living within the bond of a new faith, prayer and fasting, healings and miracles, the enduring of persecution, and missionary expansion with no resources other than the convictions of a new religious experience. And there are the African Galatians and Corinthians also, with their proneness to litigation and party divisions, their moral lapses, and their new legalisms.

At other times it is the second Christian century which we see before us in African form, with its loss of the full dimensions of the earlier Christology and soteriology, and its descent into legalism. We see too modern Montanisms, with their prophet founders and prophetesses, their New Jerusalem holy cities, their millennial hopes, and their replacement of the incarnation by the present revelations of the Holy Spirit.

When we observe the remarkable expansion of some of these African Churches, across tribal and national boundaries and spanning great distances, and when we see some of the mass movements swinging whole sections of the population into the Christian orbit, as with Kimbanguism in the Congo, Harris in the Ivory Coast, or Joseph Babalola or Garrick Braid in Nigeria, we wonder if we are watching the way the Christian faith spread and took root in the tribes of Europe and the peoples of North Africa during the first great periods of Christian expansion.

Medieval popular movements and the non-establishment wing of the sixteenth-century Reformation both reveal many similarities with current African developments. Once again people leave the established older Churches with their higher prestige and better facilities and find their spiritual home in some despised, persecuted, poor, and ill-equipped African independent Church because here they believe they find the really vital and powerful Christian religion, and the true original Church of God, uncorrupted by Western accretions and human distortions.

Many independent Churches have regarded themselves as effecting a radical reformation in a Christianity that was corrupt and powerless because it had diverged from the biblical patterns. It is possible that the radical Reformers of the sixteenth century in Europe and of the twentieth in Africa have been equally misunderstood, and that the study of the latter could be most enlightening for our understanding of the former, as for many sections of Christian history.

MISSIOLOGY AND ECUMENICS

No mission society has ever said, We will teach this African member of our mission to read, train him a little in our ways, teach him some hymns, give him a Bible, and then turn him loose and have no further dealings with him, perhaps even put obstacles in his way or let him know that we think he is far from grasping the Christian faith. After thirty, fifty, seventy years, we will re-establish relationships and see what he has done with the little we gave him.

And yet the equivalent of this experiment has been performed time and again whenever an African with some mission or national church background has voluntarily separated himself or been forced on other grounds to do so, and has proceeded to establish a Church of his own. When contact is re-established decades later we discover what has been happening when all mission or other controls and resources have been eliminated and unsophisticated Africans have been left to 'go it alone'.

Further, their idiosyncracies, eccentricities (at least from Western viewpoints), emphases and insights, misunderstandings and heresies, strengths and weaknesses, may be taken as very similar to those within the older Churches, but freed from controls and inhibitions, allowed to develop in unsophisticated ways, and so writ large for all to see. The independents therefore offer missiology a series of extensive, long-term, unplanned, spontaneous, and fully authentic experiments from which it may secure answers to some of its most difficult questions. This is a unique contribution that we are only beginning to appreciate and use.

For example, what is it that African Christians desire to retain from Western Christian forms? It is not easy to answer this question within Churches established by and still connected with a particular Western tradition, but the independent Churches are better placed to answer for us, especially as their members may be drawn from a variety of older denominations. The answer seems complex, and here we can do no more than note that the independents characteristically draw upon the symbols, vestments, rituals, and hierarchies of some of our traditions, but less upon the sacramental and sacrificial emphasis that often accompanies these; at the same time with their emphasis upon the Bible, preaching, and lay participation, they exhibit more 'protestant' tendencies.

A similar question applies to the relationship with the forms of African traditional religions and cultures. What are the continuities and discontinuities in this connection, and are they where mission policies have tended to place them? Here some of the answers are both surprising and impressive. For example, where missions have emphasized a break with African marriage systems and required monogamy, the independents have commonly accepted continuity with the past here, and stressed the break with the systems of magic as the vital point of discontinuity.

As a further question of missiological importance, we may ask what are the most consciously felt needs, and what are the less conscious but still urgent needs which a new religion must meet if it is to be accepted? Again it is the independents who help us to see the overriding African concern for spiritual power from a mighty God to overcome all enemies and evils that threaten human life and vitality, hence their extensive ministry of mental and physical healing. This is rather different from the Western preoccupation with atonement for sin and forgiveness of guilt.

As a less conscious but still vital need there is the demand for self-respect and for acceptance by the rest of the world. In the independents this is met by their conviction of their own independent standing in the sight of God, who has raised up African prophets as inspired leaders of African Churches that will yet grow and speak new and precious things to the whole of mankind. The Western missiologist had probably not expected this sense of mission to him and to his world, and finds there was not much place for this factor in his missiological theory.

As a final question of the kind currently debated by the missiologists we may choose that of how Churches grow. Some of the independents have achieved memberships to be measured in six or more figures, and some have spread over wide and diverse areas and even into the Western world itself. How have they done this without the usual resources of men and equipment organized by some sending body? The essence of the answer seems to be that they find a mandate in the revelation to their founder or prophet, and a gospel in their offer of spiritual power from the God who has given the revelation and who continues to manifest himself in healing or guidance or deliverance from the forces of evil. For their method they have preaching and testimony set in the context of joyous worship and for their chief instrument, the Scriptures. This latter is noteworthy, for it stands in contrast to the relative neglect of the sacraments.

The related field of ecumenics must be dealt with more briefly. The practice of ecumenism has been extended in our time to include the Roman Catholic Church and the Pentecostal Churches, and now in yet another direction towards the independent Churches, especially those in Africa. In 1969–70 there was the epochal admission to the World Council of Churches of the Church of Jesus Christ through the Prophet Simon Kimbangu in Zaïre. Approval of the Kimbanguist Church seems to have depended less on doctrinal orthodoxy expressed in familiar ways than upon its dynamic Christian life. This is introducing a new dimension into ecumenism and into the basis upon which Churches are prepared to recognize one another.

At the same time many African independent Churches raise important theological questions and present old and possibly new heresies with which African theologians must deal. It has been suggested that we have here one of the stimuli towards the development of an African theology, which might well find some of its distinguishing characteristics reflected in the special features of these highly indigenous African Churches.

SYSTEMATIC THEOLOGY AND CHRISTIAN ETHICS

The independent Churches of Africa present a number of questions in important areas of systematic theology, and above all in the doctrine of the Church, and in what is meant by the criteria of the Church. When an independent Church applies for membership of a Christian Council it soon appears that the four classic notes of the Church as one, holy, catholic, and apostolic are very difficult of application, and that the different credal forms, or the Reformation marks of preaching, administration of the sacraments, and the exercise of godly discipline, help us little. The dissatisfaction already felt with all these criteria in Western quarters becomes explicit in the African context. Likewise the current Western search for more dynamic criteria, indicative of the inner life and vitality of a Church, is strongly encouraged when faced with an African independent Church whose Christian existence and dynamic we can sense but never capture in our familiar categories.

It is the independent Churches again that have exposed our Western tendency to informal or unconscious use as criteria of a Church, of matters that have no business there. The main example is the common addition of the requirement of monogamy, with the implication that a body allowing polygamy, as many independents do, cannot belong to the people of God, the Church. This is an unbiblical and untheological procedure.

This same issue of monogamy versus polygamy also poses questions to our Western Christian ethics. Is polygamy marriage or adultery, within its own social system? Is there a new species called 'Christian marriage' which alone *is* marriage? Is there any difference in principle between marriage with its various systems, and the various systems of politics and economics, in the way they should be dealt with in Christian ethics? The concrete issue of polygamy in an ostensibly Christian Church context can stimulate the development of a more satisfactory theological ethic that does three things: separates this issue from the criteria of the Church, does justice to the polygamous system as a form of marriage, and yet establishes the Christian norm of monogamy.

Of other theological issues we must speak more briefly. In the realm of soteriology it is among the African independents especially that we see the 'Christus Victor' view of the work of Christ manifestly exhibited. To study the gospel of the independents expressed in terms of abundant life and divine power may open up neglected dimensions of the biblical sources of the Christian faith and of the gospel itself for our theologies.

It is a commonplace in the West to acknowledge that both the fact and the theology of the Holy Spirit have been neglected through many centuries. African independents have a pentecostal emphasis and indeed in Ghana like to be known as the 'spiritual Churches', in this sense. Without condoning their commonly inadequate Christologies we can find in them another contributor to the ecumenical search for a Christian faith and practice less defective at this point.

There is one general point I would make about the importance of the study of this range of minority grass-roots but dynamic Churches. Theology as a science depends upon access to its appropriate data in their most authentic and vital forms. If we regard the data of theology as being the revelations and acts of the Divine, the post-biblical and contemporary manifestations of these data will occur less vividly in a dispirited Western Church with declining numbers and morale. On the other hand, the data will be more evident and accessible in unsophisticated Churches where the living God is taken seriously as present in the healing and conquering power of the Spirit, with a gospel-generated growth and a spiritual creativity and confidence. Here, at the growing edges of Christianity in its most dynamic forms, the theologian is encouraged to do scientific theology again, because he has a whole living range of contemporary data on which to work. It is not that these dynamic areas of the Christian world are free from imperfection; but being full of old and new heresies they need theology and offer it an important task.

PHENOMENOLOGY AND HISTORY OF RELIGION

As a postscript to remarks that have concentrated on various sections of the Christian religious disciplines we must indicate some contributions that the study of Africa's independent Churches is making to the general phenomenology and history of religion.

For example, it becomes apparent, especially in new movements that cannot be called independent Churches, that the traditional tribal religions must also be investigated since these provide a major component of the new developments. Thus the history and phenomenology of religion are being led into an area that has largely been left to the anthropologists. For phenomenological study there is a rich reward, for these new Churches and movements present an extensive contemporary and dynamic sampling from the characteristic forms of religion. There are new holy cities, sacred mountains, local sanctuaries, and tombs of the saints; new *langues des dieux*— holy words, revealed languages, and even revealed scripts; new festivals with rituals and symbols drawn from colours or from water or other elements. The historian of religion also has ample materials for studying the rise and development of new religious traditions in bodies that share in the 'rapid social changes' of our era, and can discover the emergence of myths and legends within a single generation. All this and more awaits the phenomenologist and historian of religion who can wean himself from preoccupation with the major so-called world religions and with the religions of antiquity.

In short, I commend the study of the independent Churches and other movements of Africa, and of the rest of the world, to all the Western religious disciplines not merely as a highly specialized field of inquiry, but as a field pregnant with new ideas, new methods and procedures, new categories and points of view, for use throughout their work.

18
Monogamy: A Mark of the Church?

Since this essay was written missions and older churches have given much attention to the subject of marriage, and there has been considerable change in their attitudes towards polygamy and their rules about monogamy. This has occurred not least in Roman Catholic quarters, as witness the pioneering writings of Fr Eugene Hillman. It may be regarded as one part of the extensive re-examination of the nature of marriage and the family, of the role of women and the celibacy of the priesthood that is occurring in Western societies.

There is a widespread tendency among all Christian churches to add to the essential marks of the Church certain features drawn from their own individual traditions, and then to judge other churches by their own rather than by common basic criteria. This practice presents one of the main problems in current ecumenical relations. In Africa it is seen above all in the attitudes of the older churches, those derived from the work of European missions, which have adopted monogamy, towards the independent churches which have retained the African tradition of polygamy. Very often the first question asked about such a church concerns its position on marriage; and if it applies for membership in a Christian Council, the fact that it is not monogamous is liable to be the ground upon which its

---

International Review of Missions, no. 219, vol. 55, 1966, pp. 313–321.

application will be rejected. It is not sufficient for a church to show that it accepts the Scriptures and endeavours within its own resources to interpret and apply them in a Christian fashion, or that it affirms faith in Jesus Christ as Son of God and Lord and Saviour according to the Scriptures and so fulfils the basic criterion established by the World Council of Churches in 1948 and 1960. Whatever positions it may adopt on other matters of Christian ethics, and in many matters of faith and order, unless it adopts the monogamous position on the one question of marriage, it cannot be accepted into fellowship as a Christian Church. This in effect elevates monogamy to the status of a mark of the visible Church. Is this legitimate and can monogamy bear this responsibility? The position of monogamy as the biblical norm for the marriage relation is not the question at issue, but rather what use can rightly be made of this norm as a criterion of a Christian church.

Nineteenth century missionaries to Africa were probably not conscious of the distinction between monogamous marriage as an institution in Western culture and monogamy as the Christian norm for the marriage relationship; and they sought to replace the polygamy found in African cultures by the Western institution, as a basic necessity in a Christian church. Now that Africans have discovered the extent to which monogamy actually does control the behaviour of the peoples of the West, and especially of those who have worked in Africa, many can no longer identify monogamy with Christianity, or regard it as clearly superior to an ordered system of polygamy. The cultural argument for monogamy has ceased to be effective, and it is mentioned here only to distinguish it from other more important arguments at work in the minds of those who planted the Church in Africa.

The chief of these was a pragmatic argument. The difference between the Christian faith and the traditional pagan religions of Africa was so fundamental that it involved decisive changes in the manner of life of the convert. It was not possible to make an easy and gradual transference from one to the other, and at certain key points there had to be a radical break to mark and support the new allegiance if there was ever to be a visible church that could clearly be called Christian. In the judgement of most missionaries these key points were represented by what was known as 'medicine' or 'fetish', or the whole realm of magic and the native practitioner, together with certain African customs or institutions, of which polygamy was the most important. Traditional magic and medicine were therefore replaced by Western medicine, and polygamy by monogamy. These were the points at which no compromise was possible, and no accommodation to African cultures could be considered.

The necessity or the wisdom of this pragmatic judgement at the beginning of the Christian Church in Africa is not under discussion. A start had to be made, and a stake driven in for the new faith somewhere, somehow.

It is described here because it still represents the attitude of many of the older churches and explains why they feel the independent churches have betrayed the Christian faith at vital points. This attitude is well expressed in a stern injunction in 1933 from the then Anglican bishop of Lagos against all forms of fraternization with the 'so-called African Churches'.

> . . . I think we compromise our principles when we go to their religious gatherings, attend their weddings . . . and other functions . . . [this] is likely to lead . . . people to think we are at one with them in their teaching and practice with regard to polygamy and other like matters . . . Let these 'African Churches' take the teaching of Christ as their standard with regard to marriage instead of basing it on the custom of the country and we shall be glad to receive them back into fellowship and communion.[1]

This non-fraternization order was made in regard to the 'Ethiopian' or 'African' type of church, but would apply even more strongly to the more recent prophet-healing forms, and the chief bone of contention is clearly polygamy.

Despite the optimistic reference to acceptance of the teaching of Christ as settling the issue, this is primarily a practical argument based on a judgement as to the effects of compromise at this point. There is a formidable body of evidence aligned against it. There is first the patent failure of many of the older churches to secure monogamy among their own members: the irregularities in the sphere of sexual relationships are often an open scandal, and are testified to in the number of congregations where a majority of members are under discipline for marriage offences.[2] Further, there is widespread discussion in the courts of the older churches as to the wisdom of a rigorous stand in this sphere, and various modifications of disciplinary membership regulations have been proposed or adopted in order to come to terms with the existence of polygamy. It is also increasingly recognized that polygamy has been an integral part of a cultural and social system, and that its replacement by monogamy can occur only in the course of wider changes in African life. These are now under way and will in the end effect and confirm changes in the marriage system that the direct attack of the churches has not been able to secure. Finally, it is becoming apparent that the major issue no longer lies between polygamy and monogamy, but between any ordered system of sex relations and the increasing disorder and promiscuity that are appearing in African life, especially in urban and industrial areas, as in so many other parts of the world. In the words of Dr Taylor, 'This means that the Church should unreservedly honour and encourage faithfulness and stability wherever these are found, even where the marital pattern does not conform to what it regards as the Christian ideal.'[3]

On the other hand the independent churches that are polygamous in varying degrees, because they have been aware that a return to orderly polygamy was better than succumbing to the new licence overtaking African society, have made a different practical judgement as to where a firm stand must be made against certain features of traditional African life. Many of them have rejected all traditional and much Western medicine because they have realized that it is only too easy first to replace the traditional world of magic, and its medicines, with the medicine and doctors of the West, and then to treat these as no more than a new and more powerful form of magic. When these prove inadequate, and there has been no real discovery of faith in the Christian God, return is made to the earlier magic, and many in the older churches once more consult a traditional practitioner. This is therefore the point at which the stand must be made, and to do so many of the prophet-healing churches have rejected all medicine, both African and Western. For them the vital point of no compromise does not lie in the realm of marriage, but in the transference to faith in the one God and in His power, rather than in any man and his 'medicine'. These churches therefore do not take a stand on monogamy, although they share in the general social movement in that direction and increasingly recognize the biblical norm. They do insist on complete rejection of native practitioners and their methods, and to a much lesser extent of Western medicine, that may replace faith in God. In adopting this rigorous position they have achieved a breakthrough at the crucial point, and in doing so have gained a more basic qualification for recognition as Christian churches than monogamy could have provided.

This independent African judgement, made existentially and without theoretical consideration, is of the utmost importance for the theory of missions and for the guidance of the older churches in Africa. It is important because it has worked, in however one-sided and extreme a fashion, and because it corresponds to the biblical position in these matters. The people of Israel reached their unique religious position in the ancient world not by adopting monogamy as against polygamy, but by their faith in God alone and their rejection, at least in their leaders and official teaching, of magic, sorcery and trust in other powers to help them. In the Scriptures this is frequently made an issue upon which men must choose; polygamy is never made an issue in this way and actually continued in some Jewish communities into the medieval period or later,[4] contrary to common statements that it had been replaced by monogamy before New Testament times.

It should also be noted that the continuance of polygamy in practice does not render it impossible to establish a norm of monogamy. Israel was able to do just this, and to use the analogy between a monogamous marriage on the one hand and God as husband and Israel the faithless spouse on the other, an analogy that reappears in the New Testament in terms of

Christ and His Bride the Church. The establishment and the ultimate influence of this norm were not dependent upon a prior achievement of monogamy, any more than Christian norms in other spheres of life depend on their being first realized in the Christian community.

On these grounds the position of a polygamous independent church may be both more realistic and less opposed to the biblical position of the people of God than some of the rules and arguments to be found in older churches.

The time has come for the older churches to make a much more thorough study of their implicit use of monogamy as a mark of the visible Church. One welcome sign of this comes from a report on a retreat of Methodist ministers in Nigeria:

> . . . the Church should look carefully at its ruling forbidding polygamists the means of grace in the Holy Communion, lest the requirements of the Law take precedence over the offer of the Gospel, and we be found preaching a doctrine of salvation by works. The theological basis of our practice should be carefully examined.[5]

How surprisingly difficult it is to do this will be evident to anyone who has read Helander's *Must We Introduce Monogamy?*, including its account of the fanciful arguments adduced by Barth, Brunner, and others in support of their position.[6]

The All-African Seminar on Christian Home and Family Life, at Mindolo in 1963, boldly declared that 'a pagan polygamist upon conversion should be received into the church—he, his wives and children', and should also be admitted to the Lord's Supper but not to posts of responsibility. This, however, was too radical for the Churches of the Kenya Christian Council gathered to examine the same theme the next year at Limuru. Here the earlier position of monogamy as a prerequisite for church membership was reaffirmed by all except the independent ex-Anglican Church of Christ in Africa, which does not follow this rule.

In June 1965 the South African Churches held a national conference on polygamy and allied matters, where 'strong divergence of opinion and difference in practice became evident'. While one viewpoint expressed in the Findings opposed the admission of polygamists under any circumstances, another view favoured 'Acceptance with various limitations'. The qualifications and precautions, however, were so numerous that this acceptance was plainly a somewhat grudging 'concession' (the term used) in a practical situation, rather than a positively based decision. It would appear that changes envisaged at All-African conferences meet with much less favour at the regional level, where there is room for greater depth and clarity in the discussions.[7]

The consultation on independent churches arranged at Mindolo Ecumenical Centre in Zambia in September 1962, issued a statement which revealed one of the most positive attitudes toward this reappraisal yet seen in church and missionary circles in Africa:

> . . . We suggest that [older churches] should consider whether in those of the [independent churches], where there has been little change from traditional African patterns of marriage, there may not nevertheless be a genuine relationship to Jesus Christ. By virtue of this, may they not be recognized as churches with whom possibilities of Christian fellowship must be explored?

This statement dealt with the question in the right terms and at the right level, in fact, Christologically.

Another contribution to the discussion set in the right context comes from the Consultation on the Evangelization of West Africa at Yaoundé, Cameroun, in June 1965. It suggested that 'The crucial question is whether the Church regards polygamy as a state of marriage or a state of adultery; in Africa, as elsewhere, a vital distinction is made between the two. We can find no scriptural justification for such practice as admitting polygamous converts to baptism but not to communion.' This implies that we need a more positive and biblical way of looking at marriage systems that are not monogamous—at marriage itself in any form—and that we must ask ourselves what is meant by the term 'Christian marriage' which we all too easily assume we possess as over against the polygamous churches. It certainly cannot be equated with monogamy, and is as dangerous and confusing as the similar terms, 'Christian economics' and 'Christian politics'.

Some of these confusions are apparent in the South African findings of 1965. It states that 'Customary Union or Tribal Marriage is as valid a form of marriage as civil marriage', but requires 'penance' by a Christian woman so married before she may be readmitted to the Church (nothing is said of a Christian man so married, who is apparently not provided for). This penalty on customary union is justified, *inter alia,* by its potentially polygamous nature and its potential instability through lack of compulsory legal registration. Penance for a valid marriage because of its potential failure!—as if the most 'Christian' marriage by church rite is not also potentially open to worse disasters than polygamy, and to legally sanctioned dissolution, as the Conference itself had recognized in an earlier section on the 'Modern Decline'.

The Yaoundé Consultation made another recommendation concerning this difficult question: 'This being a problem which the white man cannot understand from within, it is very desirable that missionaries should sympathetically withdraw from discussion in which African churches seek for guidance of the Holy Spirit on this matter . . .' This sounds an admirably humble attitude to adopt in these days of autonomy of the younger churches, and if it were in connexion with practical matters peculiar to Africa, with local problems of discipline or organization or expression of the Faith, I would concur. But when the problem concerns the Christian doctrines of the Church and of marriage, the relation of ecclesiology to Christian ethics, and the biblico-theological basis for an answer, we are *all* concerned. We all have problems of whether or not to recognize as churches those that differ from us in doctrine and in practice, and on the question of marriage in a non-Christian world.

As a fresh line of approach in reappraising our answer to this problem, perhaps there is a proper and profitable analogy between the various systems of marriage represented by polygamy and monogamy in Africa, the various political systems represented by the soviets, democracy, or the fascists, the systems of international relations represented by the institutions of war and of the United Nations and international arbitration, and the economic systems found in slavery or in free wage labour. All of these, including the marriage institution, are temporal systems belonging to the passing fashion of this world; none is made an issue in the Bible, whether it be marriage, war, government, or slavery; several of them provide important analogies whereby God is known as Husband, Bridegroom, Lord, or King; all are brought under various practical controls suggested from time to time, and finally made subject to the norm for all human affairs established in Jesus Christ and His humanity. No case can be made for suggesting that marriage is different in principle from these other spheres of human life, or more integrally related to our salvation. The Christian Church has in the past existed under all forms of political, economic, and marriage systems, and continues to do so today; while faith in God and acceptance of salvation through Jesus Christ are, in the last analysis, no more dependent upon monogamy, democracy, and a free wage labour system than upon other social forms.

Although the Christian life is no more guaranteed by monogamy than it is denied by polygamy, it is at the same time clear that monogamy in marriage relations, and an ordered and peaceful freedom in political and economic systems, offer possibilities for fuller human development than is possible under other conditions. But there is no direct correlation between a measure of achievement of these goals and man's standing before God in Christ as a forgiven sinner. The Church, therefore, cannot be defined by reference to its achievements in any of these temporal spheres.

Those who cannot accept this argument from analogy must produce biblical and theological reasons to show that marriage stands in a class apart from other moral issues and forms of human existence, and that monogamy possesses such an essential relation to the possibility of faith in Jesus Christ, that any Church claiming His name must thereby also be monogamous.

In conclusion it should be pointed out that this discussion has not concerned itself with what should be done in the older Churches, nor has it suggested that they should all throw open their doors to polygamists, nor that judgement should be passed on the missions which insisted on monogamy. The question is that of recognition of independent polygamous churches as Christian churches, and the conclusion must be drawn that none should be excluded from Christian fellowship or from Christian Councils solely for this reason. C. G. Baëta has opposed this on pragmatic grounds, when he says

> . . . there can be no reasonable doubt that the affiliation of the separatist churches would mean the acceptance of the practice of polygamy for all church members. How could there be an association of churches in the same council, in which some approve polygamy and others not permit it?[8]

It, however, is difficult to believe that the result would be so extreme; but it can be well imagined that some older churches might have to re-examine their position and make a greater accommodation to the realities of the situation. This could only redound to the health of the Church, and anyway, as the cases cited above demonstrate, this is a process already under way in some churches. As for the question of association with polygamists, Christian councils already transcend in their membership weighty matters of faith and order (from Anglo-Catholics to Salvation Army and Pentecostalists), and important differences of opinion in matters of Christian behaviour (pacifist and non-pacifist, teetotaller and those who use alcohol and tobacco—and alcohol at least presents a widespread and growing problem in African life). Again marriage practice is being isolated from all other issues which divide Christians and is being made a determinant of their fellowship. The qualities of this fellowship are best demonstrated to the world when Christians with a strongly held conviction are able to stand with those whom they regard as weaker brethren and accept the shame, if shame it be to them, of personal and public identification with others who bear the essential marks of Christ, and yet are supporters of war or of communist governments, who are reactionary capitalists or extreme socialists, or the husband of more than one wife. One of the visible signs of the presence of the Holy Spirit is the ability to transcend historical and cultural differences, and even differences in the most deeply held convictions on the important matters of Christian ethics.

The question of recognition of the independent churches as Christian churches raised at the Mindolo Conference in cautious fashion urgently requires an affirmative answer based on a deeper understanding of the true marks of the visible Church in history, coupled with a more penetrating assessment of the many biblical norms which monogamous churches fail to fulfil. Let it be publicly declared that a polygamous African church may still be classified as a Christian church, even while monogamy remains the Christian norm, and that no such church will be excluded from Christian councils and full Christian fellowship solely because of its polygamy.

Notes

1. *Report* of Proceedings, Second Session, Fifth Synod of the Anglican Diocese of Lagos, 1933, pp. 10–11.
2. E.g., John V. Taylor: *The Growth of the Church in Buganda* (London: SCM Press, 1958), p. 182, calls such a church a 'monstrosity'; similarly S. G. Williamson: *Akan Religion and the Christian Faith* (London: Oxford University Press, 1965), says of the Methodist Church in Ghana that 'In spite of its rules against polygamy, the Church appears to be riddled with it.' (p. 291 of original unpublished dissertation).
3. *Op. cit.*, pp. 258–9.
4. For references, and the whole question, see the excellent but neglected investigation by G. Helander: *Must We Introduce Monogamy?* (Pietermaritzburg, 1958), pp. 25–6.
5. Papers for the Synod of the Western Region District Methodist Church in Nigeria, 1962, *Booklet 2*, p. 4.
6. *Op. cit.*, pp. 47–8.
7. For the Southern African Conference see *The Christian Council Quarterly* (Capetown), third quarter 1965, pp. 9–13; see also T. Price: *African Marriage* (London: 1954), p. 46 *et passim* for earlier evidence of the changing outlook.
8. C. G. Baëta, 'Conflict in Mission: Historical and Separatist Churches', in Gerald H. Anderson (ed.): *The Theology of the Christian Mission* (New York: McGraw-Hill, 1961), p. 298. Professor Baëta endeavours here to draw a distinction by asserting the basic importance of marriage, and depreciating the significance of war ('merely a abnormal thing') and of slavery ('a passing fashion'). In an era when both celibate and married, monogamist and polygamist live under the possibility of atomic annihilation this distinction is unacceptable. In 1962 at the Mindolo Consultation Professor Baëta agreed that Western Christians have unwarrantably added what is in effect a new 'mark' to the Church, and he criticized a church in West Africa which had recently destroyed a most promising evangelistic campaign among pagans by insisting on monogamy.

19
A Theology of Water, in Introduction to
J. Ade Aina's *Present-Day Prophets*

This material introduced the reprint of a notable pamphlet by a Nigerian aladura leader. It contains a biographical sketch, an historical outline of the situation at the time (more fully treated in African Independent Church, *volume one), and a commentary on a remarkable example of indigenous theological apologia and interpretation concerning the holy water so widely used in independent churches. It is included to draw attention to the large range of publications emanating from independent churches, especially in West Africa, and to the importance of taking them seriously.*

THE AUTHOR

Pastor J. Ade Aina was one of the longest surviving participants in the first stirrings among Christians in Western Nigeria that led to great emphasis on prayers, healing, and revelation through prophets, and finally to the many-sided aladura (i.e. 'prayer-group') movement independent of the older churches. After having been a member of the earliest group in

From *The Present-Day Prophets and the Principles upon Which They Work* (c. 1932), issued by the College of Religion, University of Nigeria, Nsukka, 1964, pp. i–v.

Ijebu-Ode about 1920, and later in Lagos in 1924, he was transferred by his employer, a leather-trader, to Ibadan. Here he discovered a kindred spirit in I. B. Akinyele, and established a similar group under the name that was by now in use, Faith Tabernacle. In 1930 the Ibadan aladura leaders had discovered Joseph Babalola, who became the most famous of Nigerian prophets, and had joined forces with the founder of another aladura group, Josiah Oshitelu of the Church of the Lord. All these were involved in the great aladura revival and mission in Ibadan and surrounding districts in the second half of 1930.

The following year saw Faith Tabernacle and the Church of the Lord part company. The former is represented today by the large Christ Apostolic Church, which had Akinyele, when he was also Olubadan ('king') of Ibadan, as its head. Aina transferred allegiance to the Church of the Lord, and became its first ordained minister, with a congregation at Oke ('hill') Bola in Ibadan, where he remained for the rest of his life. In 1935 he and his congregation seceded to form the Aladura Church, or Mission, and subsequent local divisions saw Aina at the head of the Aladura Apostolic Church in 1942, and of the Living Faith Apostolic Church from 1952.

During the three decades from the Ibadan revival Pastor Aina produced about fifteen printed publications, some of as much as eighty pages. They include hymnbooks with some original hymns, a church constitution, a catechism, a service book and an ordinal, and separate treatises on the Second Coming, polygamy, and Islam. Because this spontaneous literary activity by an African Christian was obviously of some significance, and yet remained almost entirely unknown among the older churches, the College of Religion decided to make one of Pastor Aina's earliest publications more widely available, and to draw attention to some of its contents.

His pamphlet on *The Present-Day Prophets and the Principles upon Which They Work* is a defence of the aladura movement in face of the hostile attitude of the Colonial administration and the older churches and missions in the early 1930's. It was first published in printed form about 1932, as a 16 page booklet, for threepence.

THE GOVERNMENT AND THE PROPHETS

The government had some reason for alarm. The economic depression of these years had borne hardly upon Western Nigeria, as elsewhere, and made taxes harder to collect, as well as increased the risk of demonstrations or even of rebellion. The aladura movement spread rapidly, set many travelling to find the prophets (especially the sick and diseased), and led to large and excited gatherings. This amounted to a dangerous social disturbance in the eyes of government. It was aggravated by the appearance of pseudo-prophets who counselled non-payment of taxes, no doubt with the idea of increasing the gifts and thankofferings they themselves received.

Government fears were increased by three publications of Oshitelu, containing his prophecies of doom, and warnings of divine judgment on sinners, including 'those who collect taxes and money on land'. The commissioner of police banned the pamphlets, and a top-level conference in Ibadan proposed prosecution for sedition. The Attorney-General wisely dissuaded them from this action. Oshitelu was interrogated at the local level, and cleared himself of charges of opposition to payment of taxes. Aina's defence of the 'true prophets' appears at the end of the pamphlet. It is a simple rebuttal of the charges, together with a rather elaborate scriptural support for obedience to the authorities and payment of all dues. That this defence was sincere, and was in fact representative of the main aladura movements, is borne out by the subsequent history of the aladura churches; they have proved, if anything, a-political, and seditious intent has been far from their real purposes. This section of the pamphlet is of historical value as representing a political interpretation falsely given in many parts of Africa to prophet movements that were primarily concerned with the search for a 'wonderful working power' in the Christian religion.

PROPHETS – TRUE AND FALSE

Pastor Aina's 'Fore-word' explicitly declares that the true prophets have been raised up to offer this full power of the Gospel, in face of the failure of the leaders of the older churches. This claim led to the three charges against the aladura that Aina seeks to answer in the main body of his pamphlet, and as these charges are commonly still made against independent prophet churches, Aina's answers deserve careful attention.

The first charge is that the day of prophets is past, and all aladura prophets are false. Aina counters this by recalling the pentecostal promise of Joel 2: 28–29, which was fulfilled in the time of the apostles, and again in Nigeria, and by emphasizing the importance of using the biblical criteria for distinguishing false prophets from true. These criteria have not always been easy to apply, either in biblical or in Christian history, and the genuine leaders of the aladura movement have always been greatly embarrassed by the charlatan and lunatic fringe of false prophets. The ministry of the older Churches often lacks the prophetic element, which derives from one of the three offices of Christ as Prophet, Priest and King; these same churches are also gradually learning to look with greater respect on the modern Pentecostal wing of Christianity. It is therefore less easy now than it was thirty years ago to dismiss the aladura prophets out of hand, especially when they are seen as part of the series of prophet movements which have spread across much of Africa in the last fifty years.

A THEOLOGY OF WATER

The second criticism met by the aladura is that 'mere water' is of no avail for healing or against evil powers, even though it has been consecrated by a prophet. Aina's answer to this is an impressive attempt at a theological rationale on a biblical basis by an unsophisticated African, and deserves a patient effort to understand the mind of a writer who is not using his mother tongue (as he pointed out in his foreword), and who has not been trained in theological method.

The first step in the argument is to compare three kinds of healing agent:

(1) Medicines manufactured by human wisdom, and administered by expensive doctors. Support for these cannot be found in Luke the physician, since there is no evidence that he practised this profession after conversion, nor in Paul's prescription of wine for Timothy's stomach, since Aina claims this was not medicinal wine commercially obtained, but the freely given wine of God in Isaiah lv: 1.

(2) Consecrated oil, as recommended in James v: 14–15. This is better than the medicines in (1), and has always been used among the aladura churches. But "There is a great deal of human efforts in producing such oil". The implication is that one is still relying to some extent on the human factor, instead of having faith in God alone.

(3) Consecrated water, which is in no sense a human product, but comes straight from God. To rely on this alone reveals the highest degree of faith.

The next step is the interpretation of this consecrated water in scriptural and sacramental terms as Living Water. Just as ordinary bread and wine become the body and blood of Christ after consecration, so also does common water become Jesus Christ the Living Water after it has been blessed.

The final stage is the attempt to subsume consecrated water, together with the wine of Timothy's prescription and of the miracle at Cana, under the one image of Christ the Living Water. Here the argument becomes rather confused. What is clear, however, is that we have before us a sincere attempt at biblical and Christological thinking, and an indication that the archetypal image of water is as important in the mind of Africa as it is in the Scriptures themselves, and in so much of the history of religions.

Further light is thrown on the theology of water that is here attempted by a remark in a publication by D. O. Abimbolu, the senior lay leader of the Church of the Lord in Ibadan. Abimbolu points out that in Genesis iii, "God only cursed the soil because of Adam, but not water." This seems to us to provide the clue to Aina's theology of water — that here we have the perfect sacramental element, untainted by the Fall, and thus distinguished from all substances, especially medicines, which derive from the earth. Water, the primeval element of Genesis i:2, retains its primal purity, comes direct from heaven, and serves as the vehicle for the power of God to those who have faith in him alone.

This is not the place to examine either the exegesis or the orthodoxy of Pastor Aina's argument. It is more important to recognize it as a serious piece of indigenous theology, revealing images and ways of thought with which the Western-orientated older churches must come to grips. If in some respects it should be heretical, then it is only as African theological thinking discovers this, and supplies a better account of these same matters, that the Church in Africa will articulate its own faith and stand on its own feet.

THE CHURCHES AND THE ALADURA

The remaining charge was that the prophets did not direct their followers to the older churches, and even discouraged present members from paying their church dues. Aina answers that the prophets recognize the biblical injunction to give freely, but cannot support the undue emphasis on money in the older churches, nor the methods allegedly in use to secure it. This becomes part of a general criticism of these churches as lifeless and unspiritual, and failing to meet the needs of their members, whose unchristian conduct is described at some length.

The lack of spiritual power was clearly seen when the churches "were being locked up . . . during the time of pestilence and influenza. . . . Are these churches?" This refers to what appears to have been a traumatic experience for many Nigerian Christians — the world influenza epidemic of 1918, when church buildings were closed, and Christians, both black and white, succumbed to the plague.

What was the use of a church which could not protect even its white sponsors, and which ceased to operate when its members were in great trouble? The marvel is that disillusioned African Christians did not turn away from the Christian Church, but of their own accord sought the more earnestly for the spiritual succour which they felt had eluded them. The prayer-group formed within the Anglican congregation at Ijebu-Ode was the fore-runner of the whole aladura movement, of what Aina calls a "new establishment of the Church of the Lord on earth", which will give real help to its members, and prepare them for the coming judgment at the Second Advent.

How far Aina's other criticisms were justified, and to what extent the aladura churches have been more effective in ministering to the spiritual needs of their members, cannot be examined here. Suffice it to say that the aladura attitude is similar to that of the reformer and the revivalist at many points in Christian history, and the fact that these were indigenous African protests within churches overwhelmingly Western in nature lends them added significance. Only those who forget that the spiritual health of the Christian Church depends on ever-renewed reformation will fail to give the writings of Pastor Aina, and of others like him, the attention they deserve.

20

Profile Through Preaching:
The Use of Scripture as the Criterion of a Church

These selections form a digest of a longer detailed analysis of the sermon texts used in the Church of the Lord (Aladura) across four West African countries and over a period of thirty years. The method used was evolved for the purpose and is fully described in the original publication so that it might be used elsewhere on similar data. It has been so used for two Free Church ministers in England, each with many years of preaching behind him, and also for analysis of some 9,000 texts used in the Anglican Diocese of Leicester in the earlier decades of this century. There are many similar bodies of material awaiting analysis in Britain and elsewhere. The method has theological value in the area of ecclesiology, and stands as an example of the stimulus provided by theological work in another culture.

CRITERIA OF A CHURCH

This study is concerned with the question of how we may decide that a religious body is in fact a Christian Church, especially when we remember that formal statements of doctrine and practice and confessions of faith

(From *Profile Through Preaching*. London: Edinburgh House Press 1965.)

are not necessarily accurate indications of the religious understanding that controls the life of a group claiming to be a Church. When expressed in this way, the question is germane to the decision the Christian world faces in Africa, with its thousands of modern religious movements, many of them claiming to be Christian Churches. No doubt there are similar problems elsewhere, but in Africa at least the issue is widespread and urgent.

The method of analysing sermon texts to be described in these pages is offered as a contribution towards an objective determination of what is and what is not a Christian Church. It was developed in the course of a prolonged study, in depth and from a theological viewpoint, of a West African Independent church, 'the Church of the Lord (Aladura)', which means 'the praying church'. This is one of the three main Churches which may be traced back to the various prophet and healing movements which appeared in Western Nigeria between 1918 and 1930. Its founder, J. O. Oshitelu, was an Anglican teacher-catechist dismissed by the Church on account of his unorthodox practices.

Over the years this Church has developed its organization and issued a large number of publications, including a hymn-book, a catechism and extensive liturgical material, some of which is original and the rest is adapted to the African situation from the Anglican Book of Common Prayer. The Church observes both dominical sacraments, makes considerable use of the Bible and possesses a hierarchical and mainly literate ministry, including women. Dependence on traditional magic and idolatry is replaced by reliance upon the God of the Scriptures, through faith, prayer, fasting and holy water. It is best described as a prophet-healing Independent Church with some Pentecostal features.

It is possible that many of the features we have described are little more than a borrowed Christian veneer masking a religious life that remains essentially pagan. In support of this interpretation some would draw attention to the Church's toleration of polygamy, to its excessive reliance on dreams, visions, and spirit-messages, to the selling of revelations for money, the turning of holy water into a new agent of magic and the general self-centred benefit-seeking attitude of many members. When, in addition, we remember the proximity of paganism and the evidence of its continuing vitality among members of the older or Western-connected Churches, it is not unreasonable to doubt the claim of such an independent African religious movement to be a Christian Church.

How then can a decision be made, and what criteria may rightly be used? This is the question facing Christian Councils, the older Christian Churches and missions in Africa; it is to be answered only from an intimate understanding of these African developments that is as yet extremely rare and on the basis of theological criteria that really do test the existence of an African community such as the Church of the Lord.

Effective Tests for an African Independent Church

It is inevitable that we should turn first to the familiar criteria used in Western theology, such as the classic 'notes' of the true Church declared in the ancient creeds—unity, holiness, catholicity and apostolicity. In a later theological study[1] we have made soundings in the life of this Church, and satisfied ourselves that the Church both acknowledges these notes and shows some signs of having endeavoured to express them in its life; here we can but draw attention to what has been said above about unity and mission.

Not every religious group, however, that remains united, claims the world for itself and spreads, is thereby a Christian Church. The four classical notes themselves need Christian interpretation, and when their full Christian content is given it becomes apparent that their relation to the Church in history is always eschatological; the Church believes in faith that these represent the promised fulfilment, and for the present it must repent its lack of holiness and unity, and neglect of its mission. This great difference between promise and achievement makes it possible for a Church to profess faith in the true Church through the traditional notes even when it has virtually ceased to be the Church in any effective or recognizable manner. To meet this situation there have been various formulations of the outward 'marks' or signs that provide criteria of the visible Christian Church.

Some suggest that we should use the features that were evident in the early Church as the marks or signs we apply. Thus in Acts 2: 42 there is the 'Jerusalem Quadrilateral' of apostolic doctrine, fellowship, breaking of bread and prayer; and in the whole section, v. 42–6, the further marks—performance of wonders, sharing everything in common, 'having favour with all the people', and increasing in number. The Church of the Lord passes these tests as much as many Churches in Christendom, and more than some. Another scriptural test is to ask whether the 'works of the flesh' of Gal. 5: 19–21 (adultery, idolatry, witchcraft, strife, drunkenness, etc.) have been put away, and the 'fruit of the Spirit' (Gal. 5: 22–3–love, joy, peace, temperance, etc.) made manifest. Here again the record of the Church will bear comparison with that of others to which we grant the name of Christian. Dr. Field has applied some such tests as these in her evaluation of the 'African-organized Christian cults', as she calls them, in Ghana; these:

> . . . bring a feeling of peace, refreshment and well-being . . . Their members . . . seem happier, more generous and harder-working than most of their compatriots and their zeal is un-paralleled . . . these worshippers have recaptured something of the atmosphere of the primitive Church . . .[2]

This may be a secularized form of the Scripture signs, but the testimony stands and is applicable also to the Church of the Lord.

More specific and objective marks of the Church appear in the Reformed tradition which speaks of the preaching of the Word, the administration of the sacraments and the exercise of discipline, and it is clear that the Church meets these requirements. It would also fulfil the 'South India Quadrilateral', whereby a church must accept the Scriptures as its basis and expound them, administer the dominical sacraments, possesses a ministry and a common life manifesting both growth in holiness and witness to the world. Discernible Christian forms of each of these features may readily be found, and however much room there may be for improvement, that is all that can be required.

It may be objected that in some of these activities there is only a minimal Christian content, and that they may represent no more than African conservatism maintaining the forms inherited from the older Churches, or African imitation of externals devoid of understanding; this criticism might be levelled against the celebration of the Lord's Supper in the Church of the Lord. On the other hand there is today a good deal of dissatisfaction with the rather mechanical use of these outward signs of the visible Church, coupled with a search for better criteria.

One step in this direction is to concentrate upon the relationship to the Scriptures as the main criterion or mark. Greenslade, in a discussion of how to decide whether a body is a Church or not, insists that we should ask not what it lacks but what it possesses, and declares acceptance of the authority of the Bible to be the first requisite.[3] On this basis Parrinder was able to distinguish between the Holy Ethiopian Community Church in Ibadan, which rejects the Bible, and the secession from it known as the Ethiopian Communion Church which returned to use of the Bible.[4] The former is not a Church, despite its name; the latter has adopted the first visible sign of a Christian Church, however confused its interpretation of the Scriptures may be. By this criterion the Church of the Lord, which essays to establish all belief and practice on the Bible, is definitely a Church. An account could be given of its use of 'Scripture proofs', its Bible classes and the hunger of the young ministers for 'more Bible', the formal place of the Bible in the Constitution and its regular use in worship, the injunctions to possess and use one's own copy, and the bringing of revelations and visions to the bar of Scripture. Even though much of this use is ignorant and selective, the remedy for these defects is largely contained in the Scriptures themselves, which are potent in the long run to reform their own abuse. This is undoubtedly the best single visible mark of a genuine Church among the African independent movements.

The possibility, at least, in the short run, of a completely unchristian interpretation or use of the Bible leads to the application of a further criterion at this point. Greenslade suggests formal acceptance of the Apostles' Creed as an indication of an orthodox interpretation of Scripture, but in Africa this acceptance may be no more than vestigial or imitative, and give no indication of the actual message that is being extracted from the Bible or received through it. As Barth has expressed it, what counts is not the mere possession, honouring or formal acceptance of the Bible as the law of the Church's faith and order, but whether it actually does witness to Jesus Christ.[5]

Once we have reached the criterion of witness to Jesus Christ we have left the readily visible marks of the Church. This is what Molland has done in his search for criteria when he rejects the Bible itself as the adequate visible sign, and says that:

> Any faith which rests upon and is permeated by ['belief in Jesus Christ as the Son of God, as Lord and Saviour'] must be said to lie within the limits of Christendom . . .[6]

This is similar to the criterion used by the World Council of Churches since 1948. In 1960 this was qualified by the addition of 'according to the Scriptures'. The Church of the Lord would have no difficulty in assenting to all these formulations, any more than it has in reciting the Apostles' Creed, but we do not regard this as a suitable criterion for use among the prophet-healing Churches. It is too doctrinal for Churches that do not express themselves in this way, but are only too willing to do so if required, and it does not take account of the Pentecostal forms of African church where the viewpoint is pneumatological rather than Christological. These need criteria that are more dynamic and less doctrinal.

The Use of Scripture as a Mark of the Church

It is well known that various Christian Churches possess their own characteristic tradition of hermeneutics and exegesis. Robert Friedman, in an article in 1940,[7] suggested a comparative analysis of these different traditions, in order to discover their use of the Bible and especially of the different emphases within the New Testament. He was concerned with placing the Anabaptists in relation to other sections of the Church in the Reformation period, and suggested that a more satisfactory typology of Christian groups could be established on this basis. In his tabulation he shows that the Evangelical Anabaptists, and other Evangelical groups such as Franciscans and Waldenses, together with the humanists and rationalists, favoured the Synoptic Gospels; Luther and Zwingli emphasized the four gospels, but the Gospel of John was preferred by the Eastern Orthodox Church and by mystic and spiritual groups; the Pauline Epistles were of importance both in churchly and Pietist quarters; the Revelation of John was little used except by millenarian and antinomian groups, for whom it was decisive; in addition, the place assigned to the Old Testament varied considerably and the study of this might also assist in the typology of different forms of the Christian Church.

The results of our own study of the typology of modern African religious movements have been presented elsewhere. We have not used Friedman's suggestions for our typology, although they deserve to be followed up in ecumenical studies; rather have we applied his ideas about the importance of the way Scripture is used to the more fundamental question of the criteria of a Christian Church. To do this we have developed a method whereby the use of Scripture revealed in preaching may be analysed objectively, and interpreted in a reasonably reliable fashion, to display the version of Christianity that obtains in a particular Church.

THE METHOD

Texts as an Index of Preaching

The Church of the Lord, as we have seen, desires to be a genuinely biblical church. Evidence of how far this is achieved is offered at many points in the life of a church, but nowhere more frequently and more overtly than in its preaching. It was possible to secure extensive information about the texts chosen for preaching—from the printed C.M.S. preacher's book or record of services which every congregation is supposed to possess, and from a few supplementary sources. Where records were extensive, sets of texts for complete calendar years were taken at intervals over the period; otherwise all texts over the few recorded years were used. In this way some eight thousand sermon texts were gathered. These represented preaching in many large and small churches, both rural and urban, in all four countries, by all levels and kinds of ministers, and over all three decades of the Church's life. This material is certainly thoroughly representative, and even if it does not always correspond to the actual content of the sermons based upon it, we do have a comprehensive indication of the parts of the Bible which the ministry is reading and of the particular texts that appeal most strongly.

Before proceeding further, we had to take account of a factor outside the Church of the Lord which could have influenced its choice of texts—the lectionary for Sunday lessons in the C.M.S. publication, *The West African Churchman's Calendar*, which has long been widely used. It has not been possible to compare the texts, Sunday by Sunday, with the lessons in this lectionary over the past thirty years, but in the few tests we were able to make from the 1961 *Calendar* no correlation could be found. This result was confirmed by inspection of the whole body of texts, when the influence of this or any other lectionary was excluded on the following grounds: 1. A common lectionary would have produced some identity of texts in different branches of the Church at the same time of the year; there was no such identity wherever we tested the data. 2. The C.M.S. lectionary would have produced a grouping of texts from individual books over successive Sundays, and a progression of passages through the book. There was no such grouping or progression, and texts were irregularly distributed. 3. The C.M.S. lectionary uses the Apocrypha of the Old Testament; in 1961 morning and evening Old Testament lessons for a month were entirely from this source. There were no lessons from these books in the Church of the Lord data. 4. Some books, especially in the Old Testament, do not appear in lectionaries, or only very rarely. The Psalter is not used by the C.M.S. lectionary, but supplies many Church of the Lord texts, and these also come from books such as Esther, Song of Solomon and Lamentations. 5. There is a preference for certain books in most lectionaries, so that Genesis and Isaiah, for example, are found more often than Proverbs and Ecclesiastes, or Mark's Gospel more often than the Epistle of James. As we shall see from the final results, the preference in the Church of the Lord texts, in these and in other books, is distinctly different from that of the C.M.S. lectionary. We therefore concluded that the sermon texts may be accepted as a fair indication of the mind of the Church, rather than as a reflection of some outside influence of this kind.

Methods of Analyzing the Texts

This volume of material could be handled only by mathematical methods, and we endeavoured to follow a procedure that might be adopted for the analysis of similar information in other African studies, or even elsewhere. Our first enquiry was into the comparative extent to which the different books of the Bible, and the Old and New Testaments, were used. Having ascertained the number of texts chosen from each of the books of Scripture, we had then to decide on an equitable basis for comparing the different degrees to which the books were used; for example, did the two texts from Philemon represent a greater or a lesser *degree* of use than the 126 texts from the much longer book of Jeremiah? It was evident that the only quantitatively fixed unit was the printed page. This had two disadvantages: that fractions of pages had to be gauged accurately, especially in the smaller books, and that the resultant figure of number of texts per page varied according to the edition of the Bible used in the enquiry. This variation also meant that the figures used in one enquiry would not correspond to those of others, but this was of no importance, for the figures had no significance in themselves, but only as a means of comparison of one book against another. Any printed text would provide a table of degree of use of all the books of the Bible that was strictly comparable with any other table drawn up by the same method but from another printing.

For the purposes of our table we have treated Genesis Chs. 1–11 separately from the remaining historical chapters, with a result that is significant. We have also allowed ourselves one adjustment in the position of a book: Malachi proved to be first among Old Testament books and fourth in the whole Bible, but this was found to be due to unusually extensive use of 3:8–10. This passage on tithing was used no less than fifty-two times out of a total of seventy-three sermons from Malachi; we concluded that this text happens to have become the basis for financial appeals, and that its elimination would give a fairer estimate of the use of the book. This kind of adjustment is necessary only for a small book and was not required apart from Malachi.

When the table of degree of use has been constructed, an attempt must be made to explain the relative positions of the different books and why some appeal more than others. To do this we must examine the material used within each book and, especially where a book contains diverse material, we must seek out the parts that are most used. For this kind of internal analysis the page unit is too large, and we have fallen back on the number of texts or selections per verse. With this procedure we are able to analyse, say, the doctrinal as against the ethical sections of the Epistle to the Ephesians, and to discover that the former averages .33 selections or references per verse, but the latter averages 1.4, and so may be said to be used over four times as much, a result with a significance which we hope to set forth below.

It should be pointed out that a proportion of the texts or references consist of more than one verse, and occasionally of a passage of six or seven verses. We have regarded all references, long or short, as one instance representing one sermon and, since practically all favourite texts consisted of a single verse, we have found no special difficulty at this point. We should also make it plain that although mathematical methods have been used, with results sometimes expressed to two places of decimals, we draw our conclusions not from these figures in themselves, but only from the comparisons they provide between the use of different parts of books of the Bible.

CONCLUSIONS

The Profile of the Church of the Lord

The results of our main analysis of the use of books of Scripture, together with a selection of our sectional analyses, are presented in visual form in the profiles appended. It must be distinctly remembered that these do not depict the number of texts from the various books or sections, but the *degree of use* measured by the index we have described. The general results of this study may be summarized as follows:

1. The Church of the Lord does use the whole Bible, in all its books, as a basis for its preaching and in expression of its desire to be a biblical Church.

2. There is considerable difference in the extent to which different types of books, and different kinds of material within individual books, are used, and these differences are usually correlated with particular features of the

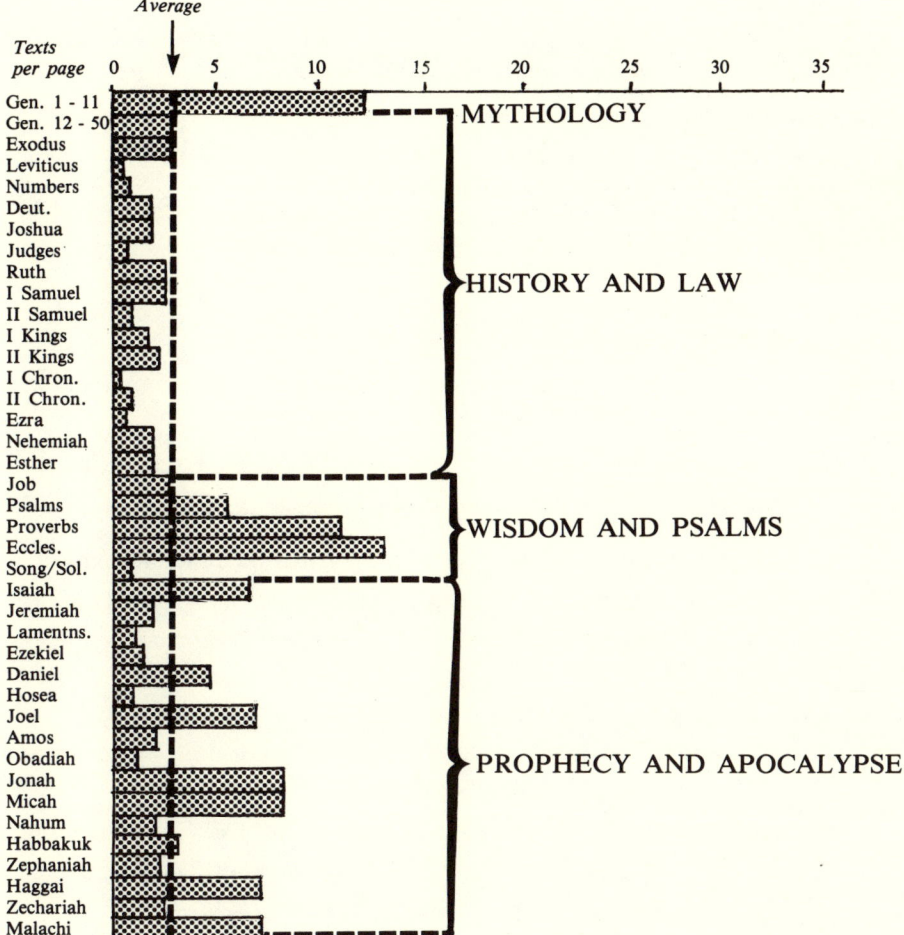

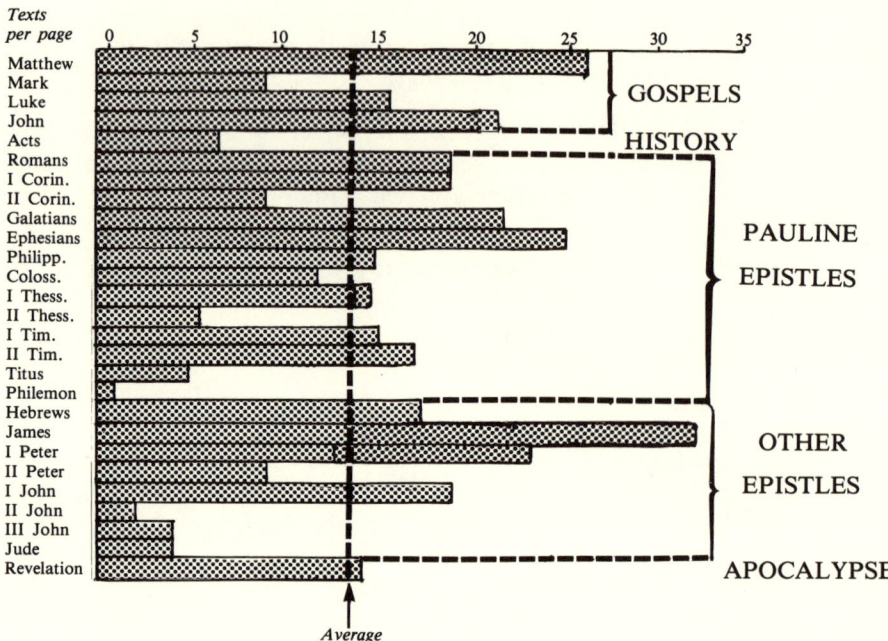

Church (such as tithes, vows, fasting, barrenness, healing, etc.), or with its interpretation of the Christian faith as a whole.

3. The order of preference among the different types of literature is:

    a. Wisdom, and practical teaching, moral or religious, including James.

    b. Gospels and Epistles, with the emphasis on the didactic and ethical.

    c. Mythology, as in Genesis 1–11, to which might be added individual stories from the historical books of the Old Testament treated as archetypal stories.

    d. Apocalyptic books, not because of the apocalyptic and symbolic material, but on account of the related elements of warning, judgment and deliverance.

    e. Prophetic literature.

    f. Historical, legal and personal material, whether in the Old Testament, the Gospels, Acts, or the Epistles.

4. The New Testament is used three times as intensively as the Old, and fairly evenly through its major divisions.

5. The themes of the Kingdom of God in the Gospels, of justification through faith in the Pauline Epistles, and of the person and work of Christ in the New Testament as a whole, escape attention, but emphasis is given to the themes of life and of the spirit in John's Gospel, and to the Resurrection in various books.

6. The Christian faith is interpreted as a new moral and religious law, which can be obeyed only through the gracious help of God given especially through the Holy Spirit, and also through Jesus Christ the teacher. Those who confess and repent of sin, and obey God, are rewarded by deliverance from the present evils of this world and by enjoyment of God's blessings, but they must continue in their endeavours, ever mindful of the final judgment, beyond which lie further blessings for the faithful and punishment for all others.

This is what the Church of the Lord is actually hearing through the Scriptures. It may seem to contain only a muted testimony to Christ, and a very legal and moral emphasis, but however unbalanced or distorted, the preaching remains a form of Christian exposition and proclamation—it cannot be called Jewish, Muslim or pagan preaching. No sufficient reason emerges from our study of the use of Scripture by this African body to justify a refusal to admit it into the category of a Christian Church.

The version of the Gospel described above is also remarkably similar to that found in Independent Churches in Northern Rhodesia and in parts of South Africa, as reported by Taylor and Lehmann,[8] by Pauw,[9] and by Monica Wilson.[10] We suspect, therefore, that this interpretation of Christianity is common to many of the newer Independent Churches in Africa, and may indeed be more widespread among the older Churches and missions in this continent, and elsewhere in the Christian world, than we have yet recognized.

Method

When we began the analysis of the 8,000 texts we had little idea of where it might lead us or the methods that would be developed. If the selections, made by a largely uneducated ministry, were in fact haphazard, with small relation to content or meaning, then there would be little variation over the various parts of Scripture, and no significant pattern would emerge. At the other extreme, one could imagine a Church with an educated ministry, very conscious of its own form of the Christian faith, and seeking to inculcate this in the members through preaching as in other ways; here we should expect a highly selective use of Scripture which

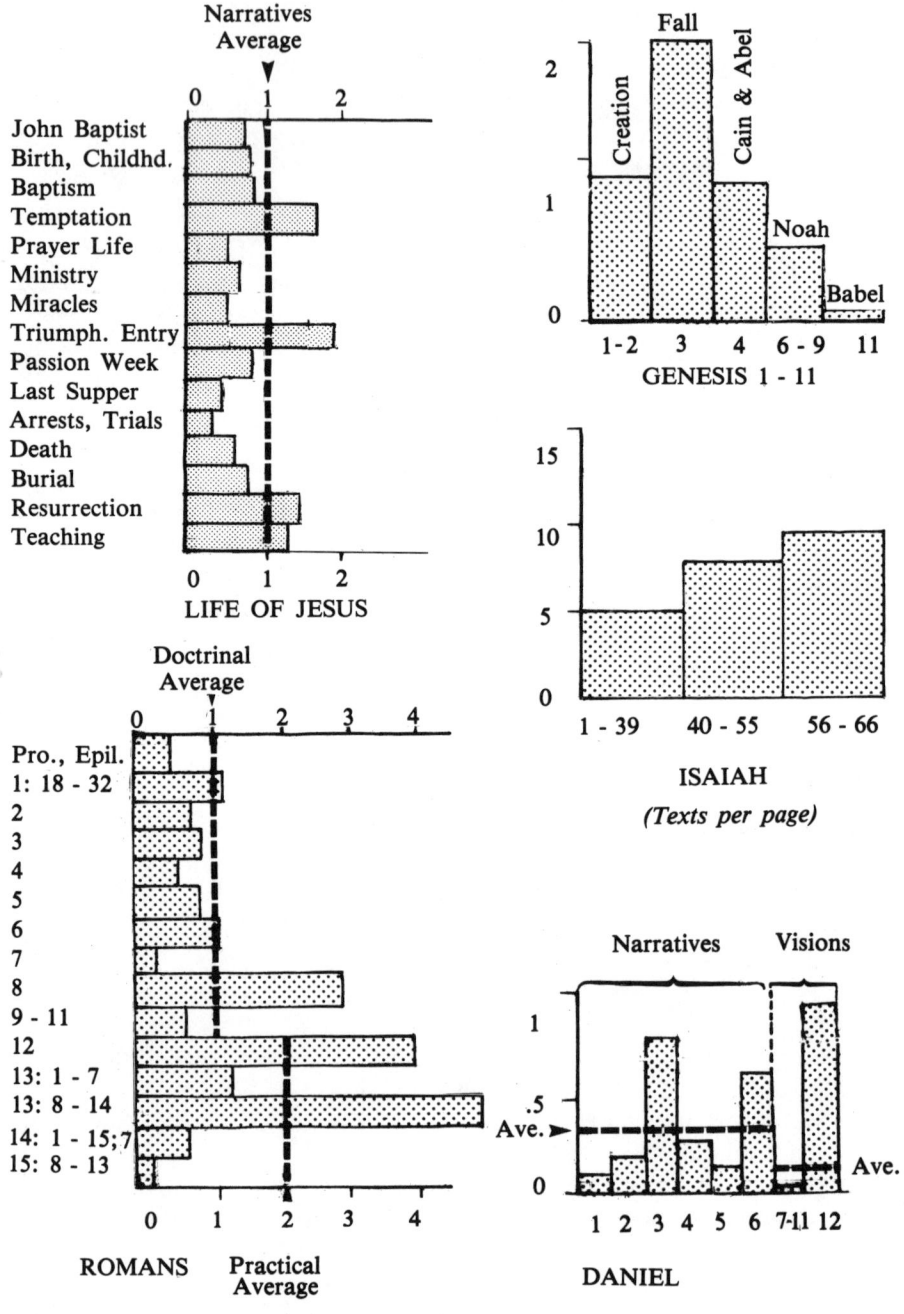

mirrored the predilections of the Church rather than its actual existence. The Church of the Lord certainly has a special view of the faith which it seeks to propagate, but we doubted whether the ministry was sufficiently sophisticated to use the Bible in this way. In between these two positions there is the possibility of a less self-conscious use of Scripture, whereby the texts chosen reflect the understanding of Christianity that operates in the Church as a whole; in this case the Church as it were unconsciously 'gives itself away', if a sufficiently large number of its preaching texts is examined. We hoped that this might be so in the Church we were studying.

It soon became apparent that there was a definite correlation between the choice of the texts and at least some of the features of the Church of the Lord, so that we were encouraged to pursue the analysis with as much thoroughness as we could command. Naturally some sections have proved more rewarding than others, but as the results now stand before us we feel that the lineaments of the Church can be traced, here more clearly and there more faintly, but almost always evident to some degree, throughout its use of the Bible. As we have sought to follow the impress of the Church in its choice of texts, its own features have become more plainly revealed to us in what we may call a Church profile, based on the shape of its preaching texts.

We would point out that the Church we have studied is fairly uniform in its interpretations of the Christian faith; the application of this method to a Church with little theological homogeneity might produce results neither clear nor reliable, for those from one party would mask those of another, and the overall profile, while mathematically correct, would represent an interpretation of the Scriptures that had little relation to the life of the Church.

If within these or other limits that may appear, this method helps us to follow up Friedman's suggestions, and to place the comparative study of Churches on a more systematic basis, there is no reason why it should be limited to African studies; given the further development and refinement that it no doubt requires, it might well become useful in ecumenical church study, providing, of course, that the high correlations we have found in one case obtain also in a number of other Churches. If we may allow ourselves a speculation here, it is conceivable that from a large number of such church profiles it would be possible to establish a 'normal range' within which an identifiably Christian Church should lie, and within this range certain 'type-profiles' associated with the various Christian emphases and ecclesiastical forms. Thus it might be found that there was a typical Lutheran, Roman Catholic, Methodist, or Pentecostal profile, and that there were other profiles representing older or younger Churches, African, Asian, or Western Churches. It is also possible that deviant bodies such as the Mormons or Jehovah's Witnesses would be revealed as such by the extreme distortions or variations in the graphs of their use of Scripture, which would then help to establish the limits of a Christian profile. If this were so, then we should have a new instrument for studies in typology and in comparative ecclesiology, for in the shape of the preaching there lies a portrait of the Church and its Gospel.

Notes

1. *African Independent Church* (1967), especially vol. 2.
2. M. J. Field, *Search for Identity*. London: Faber & Faber, 1960, pp. 77–78.
3. S. L. Greenslade, *Schism in the Early Church*. London: SCM Press, 1953, pp. 214–217.
4. E. G. Parrinder, *Religion in an African City*. London: Oxford University Press, 1953, pp. 127–129.
5. K. Barth, *Church Dogmatics*. Edinburgh: T. & T. Clark, 1956, vol. IV (1), p. 723.
6. E. Molland, *Christendom, the Christian Churches,* ... London: A. R. Mowbray, 1959, pp. 355–356.
7. R. Friedman, The Concept of the Anabaptists, *Church History* 9 (4), 1940, pp. 341–365.
8. J. V. Taylor and D. A. Lehmann. *Christians of the Copperbelt*. London: SCM Press, 1961, pp. 296f.
9. B. A. Pauw, *Religion in a Tswana Chiefdom*. London: Oxford University Press, 1960, pp. 141–144.
10. M. Wilson, *Communal Rituals of the Nyakyusa*. London: Oxford University Press, 1959, p. 187.

21

The Litany of an Independent West African Church

This essay was my first attempt at analysing material from an African independent church. The theological results, and the relationships to Anglican Western and to African cultures that were revealed, proved so interesting that I felt encouraged to further enquiries into the life and documents of the church with which I was becoming involved. Probes into other aspects of the church, such as its catechism and then its preaching (as in the previous essay) produced similar theological results so that each study began to confirm the accuracy of the others. The fullest treatment is contained in volume two of African Independent Church, *although this does not include the analysis of the sermon texts.*

One of the West African independent or separatist churches which has spread from Nigeria to Sierra Leone, has produced and published what it calls "The Holy Litany".[1] This litany invites examination for various reasons. The Church is one of the many similar bodies that have emerged from the Anglican Church in Nigeria, and therefore we may expect

---

Sierra Leone Bulletin of Religion 1 (2), 1959, pp. 45–55; reprinted in *Practical Anthropology* 7 (6), 1960, pp. 256–262, and in *African Independent Church*, vol. 2, pp. 161–168.

to find the origins of such a litany, at least to some extent, in the Book of Common Prayer. The litany itself is published as the work of the founder and head of this particular church, and so may be accepted as having authority and as representative of this church's outlook. And finally, since a litany is a very flexible and adaptable liturgical form, examination of this example may be expected to reveal something of the way in which an African church adopts Western liturgical material and adapts it to local needs and ways of thought.

The "Litany or Penitent Supplication before God during Lenten" is used in Lent and on other special occasions. The title contains echoes of the first rubric of the Litany in the Book of Common Prayer. The latter then commences with its invocation of the Trinity, Person by Person, to "have mercy upon miserable sinners". The African litany also follows a three-fold pattern in its opening section but without any reference to the Trinity. The three-fold form is merely repetitive, as follows:—

Priest. We use our mouths like broom before Thee.
Cong. *Good Lord, have mercy upon us.*

This is repeated twice more, all kneeling and bowed to the ground throughout, and then concludes:—

Priest. We great sinners humbly supplicate before thee.
Cong. *Good Lord forgive us.*

The whole litany is built around this unit, which divides the litany into its three main sections and also provides the conclusion; thus it occurs four times altogether. However different this introduction may seem from that in the Prayer Book, the theme, mercy upon sinners, is the same.

This theme is then developed in the first of the three sections of the litany, devoted to the confession of particular sins named in fifteen versicles, with the standard response, *Good Lord, forgive us.* At this point the Anglican litany proceeds to a series of deprecations, beseeching deliverance from various evils, including sins, but not directly confessing these latter. The African litany has clearly borrowed from this section, for six of the versicles show a direct derivation from the parent litany, and two others embody phrases found elsewhere in the Prayer Book. Three versicles suggest emphasis relevant to West Africa or to special teaching of this particular church—"our sins of pilfering and stealing . . . despising prophesyings . . . disobeying the Voice."

After a repetition of the introductory broom-theme there follows the second main section, a series of fifteen deprecations. These follow the same themes as those to be found in the corresponding section in the Book of Common Prayer, except for those which have been covered already by transference to the first sections as sins to be confessed. The versicles either repeat the Anglican phrases, or else expand or adapt them. These changes are of two kinds. The first is by way of application to the African situation; the particular evils from which deliverance is sought now include witches and wizards, poisonous locusts, flies, drought, and more curiously, black butterflies and birds. The second change would seem to be an expansion of the single reference to the day of judgment in the Prayer Book deprecations. This is now developed at some length through six versicles based on Biblical language drawn from apocalyptic passages, especially Joel ii–iii, which is a favourite section in this church. We find prayers for deliverance from the days when there shall be "intense darkness" (Joel ii. 2), "war and rumours of war" (Mt. xxiv. 6), "the sun . . . become dark" (Joel ii. 10, 31; iii. 15; Mt. xxiv. 29), "the moon . . . become blood" (Joel ii. 31; iii. 15; Acts ii. 20), and when "the stars . . . shall fall down" (Joel ii. 10; iii. 15; Dan viii. 10).

The concluding prayer is for deliverance "on the day of thy Holy appearance."

Once again the broom-theme appears before the next main section. From this point there seems to be an almost complete divergence from the pattern of the Anglican litany. This proceeds through observations based on the life and work of Jesus Christ, a long series of intercessions, and further petitions, to the Agnus Dei, a Kyrie eleison, and the Lord's Prayer, followed by further supplications incorporating the Gloria. Only the Gloria remains of all this, together with a few references to themes found in these intercessions or petitions, but now included in what is the longest of the three sections of the African litany, a series of twenty-seven versicles on the theme of "victory" over various evils.

Although this "victory" section contains no more than three specific references that could have come from the Anglican litany, the whole may be regarded as a peculiarly African development of two related themes in the latter part of the parent form. The first of these occurs in the collect after the Lord's Prayer: ". . . hear us, that those evils which the craft and subtilty of the devil or of man worketh against us, be brought to nought." The second follows immediately in the Prayer Book in what were originally special intercessions in time of war, with "From our enemies defend us, O Christ" as its central petition. The African litany prays for victory over a great range of enemies, both fleshly and ghostly, which have been the traditional disturbers of African life. In only three of the twenty-seven versicles are the enemies of an impersonal nature—"death", "bad talismans", and "blood enemies and unknown disease". All the rest are personal evil powers, ranging from Satan through "wizards and witches", "magicians and necromancers", "wicked juju men", "soothsayers and those who curse us", "quack doctors and herbalists", to the more prosaic "talebearers and gossips", and those "who feign friendship with us".

Thus even where the African litany might seem to depart most widely from the form and content of its original, it still keeps company with it in spirit and intention. If we could realize more vividly just what were the evils which the England of four hundred years ago believed "the craft and subtilty of the devil or man" worked against it, we should almost certainly find still more in common between the African and the English worshippers as they used their respective litanies.

"The Holy Litany" then concludes with the broom theme and a Gloria identical with that in the latter part of the Prayer Book form.

With the "shape of the litany" now before us, let us consider its literary form. Its general arrangement is similar to that in the Book of Common Prayer and we have seen that its vocabulary is also somewhat similar. Its structure, however, is much simpler, with three sections each of which is a unity both in form and in theme, and with the fourfold "brooming" introducing, punctuating, and concluding the litany. In comparison the English form is more complex, especially after the Lord's Prayer, and to that extent lacks an easily appreciable unity. It has been suggested that what is really a second litany, after the Lord's Prayer, would be better omitted, and the 1928 proposed Prayer Book took the step of separating this section as an optional supplication.[2]

That the African litany has moved in the direction of a more primitive, simpler literary form is to be seen most clearly in the short sentences of the versicles, each with its own response of roughly equal length. This was the usual form of the pre-Reformation litanies of the West before several versicles were combined and the number of responses reduced accordingly.[3] Cranmer combined the versicles of his sources, and produced the threefold biddings found in the deprecations in his English litany. Similarly, his biddings to intercession are almost all much longer than their responses. This increase in brevity and rapidity has been described as a doubtful gain.[4] The African form is highly antiphonal and rhythmical, and of course has a larger part for the people. Is it too much to suggest that there is a sound liturgical instinct at work here, and at work in the same direction as that to be found in a number of modern service books?[5]

The theological content of these African prayers must now be noted. As compared with their English counterpart the range of prayer is severely restricted by being confined to confessions with prayers for forgiveness, and to petitions for protection and victory, with a total absence of the intercessions that form one of the finest features of Cranmer's litany. This omission cannot be due to an indifference to intercession, for in other services prayers are regularly offered; e.g. for "the Archbishop of Canterbury and for all ministers throughout the world". It is possible that there has been a failure in adaptation at this point, a point where the prayers of a long established church in Europe are too remote from the situation and the present stage of development of a comparatively new separatist church in West Africa. Several illustrations of this might be offered. English worshippers knew what they were doing when they prayed for the Royal Family at some length, and for the "Lords of the Council and all the Nobility", together with "the Magistrates". What immediate equivalents would suggest themselves to African worshippers in a small sect under a colonial regime? And again, "the fatherless children, and widows" whom God is asked to defend in England, need no such defence in traditional African society, which has its own ways of providing for its less fortunate members. And finally, while the fine flower of the Christian attitude is to be seen in the intercession of the Prayer Book for "our enemies, persecutors, and slanderers", African Christians are more concerned with deliverance from a very extensive range of deadly enemies. The African litany fails to maintain the achievement of the Anglican litany at this point, and reverts to the level of the ancient litanies in their preoccupation with deliverance from dangers.

A theological restriction of a different kind is to be found in the form of the approach to God. God is addressed throughout as "Good Lord", and the only reference to the Trinity is in the concluding Gloria, which is more of a praise-ending than a basis of approach to God. The English litany of course uses "Good Lord" regularly in its responses, but not exclusively. There are also responses where the address is to the Persons of the Trinity, and other sections where the approach is to Christ as in the Agnus Dei and the Kyrie, and above all in the obsecrations where our deliverance is specifically based upon the work of Christ on our behalf through reference to about twelve aspects of his life and work. All this is absent from the African litany. To this extent it is less specifically Christian, and would be more capable of use by any theist and by the semi-pagan.

The view of God implied in this litany may be described as follows. God is in control of all society, nature, death, and evil powers including Satan, and God will act to reveal his control both now and in the future consummation. God is good and demands both an inner and an outer morality in men, and a morality that shows derivation at some points from the Christian ethic. God is merciful to those who confess their sins. And finally, there is at least formal recognition that God is triune. This theological outlook would seem to pass beyond the boundaries of traditional African religious thought, even though they clearly have much in common. The direct reference of all men's needs to the supreme God, and the strong repudiation of all other spiritual powers as sources of help, is a major change. The specifically Christian features in the ethical outlook of the litany are harder to trace, but the references to heresy and schism as sins, to the sins of thought, of pride and selfwill, of stiff-neckedness and hard-heartedness, suggest Christian or biblical sources. The eschatology is clearly biblical in its expressions. The Gloria likewise represents a distinctively Christian element.

The indigenous or specifically African nature of the litany remains to be considered. The best approach to this is to be reminded first that the Anglican litany grew out of the particular situation and needs of England towards the middle of the sixteenth century. A succession of troubles, bad weather, disease, and wars, had led Henry to issue a letter in 1543 desiring the people to pray for deliverance from these continuing evils. The small response was explained as due to the people not understanding the Latin prayers used, and so Cranmer was asked to prepare prayers in the vernacular that would be more effective. He did so by adapting earlier material from England and the Continent, and adding his own important contributions. The Litany of 1544 was therefore an attempt, and a successful one, to adapt the old to a new situation; and it properly reflects the particular state of England at the time. The occasional prayers that follow in the Book of Common Prayer, and that may be used to supplement the Litany, reveal this situation quite clearly, with their themes of rain, fair weather, dearth and famine, wars and tumults, and plague or sickness.

The African litany is also an attempt to adapt the old that it has received in order to meet the needs of the new situation in which such an independent church finds itself. There is first a recognition that a church does need the support of liturgical forms, but that these must speak to the people who use them. If with this in mind we examine the contents of the first section of prayers of confession and for forgiveness, we notice the particular sins referred to above deriving from the special teaching of this church, and also a group of sins not usually included as relevant in Western confessions—"pilfering and stealing", "murder by word and deed", "adultery and fornication". There is some reason to believe that the members of this church have a record above the average on these matters. At the same time it is clear that petty theft and sexual irregularities are among the most common moral failures in "areas of rapid social change" such as those where this church was founded and where it works. Is there possibly a vicarious aspect to the inclusion of these sins? There is certainly a very direct reference to the social context of the Church.

A still more clearly indigenous aspect of this litany is the overwhelming emphasis on deliverance from and victory over a wide range of evil forces. This theme might be said to occupy about fifteen per cent of the Anglican litany, but no less than about seventy-five per cent of the African. While it has been suggested above that the medieval Englishman and the modern African might have much in common in the *kind* of evils they faced, the *range* of evil powers and the general insecurity of life would seem to be much greater for the African. It would be wrong to imagine that the pre-occupation with evil powers in this litany is an archaic element, a reference to the insecurities of life in the African past, and a failure to enter into the emancipation offered by the Christian Faith. Many observers agree that in certain fundamental respects life was never more insecure, more bewildering and uncertain, than it is to-day for Africans in the areas that have changed most. They have to deal with the meeting of two cultures as the medieval Englishman did not. One of the chief signs of this increase in insecurity is the widely remarked upsurge of witchcraft in those parts of Africa where it was most expected to vanish before the impact of education, medical care, industrialization and urbanization.[7] A litany that is extensively concerned with all the practitioners of evil medicine and witchcraft and that repudiates them so strongly, is both Christian and relevant to its own social environment.

There remains one particularly interesting indigenous feature that deserves further comment, that of the "chorus" with its symbolic action, "we use our mouths like broom before Thee". The kneeling worshippers are bowed with their faces to the ground, where some actually do brush the floor with their lips as they pray, while others are content with action a few inches away. Various explanations as to the meaning and origin of this practice have been offered to the writer. Intelligent Yoruba youths, not members of this church, explained it as a sign of humiliation and penance before a powerful Yoruba king in former times, a performance which might be voluntary or might be commanded by the king as a punishment. As this church is Yoruba in origin, we could expect this historical background to be relevant. A prominent leader in the church, while recognizing the truth of this, proffered direct relevation to the founder of the church as the origin of this element in the litany; he also suggested, as other members of the church have done, that our speech needed sweeping clean and that this was akin to the story of Isaiah, the man conscious of unclean lips. (Isaiah vi. 5). If we are to take the symbolism literally it seems rather inverted, for it is the floor that is swept with the lips as broom, rather than the lips and their speech that are cleansed. Such niceties, however, are probably irrelevant. It is more likely that here we have an introductory element, representing both reverence and humiliation before God, and also the need for cleansing, before proceeding to the prayers. If this is true then we have an example of a congenial African cultural element, being developed and applied in terms of a biblical image. The whole process, consciously or unconsciously, suggests an insight into one of the profound emphases of the Bible, on the importance of speech and on the extensive evil effects of the Fall on the work of the tongue (James iii).

We may gather up the results of our survey of "The Holy Litany" in four propositions:

1. The Christian form and content, largely derived from the Litany in the Book of Common Prayer, have been simplified as to form and reduced in Christian reference as to content.

2. African interpretations and references have been widely introduced to make the litany relevant to the outlook and needs of the worshippers who use it.

3. A distinctively African symbolic rite has been developed on lines at least congenial to the Bible and appropriately incorporated in the litany.

4. Incompatible ideas from African traditional religion have not intruded, but have been avoided or specifically rejected.

Notes

1. *Catechism of the Church of the Lord (Aladura) . . . And The Holy Litany . . . with the Church Prayer Drill,* Ogere Headquarters, Nigeria, 19. 8. 48.
2. Procter and Frere, *A History of the Book of Common Prayer,* 3rd edn., 1949, p. 425.
3. For an excellent example of earlier forms, see W. D. Maxwell, *Concerning Worship,* 1948, 29 ff., quoting in abbreviated form "The Litany of Dunkeld", ninth century, from J. Cooper, *Reliques of Ancient Scottish Devotion,* 1913, pp. 24 ff.
4. Procter and Frere, *op. cit.,* pp. 415 f.
5. For an African example developed under missionary auspices, see the litanies in *A Christian People's Worship,* Tigerkloof, 1952, pp. 61 ff. This is a translation of *Kobamelo* in Tswana, for the Church in Bechuanaland.
6. Procter and Frere, *op. cit.,* pp. 31–32, on the circumstances of Cranmer's litany.
7. For example: special issue of *Africa,* viii, 4 (1935); Barbara E. Ward, Some Observations on Religious cults in Ashanti, *Africa,* xxvi, p. 47; M. J. Field, Some New Shrines of the Gold Coast and Their Significance, *Africa,* xiii, (1940) 138 ff.; Max Marwick, The Continuance of Witchcraft Beliefs, in P. Smith (ed), *Africa in Transition,* 1958, pp. 106 ff.; E. G. Parrinder, *African Traditional Religion,* 1954, pp. 133, 144; M. A. C. Warren, *C.M.S. Newsletter,* July, 1957, *passim.*

F. MISSIOLOGICAL

This section opens with a general statement of the place of the religions of primal societies, and of their new religious movements, in the whole sweep of Christian history. Then follows a detailed case study of one of the chief problems in cross-cultural communication between sophisticated and primal societies, a problem that emerges very clearly in many of the new religious movements. The third essay presents a general consideration of two-way missions between the West and Africa, and is in a more popular vein. Most of the material in other essays has missiological relevance in varying degrees, but especially in essays one, thirteen and fourteen, and seventeen to twenty.

22

A Further Dimension for Missions: New Religious Movements in the Primal Societies

An attempt is here made to explain the phenomena of new movements to the Christian mission constituency for which this journal caters, and to show their significance by setting them in the widest historical context, that of Christian expansion since the first century. It was assumed that readers might know nothing of these developments; some of the basic explanatory material has been deleted since it is dealt with in other essays.

The tone is perhaps somewhat aggressive since the aim was to stir fellow-believers into action! It also boldly uses our domestic anagram or code-word for the phenomena — NERMS, for New Religious Movements. *The brief outlines of particular relations between missions and NERMS needs expansion to present a full view of the increasing number of projects taking up this new task. A similar but briefer version appeared in* Milligan Missiogram *(Milligan College, Tennessee) 2 (1), 1974, pp. 13–16.*

    The setting for this essay is provided by a vivid image from Professor Alan Tippett when he pointed out a new 'fact of global significance — that the great animist world is "turning over" like an iceberg in our day,

---

International Review of Mission no. 247, vol. 62, 1973, pp. 321–337.

and taking up a new position which may be a determining factor in world history for the next century. Whether we like it or not, millions of people are changing from something old to something new . . . culturally and spiritually this is their "fulness of time".[1]

We shall outline the peculiar place 'the great animist world' has held in the history of Christian expansion, the changes and disillusionments that are occurring in this world today, and the emergence of its own vast range of new religious movements subsequent to encounter with the Christian faith in modern times. Against this backdrop we shall explore the new historical, ecumenical and missiological perspectives they provide. Finally, the new movements will be examined as a further dimension of missionary action, with some account of beginnings that have been made.

I. CHRISTIAN EXPANSION AND THE PRIMAL SOCIETIES

Since there are objections to the use of terms such as 'tribal', 'primitive', or 'animist' we are using the more innocuous and we hope accurate word 'primal' for the religions and societies concerned. It is these primal peoples who appear to hold a unique place in Christian history. Any overview of this history reveals a geographical expansion in two great waves. The first gathered up the Mediterranean world and spread out to include the continent of Europe; the second arose with the expansion of the Christian European peoples into most of the rest of the world from the sixteenth to the twentieth centuries. As a result both of their missionary labours and of their settlement abroad the Christian faith has become established in almost every region of the globe.

Closer examination reveals that there is no room for triumphalism at this 'great new fact of our time', a world-wide church, for the remarkable geographical extension has been accompanied by an equally remarkable cultural constriction. In no major cultural area has there been a general replacement of any of the 'higher' or more sophisticated religions in its own territory by the Christian faith. The great Asian religions and Islam are not only intact but have revealed remarkable capacities for further development. We are not forgetting the notable Christian communities planted in their midst, but these remain tiny minorities, even though their influence is often out of all proportion to their size.

By and large the only cultural areas to accept the Christian faith have been those where the prevailing religions were of the primal kind. The public and popular religions of Greece, Rome and much of the ancient Near East were essentially primal in nature, albeit associated with sophisticated cultures. The religions of Europe were also primal, like those of all the other areas where Christianity has made great advances. These include Oceania — already a Christian culture area, and Black Africa which promises to become the first new Christian sub-continent. The Americas and Australia became Christian areas through European Christian expansion rather than by the conversion of the indigenous peoples. It is significant that in Asia the only major responses in terms of whole areas or peoples have again been among the primals, especially the 'hill tribals' of Taiwan, Southeast Asia, and India (e.g. the Nagas, nearly half a million of them and over half of these Christian), but also in parts of Indonesia and especially in the Philippines, 'the most Christian part of Asia'.

The Christian world has not yet reckoned with this striking fact, that its main expansion so far has been either into primal cultures or into those more sophisticated cultures that retained a primal form of religion. As a consequence Black Africa and Oceania represent only the second substantial expansion of the faith into a major geographical and cultural area, comparable to the first extension into the Mediterranean and European peoples. And further: after the initial spread into the Mediterranean world, Christianity has depended in each of these advances upon alliance with a culture more sophisticated than that of the peoples it was winning. It moved into Europe in association with a Christianized Graeco-Roman culture, and into the wider world of the primal societies in alliance with the successor Western European culture it had helped to mould.

II. THE NEW SITUATION AMONG THE PRIMAL PEOPLES

The primal peoples form a substantial part of the Third or developing world, and we have some familiarity with the great changes associated with the ending of the colonial era, the advent of political independence, and the commencement of modernization. These changes have their own import for the relation between Christianity and the primal societies, in alliance with other less evident aspects of the new situation which have immediate bearing upon the thesis of this essay. Five of these deserve our attention.

A. Christianity is no longer coincident with Western culture, nor indeed with any sophisticated culture. It is ceasing to enjoy the benefits of such alliance and is being forced to stand on its own merits and even to move into opposition to the culture in which it has thrived for so long. The further advances of Western culture into the world of the primals through its politics, economics and technology will no longer bring with them an advance of the Christian religion; indeed, the effects of this further influence may well be exactly the reverse.

B. Western culture itself no longer commands the awe and admiration it once did among the primal peoples, for in many areas these have given way to profound disillusionment as acquaintance with this culture has increased and the full effects upon the primal world become manifest. Too many of the Western peoples seem unable to manage their own affairs. While most of the white nations have grudgingly brought the colonial period to an end, their economic domination remains and their affluence advances at the expense of continuing poverty in the Third World. In view of the increasing disjunction between Christianity and Western culture this disillusionment might augur well for Christian advance among the primals, were it not for their continuing identification of the two, and their ignorance of the new Christian forms in other cultures more like their own.

C. The loss of confidence in Western culture and its peoples is manifest in the new consciousness of their own identity and the new aggressiveness occurring among the primal peoples. We are familiar with this on the international political scene, as well as in such concepts as 'negritude' and 'Black is beautiful', and in the many efforts at the revival of indigenous arts, crafts and other cultural forms. This new confidence and aggressiveness are nowhere more striking than among a small and weak minority in one of the largest and most powerful Western nations of the world — in the Indian peoples of the United States. Similar awakenings are occurring among primal minorities in like situations — among the Australian aborigines, the New Zealand Maoris, the inhabitants of New Guinea, and tribes in Amazonia or Alaska. In this, their 'fulness of time', these primal peoples 'are preparing to make their appearance on the horizon of greater history (that is they are seeking to become *active subjects* of history instead of its *passive objects*, as they have been hitherto) . . . the peoples of the West are no longer the only ones to "create" history . . .'²

D. On the other hand, a still further disillusionment, partly compounded from the changes we have outlined, is beginning to appear in parts of the primal world where political independence has suddenly replaced a colonial situation. The rising tide of expectations generated during the nationalist struggles for freedom has not been matched by results, and has for some turned into a flood of new disillusionments, conflicts, and frustrations. The post-colonial situation is of course exemplified most in Africa. Here it is possible that there is more sickness and malnutrition, more insecurity and strain, especially in the great urban areas, a greater gap between the rich and the poor, more confused, frightened, and displaced people, more actual refugees from their own homelands, than ever before in its history. This is not to denigrate the achievements of independence which form an impressive catalogue. It is merely to realize that the situation continues to bear heavily upon so many among the primal peoples, in spite of their recent hopes for better things as free nations.

E. Finally, as a further loss of confidence there is also a certain disillusionment with Christianity itself. The new religion often failed to fulfil what were taken, rightly or wrongly, to be its own bright promises to the primal world — a new life of power and abundance in equality with white Christians under the one God, or even the early reunion with their beloved dead in a renewed earth. When neither Christ nor the dead returned many primal peoples have sought for the New Age in their own millennial cults. When the Bible has failed to reveal all the secrets of Western knowledge and power, or has become suspect as a limited or substitute version designed for natives only, prophets have arisen with their own direct revelations from God. When the broken history and manifold denominationalism of Western Christianity are discovered, some in primal societies have begun their own search for the true original Christian Church. And in face of the apparent inadequacies of Western medicine, even in Christian hands, to deal with old and new sicknesses, healing movements of varying religious complexions have appeared. All these developments pay tribute to the effect of the new faith; primal peoples felt there was more in it than they had been given or been able to apprehend from the manner of the missions, and so they sought for its still hidden treasures in their own way.

Other primal peoples 'were tired of Christianity and wanted to have a rest for a while', or else turned to new imported and non-Christian faiths. Thus the Mormons have long had a large following among the Maoris and an intricate relationship with North American Indians; Jehovah's Witnesses have had considerable influence in various parts of Africa, and claim an annual increase of around 8% in Papua-New Guinea; there the Baha'i faith has also been expanding, especially since 1963, as it has in parts of Africa and among Canadian Indians, where it finds nearly half its national membership. A further alternative appears in the revival of magical and occult practices, or in witch-eradicating movements. But whatever the alternative it is likely to represent a loss of confidence in the Christianity encountered earlier.

It seems there is little experience from the past to guide us in this new situation facing the Christian faith in the world of the primal peoples. In the rest of this essay we shall concentrate upon the specifically religious aspect of the situation, represented by the new religious movements that have appeared over the greater part of the primal world as an unrecognized and unexpected consequence of Christian mission and other contacts. We shall call them simply new religious movements among primal peoples, and for convenience assign them the acronym of NERMS.

III. NEW RELIGIOUS MOVEMENTS AMONG THE PRIMAL PEOPLES (NERMS)

As a rough indication of what is included we may mention representative movements across the primal world, using the names most commonly applied to each. There have been some dozen Maori prophet movements in New Zealand, one at least of which has issued in a large independent church; in Polynesia and Melanesia there have been prophet and millennial movements, an important independent church in the Solomons, others in Hawaii, and in the New Guinea area there are the much publicized and numerous cargo cults; the hundreds in the Philippines range from independent churches to highly syncretistic nativistic movements; new nativistic religions often with millennial features have appeared in the Indonesian archipelago, and a few among the hill peoples of Southeast Asia, and of India (in distinction from the Hindu population). In Russian Asia there has been the millennial Burkhan movement in the Altai Mountains since 1904, and in Europe proper the only clear example seems to be the 'Big Candle' cult among the Cheremis of the Upper Volta from the 1870s.

The earliest of all recorded movements occurred in Latin America, commencing in Colombia under the Spanish in 1546, and leading to a whole range of imitation churches, man-gods, second Christs and other messianic forms in subsequent centuries; one of these, the Hallelujah religion in Guyana, has roots nearly a century old, while another, Mama Chi in Panama, began only in 1961. Others have arisen among the imported Negro peoples, such as messianic movements among the Bush Negroes of Surinam, and the complex range of Afro-American and spiritist cults among the Negro and mixed peoples of the Brazil littoral, and of the Caribbean. In North America the Indian peoples produced prophets with highly syncretist and nativistic movements from the mid-eighteenth century, including the famous Ghost Dance of the 1880s. Three important continuing movements are the religion of Handsome Lake among the Iroquois, founded in 1800 and now the oldest continuing prophet movement in the world, the nativistic Indian Shaker Church of the northwest since the 1880s, and the Native American Church or peyote cult which is now about a century old, and as the largest pan-Indian movement of any kind has spread into over fifty tribes. The USA also possesses the oldest independent church among a primal people, continuous since the 1740s among the Narragansetts of Rhode Island; other independent churches may be found among the Seminoles of Florida, the Creeks and many others in Oklahoma, the Hopis, the Apaches and others in Arizona, and in some of the great cities. Similar movements among the Canadian Indians and the Eskimos occurred from the eighteenth century onwards, but have mostly been local and short lived.

It is in Black Africa, however, that the largest concentration of NERMS occurs. Here again the earliest European influence was attended by prophet movements, such as that of Béatrice who was burned in the Portuguese-dominated Kingdom of the Congo in 1706. White settlement in South Africa led to millennial movements among the Xhosa and Ndhlambe peoples; similar movements later produced what the colonial authorities regarded as 'disturbances' and in some instances actual revolt, such as Chilembwe's Nyasaland rising of 1915. From the 1880s there developed independent all-African churches in south and west Africa, and then in east and central Africa. From the second decade of the present century there began a vast proliferation of movements of a different kind, prophet-healing in their main concerns, much more Africanized and often highly syncretistic, and shading off into other groups that are neo-traditional in emphasis and sometimes anti-Christian also.

At first sight it might seem that we have here no more than a motley collection of unrelated developments, with nothing more in common than their appearance as epiphenomena related more or less loosely to the history of Christian expansion or of colonialism. Elsewhere we have set forth the reasons why these NERMS may rightly be regarded as in some important senses one single phenomenon that constitutes a new field in the history of religions.[3]

The phenomenological similarity of NERMS may be indicated by listing some of the characteristic features that are likely to be found no matter what the period or the area in which the movement has appeared. Many of these will be less characteristic of those independent churches that stand close to the Western Christian forms, and will be more evident in the millennial and prophet-healing movements that represent the greater part of the whole range.

1. An individual with some Christian background or contact has a new spiritual experience of a mystic nature — commonly in dream or trance he visits heaven and receives a new revelation and commission from the supreme God, Jesus or the angels. He returns with a new message, rituals and powers; the old spirits and divinities are ignored, demoted, or reinterpreted in relation to the one personal God.

2. As a preacher, prophet, messiah, healer or political leader he attracts followers into a movement that bears his distinctive stamp. Especially notable is the frequency of women founders and leaders, particularly in Africa. The charismatic leader is complemented in due course by others with organizational gifts and the movement consolidates.

3. There is a dramatic break with some of the traditional ways, especially those connected with magic. Ritual objects and fetishes may be burned, and the traditional economic basis of life destroyed; or else new villages are established with economic activities which move in the direction of modernization. Moral reform is a prominent theme, sometimes by strengthening traditional sanctions and norms, or reinforcing and extending these through the Christian ethic; an ascetic element is common, together with the prohibition of alcohol and tobacco. Some traditional practices such as polygamy, the eradication of witches, and the reliance on dreams

may be defended before Western Christian criticism; less commonly monogamy may be required.

4. Considerable religious creativity is evident in new rituals and symbolisms, drawing upon both the religious traditions involved. Likewise new organizations of a voluntary type, on a spiritual rather than a kinship basis, and often with a trans-tribal membership, replace the traditional groups.

5. Specific practical benefits are offered here and now through healing, divine guidance, or protection from evil powers, or else in the nearer future in a promised New Order of peace, freedom and prosperity. This new age will appear through some supernatural spiritual agency if the members are faithful to the way of life of the new religion.

6. The new faith is commonly regarded as potentially universal, and where this becomes explicit and the membership transcends tribal boundaries a remarkable missionary zeal may appear and the movement may spread over a wide area and even become international. This is a quite new feature not found in primal religions.

7. In general there is a deep concern for personal and corporate spiritual renewal, together with the recovery of self-identity and self-respect and the establishment of a position of responsibility and dignity in the eyes of the whole world. Some movements have assumed more political forms of revolt or of nationalism; some become anti-white or anti-Christian; others, however, aspire to the contribution they believe their people can make even to the more sophisticated peoples of the world.

In presenting these characteristic phenomena we do not forget that the pathology of religion is as evident in NERMS as in the rest of us; there are the charlatans and quacks, the deranged and the renegade among them, and movements may degenerate, or mutate into pseudo-religions. These, however, are less calculated to introduce us to the real significance of this vast religious development not only as a 'new field in the history of religions', but also for Christian missiology.

IV. NEW DIMENSIONS OF CHRISTIAN HISTORY, ECUMENICS, AND MISSIONS

This significance begins to appear when we recognize that none of these movements would have come into being apart from the interaction of the Western and Christian world with primal peoples. Now they present us with a whole new range of possibilities for reflection and for action which we can best explore in terms of three different yet inter-related perspectives or dimensions — the historical, the ecumenical and the missionary.

A. From the point of view of Christian history we can discern new reaches of Christian influence, beyond the familiar areas of missions and the churches these have planted, beyond these to the new religious creations of the primal societies that we have so strangely ignored or shunned. We have been unwilling to see even the independent church of indigenous origin as belonging to the Christian story — sometimes merely because it tolerated polygamy. Our restricted or rigid Western categories have blinded us to the Christian impress or influence that may be discovered right across the great variety of unexpected and strange forms found among NERMS. Some of these may even be the direct inheritors of missions that might seem to have failed: the work of Jesuit missionaries among the Yaqui of north-western Mexico ceased with their expulsion in 1767; it continues, however, in the Yaqui church, a reworking of the Christian and Yaqui traditions into a new form that has remained at the centre of Yaqui communities even when they have migrated into Arizona in the present century. Their renovated 'temple' south of Phoenix stands right next to the Catholic church as if asking to be included in the Christian history to which it belongs. A whole new dimension of Christian history taken in the widest sense calls upon the conventional church historians to venture beyond some of their well-trodden fields into new and exciting regions that can no longer be left to the secular disciplines.

B. The ecumenical dimension appears when we discover that only a minority of NERMS are specifically anti-Christian and that a surprisingly large number regard themselves as Christian, or as the true form of Christianity for their own people which is quite different from that for Westerners. Even where the Christian aspects are slender or distorted it is the intention that is often of the greatest significance. No one could say that the Native American Church is entitled to use the word 'church' in any historic or theological sense; it might be called a neo-traditional or highly syncretistic cult. And yet it has been bitterly opposed by many traditionalists, has an impressive moral effect upon individual members, uses the name of Jesus and sometimes the Christian Scriptures, interprets its use of peyote as a God-given sacrament equivalent to the Westerners' use of bread and wine, and calls itself the Indian version of Christianity. There is an intention here that we must appreciate and make our starting point, even though we may disagree with much of the movement's self-interpretation. To this limited but important extent even the peyote cult belongs within the Christian orbit and the ecumenical attitude applies.

Support for this radical ecumenism is to be found in the overall tendency for NERMS to move across the spectrum from the neo-traditional or highly syncretistic end towards a more orthodox or recognizably Christian form. For example, both the Native American Church and the Indian Shaker Church started with their own new revelation replacing that of the Scriptures, but now some sections are using the latter. The Kimbanguist Church, now sitting in the World Council and training its leaders under a European theologian, was usually described even in the early sixties as a reversion to paganism with Simon Kimbangu as a new Black Messiah for Africans. And all over Africa the independent churches are reaching out for Christian fellowship and for help in understanding the Bible and in training a better ministry, and some have been admitted to Christian Councils; in New Zealand the century-old Ringatu cult has begun to move in a Christian direction, and the fifty-year-old Ratana Church has had some relationship with the National Council of Churches. A long established movement seldom develops in the opposite direction.

The Western Christian must, however, beware of thinking that this means 'everything's going my way', just as no one can genuinely participate in ecumenical relationships with this attitude or expectation. It will surprise and even alarm some to learn that many NERMS regard themselves as having attained a more effective and authentic Christian form than that of missions and local churches with which they are familiar, or of the Western countries they occasionally visit. In this way they claim to represent a reformation, a rediscovery of the power of the Christian Gospel and of the true original Christian Church. Some who have studied certain of the independent churches of Africa would recognize a measure of truth in this claim and would find a parallel in the long forgotten or despised 'radical reformation' of the sixteenth century. It may be no accident that modern Mennonites have shown a peculiar capacity to work sensitively with independent churches in Africa.

C. The missionary perspective or dimension is the one most readily discerned by many of us, and, as some of the above remarks would suggest, possibly for the wrong reasons. It is evident most clearly, of course, in the anti-Christian movements and in the forms we have been describing as neo-traditional or highly syncretistic. There are other movements which may be identified as having achieved a position corresponding to that of Israel in the Old Testament period, with commitment to one supreme creator and saviour God who demands a high morality. Some NERMS actually make this identification and call themselves Israelites as in South Africa and elsewhere, or Bayudaya (people of Judah) as in Uganda, or the Aaronista in Peru. Others again are in some sense Christian churches, but reveal such serious misunderstandings or distortions of the Gospel that they could not be accepted into Christian Councils. With these a quite substantial ecumenical relationship is possible along with the exercise of an evangelistic missionary responsibility, and experience suggests that the two attitudes are not mutually exclusive but in fact can reinforce each other. However this may be, we are certainly presented with a large new area of missionary duty running across the continents, with a complexity born of the peculiar place NERMS hold in Christian history, and an urgency springing from the pace at which changes are occurring in the world of the primal peoples.

V. A NEW AREA FOR MISSIONS

We have already identified the sense in which these movements present the Christian world with a new dimension of missionary responsibility, where there are few precedents to guide us. This area requires a different approach, a new kind of missionary, unfamiliar methods, and a much more flexible and adaptable policy on the part of sending agencies. To guide these adjustments considerable research is required in this strange field itself, and in the history of the tentative efforts that have been already made to enter it.

We could, for instance, examine a Christian attempt in the 1960s in the border areas of upper Burma and Thailand, where the millennial Buddhist-influenced Telakhon ('fruit of wisdom') cult had waited for Ywa, a withdrawn high god, to deliver the Karens. In Telakhon mythology this deliverance would be heralded by their white 'younger brothers' returning their own Golden Book, lost through their ancestors' disobedience to Ywa. Missionaries of the Church of Christ in Thailand and the United Christian Missionary Society heard that the Telakhons believed this was now about to happen. They decided that here was the great opportunity, arranged contacts through an influential Karen, and set out on elephants provided by the Telakhon bearing as gifts Bibles printed in the Burmese-Mon alphabet and in two vernaculars. They were welcomed with great hopes on both sides, and the contact continued over the years 1962–65 during which the Telakhon numbers trebled to some 10,000, and the missionaries prepared to open a clinic and school. Disillusionment, however, intervened on both sides. The Bibles proved to be in a script the leader could not read, did not reveal the secret of Western power, and so could not be the real Golden Book. The leader abandoned the ascetic ways of a celibate monk and assumed a regal style of life in preparation for the new age when all Karens would join Telakhon under him. New revolts against the Burmese led to his capture and death in Burma. Leaderless, the Telakhon awaited his supernatural return and rejected further overtures from the missionaries, although a Karen evangelist was accepted by one village in 1970. The missions had done the best they knew, but had not fully understood the Golden Book and the nature of similar movements among the Karen over the past century and a half.[4]

A different result attended the encounter between the British Wesleyan Methodist Mission and the followers of the Liberian prophet Harris. In 1913–14, he had turned many thousands of lower Ivory Coast primal peoples away from their traditional cults and left them waiting for the coming of the white man to teach them the Bibles they bought but could not read. No one in the Western Christian world took note of this for a decade, until the Methodist missionary, W. J. Platt, accidentally heard of it in 1923, not from the small Methodist work he was visiting from his base in Dahomey, but from French colonial officials who were concerned about the Harris movement. When he returned in 1924 to study the situation more closely he was met everywhere by enthusiastic crowds and treated as the white messenger Harris had promised. Groups of congregations were handed over to the Mission and Platt persuaded a financially embarrassed Society to respond with a major move into the Ivory Coast. Two years later there were 160 Methodist churches and 32,000 enrolled adherents, and the great Methodist community today has been built on this unexpected inheritance from a lone prophet.[5] Further offshoots of the work of Harris are to be found as healing cults and independent churches in the Ivory Coast today. Now for the second time Harris Christians may be open to help from the West; the main independent Harris church has been discussing various problems with the Mennonite Church of the USA.

The Mission Board of this Church has already pioneered with distinction in this sensitive realm since 1959 when Edwin and Irene Weaver responded to an unsolicited invitation from the leader of a group of independent bush churches in Eastern Nigeria to come and help them. After a period of mutual disillusionment the Weavers commenced the process of adjustment to a situation unique in the experience of their Board, and worked out a new form of missionary action with substantial results, until the civil war imposed a temporary withdrawal.[6] From 1969 to 1971 the same couple explored yet another form of approach to a whole range of independent churches in Ghana, and enlisted the older churches to assist in giving Bible study and leadership training; and from 1970–76 the Mennonite Board supplied the first tutor for the fledgling seminary of an independent church in western Nigeria. In various parts of Africa similar help is being given by other bodies — to the Kimbanguist Church in its theological seminary through Marie-Louise Martin and others in Zaïre, to the Shona independent churches in Rhodesia where Marthinus Daneel is working out forms of self-help and development, through the correspondence courses of F. H. Burke, an American missionary in South Africa, and especially through the manifold efforts over a recent decade of the Christian Institute for Southern Africa in correspondence courses and a special seminary belonging to the independent churches themselves.

This wide-open situation in many areas of Africa has some counterparts elsewhere, and in so far as the movements concerned may be called independent churches the approach is as much ecumenical as missionary. A different situation exists with movements of the more neo-primal kind, but even here there are signs of the necessary adaptability among missionaries. In Guyana, for instance, the Anglican mission among Indians of the interior is co-operating with the Hallelujah religion mentioned above and is open to incorporate it within the Church as a prayer tradition with a strong moral discipline. Among the Plains Indians of the USA new approaches to the Native American Church or peyote cult are being tried by Catholic priests who have made a sensitive study of traditional religion; something similar has happened with the Ringatu cult in New Zealand, and there must be other examples to be discovered and studied.

We are familiar with attempts to identify 'the Christian approach to the Jew', to the Muslim, the Buddhist or the Hindu, and also to the 'animist'. We are now faced with exploring the Christian approach to the peyotist, to the Indian Shaker, to the voodoo worshipper and the Ras Tafarian, to the Umbandist or spiritist in Brazil, to the cargo cult member in Melanesia, the Mama Chi adherent in Panama, or the members of indigenous independent churches in the Solomons, the Philippines, Arizona, and Black Africa. These represent not only a special sphere of Christian responsibility but also a new potential for Christian advance in non-Western cultural terms. This requires considerable research in order to know what we are doing, together with a new type of missionary to do it, more professionally equipped and prepared to work in strange ways and on a long term basis. Here are movements that exist in their own right as creations of the human spirit, and, we believe, never devoid of the presence of the Holy Spirit. They can be neither dismissed, replaced, dominated, taken over, nor infiltrated in the interests of individual conversions to a more seemingly orthodox Christianity. The first task may be to break through the image and pattern of their relation to missions and churches in the past. As one of the Catholic priests referred to above has found, it might even be possible to remove some of the asperity between traditionalists and the new movements, and to see this also as part of the 'strange work' of Christ the Reconciler.

The manifold difficulties of this enterprise are attended by less obvious dangers. The sudden discovery of this somewhat exotic field shows signs of producing a rash of ecclesiastical and ecumenical tourists, especially in Africa, and this can do nothing but damage to the movements themselves. The awakening that has begun in mission circles could lead to a scramble by would-be enlightened mission agencies to join this particular bandwagon, for fashions are as powerful in missiology as elsewhere. Efforts to atone for former neglect could occur at the expense of continuing responsibility to the older mission-founded churches, and especially to the extensive research urgently needed if their history, inner life and real needs are to be better understood. Quick impressions can lead to hasty generalizations as has happened especially in Africa — by forgetting that Sundkler's pioneering work was confined to the Zulus, by employing messianic or other concepts too freely, by uncritical acceptance of Barrett's suggestive theses, or by assuming that the growing point of Christianity in Africa lies mainly with the independent churches.

Neither difficulties nor dangers must be allowed to obscure this new dimension of the mission task that opens out before both Western sending agencies and the churches of the Third World. If our interpretation as a distinctive but neglected area is correct then it can be accepted as one of four main areas where the missionary action of the world Christian community can be identified:

1. There is the continuing 'classic' work of missions to the 'untouched' peoples who still exist in remoter areas, or in the great world culture-religions, however refashioned by dialogue, mutual participation or other approaches.

2. To this we must add the newly developing exercise of mission by Christian communities to one another across the nations and cultures of the world, in which some of the more developed independent churches we have mentioned may have a special role to play.

3. Now we are discovering the wide-ranging complex of new religious movements from the primal societies with their own peculiar call to mission.

4. And finally it is clear that Christianity is ceasing to be a culture religion in the Western world and is entering into a mission situation in relation both to the post-Christian West and to the new international secularized culture derived from it.

For the most part the Christian community has not extended its concept of mission beyond the first or classic era, and on occasion even this is in danger of constriction through the closure of some traditional overseas fields and the changed situation in those that remain. Those who carry the missions concern in the churches may well revive a flagging cause by extending the horizon to the further areas we have indicated, and especially to the fascinating realm of new religious movements among the primal peoples. Then the Christian world may discover that, far from being over, the great age of missions — of missions more varied and complex than we have ever envisaged — is just beginning.

Notes

1. *Church Growth Bulletin* 4 (5) May 1968, p. 10.
2. M. Eliade: 'History of Religions and a New Humanism', *History of Religions* 1 (1) 1961, p. 2.
3. See Harold W. Turner: 'A new field in the history of religions', *Religion: Journal of Religion and Religions* (Newcastle upon Tyne, England), 1 (1) 1971, pp. 15–23.
4. See T. Stern: 'Ariya and the Golden Book', *Journal of Asian Studies* 27

(2) February 1968, pp. 314–27; articles and reports by Emilie Ballard in *The Thailand Tatler* (American Baptist Mission) May 1969, February etc., 1970.
5. See G. M. Haliburton: *The Prophet Harris* (London 1971), especially chs. 11–14.
6. See their *The Uyo Story* (Elkhart, Indiana: Mennonite Board of Missions, 1970).

23
The Hidden Power of the Whites:
The Secret Religion Withheld from the Primal Peoples

This essay is a rather sad and cautionary tale of inevitable and endless misunderstandings of Western culture, of the Christian religion and its Bible, and of the relation between this culture and this religion. These misunderstandings mark primal societies in all parts of the world, and they become especially evident when they lead to the development of NERMS; they also exist in the midst of much mission work and even within secular education. There are, therefore, warnings here for all engaged in cross-cultural communication. Fortunately for the Christian religion it seems able to spread in spite of (even by means of?) these handicaps, and as it takes root gradually to overcome these misconceptions.

The interaction between Western culture and its Christian religion and the primal cultures of the world has been proceeding with ever accelerating speed ever since the era of European expansion commenced late in the fifteenth century. In this interaction it is inevitable that the

---

This essay was first read as a paper at the International Congress for the History of Religions at Lancaster in August 1975, and in 1976 formed one of the Burns Lectures given in the University of Otago in New Zealand. A slightly shorter version will be found in *Archives des Sciences Sociales des Religions* 46 (1), juillet-septembre 1978, and a Hungarian translation in the journal *Világosság* in 1978.

stronger and more sophisticated culture is encountered, assimilated and understood only in a selective and modified fashion. On the part of the stronger culture, which becomes more donor than recipient, this selection and modification are partly unconscious and partly a matter of policy, where certain elements are withheld for reasons of political control, prestige, paternal kindness or a desire to minimize the culture shock arising from the encounter. The weaker primal culture also makes its own selection from what is offered to it, and adds its own interpretations and modifications. The interaction process, therefore, in the contact of cultures is exceedingly complex, no one ever knows exactly what is happening, and serious misunderstandings occur on both sides without anyone realizing that they are misunderstandings.

Western cultures are never received as integral wholes but only through selections from their political, judicial, commercial, educational and religious systems, and from their technologies, selections abstracted from the histories, values and meanings of the total context in which they can be understood, and from which these systems receive their power. Hence the real source of the powers of the white peoples is never fully seen in the recipient area. When the selected aspects of white culture transplanted into primal societies do not speedily bring the full knowledge and power of the whites to the primal peoples, the latter may explain the mystery in a way that is rational and quite correct — there must be more to it than we have seen, and the whites are withholding something important from us. This situation has occurred in all five continents of white Christian expansion and missionary activity and is expressed in beliefs to be found in primal societies across the world, and especially in their own new religious movements, beliefs that the whites have neither revealed the full secrets of their Christianity nor given the local peoples the full or the true Bible. The suspicions are focussed on these, the spiritual dimensions of white culture, since for most primal cultures the ultimate sources of power are magical and ritual, mystical or spiritual; it is only through full access to the white man's religion, therefore, that the local people can both explain and share in the power of the whites.

I recognise that there are many exceptions to this thesis, as, for example, the Niger Delta people who as early as the 1870s petitioned for secular subjects rather than religious teaching in mission schools. But this religious interpretation of the sources of power is only the first of many ways in which primal cultures are strongly preconditioned to misunderstand the Christian religion of the white peoples. As a further cultural factor there is the common belief that power is related to secret knowledge possessed only by the magician or the priest, or by those who have been initiated into one of the secret societies so often found among primal peoples.

It was only to be expected, therefore, that the source of this impressive power of the Europeans would be most closely guarded or known only to the few. We are told, for instance, of an old and serious-minded Maori warrior in New Zealand who consulted W. E. Gudgeon on the subject of the Scriptures. After forty years' studying them he had concluded there was nothing in them available to him, and that the key to the great book was in the hands of the bishops, who selfishly kept to themselves all that was of real value. When Gudgeon protested that he had never heard of any such thing he was cut off with the sarcastic remark that since he was not a bishop it was hardly likely that he would know anything about it. "For", said the old warrior, "it is not the Maoris only who are being defrauded, but the Europeans also." The reasoning is clearly culturally based: the Maori tohungas (or medicine-men) kept their powerful incantations in their own hands, and likewise the bishops, as a superior class of tohunga, would keep the really powerful parts of the Bible from the lower clergy and the laity.[1]

From Papua New Guinea we have current reports of the same explanation being found for any successful secular activities on the part of an individual. In Bougainville in the 1960s Paul Lapun who had long been a Catholic teacher became a successful political leader in the national assembly by his own abilities and the ordinary political processes; many of his supporters, however, attributed his success to secret knowledge and magic powers he had learned as a school teacher from the Catholic missionaries and the sacred Christian books.[2] Likewise the same explanation was offered when another ex-teacher in a Catholic school in the S. Madang District made a conspicuous success of his trade store, instead of failing as so many local entrepreneurs had done; it was not a matter of rational organization, hard work, or business acumen, but of spiritual and secret knowledge learnt from the priests.[3]

This notion of a secret wisdom, or of a knowledge as yet undiscovered that would provide the way to success or the answer to current misfortunes, pervades many primal cultures; it provides striking testimony to man's belief that his life can and should be better than it is, and supplies some of the dynamic for innovation even in the apparently conservative primal societies. And cannot exactly the same things be said of our Western attitudes to our problems, and to the knowledge we seek for their solution?

As a third cultural factor leading to misunderstandings there is a common belief in an original wisdom or knowledge, sometimes even contained in a book, that was given by the gods at the creation and included all the things known to the whites and more, but which has been the victim of some primeval misfortune, or subsequent human wrongdoing. Among one group of Karen hill peoples of Burma the sacred book was believed to have been preserved but they had forgotten how to read the script; when in 1928 the first Christian missionary entered their area they hopefully approached him with what turned out to be a much revered copy of the Anglican Book of Common Prayer.[4] Even more pathetic is the current belief of the Telakhon cult among these same Karen, that Ywa the High God had in the beginning set aside the Book of Gold for the Karen. They, however, were too busy with mundane affairs to come and collect it, and so it was entrusted instead to their younger white brothers, who had profited from it in the meantime but would in the end return and share it with the Karen. There was great excitement in the 1960s when a formal invitation went forth from the cult to missionaries in Thailand to bring their Bible, which was undoubtedly the Book of God, to the cult leaders; and even greater disappointment when it was discovered that the Bible did not tell how to repair a radio much less all the mysteries of Western science. The missionaries were then accused of withholding the true Golden Book.[5]

The trickery of the whites in securing the original wisdom meant for all appears as a theme in a number of mythologies. Some North American Indian peoples assert that the Christian religion of the white peoples was originally in the possession of the Indians whose sacred records were stolen by the whites and kept to themselves.[6] The almost total failure to translate the Scriptures into Indian vernaculars over nearly five centuries of Christian contact lends some support at least to the second part of the indictment. A similar charge has appeared in the possession cults that have appeared over the last ninety years among the Isoko people of the Nigerian Mid-West: they had been given the original Bible, far fuller in content and more powerful than the present version, but this had been taken away and either lost or destroyed by the missionaries.[7] The same notion attached to the Book of Life, the secret book allegedly given Alice Lenshina, the prophetess in Zambia, when she visited heaven; her followers had never seen it and in 1955 the rumour spread that a Presbyterian missionary had stolen it and sold it to the Pope![8]

Clearly the important idea running through so many different mythologies and legends is that the whites outwitted or cheated the other peoples either at the creation or in subsequent allotments of spiritual and powerful gifts to men; and they are still doing so within the Christian religion.

As a fourth and final cultural factor often involved in these misunderstandings we may mention the ways in which pre-literate cultures often interpret the nature and purpose of writing. Written words used in a sacred context may be regarded as even more powerful than the spoken words used in their own traditional rituals, whether religious or magical. Literacy, therefore, does not destroy the mystic power of such words as in our simpleminded white assumptions — it may even enhance it. Thus the Toba people of the Argentine treated the Bible as a fetish object and tied it to their sides while dancing or placed it on the sick for healing, and when the Bible began to be translated from a vaguely understood Spanish into Toba its mystique decreased.⁹ They often complained to the Mennonite missionary that he had not shared his deepest religious knowledge with them, and when they asked for Bible study it was for this special secret knowledge that the missionary had of the Bible, rather as an object to be exchanged than a personal insight to be sought and applied.

The ritual use of documents as power-filled objects extended to all kinds of writing — hence the great concern with letters, letterheads, rubber stamps, receipts and certificates for the most trivial things common among peoples under white colonial administration. But it was the Bible, the great document of the religion of the whites, that attracted this attitude above all other forms of writing.

The eager response to the teaching of reading and writing that marked the first phase of so much missionary activity often, therefore, had other motives than those which governed the mentors, and inevitably led to disillusionment. As Professor Parsonson of Dunedin summed it up in a study of "The Literate revolution in Polynesia": "The Polynesians had plainly believed that the art of reading and writing was the real source not merely of the technological capacity of the European but also of his military and political strength, his *mana*, and that they need only master these skills to secure a like pre-eminence. Then they discovered that these were not enough or at least while they apparently worked in European hands they dismally failed in their own."¹⁰

Judith Binney made the same point in writing of the Maoris in the first missionary period up to 1840, here "literacy became fashionable because of the desire to master the secrets of the European world, which, it was assumed, were contained in the ritual words. . . . The Bible was adopted . . . because they considered the words themselves contained the power . . . , by an exact recitation of the texts the desired goal, communication with the supernatural, would be achieved. Hence . . . the actual content may well be irrelevant. . . . What they expected to gain is most blatantly revealed in the heretical cults: material wealth, power, and the knowledge of the Europeans, which were given by God."¹¹ After all, did not the sacred book itself say "Seek ye first the kingdom of God . . . and all these things shall be added unto you."? Seeking the Kingdom of God was readily translated into ability to read and recite the sacred text, but it did not work.

There is a story often found in missionary literature of North America concerning the Flathead Indians of Oregon on the west coast. They had been visited by a missionary with a Bible from which he taught, very early in the nineteenth century, and never forgot the effect he had created. In 1832 four of them set off east some two thousand miles to the military post of St. Louis where they asked for a copy of the white man's Book of Heaven. The commandant received them kindly as a Roman Catholic, as also did the priests to whom he referred them. But as in the manner of the day there was no Bible to give them. As one of the Indians sadly expressed it at a farewell dinner: "My people sent me to get the white man's Book of Heaven. You took me to where you allow your women to dance, as we do not ours, and the Book was not there. You took me to where they worship the Great Spirit with candles, but the Book was not there. You showed me images of the good spirits and pictures of the good land beyond, but the Book was not among them to tell us the way.... You make my feet heavy with gifts, yet the Book is not among them." Of the four Indians only one survived the rigours of the journey to report his failure to his people.[12] It is natural that in mission circles this story reflects the hunger of the heathen heart for the true Word of God. Without doubting something of truth in this it would be surprising if the Indians had not also been driven by completely different understandings of what a book could do, understandings that would have shocked many a missionary and perhaps lent some justification to the former Catholic practice of avoiding indiscriminate distribution of the Bible.

In particular primal cultures there might be other factors at work to create this basic misunderstanding of the Christian religion and its Scriptures, besides the four very widespread factors that we have indicated. These lead to the disappointment with Christianity that often marks the second and third generation, and that runs parallel to the disillusionment with many of the white man's schemes for social and economic development after the first high and unrealistic hopes, whether these schemes came through colonial administrations or now under newly independent governments. Clear indications of this occur among the cargo cultists of Papua New Guinea. As a commentator on the Peli cult put it, the local people had tried all the government schemes of the whites without achieving anything like equality with the whites. They had undertaken cash cropping with rice, peanuts, and coffee, and secured a little cash income. Their young men had walked an hour and a half to school daily for six or seven years, and now hung around the villages unemployed. They had accepted the setting up of a local government council, but all it did was collect taxes and the roads were worse than fifteen years ago. A chain-letter get-rich-quick scheme called Australian Bonanza had raised new hopes and secured a big response, and must have been the real road to affluence and power for government went and banned it. So they had turned back to their own magico-religious methods in a new money-doubling cult.[13]

These disappointments arise partly from false expectations, as with the New Caledonian who complained to the first Marist Fathers, "You do not give us rain. Your brothers the white men keep it away from us in their own country. Come and see our crops. They are dying . . . the ground is dry."[14] The disappointments might also be due to over-expectations: when the Queen of England paid a state visit to Sierra Leone in 1961 the rumour went round that England had not sent the real queen, who would have had grander clothes and not travelled around in an open car so close to the people; the mystique was missing, kept back from the local people.

It is possible that misunderstandings about the spiritual secrecy of the whites are encouraged by the reserve about religious matters characteristic of much modern white culture, and by the lack of any signs of religion on the part of whites who are in fact non-believers, and who may even show hostility to it. It is concluded that the white man is deliberately hiding his secret spiritual power or declaring there is no such thing; some white agnostics might be astonished if they knew the mystic religious powers with which they are credited by their associates in primal cultures!

In the general life and practice of Christian missionaries there is much that is open to the kind of misinterpretation that we are examining. No matter how simple his life style by his own standards, or how little power of any kind he wields in his own country, in the eyes of a primal society he appears rich and powerful, and this because of his religion; but when the local people accept the same religion they remain weak and poor. He may commence schools using his own European language and then for good educational reasons change to the use of the vernacular; clearly he has decided to protect the secrets contained in his own literature. Or he may concentrate on only sufficient literacy to read the Scriptures and otherwise emphasize practical and manual training; as a result those he has taught cannot share his full literary wealth, nor do they have sufficient practical skills to make for themselves the wonderful technical equipment he possesses. He may operate a trade store to bring basic Western goods within their reach, and then close it when mission policy turns against such trading or it has been replaced by secular commercial developments. His very first contacts may have been established by goodwill gifts or bartering to meet his own needs, and then he closes this channel for the sharing of his wealth with them. Once the mental set, the cultural pre-disposition, is there, his most innocent or entirely appropriate actions are open to interpretation as one more example of something being kept back from the local people.

The whole practice of a mission station might appear at first to proclaim that here was a new and more powerful witch-protection movement with its own attack on previous movements or methods, replacing them by its new rituals and "medicines", its new confessions of sin and malice, its new promises of a golden age to come when evils will vanish. Its methods are all of a piece: the new powerful "medicines" in the medical clinics, poured over one in baptism, eaten and drunk in the Holy Communion, and the mysteries partly shared in the classroom and the workshop

— all part of the new and powerful movement. One could share in it up to a point by learning to read and to use carpenter's tools, by becoming a member of the church and paying dues, but at the end of all this one was still left without the real cult secrets for oneself.

The most explicit example I have found occurs in L'Eglise de la Foi founded in Zaïre in the 1960s, by Bakwafula. He asserts that the power of the whites lies not in their various secular organizations but in their religion and its rites. These are not the public religious rituals of the mission churches but other more secret rites performed in cemeteries at night. Through him God has revealed these secrets so that Blacks who join his church can benefit from them and become rich like the whites. Interestingly enough his appeal is mainly among the more sophisticated bourgeoisie, the very people who have learned most of Western secular wisdom and skills and yet who feel they are still poor and powerless in comparison with the white nations.[15]

Wherever there has been criticism of one mission by another further doubts have been cast on the authenticity or the fulness of the Christian religion offered by one's own missionaries. This is especially acute when a new mission body arrives and competes with the earlier mission by openly declaring that it is 'The FULL Gospel Church' or the real Jehovah's Witnesses that will give people the true and complete meaning of the Bible for the first time. Even if the authorities of the mission have no such thoughts it has happened that, for example, African agents of the Salvation Army have operated in their own cultural terms and announced that they brought important truths of the Bible that earlier missions had concealed from Africans.[16] The 'scriptural gymnastics' involved in some of these new teachings may impress for a time, but of course an even more bitter disillusionment is likely to ensue in the end: the Bible still hasn't shown how to make radios!

Basically there is nothing new or confined to primal societies in this notion of a secret knowledge confined to the inner few to whom it was given by Christ at the beginning. The New Testament itself seems to support the idea. After the parable of the sower, in Mark's Gospel ch. 4:10 we are told that 'When he was alone the twelve . . . questioned him about the parables. He replied: To you the secret of the kingdom of God has been given, but to those who are outside everything has been given in the way of parables, so that . . . they may look and look and see nothing. . .' And again in v.34: 'privately to his disciples he explained everything.' It is not entirely surprising, therefore, to learn that the Tokoist or Red Star independent church in Angola explained why the Protestant missions taught their converts to pray with their eyes shut: it was so that they would not see the Holy Spirit or the truth that the whites hid at all points.[17]

Belief in a secret tradition stemming from Christ appears right at the beginning of Christian history in the account of Acts 8:9–24 of Simon the sorcerer who tried to buy what he recognized as a superior power. It has been fostered in all gnostic versions of Christianity and emerges again in our own day in diverse areas of the world, and especially in primal societies. We learn of the Society of the Secret Power of Jesus in Ghana which aimed to discover the secret wonder-working magic by which Jesus worked miracles;[18] or of the secret prayer groups in Soweto, the huge African slum area by Johannesburg, which claims to know the hidden meanings of the Bible and to stand in a succession of such secret prayer groups right back to Christ and the disciples;[19] or again of the first missionary to visit the village of Iokea in Papua in 1912 — he was received as a 'big man' and expected to produce the symbol of his wonder-working powers, and there was great disappointment when like Paul and Barnabas on an earlier occasion he insisted that he was but human with a nature like their own, and that they would learn by way of Christ and not through any secret knowledge transmitted through him. It was in this same village that the best known of the early cargo cults broke out a few years later, the so-called Vailala Madness.[20]

It is on the Christian Scriptures that most suspicions of double-dealing by the whites are focussed. These suspicions may arise quite innocently in the course of an individual's own searching among religious books of all kinds. I think of a young Nigerian man who assured me that he was prepared to buy books rather than eat, an even more drastic alternative than in the European exhortation to sell one's bed. He had the English Authorised Version, and his own vernacular Bible in Yoruba, but had found that these did not tell the whole life of Jesus — he had found accounts of the missing years of his boyhood and his sojourn in Egypt in *The Aquarian Gospel of Jesus the Christ* which is full of apocryphal and occult material; we may never have heard of it, but many West Africans and others have. Then he found further that there were many unfamiliar stories of Abraham and others in Polano's *Selections from the Talmud*. Still further reading, this time in the Douai English version of the Bible used by Catholics, had revealed books that were not in the Protestant Bible at all — he had discovered the Old Testament apocrypha; and still further that even in books common to both Catholic and Protestant Bibles there may be differences, as with Esther where thirteen verses in ch. 10 of the former are represented by only three verses in the latter. There were, however, self-imposed limits to this extensive research, for although he had heard of the *Sixth and Seventh Books of Moses* he refused to explore these for, as he put it, "If I go deep I have two minds, half occult or magic." Others, however, are fascinated by this hotch-potch of ancient Egyptian and mediaeval European magic and occult literature, and not least because they contain a detailed key to the use of the Old Testament

Psalms, one by one, for all kinds of practical healing and other purposes. Here, then, we have a wide range of quite specific evidence that when used without adequate understanding proves that the whole Bible has not been brought by missionaries.

This whole problem is compounded by the inevitable process of providing the scriptures in vernaculars in various stages and selections. I have long held the opinion that Bible Societies and their translators have not taken the full measure of the effects of the particular selections they are forced to make. I have no wish to do other than honour the immense labours in these directions, but I am forced to raise these further questions after seeing at first hand the disastrous confusions attending anything less than the full Bible, together with the Apocrypha and all the other associated fringe and pseudo-scriptures, all being set in the context of education on their history and contents. No one can rest content merely with the Gospels and Psalms, for instance, for long, and the appropriateness of even these as first offerings should receive much more research.

Some examples must be given of other ways in which primal peoples think the whites have not brought the whole Bible. It is not uncommon to say that the first pages had been removed, for in these the local people had been mentioned by name as within God's plan of creation; or else other pages had been cut out wherein it was shown, for example, that Jesus Christ was a member of the local tribe in Irian Jaya,[21] or identified with a local culture hero – thus in the Letub movement in the Madang district of New Guinea of the early 1940s Jesus and God were identified with two traditional divinities, Dodo and Manup, and this was what the whites had kept secret.[22] The same identification occurred in Fiji in the Tuka movement of the 1870s when the Bible was believed to be really a book given to the whites by the mythical hero twins, who were important figures in Fijian religion, but the white men could not pronounce their names in this book so they had replaced them by Jesus and Jehovah.[23] In other areas it may be the last pages of the Bible that have been removed wherein God tells Papuans how they may secure factories and ships and cargo,[24] or Africans in Angola that Jesus Christ at his second advent will be in the form of a Negro.[25]

A variant on this theme is that the missionaries do not teach the whole Bible that they have brought. Listen to a complaint from Zambia: "When I asked about the Bible they could not give me true answers. I was very much puzzled about Daniel and Revelation. But they said, 'These are only dreams. You need not read those books. They are very hard and nobody can understand those books. It is better to read the Gospel.' But there was a great demand in my mind to understand these. I saw the beast coming out of the sea. I saw the beast with ten horns. I wanted to know."[26] And so he should, but what *is* the poor missionary to do towards such instant understanding?

Whatever he does he will be accused of hoodwinking people by teaching only parts of the Bible. The independent Church of the Ancestors in Malawi charge him with ignoring those passages in the Old Testament which show the great importance of the ancestors in religion, and many others accuse him of avoiding the presence of polygamy among so many famous figures in the Bible and teaching his own European system of monogamy, or of ignoring subjects like dreams and fasting. The whites had never allowed the local people to discover how close the Bible really was to their own culture.

Even more drastic is the suspicion that the whites had not brought the true or the real Bible but have left this, like "the real Queen", in their own country and brought only a specially prepared and innocuous version for the primal peoples. A parallel example of the same attitude occurs in the story from Zaïre of the Catholic priest newly arrived from Europe who lost his breviary and found that a newly-ordained African priest had borrowed it to compare it page by page with his own and so make sure that he had not been given an inferior version.[27] Also from Zaïre, but from the independent Kimbanguist movement, comes the report of how the Kimbanguists, in the minds of some of them, acquired their spiritual basis: "Before independence Diangienda [son of the prophet and head of the Church ...] went to Jerusalem where he was taken to a secret location by a white-haired old man. He was given the key to a box before him. He opened the box and inside it was another box, inside of that another, and so on until seven boxes had been opened. When the seventh box had been opened Diangienda found the true Bible which had been hidden from the Africans by the missionaries."[28]

If the true Bible has not been brought it has been replaced, according to a suggestion made in the Paliau movement in the Admiralty Islands off New Guinea, by a reinterpreted version put into secret and figurative form by a group of whites so that it cannot be understood; it was quite clear before it was tampered with.[29] Others again have used a much simpler agrument: this cannot be the true Bible because it is not the one the missionaries obey as the real Word of God — see how not a single missionary woman covers her head when praying.[30] No doubt there are many more places where missionaries have been caught out, with a logic that in its own terms is impeccable.

Even a new translation of the Bible, among primal peoples exactly as among Westerners, produces suspicion that it does not represent the real original, but may well have been changed or omit some important parts, or make errors in translation into the vernacular, as has sometimes occurred in spectacular and disastrous ways. On the other hand there has been a special suspicion of the Roman Catholic Church for its traditional policy, now changed, of not translating into the vernacular, whether it be the Bible or the Liturgy. At times this may be justified by explaining that the Bible is too powerful to be read or known by anyone but a priest, who has therefore to treat it as a secret book not safe for all to use. That is simply a local cultural version of the argument that has in fact been used in the past by the Church itself; and it is supported when people see priests privately reciting the offices for the day from their Breviary.

At the same time this situation feeds the very resentments and misunderstandings we have been examining. When I was collecting the life histories of individual members of the Church of the Lord (Aladura) in West Africa in the late fifties many proved to be ex-Catholics and voiced a common complaint — that they had been put off with Bible histories and catechisms and not been given or been taught the Bible itself; their hunger had first been satisfied when they discovered the particular ways in which this independent church emphasized and used the Bible.

An interesting variant on this theme occurs in the charge brought by Silas Eto against the Methodist Church in the Solomon Islands, that it had not been teaching the true doctrines of John Wesley! He had come across that widely read book of Sargant, *Battle for the Mind,* and its accounts of enthusiasm attending the Wesleyan revival and of similar phenomena in Africa and elsewhere, but none of this was allowed by the later sober generations of Methodist missionaries, who were therefore no true representatives of the authentic Methodist tradition. So he formed his own independent Christian Fellowship Church, where the Spirit was allowed free play and worship assumed the usual features of possession cults and ecstatic Christianity.[31]

Most white missionaries have probably had some assumptions about people in primal societies being prone to emotionalism and to various uncontrolled or ecstatic forms of religious behaviour; their own behaviour has been devoid of any such suggestion and they have discouraged what we now call pentecostal features in religion. Silas Eto has not been the only one to feel that the whites have been keeping something back at this point, hiding the real power of the Holy Spirit. Similar reports can be found from Rhodesia among the Shona, from the Ibibio of eastern Nigeria during the great Spirit movement from 1927, from South African Bantu, from Papua New Guinea and many other areas. Sometimes this power is associated with what is called "a Jordan baptism" which the whites have had but which they have not shared with others in their mission forms of Christianity. I have no evidence as to whether the more recent Pentecostal missions avoid these charges.

No mission, however, which introduces the Bible can avoid the kinds of misunderstanding we have been surveying, and which may arise from the most incidental things. Thus in 1919 a rumour went round western Nigeria "that an angel has marked all Yoruba Bibles on page 928". It had to be explained that these marks at the foot of the page were used by the printers to help fold the pages aright for the bookbinding.[32] More serious are the interpretations given to many passages in the Bible which promise greater religious power even than that recorded in its pages: Jesus himself had said that his followers would do even greater things than he had done (John 14:12), and promised the gift of the Holy Spirit to lead them into fuller truth (John 16:13) by revealing the further secrets, for "there is nothing hid that shall not be known" (Luke 12:2). The missionaries had retained for themselves the secrets of these powers and this knowledge. How one is tempted to purge the Scriptures of these awkward passages! And of the declaration at the end of John's Gospel that "there were indeed many other signs that Jesus performed . . . which are not recorded in this book." (20:30).

The search for these further spiritual powers is therefore pursued through other books, especially the apocryphal, occult or gnostic literature that has a distribution much wider than one might suspect; we have already mentioned a number of these, such as the *Aquarian Gospel of Jesus the Christ* and the *Sixth and Seventh Books of Moses*. This latter was something my university Old Testament class in Sierra Leone soon asked me about; they mostly knew of it — I, their Old Testament teacher had never heard of it! Or perhaps some thought I was only feigning ignorance in order to retain its powers for myself. Sometimes even secular literature may be mistaken for one of these further books not in the ordinary Bible: Yaliwan, a leading figure in a current cargo cult in New Guinea, was noted as possessing a copy of Agatha Christie's detective story *Evil under the Sun* — here, no doubt it might be expected to find Christ's further secret ways of overcoming all evils.[33]

In default of discovering the secret literature of the West the primal cultures have often proceeded to produce their own sacred books with the further knowledge that they need. A sophisticated example is Birinda's *La Bible secrète des Noirs selon le Bouity* published in 1952 by a Gabon national; the Bwiti cult is a complex independent religious movement in Gabon. This turning to their own spiritual resources marks the emergence of the great range of new religious movements among primal societies across the world subsequent to interaction with, especially, the Christian faith. From these it is possible to present a host of examples of new revealed scriptures that supplement or replace the Christian Bible. Some of these were openly displayed and used alongside the Bible, as with the work entitled *Narito Na Ako* ("I am Here") in the Iglesia Sagrada Ng Lahi of the Philippines since 1949; this was written by Placido Bronto from a revelation allegedly given by the Malay god in ancient times.[34] In

Rhodesia there is *The New Revelation of the Apostles* which contains the important visions of Johane Maranke, the founder of the African Apostolic Church (the "Vapostori"), in 1932 — one vision tells of his being given two books in a foreign language which he could understand through the Holy Spirit, and which contained the message of eternal life; this shows his independence of the missionaries who had been accused of withholding the Holy Spirit and has provided a canonical addition to the Bible.[35]

Somewhat more uncertain is the use made of other alleged scriptures, such as the leather-bound book with musical notation and text which Simbinga, the founder of the Bituma cult in Zambia over forty years ago, claimed had been given him by an angel, and from which he read when in trance; it proved to be a copy of the Psalter in Afrikaans, and although he had worked in Johannesburg it is doubtful whether he could actually read it.[36]

Other scriptures or their equivalent actually replace the Christian Bible, as in one of the very earliest of new movements in primal societies ever recorded, the Indian "church" set up about 1583 in Brazil in imitation of the Jesuits, complete with sheets of tree bark covered with marks and claiming to be Bibles.[37] Similar endeavours appear in the Delaware prophets in North America one of whom (probably Neolin) in 1762 showed the Quaker trader, James Kenny, "his own book containing their new religion, being a favour, I think that no white man has received here beside me: ... he also said his prayers by his book."[38] Similarly on the American West Coast a Squamish Indian prophet in the 1840s had a drawn "map" from which he preached; it probably showed in pictorial or diagrammatic form the history of the world from the creation, in imitation of a certain device used by early Catholic missionaries in the area.[39] A little later Smohalla, another Indian prophet, had a book containing mysterious characters probably like our alphabet, recording his experiences and his teaching.[40] Some of these new religious documents actually did have a new script of a semi-alphabetic kind, which had allegedly been revealed by the Spirit, as in the Pau Cin Hau movement in 1902 among the Burmese Chin People. The most notable example is the new revealed language and script, with thirty-two symbols, of the Obere Okaimi church in east Nigeria in the 1930s, which actually began its own schools for religious teaching in this language.[41]

A quite pathetic instance occurred some time in the middle of the last century in the rather obscure beginnings of what is now the remarkable Hallelujah Religion in the hinterland of Guyana; it is believed that an Indian called Bichywung was taken to England by an Anglican missionary, but the latter had fooled the Indian by hiding God's word from him.

In consequence God gave the Indian his own piece of white paper with the Word of God on it.⁴²

Sometimes the new scripture will assume a form dictated by the local culture rather than by that of the white man with his books and paper. This is probably the case with the Kurrangara or Worgaia movement among Australian aborigines; these are reported to have a "holy book", an aboriginal Bible, kept at Myroodah on the Fitzroy River in a secret spot in the bush, much like a sacred churinga tablet which it probably resembles, and containing the story of Noah in local terms.⁴³

The idea of a secret book from God given to the founder but never seen by the members is not uncommon in African independent churches. Various forms of this notion attach to the initial revelatory experiences of Alice Lenshina before she founded her Lumpa Church in Zambia in the 1950s. Some believed that Jesus had shown her several books and one of these she had brought back to earth, and that soon this secret book would be given to her members as their own holy book. Likewise there were members of Shembe's Zulu church who believed he preserved secret scriptures in his own house.

As a further variant on the possession of supplementary or alternative scriptures we find the claim to possess a new god-given means of interpreting the Christian Bible, and in two notable cases through hallucinogenic substances. One of these is the peyote cactus button; earlier this century some of the more Christian-influenced members of the peyote cult introduced the belief that peyote opened the Bible to the understanding of the American Indian people. This, however, has never been general in this movement, now known as the Native American Church; it is more usual to accept the peyote as giving direct communication with God apart from Scriptures — it is the whites who have to seek God through the more indirect way in the Bible, as a punishment, some would say, for having killed Christ.⁴⁴

The other striking use of a hallucinogen occurs in the Rastafarian movement of Jamaica, with its smoking of marijuana. Here the Bible contains the Word of God, but a white man, King James of England, translated the Bible and distorted its message. Now under the divine influence exercised through the "holy weed", they have the key to the Bible and can easily detect the false passages put in by the whites; the real Word of God is contained in a limited number of passages which the Rastafarians can identify.⁴⁵

If we remember that there are also members of primal societies who do not share in these suspicions and misunderstandings, and who use the Bible within a church community much as any white Christians, then we have before us the full spectrum of reactions to the Christian Scriptures. This is now seen to run from this more orthodox position through those who accept the Bible but select or interpret for their own purposes in highly unorthodox ways, to those who virtually extend the biblical canon by the addition of their revealed books, and then further to those who replace the Bible entirely by their own equivalent, or, finally, to those who simply reject all scriptures and rely on other modes of revelation.

Behind and explaining so many of these phenomena lies the basic suspicion that the white peoples have not shared their most valuable knowledge or spiritual power with those in primal societies, and the basic cultural misunderstanding that every single aspect of white affluence and power depends directly on the Christian religion and is somehow related to its possession of the Book of God.

Our survey has revealed the many overt forms in which these suspicions and misunderstandings are expressed, and especially and most explicitly in the new religious movements among primal societies. At the same time we can be reasonably sure that these culturally-based reactions are not confined to the ranks of the independent movements, but also lie hidden much more than anyone realizes among other members of the missions and older churches also.

Other major religious traditions have not had to face this problem, and for various reasons. They have not been associated with such a technologically advanced, powerful and wealthy culture as that of the West, or their encounter with the primal cultures has been geographically and quantitatively much more limited, or there has been no policy of widespread distribution and vernacular translation of their sacred scriptures. It is the Christian tradition above all others that has encountered this problem and with such devastating results.

At the same time most of the reactions we have been examining testify to the great impact these Scriptures have had in primal cultures, and not least in their own new religious movements where there was no outside constraint to take any further account of the Bible. And yet this is what they have done and conspicuously so, in seeking a Bible-based religion. There is therefore no possibility of withdrawing from these problems, either on Christian theological or on local pragmatic grounds. And yet in some ways only the outer edges of the problem have yet appeared, fostered by the discovery of some of the other ancient or esoteric books that we have mentioned; the effects of the fuller discovery of Western biblical criticism remain to be seen. There is, however, no stopping short of the fullest possbile sharing of all Western knowledge and especially of Christian resources, for all the intermediate stages of cross-cultural relationships are fraught with the kinds of selection and misinterpretation here surveyed. And as this process proceeds it is possible that the reverse effect will be set in motion and we of the Western cultures will be struggling to understand different interpretations of Scripture occurring in Christian communities in the non-Western world. Then perhaps some at least of those who have reduced the Scriptures to the status of no more than one among other Ancient Near Eastern documents will be found searching for the secret of how the Bible seems to provide spiritual power for churches in other cultures at the dynamic, growing edge of the Christian faith. Initially, perhaps, we shall be no more successful in fathoming their secrets than they have sometimes been in understanding ours.

Notes

1. W. E. Gudgeon, *The Maori: his customs and folklore*. n.d. [1905?], section on Maori superstition, pp. 2–3.
2. E. Ogan, Cargoism and politics in Bougainville, 1962–1972, *Journal of Pacific History*, 9, 1974, pp. 118ff.
3. T. Ahrens, Christian syncretism, *Catalyst* (Goroka) 4 (1), 1974, p. 9.
4. T. Stern, Ariya and the Golden Book, *Journal of Asian Studies* 27 (2), 1968, p. 305; E. Galusha, in *The Missionary Register* (London), August 1831, p. 355.
5. Stern, *op. cit.*, pp. 318ff.
6. A. F. Chamberlain, New Religious Movements among the North American Indians, *Journal of Religious Psychology* 6 (1), 1913, p. 4.
7. S. Barrington-Ward, The Centre cannot hold . . . , Paper at Seminar in School of Oriental and African Studies, London, May 1974, p. 6.
8. C. Heward, The Rise of Alice Lenshina, *New Society* 4 (98), August 1964, p. 7.
9. E. S. Miller, The Christian Missionary: Agent of Secularization, *Missiology* 1 (1), January 1973, p. 102.
10. G. S. Parsonson, The Literate Revolution in Polynesia, *Journal of Pacific History* 2, 1967, p. 57.
11. J. Binney, Christianity and the Maoris to 1840, *New Zealand Journal of History* 3 (2), 1969, p. 155.
12. E.g., J. W. Bashford, A Romance of Modern Missions, *Missionary Review of the World*, N.S., 1 (7), 1888, pp. 481–483.
13. W. R. Stent, *An Interview with a Cargo Cult Leader*. La Trobe University Department of Economics Discussion Paper No. 3/73, 1973, pp. 43–44.
14. J. Guiart, The millenarian aspect of conversion to Christianity in the South Pacific, in S. L. Thrupp (ed.), *Millennial Dreams in Action*. The Hague, 1962, repr. New York, 1970, p. 127.
15. G. Bernard, La Contestation et les églises nationales au Congo, *Canadian Journal of African Studies* 5 (2), 1971, pp. 150–152.
16. E. Andersson, *Messianic Popular Movements in the Lower Congo*. London, 1958, p. 132.
17. A. Margarido, L'Eglise Toko et le mouvement de libération de l'Angola. *Le Mois en Afrique* 5, mai 1966, p. 83.
18. M. J. Field, *Search for Security*. London 1960, pp. 267–268.
19. A. G. Schutte, Thapelo ya sephiri: a Study of Secret Prayer Groups in Soweto, *African Studies* 31 (4), 1972, pp. 245–260.
20. G. Cochrane, *Big Men and Cargo Cults*, London 1970, p. 52.
21. H. Pos, The Revolt of Manseren, *American Anthropologist* 52 (4:1), 1950, p. 561; F. C. Kamma, *Koreri*. The Hague, 1972, pp. 161, 206.

22. R. Inselmann, *Letub: the Cult of the Secret of Wealth*. Hartford Seminary Foundation M.A. dissertation, 1944, *passim*.
23. B. H. Thomson, *The Fijians*. London, 1908, p. 142; A. R. Tippett, Religious Innovation in the Fiji Islands, Paper, International Association for Mission Studies, Frankfort 1974, p. 51.
24. G. Oosterwal, Cargo Cults as a Missionary Challenge, *International Review of Missions*, 61 (224), 1967, p. 474.
25. C. Tastevin, Nouvelles manifestations du prophétisme en Afrique et en Angola, *Comptes Rendus de l'Académie des Sciences coloniales* 16 (3), 1956, p. 153.
26. J. V. Taylor and D. Lehmann, *Christians of the Copperbelt*. London 1961, p. 287.
27. R. M. Slade, *The Belgian Congo: Some Recent Changes*. London 1961, p. 35.
28. J. M. Janzen, Literacy and Culture among the Bakongo. Paper. Canadian Association of Africanists, Waterloo, February 1972, p. 4.
29. M. Mead and T. Schwartz, in B. H. Schaffner (ed.), *Transactions of the Fourth-Fifth Conferences on Group Processes 1957–1958, Princeton, N.J.* New York, 1960, p. 130.
30. C. Kraft, Towards an Ethnotheology, in A. R. Tippett (ed.), *God, Man and Church Growth*. Pasadena, 1973, p. 114.
31. A. R. Tippett, *Solomon Islands Christianity*. London, 1967, p. 214.
32. *In Leisure Hours* (Lagos), May 1919, p. 48.
33. L. Hwekmarin *et al.*, The Yangoro Cargo Cult, 1971, *Journal of the Papua and New Guinea Society* 5 (2), 1971, pp. 25–26.
34. D. J. Elwood, Contemporary Churches and Sects in the Philippines, *South East Asia Journal of Theology* 9 (2), 1967, p. 71; *idem*, Varieties of Christianity, in G. H. Anderson (ed.), *Studies in Philippine Church History*. Ithaca, 1969, p. 385.
35. M. L. Daneel, *Old and New in Southern Shona Independent Churches* vol. I. The Hague, 1971, pp. 316, 321.
36. W. M. J. Van Binsbergen, Bituma: Preliminary Note on a healing movement... in Zambia. Paper, Lusaka Conference on Africa Religious History, 1972, p. 5.
37. R. Southey, *History of Brazil*. London 1822, vol. I, pp. 371–373.
38. Journal of James Kenny, 1761–1763, *Pennsylvania Magazine of History and Biography* 37 (1), 1913, p. 173.
39. W. Suttles, The Plateau Prophet Dance among the Coast Salish, *Southwestern Journal of Anthropology* 13, 1957, pp. 385, 386–387.
40. W. La Barre, *The Ghost Dance*. Garden City 1970, p. 29; see also Kennekuk, p. 215.
41. R. F. G. Adams, A New African Language and Script, *Africa* (London), 17 (1), 1947, pp. 24–34.
42. A. Butt, The Birth of a Religion, *Journal of the Royal Anthropological Institute* 90 (1), 1960, pp. 69, 75, 83.
43. H. Petri, Postface, in H. Nevermann *et al.* (eds.), *Les Religions du Pacifique et d'Australie*. Paris 1972, p. 369.
44. P. Radin, The Peyote Cult in the Winnebago Tribe, *37th Annual Report, Bureau of American Ethnology for 1915–16*. Washington 1923, pp. 420ff.; also W. La Barre, *The Peyote Cult*. Hamden, Conn. 1964, p. 159.
45. M. G. Smith *et al.*, *The Ras Tafari Movement in Kingston, Jamaica*. Kingston 1960, p. 48.

24
Dynamic Religion in Africa

After the warnings in the previous essay this is a brief and more cheering statement written for schoolteachers concerned with the place of Christian studies in religious education. It introduces the existence of new forms of Christianity that challenge Western Christian communities to benefit from their spiritual vitality even while seeking ways of offering Western resources to others in their further spiritual searching.

By bringing the religions of the world into our midst the immigrant communities in Britain have been playing into the hands of all teachers seeking to broaden their syllabuses and their field work. Some of these immigrants, however, bring with them new forms of the christian faith drawn from its grass-roots manifestations in the West Indies and in black Africa. Since these are little known in this country they are liable to be overshadowed by the apparently more exotic activities of Muslims, Sikhs and Hindus. When a patient entering a local hospital gave as her religion 'Cherubim and Seraphim' it was difficult for the staff to take her seriously; they naturally asked some of the Pakistani doctors if they knew what this was. In fact she belonged to a British branch of a new all-African denomination dating back to the mid-twenties in western Nigeria, and now numbering (according to the latest doctoral dissertation on it) some 100,000 members scattered in 1,500 congregations across its various

---

Learning for Living, 12 (5), 1973, 3–7.

secessions and divisions, spilling over into other West African countries, and now operating here to liven up the staid British scene.

The writings of Clifford Hill have made information available about the three main movements of West Indian origin — the New Testament Church of God, the Church of God of Prophecy and the Apostolic Church of Jesus Christ. There has been little more than passing mention of the movements from Africa, although two graduate dissertations have been prepared on the Church of the Lord (Aladura) branches, and on the Cherubim and Seraphim, both in London. The West Indian and African churches no doubt have a good deal in common, and together they too provide a new potential for religious education, although in a very different direction from that of the Asian religions.[1]

MANY FORMS OF CHRISTIAN FAITH

First of all they demonstrate something of the great diversity of christian forms throughout the world. The christian faith is much more varied than one would ever guess from observation of the churches in Britain. We have taken our own form as being Christianity in itself, and expected the rest of the world to be like us — yes, even the liberal readers of this journal are much more ethnocentric than they have ever realized. The truth is that we have only one tribal form, that of the Western Europeans, albeit with minor variations as between the clans. Other peoples, other cultures bring out possibilities in the christian faith that we have never known, or at best have long forgotten. This serves to put both ourselves and the christian religion into a truer perspective. The hope, therefore, should not be that these immigrant African forms gradually assimilate to our own, but that they should have full opportunity to be their own authentic selves in order that we might learn from them the further dimensions of our common tradition.

VITALITY OF CHRISTIAN FAITH

Secondly, the vitality of the immigrant denominations which enables them to operate here in spite of the frequent lack of church buildings of their own is but one facet of the great dynamism these movements display in their own countries. While we are plagued by a sense of the decline and insignificance of religion in our midst, and of our apparent powerlessness to do much about it, it remains true that the christian religion has never spread faster than in our own lifetime, and that if we have lost a cutting edge to our faith this is not so in many other parts of the world. The tremendous explosion of vitality and development in black Africa in the last twenty years is represented in the religious dimension also, and is seen in the growth of the churches we do know about there (planted by our Western missionary societies) and especially in the further proliferating grass-roots forms with names that are still strange to us. This evidence of the continuing vitality of the christian faith is now before us in some of our British cities. And be it noted that the members are not illiterate bush peasants who are still simple enough to fall for the christian message, but the elites of their countries, those who are sent to the Western world as diplomats, business men or students. Their opposite numbers in our own society may assume that religion is finished for the likes of them; but this is just another example of our ethnocentricity and its takes these Africans to show it.

A MISSION TO BRITAIN

And thirdly, here is a striking feed-back from the whole mission enterprise of the past century and a half. If the Christianity our missionaries have planted overseas has really caught on then it should be something that goes with these other peoples wherever they go, and that fits their lives and needs and cultural forms; otherwise it is merely an imposed Western veneer that can be peeled off as soon as our imperial power departs. The advent of these African and other forms in Britain is proof that the veneer theory is wrong. But they do more than confirm that our good works overseas have been successful. There is another kind of feed-back that has scarcely begun to appear as yet. Some of the African churches have a sense of mission towards us! They see how static and ineffective we are, and how little we share some of their own central convictions about prayer, fasting, healing, the power of the Spirit and the joy of worship. They ride on the crest of a religion that works. They share also in the new-found African convictions of having an important contribution to make to the nations of the world, especially in the realms of human relations and of the spiritual where we are increasingly dessicated and inadequate. One sign of the authenticity of their christian faith is a desire to share their discoveries and open up to us again the dynamic of our mutual heritage. We may yet see African missionaries to darkest Britain. The real test will come when we who still monopolize the material resources of the world are prepared to pay for these missionaries to ourselves, for those with the dynamism but not the wealth to bring to us the revival we need.

Christian Expansion and Mission

This, however, will seem a wild anticipation to those familiar only with the British scene, and it is more relevant in the first place to try to understand the background of these African movements. We will see this if we start with an overview of the history of christian expansion from the beginning. Then we see that its main expansion has been either into tribal cultures or into sophisticated cultures that still possessed a tribal type of religion; and further, that black Africa (not forgetting Oceania) represents only the second great expansion of the faith into a major geographical and cultural area, comparable to the spread into Europe.

This provides us with a broad backdrop against which to examine a new phenomenon that has appeared in the course of this second expansion into tribal societies in modern times, and that includes the African independent churches as its most extensive example. We now have to learn how to take the denomination of the Cherubim and Seraphim into our company, and to learn from them even while we seek to share the experience and learning we have derived from our much longer christian history. With the more syncretistic forms we are faced with an attempt to understand people like the peyotists who feel they have already appropriated the christian gospel in their own way, and who indeed have made some move in this direction, but who are patently far from anything we could rightly call a christian church. At the further end of the range there is the even more difficult problem of relating to movements that explicitly reject the christian religion from which they have borrowed much of their new system, such as the Godianism religion of midwestern and eastern Nigeria, or the Handsome Lake religion of some 5,000 Iroquois Indians in eastern North America. . . .

The sheer size of some of these new bodies compels attention, as also the number of different groups. For Africa as a whole the suggestion is that some six or seven million people find their spiritual home in perhaps 6,000 of these new bodies, and in some areas they are steadily increasing. I think there is also a tendency for movements to shift in the course of time across the spectrum from the more traditional highly-syncretistic forms towards the more orthodox christian position. This is evident in the widespread demand for the Bible and for help in understanding it, as also in the training of leadership. No one wants to be left behind in the rapid development that is occurring in Africa, and many of these groups are aware of their poor resources in equipment and education, even while confident of their spiritual strength.

OUR IMAGE OF MISSION

If the cause of christian missions has lost some of its appeal in our churches and is not a live or contemporary subject in our syllabuses, it is not because the great day of missions is over but because we are not sufficiently in touch with what is really happening elsewhere. It is not missions that are out of date, but our image of what is involved. And we cannot suggest that all responsibility along the new front that has now appeared should devolve upon the local national churches. For one thing, they are still struggling to meet their own needs by way of development; and for another, they stand in a specially sensitive position in relation to the new movements that have seceded from them or in various ways stolen their thunder, especially through more rapid and visible indigenization. We who are not so involved at this point are often freer to make an approach that is acceptable; and in any case we are responsible for the only too Western forms of Christianity introduced into African life (what else could we bring, God help us!), and it is against these that much African independency is reacting. Even in trying to help the independents we will do it again (God save us!), unless we take them seriously as authentic forms we need to understand and even learn from.

This is all part of our whole effort to understand and appreciate that wide section of mankind whose cultural background is of the pre-literate and tribal form. The chief difficulties lie in our inbred Western christian superiority over the 'crude life of primitive and savage peoples', coupled with our ignorance of their cultures, religion and sheer humanity. Their own new religious movements, above all in Africa, reveal the dynamic, creative, and revitalizing capacities of these peoples, able to produce their own innovators and their own transitional forms between the cultures of the past and the new cultures that are now being evolved.

Notes

1. The relationship between these immigrant groups and the white churches in Britain is being explored by a new Project on Partnership Between Black and White established in late 1978 at the Selly Oak Colleges, Birmingham, under the direction of the Rev. Roswith Gerloff.

G. SOCIO-CULTURAL

For some this may be the least expected section, with its themes of modernization, education and development. The often-assumed irrelevance of "off-beat" religious movements, and the merely secular nature of these processes are here questioned in the interests of a profounder understanding both of development and of the movements themselves.

25

The Place of Independent Religious Movements in the Modernization of Africa

> *This essay seeks to counter the image of these movements as ignorant and reactionary, compensating people for their miserable lot in life in a turbulent Africa, but diverting energies from national development and modernization. The deeper dimensions of the cultural changes necessary for such development are explored in relation to the new forms of life and the new world views offered by the new religious movements.*

The eruption on to the world political scene of some thirty new independent nations in the continent of Africa within something like a decade is surely one of the most unexpected, exciting and significant political developments of our time. This essay is concerned with the religious background to this development in that part of the continent known as sub-saharan or Black Africa. Here the main religions involved have been the ethnic or traditional religions of the African tribal peoples in their interaction with the immigrant Christian religion associated with the invasion of Western culture, although in the northern and eastern reaches of this area Islam has long been a significant political influence.

The contribution of the Christian religion commences with the churches brought by freed Negro slaves first to Sierra Leone in the late eighteenth century and then to Liberia early in the nineteenth century, and continues through the great missionary expansion and the resultant range of autonomous churches that have produced a Christian population of some 43 million (excluding Ethiopia) south of the Sahara. It is not our present intention to examine the extent to which Christian missions and churches, through their own teachings, through their pioneering in education, and through their association with Western culture and its political forms and ideas have been a major factor in the growth of nationalist sentiment and the achievement of political independence. The outlines, at least, of this history are often recognized, and for recent evidence one need only enquire into the education received by most of the founders or first heads of the new nations.

We shall narrow our purpose to an examination of the relation between the modern secular nation-states and other less-known religious groups in Africa — the post-missions independent prophet movements and churches, most of them claiming to be Christian, that have emerged from the older missions and churches in increasing numbers since the end of the last century. The religious content of these movements varies considerably, from those which are plainly neo-primal revivals of traditional religions, to those which closely resemble the parent Christian body from which they sprang; but in some sense they all stand between Western forms of Christianity and the ethnic religions of Africa, and to that extent have more indigenous roots and may serve as a specially valuable indicator of the relation between religion and politics.

RELIGIOUS INDEPENDENCY AND THE RISE OF NATIONALISM

The history of the spirited reaction of African peoples against invading white rulers reaches back to the Xhosa of South Africa, who at various times between 1815 and 1857 sought deliverance from the foreigners by a holy war under a divinely-raised leader who was influenced by Christian ideas and sometimes promised his people a glorious future. This general pattern may be traced in many subsequent revolts against European rulers or colonial powers: those of Witbooi and Stürmann in South West Africa around the turn of the century; Enoch Mgijima in South Africa after the first World War; John Chilembwe in the then Nyasaland of 1915; the various revolts in the Belgian Congo from the Epikilipikili movement of 1904 to the Kitawala troubles from 1925 onwards, and the whole range of disturbances associated with the many forms of religio-political groups deriving from the prophet Simon Kimbangu imprisoned in 1921; the revolt of the Religion of the Ancestral Spirits (Dini ya Misambwa) in Western Kenya in 1948–50, and the Mau Mau revolt in 1952 among the Kikuyu; the Uganda riots in which Reuben Spartas, founder of the African Greek

Orthodox Church, figured in 1949 — these are but the more obvious examples of uprisings of a political nature intimately associated with or springing from prophet or messianic movements or independent churches.[1]

Less violent or more concealed forms of national feeling could be traced in many independent religious movements stressing Africa for the African and deliverance from white domination, such as James Limba's Church of Christ founded in 1910 in South Africa and numbering some 120,000 members in 1964, or the National Church of Nigeria with its anti-Christian religion of the "God of Africa".

The relation between the religious and the political components in these independent movements varies from one to another and at different periods in the history of any one group, so that generalizations must be treated with the greatest care. Some movements have been primarily religious in their original concerns and activities, but have been forced into political action or revolt when colonial authorities have misinterpreted them as centres of subversion, insofar as any new independent African activity and organization was regarded as politically dangerous. This seems to have been the fate of the genuinely religious healing movement of Kimbangu, although no one can say that it would never have developed political concern if the Belgians had not greeted it with severe repression. Recent evidence suggests that political interest was being forced on Simon Toko's resolutely a-political "Red Star Church" by the oppressive attitude of the Angolan authorities. On the other hand there are political movements with a religious aura where the political component has declined in importance and the ordinary religious functions have become the main activity. The famous prophet Harris began as a religiously-inspired political rebel against the Americo-Liberian government, and then became a sincerely a-political leader of a mass movement from traditional religions to a latent form of Christianity. Other examples of the same transition may be found in Spartas' African Greek Orthodox Church in Uganda, André Matswa's movement in the Congos, the Kitawala movement in Zambia, and the National Church of Nigeria.

The most that can be said is that a considerable number of independent religious movements in Africa have actively contributed to the development of political nationalism at some stage in their history. At the same time it must be remembered that there are nations such as Malawi, Ghana and Sierra Leone which have become independent without any background of support from independent religious movements (although Malawi and Ghana had plenty on which to draw), and that there are many prophet-healing churches which have shown no political interest through several decades of their existence. On the other hand, the mere existence of new independent and indigenous forms of religion inevitably provided indirect support for independence in the political sphere also.

INDEPENDENT RELIGIOUS MOVEMENTS AS AGENTS OF UNIFICATION

The divisive influence of tribalism within the new national political units has been painfully in evidence since the achievement of independence, and threatens the existence of Nigeria, the largest nation in Africa, as this is written. One of the striking features of the independent religious movements is the extent to which so many have succeeded in transcending the limitations of language, tribe, and region and have achieved a wider community. It is true that some, especially those at the neo-primal end of the spectrum, are clearly attempts at rebuilding a tribal unity shattered by the impact of the Western world. The early Xhosa prophets, the Dina ya Misambwa among the Kitosh and Busisi, the Bwiti cult among the Fang of Gabon, these remain essentially tribal in scope. Other movements have remained predominantly within one people, such as the Lumpa Church among the Bemba of Zambia. On the other hand, among the Nilotic peoples of the Sudan some of the earliest prophet-figures who arose in resistance to invading cultures, European or Arab, began to have more than local or even tribal significance by the end of the nineteenth century. They represented a transtribal political unity amounting to a structural change that was a form of modernization.[2]

More recent movements are often remarkable for their ethnic and linguistic variety, and their geographical spread beyond the limits of both tribe and nation, without losing their local basis. Kivuli, founder of the African Israel Church in Kenya, spoke some five vernaculars, encouraged intermarriage between Luo and Ragolu, and used both these languages in services. The Church of Christ in Africa, founded in 1957 as a Luo church, by 1964 had members in a large number of tribes or sub-tribes of Kenya, Uganda and North Tanzania and clergy from at least three major tribes traditionally hostile to the Luo. It has been said that it was the inter-tribal aspiration of Chilembwe's movement in 1915 that, as much as any other factor, caused it to fail; in this respect it was ahead of its time. The Church of the Lord (Aladura) has spread from Nigeria through many of the peoples of Ghana and also of Liberia and Sierra Leone, thus spanning some eighteen hundred miles and many linguistic and political barriers, and encouraging intermarriage at least among its ministers. South African churches have spread up into Central Africa, and it has been remarked that in the Congo area, Zambia and Malawi, religious independence is usually not correlated with tribal grouping. Indeed, even race has occasionally been transcended: an Indian woman has been reported in Shembe's Church in Natal, and some six or eight whites in the Kimbanguist church at Matadi. One observer, therefore, declares that once an independent religious movement has appeared within a tribe, "the character of the whole movement changes from tribal to universal; tribal differentia recede in importance; membership is extended to other tribes, among whom missionaries are now sent; city congregations become multi-tribal; the appeal becomes universal".

This is a contribution of the utmost importance for the future of Africa, but it should be noted that the wider community emerging within these religious groups seldom if ever coincides with the new national communities whose future is so uncertain. At the most they may be regarded as a form of proto-nationalism. The idea of the nation is still tenuous and lacks the necessary history and mythology to support it, as an adequate focus for self-identity. Many of the new religious movements have been able to replace the tribe and its mythology by a new "place in which to feel at home", the independent all-African church, founded in Africa by Africans and for Africans, under the prophetic leader specially raised up in Africa by God himself. Here we have the beginnings of a new sense of identity over against other races and their churches, often coupled with the vision of a great African church that will command the respect of the whole world and make its own special contribution to the religions of mankind. This church finds its mythology in the 'Ethiopian' concept, derived from the biblical references to Ethiopia and embodied in the ancient Christian kingdom of Ethiopia — an African nation not dependent on Europeans for its religion and even able to defeat them in battle, as proved in the defeat of the Italians at Aduwa in 1896. In spite of the fissiparous nature of these religious movements this sense of belonging to a great African spiritual and Christian community seems to be more conspicuous than notions of a single church for the nation. Even the early nationalists in West Africa in the days of E. W. Blyden and the foundation of the first independent churches in Nigeria in the 1890's were moved by the idea of a single all-African Christian church for West Africa, for as yet there was no concept of "Nigeria".

It is true that there have been occasional signs of a national church in Chilembwe's vision for Nyasaland, in the neo-primal National Church of Nigeria, in the reported attempt by some Kimbanguists to have their church become the official church in the new Congo republic, or in the endeavour in 1965 of an association of independent churches in Kenya to secure Kenyatta's support for recognition as the national religion of the independent state.³ These, however, seem to be the exceptions, and it is left to the older churches and missions to pursue their ecumenical visions of one church for the nation, of the correlation between the religious and the political units with which they are familiar in the Western culture from which they derive. While the need for national unity in African states is obvious and urgent we should not lament the fact that these religious movements do not directly provide a spiritual sanction and support for the nation; rather should we recognize how artificial many present political units are in African eyes, how much deeper are the unities of race and of similarities of traditional cultures, and how this wider sense of community expresses a genuine insight into the universal claims of the Christian religion, and also corresponds to the groping efforts of many modern nations to establish supra-national forms of political organization.

Although, historically speaking, many of the independent movements provided "a home for nationalistic enterprises" their further history usually reveals a refusal to be regarded merely as nationalistic enterprises. The most explicit examples of this distinction are to be found in the clashes between the governments of newly independent states in Africa and some of their own independent religious groups. Thus in the Congo (Brazzaville) the André Matswa movement began as a purely political activity and then developed more as an independent church, which the nationalist politicians tried to turn to their own purposes; the opposition it presented to the colonial government was continued under the independent régime of Fulbert Youlou by refusal to pay taxes or make census returns, so that the African government had to use the same measures as those of the former French masters, and imprison some of the leaders. In Tanzania, the Dini ya Jehovah na Michael is reported as a religious movement appearing in 1963 in protest against the ruling political party. One of the causes of the rebellion of Alice Lenshina and the Lumpa Church against the African government of Zambia in 1964 was her advice to her followers two years previously to take no part in political activities, and the subsequent attacks on them for not joining the dominant nationalist party. These examples alone would be sufficient to query the view that independent religious movements are no more than disguised forms of nationalism or of protest against colonialism; they have their own specific religious dynamic.

THE DE-SACRALIZATION OF POLITICS

Even more important than the transcendence of tribalism achieved by so many independent religious movements is the effect they have had on the whole concept of government and society. In most traditional societies of Africa the tribe itself and its rulers and institutions were set within a sacred cosmic order. The patterns and the sanctions for political organization were often derived from a religious cosmology and the mythology that expressed and supported it, and the political leader or head was the channel through which ultimate or cosmic forces operated for the welfare of the society. Sacral kingship has been widespread, and sharp separation between religious and political institutions and activities has been rare. Such a society may be called ontocratic.

It was therefore only natural that there should have been an intimate and sometimes even a structural unity between the earliest forms of independent church and of nationalist political movement. This natural tendency was powerfully reinforced by the fact that the leaders of anti-colonial political movements had so often received their educational equipment and even their radical ideas from Christian schools. It is not surprising therefore that so many African political organizations during the struggle for independence have clothed themselves in Christian forms, using hymns, prayers and catechisms and extensive quotations from the Bible. The clearest case of this unity of religious and political independency is probably Chilembwe's movement in Nyasaland, but the same conjunction may be seen in different degrees in the early Nigerian "African" churches in Lagos and in Reuben Spartas' church in Uganda, as well as in those political movements allied to a neo-primal form of religious independency, such as the early Zikist movement with its National Church of Nigeria, the Mau Mau movement with its distortions of the originally Christian Kikuyu independent churches and schools, and the Comité Mixte Gabonais (and later names) with its association with the Bwiti cult by which Léon Mba was both a political and a cult leader.

If such associations had become general there would have been a tendency to perpetuate an ontocratic society with a national religion interwoven with its political structure. In the event, however, the religious and the political manifestations of independency have tended to move apart, with the former becoming one church among others, including the older mission-connected churches, in the nation, and the latter taking the usual Western forms of secular trades unions and political parties. This differentiation of the spheres and structures of religion and politics amounts to a secularization of the latter that is a most important new departure in African cultures. It implies a radical desacralization of African society, of tribe and authority and government, a basic and essential transformation from ontocratic to modern forms of society. It also serves to clarify the distinction between Christianity and the colonial powers, for in African eyes the distinction between the religion and the politics of their European masters was by no means as clear as colonial governments liked to think.

At present a partial exception to this development is found in the peculiar position of the independent churches of South Africa, whose members are denied a share in political activity and secular government, and unable freely to express political criticism. In consequence some of the churches show an uncritical acceptance of the political powers, and are prepared to co-operate with the government and its apartheid policy while continuing much as a traditional ontocratic society among themselves, with the religious leaders replacing the traditional chiefs and diviners, and the life of the community organized on a more ontocratic pattern. This is a distortion of the development found in most other areas.

Even though African independent religious movements have not provided new national or state religions, it is sometimes claimed that the new political parties and leaders themselves serve a pseudo-religious purpose, especially where authoritarian politics tends to pervade the whole of life and the founders of independence are given a messianic status. If this were the trend of events it would be a serious qualification of what we have said about the transformation from an ontocratic to a modern society. It might seem to be supported by the public attitudes and also by the actions on occasion of independent churches themselves towards the political leaders of the last decade; one could quote the ways in which Nkrumah, Azikiwe, Banda, Kenyatta, Houphouët-Boigny, Lumumba, and also the older leader, Tubman in Liberia, have been given messianic and sometimes almost divine status. It is sufficient, however, to recall the nature of African praise-orations as traditionally delivered to prominent figures or even to much embarrassed Western visitors, and also the extremely short-lived glory of Nkrumah, the most messianic of these leaders, to realize that these apparently religious features are more superficial than substantial and do not belie the radical secularization and modernization that have occurred.

Where there is association between new governments and independent religious movements it appears to be more informal and loose, as in Kenya, or in the Ivory Coast where the government of the Rassemblement Démocratique Africain sent a representative to the special independence ceremony of the Harristes. Probably the most significant evidence on this point is to be found in the former Belgian Congo, where the various Kimbanguist groups had been deeply involved in the struggle against the colonial power. The Association du Bas-Congo (Abako) movement led by the first president, Kasavubu, is reported to have been closely associated with the Kimbanguist church, included Kimbanguists in its official candidates and in the committee drawing up the new constitution, and the eldest son of Kimbangu in the cabinet of Lumumba. This church has also had its full share of access to the national radio and of army chaplaincies, and Simon Kimbangu himself has been the centre of a growing body of legend in which he figures as the father of the modern Congo. It is therefore all the more surprising that recent reports indicate that the church has not been conspicuously partisan, but seems to be content to become one recognized body among the other churches, and to be following a policy of "render unto Caesar the things that are Caesar's and unto God the things that are God's."

This is the formula widely used to acknowledge the differentiation between religion and politics, not only among those who might have been tempted otherwise, but also among the many independent religious movements that are clearly a-political. Noteworthy among these are the Malawi and Ghana movements, most Nigerian movements especially the prophet-healing types, Kitawala in Zambia, the Lassyists in Cabinda and Simon Toko's church in Angola, and a substantial proportion of the Bantu independents in South Africa.

A particularly interesting example of the distinction between religious and other activities is perhaps to be found in the recent history of the new town of Aiyetoro ("Happy City") founded in 1947 by an aladura group in Nigeria. It began as a highly integrated community where religious activities were identified with the strenuous economic labours that achieved an astonishing development within a decade. Since 1963, under the second head, it is reported that specifically religious activities have increased, and that the head is now more like a bishop concerned with mystical "instructions" from God, and leaving daily practical business to a council and committees. If so, this community in its own short history is demonstrating the transition we are examining.[4] Similar developments are reported within Kimbanguism. Since 1959 when it became properly organized it has embarked on many secular activities to which we refer below; this produced an early reaction, the Prophetic Church of Mayumbe, which seceded in 1960 in protest against such worldly actions, and sought to confine itself to religious functions as the true work of a church.[5]

These religious movements are therefore helping Africa to achieve within one life-span the passage from an ontocratic to a modern secular state and religiously plural society that has not yet been quite completed after over a millennium of experiment and endeavour in Europe. When we think of the time spent over the great mediaeval experiment with a Christendom, and the struggles to eliminate the "divine right of kings" and all sacral monarchies, to secure religious toleration and pluralism, and to deal with the new mystiques and mythologies of the totalitarian states of the present century, then we realize the value of these indigenous grass-roots African movements that have so largely undermined the traditional mystiques of chiefship and ethnic group, established specialized societies for the purposes of religion, and allowed political development in independent Africa to proceed on an increasingly secular basis.

They have done this of course only because they have been able to resacralize so much of the common life of their members within the context of the new religious community, with its own religious mythology, charter, and sanctions. While encouraging the secularization of certain spheres of public life in new political institutions, they have not succumbed to secularism as an ideology, but have retained the religious dimension in the new form of a church, a single religious authority and institution distinguished from the diffused forms of religion that were integral to traditional society. From this position they may be able to develop a critique of the political, and if necessary an active opposition to any tendency to absolutism or the creation of a new political religion, as well as a critique of the old traditional societies and of attempts to revive them.

INDEPENDENT CHURCHES IN THE TRANSITION TO SECULAR POLITICS

An example of the contribution we have been outlining is to be found in a study of these religious movements among the Tiriki people in Western Kenya by W. H. Sangree.[6] It appears that there has been considerable secularization of the political life of the Tiriki. The elders who formerly administered the ancestral cults, and in so doing gained authority and status from supernatural forces, are now set free from their ritual duties by the decay of these cults. While they still administer the traditional initiation ceremonies and thus preserve some of their former status, these are not so clearly backed by supernatural sanctions, and the main source of the authority of the elders is increasingly derived from the judicial roles assigned to them in the new secular forms of government bureaucracy.

Sangree describes the problem of transition from the old to the new political forms in terms of the conflict chiefs and leaders feel at two points. Traditional leadership dealt with "particularistic and functionally diffuse kinship and clan obligations" — with all the affairs of a limited group intimately related to them; modern bureaucratic office imposes tasks that are "universalistic and functionally specific" — concerned with only some of the affairs of life, but with these affairs in the lives of all residents in an administrative area even if not related or known to the leaders. Leadership roles are therefore more limited in range or scope in one sense, but more extensive in another sense and at the same time more impersonal.

The church groups, especially the independent indigenous movements, are described as making an important contribution in this transitional process. They "provide a ready-made framework within which a leader can fulfil some of the particularistic relationships traditionally expected of men in authority, while at the same time, with the aid of Christian ritual and symbols, increasingly eliciting more universalistic and functionally specific relationships in those areas where social, economic and political patterns have been most modified and broadened by European contact" (p. xxxi). Government has encouraged traditional leadership to follow the new secular administrative pattern, and at the same time has welcomed a parallel administrative development for the better organization of the independent churches. These have therefore provided new opportunities for leadership that is specific in function but universal in its human outreach. They have done this for entirely positive reasons and as part of the whole political and social development of the Tiriki, and not, as Sundkler describes in South Africa, because this is the only avenue of expression for men denied their normal share in the political leadership of their people.

It is also significant that the chief who has played a major part in recent political leadership of the Tiriki was educated in mission schools and at one stage was a prominent church member. Since resuming beer-drinking and becoming a polygamist he is no longer a member of any of the churches, but retains the respect of both Christians and others, alike for his personal qualities and modern leadership. He describes himself as "a man of God and a believer in Jesus Christ, but a man without a church." His story and his religious position are not unlike that of many of the leaders of the new African nations, and perhaps it is better that these be not too closely identified with existing religious bodies at this stage of the development of secular politics.

A further illustration of the relation of independent churches to politics may be drawn from the one best known to the writer, the Church of the Lord (Aladura) in West Africa.[7] When it arose in the later nineteen-twenties the earlier conjunction between religious and political independency of the Blyden period had already passed, and there were never any connections with nationalist movements or leaders. At the same time the founding prophet, Oshitelu, preached and published judgment upon all and sundry, including the white race and the colonial power; on the face of it at least this was dangerously subversive and he narrowly escaped government suppression. This more violent attitude gave way to a long period of withdrawal from concern with politics and concentration on the religious mission of the church and its expansion across West Africa. This is epitomized in the prophet who in 1969 headed the Church in Sierra Leone; he had been embarked in Nigeria on a political career with the party known as the Action Group but abandoned politics for the ministry of this Church and then described himself as "belonging only to Jesus' party".

For well over twenty years there was no interest in politics as such, and contact with political leaders was confined to moderately successful attempts to secure patronage or assistance of traditional rulers in Nigeria, of chiefs or members of the legislature in Ghana, or of the President in Liberia. With the coming of political independence a new interest in political matters began to appear. There were protests against the French atomic explosions in the Sahara, congratulations to the heads of the new states, a three-day fast with "strong prayers" for the Congo and Algeria in their current problems, and the following resolution was passed at one of the annual conferences:

> "That letters be sent to the . . . Independent Countries of Nigeria, Ghana, Liberia, Sierra Leone, Guinea, etc., of the necessity of a

National Church or Spiritual Organization of this type to supply much needed inspiration and guidance, as Political Independence without a Spiritual National Church is a farce".

This must not be interpreted as a design for a state church so much as a recognition of the need for both secular government and a religious basis for the community. The present head of the Church, Adejobi, believes that the Church must be above party allegiances and has its own work to do alongside that of the state. This may include criticism of acts of the government, and we could quote instances of this at the height of the Nkrumah régime in Ghana. In Sierra Leone the lay head or "General Warden" of the large Freetown congregation was for long an important trade union leader and later a member of parliament. In 1955 the commission investigating the serious riots in Freetown early in the year laid most of the blame on this church leader (in our opinion quite unjustly). What is remarkable is that he has not attempted to use his church position for political purposes, although he has endeavoured to bring his religious convictions to bear on his political activities — he describes how he prayed and fasted before taking the serious decision to call the strike that precipitated the riots. It would be difficult to take exception to this thoroughly modern form of the relation between religion and politics.

The Church of the Lord has also demonstrated the capacity of Africans for new types of organization that are both "universalistic and functionally specific" through its hierarchical administration of a religious body transcending ethnic boundaries and extending across so much of West Africa and yet retaining its unity. We once had the opportunity of drawing the attention of Nkrumah to this religious parallel to a "United States of West-Africa" at the time when he was setting up the Ghana-Guinea Union and campaigning for Pan-African unity; but our remarks were coldly received!

FROM MYTH TO HISTORY:
INDEPENDENT CHURCHES AND PROGRESS

Behind the institutionalizing of religion in churches and the secularization of politics there lies the fundamental cultural transformation from a mythological (and hence a sacral) society and world-view to a modern society set within a historical view of life. This semitic outlook has been introduced into Africa through the impact of the Bible and of the Western civilization that has the biblical attitude to time woven into its fabric, and that thinks in terms of the future and of progress towards a goal. In spite of all the flux and change in the history of African peoples their societies may be described as essentially static, looking along the lines of lineage and genealogy into the mythical past and finding there, in common origins, whatever unity there might be for present sections of society. The future would see the segmentation of society proceeding still further but all development would be repetition of the present pattern, and there was no prospect of society being unified or improved in the future. As in archaic societies, the source and sanctions for life lay in the mythical past, and religion was concerned with the regular renewal of the vitalities of man and nature but not with their radical transformation or extension. Into this repetitive, conservative society there came the view that life is tied neither to the past nor to the levels of the present, but can progress to a paradisal consummation in the future. This is the revolution in world-view represented in secular form by schemes of development for undeveloped nations, and in religious form not only by the explicit millennialisms but also by the ordinary evangel and achievements of the independent and the older churches. The widespread penetration of this outlook accounts for the mounting demand for the better human existence that so many Africans see should and can be theirs.

It must be emphasized that the resultant modernization is not to be identified with westernization, for the new culture and way of life being born in Africa will be generated both from traditional sources and from Western and other influences; what the outcome will be no one can as yet foresee. In this process of drawing from both local and invading cultures the independent churches serve a valuable purpose. They operate at the grass-roots level, with peasants and artisans, literate and illiterate; their forms of worship, of church life and religious proclamation are their own new, yet still African, creations, not "promoted" as "Africanizations" by well-meaning Western Christians or self-conscious African ministers in the older churches, but springing from the vitalities of African existence in response to the impact of the biblical message; and if the latter may appear submerged at times or syncretized, there are signs that it contains its own corrective, and that this is already at work. This capacity to synthesize traditional forms and values with new modes of life and organization, and to do so within the new historical mode of thought, makes the independent churches important agents of modernization, yet accommodated to their members' readiness for change, and cushioning the impact upon them of the disturbing forces from the outside world.

We have mentioned the necessity of a religious tolerance and pluralism in a modern society, and it does seem that the independent movements are increasingly willing to accept recognition as churches among the other churches, while retaining a vision of the great African Church that is to be. Harris movements that were hostile to the older churches in the Ivory Coast are now reported to be much more ecumenically minded, and this seems to be a general tendency; indeed some of the independent churches would desire nothing better than to be fully accepted as members of inter-church Christian Councils, as seven were in the Christian Council of Kenya by 1966. Others have formed their own ecumenical associations, in Kenya, in Nigeria, and in South Africa, and it is by no means true that this movement is a hopelessly fissiparous mass of "sects" unable to organize effectively for life in a modern society. The divisiveness itself, however weakening in its current excessive forms, also serves to establish a religiously plural society, based on free individual choice, and is checked by the ecumenical developments that also occur. It must be remembered, of course, that the traditional religions of Africa, like most archaic religions, were not intolerant or exclusive; but then neither were they missionary, with a gospel to preach, and it is this achievement of a religion that is both tolerant and missionary (even to the extent of opening branches in London!) that is an important modern development.

The modernizing contribution is not confined to the sphere of religion. It may be traced in the impact upon traditional polygamous marriage systems, for although the practice of polygamy may be retained and may be a valuable bulwark against contemporary developments of promiscuity, the emphasis is changed and a new monogamous ideal is being recognized, and will have its effect by progressive adaptation. Likewise there may be changes from endogamy to exogamy in the transtribal communities of the independent churches. Most remarkable of all is the open attack on the matrilineal family and inheritance system that is reported to have occurred in John Ahui's Harris church in the Ivory Coast.[8] Both Roman and Protestant missions and the government itself had been campaigning with little success against the matrilineal system. Ahui ignored the jealousy of nephews to send his own son for education in France, and has written into the church catechism the comprehensive duties of parents to their own children. One of Ahui's leaders bequeathed by will his material possessions and his church responsibilities to his eldest son. And this has happened in a society where 80% of the privately-supported Ivory Coast students in France between 1950–60 were dependent on their maternal relatives, or where a student's cousins might force him to reimburse them with the amount that his own father had spent on his education!

In the medical realm the contribution of the prophet-healing churches has lain in the extent to which they have relieved the overstrained government and mission medical services by providing their own assistance, especially and often successfully to women anxious over their childlessness and to those with the wide range of psychosomatic troubles to be found in a rapidly changing society. These churches and prophets have done this at the same time that they have condemned all recourse to magic and the more harmful traditional forms of treatment. Even if some of the new "Christian" forms have themselves been magically interpreted, the use of prayer, faith, fasting, and holy water or blessed oil represent a distinct advance over alternative treatment that might otherwise have been used. The break with traditional practices at this point is one of the most impressive achievements of the better examples of these movements.

The economic modernization of Africa is in the forefront of world attention, but is not always realized how insufficient or even harmful external economic aid in isolation from other social and cultural changes may be for underdeveloped countries. The economic achievements and consequences of some of the independent churches should not be overlooked, as they usually are in plans for economic development. There is a widely reported testimony to the reliability and industry of employees belonging to these churches — whether among some of the Zionists of South Africa, the Toko church members of Angola, or the Kitawala of Zambia who refused to take part in politically-motivated strikes. The common prohibitions on the use of alcohol or tobacco are also of substantial economic significance in underdeveloped countries, where what may be afforded as a luxury in affluent societies becomes a serious economic and social liability. Some of the leaders of South African independent churches have inaugurated large agricultural or commercial enterprises and become wealthy men, and the 1967 annual Easter assembly of the Christian Catholic Apostolic Church in Zion (Bantu) actually had at the same time a kind of agricultural show organized by its secretary, an employee in the government agricultural department; the African Congregational Church has its own housing scheme in a Pietermaritzburg suburb.[9] Some churches have founded their own new villages supported by manifold economic activities, as Shembe's Ekuphakamene (with its home industries) and Lekganyane's Zion City Morija in South Africa, Wovenu's Tadzevu in Ghana, and above all the Nigerian Aiyetoro town to which we have already referred.

Perhaps the most comprehensive range of modern activities is that reported in 1966 in the main Kimbanguist church in the Kinshasa area; this now has schools, youth movements, workshops, dispensaries, a cooperative, an agricultural community, a community development centre, etc., and even if some of these are rather elementary and struggling with inadequate resources and personnel, such as the newspaper that had to cease publication, there is no gainsaying that here is an important channel whereby new ideas and techniques may flow into the more rural areas of this church, where people can learn to plan and to use money, supported by incentives and governed by controls that a religious body can provide.

AMBIVALENCES AND UNCERTAINTIES

It must also be recognized, however, that these movements may be somewhat ambivalent, with certain consequences that are reactionary or dysfunctional. This certainly happens where the emphasis on healing by prayer, holy water, etc., precludes the urgent surgical treatment that alone may save a life. The economic effects also deserve a comprehensive study from this point of view. For example, a member of the Kokamba movement in the Ivory Coast explained that it had saved him from extensive expenditure on fetishes and sacrifices, so that he had been able to buy a powered bicycle. Yet this same movement had forbidden the cultivation of yams and replaced these with the less nutritious cassava, thus aggravating the serious problem of African malnutrition.[10] The time and energy devoted to long and strenuous meetings for worship often far into the night, the warnings against certain quite normal actions or journeys, conveyed in dream or prophecy, the unrealistic attitudes to one's own status or capacities engendered by belief in having now enlisted the "power of the Spirit" on one's behalf — the physical and economic effects of these features can hardly be said to contribute to modernization, and require further study.

Roger Bastide raises the question of the ambivalence of what he calls messianic movements in rather different terms.[11] Since they are in various degrees syncretistic they contain within themselves the possibility of developing in a traditionalist or nativistic direction, thus opposing modernization, or of furthering this process by progressively replacing the closed and magical world of myth and dream with the open historical world of rational planning. In addition, the same movement may further the latter process under a colonial régime (by strengthening the demand for independence) and then become so opposed to the new African régime's plans for development that it begins to strengthen the forces of traditionalism. Bastide describes this as ceasing to be a "movement" and becoming a "sect" characterized by rigidity and by separation from what is happening in the world.

A somewhat similar view has been developed by Albert Doutreloux,[12] who claims that "Marxist theory is correct in asserting that, in a given socio-cultural context, prophetism may be a positive factor of conscious orientation [to social development], but that at a later stage its role becomes negative as it channels the energies thus liberated into utopian directions." What Doutreloux calls "prophetism" is ultimately concerned with establishing an autonomous religious reality that correlates with social development only indirectly and against its own basically non-social intentions. He illustrates this with the progressive dissociation from politics seen in certain movements in both the Congos and the Central African Republic — in Matswanism and the Kimbanguist Prophetic Church.

While Doutreloux avoids the reduction of the religious to non-religious categories that has distorted some studies of these movements, he operates with a view of the "pure" religious as essentially other-worldly, and therefore as escapist. It is questionable whether this does correspond to the prophetic form in the history of religions, and it is certainly contrary to the Semitic form of prophetism that has invaded most of Africa and to the specifically biblical form that has penetrated in various degrees the religious movements we are considering. It would also seem ill-matched to the strong this-worldly concern with present blessings characteristic of these movements, and the ever-widening range of the benefits that are sought.

Bastide also recognizes the tendency to escape into utopia found in many of his messianic movements but points out that there are positive elements even in this process. The dreamed-of utopia contains the goods or benefits brought by white civilization and therefore implies an acceptance of new needs, a criticism of the old order that failed to supply them, and an attempt, albeit unrealistic, at a more modern reconstructed order.[13]

The relation of Africa's new movements to modernization is therefore exceedingly complex, with negative as well as positive aspects, and with the possibility of the balance of these in any particular movement altering from one social and historical situation to another.

THE FUTURE: PROBLEMS AND DANGERS

The outline we have offered is a necessarily over-simplified account of what we believe to be important contributions to the modernization of Africa, and is based for the most part on evidence from bodies at the more Christian end of the scale of independent movements. Our justification for this is that the most clearly neo-primal movements have usually had a shorter life or have declined in importance, and seldom attract the new élites for long — these are more likely to be involved in new imported forms of occultism and magic. It also appears that some of the more syncretistic movements show signs of development towards a more Christian content, although we cannot set too much store by this at present. On the other hand the number of Africans who are adherents of the traditional ethnic religions is possibly increasing with the rapid increase in the population, just as the practice of magic may be increasing through the adoption of more sophisticated forms in the urban areas. The task of modernization therefore does not decrease and the role of the independent churches remains important.

Whether they can hold and consolidate such transcendence of tribalism as they have achieved, against its recrudescence as in Nigeria, remains to be seen. Likewise the further development of the differentiation between religion and politics — will this lead to the right kind of re-engagement with political responsibility, or into an escapist religion concerned only with immediate individual benefits and otherwise socially conservative or indifferent? As yet much of the new aspiration in Africa is foreshortened, especially among the independent churches, to concern with present benefits such as the type of healing they offer, to a sense of the power and presence of the Spirit manifest in the more ecstatic ways, to protection from the traditional spiritual evil powers and the provision of a general sense of social and spiritual security through having a new community in which to feel at home. These benefits do not seem to depend on what the politicians do or fail to do. But as the sights are raised and the full benefits of the modern world come into view more clearly there may come a greater interest in politics, and a disillusionment with the situation after independence — the poor quality of education, the lack of medical care, the extent of corruption, and social diseases such as unemployment, prostitution, and increasing crime. Whether this disillusionment will produce reactions or revolts akin to those prompted by the miseries of colonialism, or a more extreme escapism into "spiritual" religion, cannot be foreseen, unless the tendency to live with apartheid and become "the Church apart" that we have mentioned in South Africa is taken as a sign of things to come. South Africa, however, is the exception in Africa, representing neither a colonial nor a post-colonial situation, and it may well be that the independent churches elsewhere will continue their manifold functions of mediating between the forces of tradition and the forces of change, so that the benefits of secularization can be secured at the same time as the profoundly religious nature of African life is protected against the inroads of a materialistic secularism and reformed within a modern historical world-view. In any case we may agree with M. M. Thomas that "the future of the struggle for a modern ethos in non-Western lands lies ultimately with the indigenous movements which are seeking to transform traditional cultures from within."[14]

Notes

1. For literature concerning these and movements subsequently mentioned see the relevant region or country in our *Bibliography of New Religious Movements in Primal Societies. Vol. I: Black Africa.* Boston: G. K. Hall & Co., 1977.
2. Butt, A., *The Nilotes of the Anglo-Egyptian Sudan.* London, 1952, 155.
3. Kaufmann, H., Zwischen Zauberei und Christentum, *Frankfurter Allgemeine Zeitung* 134, 12 Juni 1965. One new church, the Maria Legio, was widely assumed to be the church of the government when independence arrived; for the denials in parliament see Kenya Government, *House of Representatives Debates Official Reports* 3 (1), 1964, columns 775–6.
4. McClelland, E. M., The experiment of communal living at Aiyetoro, *Comparative Studies in Society and History* 9 (1), 1966, 14–28, and G. Shepperson's comments, *idem*, 29–32.
5. Doutreloux, A., Prophetism and development, *African Quarterly* 6 (4), 1967, 335.
6. Sangree, W. H., *Age, Prayer and Politics in Tiriki, Kenya.* London, 1966.

7. Turner, H. W., *African Independent Church*, 2 vols., Oxford, 1967, see index "politics" in both volumes.
8. Amos-Djoro, E., Les églises harristes et le nationalisme ivoirien, *Le Mois en Afrique* 5, Mai 1966, 35–6.
9. Information from the Rev. H.-J. Becken of Mapumulo, Natal.
10. Sirven, P., Les conséquences géographiques d'un nouveau syncrétisme religieux en Côte-d'Ivoire: le Kokambisme, *Cahiers d'Outre-Mer* 20 (78), 1967, 130, 136.
11. Bastide, R., Messianisme et développement économique et social, *Cahiers internationaux de Sociologie* 31, n.s. 8e. année, 1961, 11–12; Eng. trans. in I. Wallerstein (ed.), *Social Change: the Colonial Situation*. New York, 1966, 467–77.
12. Doutreloux, *op. cit.*, 341 *et passim*.
13. Bastide, *op. cit.*, 13.
14. Thomas, M. M., Modernization of traditional societies and the struggle for new cultural ethos, *Ecumenical Review* 18 (4), 1966, 436; similar conclusions will be found in A. J. F. Köbben, Prophetic movements as an expression of social protest, *International Archives of Ethnography* 49 (1), 1960, 151–3, and for the little-known movements of this kind in India in S. Fuchs, *Rebellious Prophets*. London, 1965, ch. 11.

26
African Independent Churches and Education

> *Like the previous essay this study also sets out to examine critically the common image of naive independents concerned more with ecstasies and the other world than with education for this world. The realism of the independent bodies inevitably led to interest in education, and some of their leaders made notable contributions and even sought to reform the education provided by the missions and older churches.*

To think of the planting of Christianity in Africa and the work of missions and churches is to think of schools, of these agencies 'throwing across tropical Africa their gigantic fishing net of primary and secondary schools'.[1] And to think of the African peoples themselves over the past century is to recall the swelling demand for education above almost everything else. Back in 1902 this was well expressed in the exhortation of King Lewanika to his Lozi council: 'Marotse, leave your shades, abandon our paganism. Send your children to school so that we also can become a nation.'[2] The school has undoubtedly been the most universally appreciated Christian contribution to black Africa over the past century and more.

On the other hand, to think of African independent churches, or any of the wide range of new religious movements, carries with it no such image. We might even say it produces this image in reverse — of illiterate peasants and villagers influenced in their naïvety by founders and prophets who relied on visions and personal charisma rather than on education or

The Journal of Modern African Studies, 13, 2 (1975), pp. 295–308.

professional equipment, and who exhausted their followers in enthusiastic worship rather than modernized them through education. The contrast with the older churches and missions is confirmed when we observe the large part that the school plays in the histories of these bodies, and the very small reference to education in the extensive literature on the newer religious movements. The same contrast is crystallised in parts of South Africa where members of the older churches are referred to as 'School people' and those in the independent churches as 'Red people', those fresh from the tribal areas and with almost no schooling. There would seem to be some basis for the confident remark of an African headmaster to Dr. M. L. Daneel in Shonaland: 'these independent churches will vanish as the general standard of education is improved'.³ One recalls similar predictions about these new movements once the colonial era had passed, and we all know how false such prophecies have proved in the event. Perhaps the relation to education will be equally surprising once it is examined more thoroughly.

EDUCATIONAL EMPHASES

It must be granted that there is considerable truth in the general impression of a less educated membership in the independent churches. A few studies in recent years have demonstrated this in detail. J. D. Y. Peel showed that Yoruba Anglicans had post-primary education among a third of their members, while only a fifth of the two prophet-healing congregations had gone past the primary stage, and that some 30 per cent of their members were illiterate compared with only 17 per cent among the Anglicans.⁴ Mary Aquina for central Karangaland,⁵ and Daneel for the Shona churches in his area,⁶ have revealed a greater contrast: illiteracy among the independents was twice that in the older churches, and the latter had up to twelve times as many members with post-primary schooling. There may well be less extreme contrasts elsewhere, but the overall picture is sufficiently represented in these three studies.

There are, however, two qualifications to be made. The first is that even an independent church with a low general educational level may yet possess a few highly educated members — university graduates and professional people. This is especially true in Ghana, but also in Nigeria, and further examples would be found in South Africa.

The second qualification concerns the founders of these movements. A few have been described as illiterate — Moses Orimolade, co-founder of the Cherubim and Seraphim in Nigeria, Isaiah Shembe of the Amanazaretha Church in Natal, and Alice Lenshina of the Lumpa Church in Zambia (although the same source goes on to say that she was at school with Kenneth Kaunda). One is not sure how to classify the head of the

'National Church of Africa' who defined his education to B. G. M. Sundkler as having 'served in the chaplains' mess during the Great War'.[7] By far the greater proportion of founders have been literate, a large number have been teachers in the schools of the older churches, often teacher-catechists, and a few have reached higher educational levels, such as Charles Domingo and John Chilembwe at an earlier period in Nyasaland, and Bishop Ajuoga in Kenya today.

So it is clear that education and the independent churches are not incompatible. A further clarification emerges if we enquire as to the degree of education across the various types of independent church. For convenience, if not for complete accuracy, I shall use some of the common distinctions and refer to the Ethiopian type and the prophet-healing forms, otherwise variously called Zionist, *aladura,* spiritual, and so on. Mary Aquina has suggested a kind of educational gradient running across the spectrum of religious bodies: 'education plays a significant part in fixing groups within the social scale of churches, as they are viewed by Africans themselves. As the level of education sinks, more and more African elements penetrate the various forms of Christianity.'[8] Her figures for central Karanga-land for 1963 certainly show such a gradient running across the spectrum from the mission churches, through Ethiopians, Zionists, and Apostolics to the pagans — to use her classification. Something of the same pattern might be seen in the breakdown of Peel's figures for the Yoruba churches, and could probably be found in South Africa also. There are, however, other factors at work besides the type of independent church, and I use this evidence to suggest that there may be great variation concerning the educational position of the independents, rather than to impose a universal pattern.

As a corollary it might be possible to put forward the thesis that there is some correlation between the degree of interest in education and the two main ways in which independent churches come into existence. There would seem to be more educational concern in those churches that have originated by secession from a parent church or mission: they commence with a more literate membership, are in competition with the older body to retain their members and to gain new recruits, and have to justify themselves as 'real' churches in terms of the model supplied by the parent movement. On the other hand, those independents which begin in a different fashion and gather their members from more diverse sources, including the traditional cults, possess fewer educated members, and are less concerned to attract further literates. They justify their existence more by contrast to the older churches than by imitation of them, by stressing their charismatic leadership and their spiritual power, and by criticising the older churches for their weakness at these points.

We may now risk a broad generalisation concerning the two main forms of independent church, the Ethiopian and the prophet-healing. The former seems to have had a substantial concern for education from the beginning, and to have maintained this along with the growth of demand for education in the community at large. One can name the African Greek Orthodox Church and Reuben Spartas, who began in 1926 by starting a school in the best mission manner and by 1936 claimed 23 church schools; the high educational level and concern for its maintenance in the African churches of Lagos from the 1890s; the similar position among some of the early Ethiopian churches in South Africa and among their recent representatives, who have co-operated with the Christian Institute for Southern Africa in the education of their ministry; the strong educational emphasis of prophet Wovenu in his Apostolic Revelation Society in Ghana, and the earlier efforts of men like Mark Christian Hayford with his independent schools and Baptist churches also in Ghana — he had opened a secondary school at Cape Coast as early as 1898.

Above all, one must recall the schools and churches created by the efforts of the wave of independent leaders in Malawi from the end of the first decade of this century, and the similar combination — but with even greater emphasis upon schools — in the independent movements in Kenya among the Kikuyu from 1929, especially the Kikuyu Independent Schools Association and its African Independent Pentecost Church. It is noteworthy that two later secession bodies in Kenya stressed this combination in their titles: the African Independent Pentecostal Schools and Church (note the order!), formed from the Methodists in 1944, had eight schools in Meru by 1952; and the African Christian Church and Schools, which emerged from the Africa Inland Mission at the end of the 1940s over the issue of educational policy, had 13 schools by 1952.

AMBIVALENT ATTITUDES IN PROPHET-HEALING CHURCHES

On the other hand, the prophet-healing type of independent body was more African in its orientation, and therefore less congruent with education which usually meant westernisation at the same time. It was also dependent on the charismatic leader rather than the trained professional or organisation man, and on divine power rather than human wisdom and skill. This does not mean that it was necessarily a reactionary influence as far as modernization was concerned, for churches of this type emerged to help Africans cope with the challenges of the new situations in which they found themselves, rather than to resist or escape from the changes that were occurring. It was a case of coming to terms with this new world through a different set of resources and in different ways from those found in the missions and older churches. It was possible to help their members to adjust and to abandon many of the old ways even while opposing western influences, and while viewing schools as worldly institutions or as works of the devil. In this way one might find a parallel with some of the so-called sects in the West, which are not necessarily the reactionary or conservative influences they are often thought to be, as witness the considerable economic success of some of their most devoted members.

It is equally important to note the significance of this combination of aversion to western education and determination to make the Christian religion their own, in no matter how erratic or apparently heretical a manner. The school Christians of Africa are readily equated with the rice Christians of Asia or elsewhere, but here is one substantial section of African Christianity (of some sort) that gives the lie to the argument that the main appeal of Christianity was as a source of education and so of personal advancement. Without underestimating this latter appeal, which is obviously considerable, the extent of another more inherently religious appeal must also be recognised; and it is the prophet-healing independents who make this plain.

Having, as it were, got their priorities right as between religion and education, the prophet-healing churches do not continue to ignore the educational issue, but come to terms with it in a great variety of ways. Sundkler points out that after the passing of the Bantu Education Act in South Africa in 1953, the attitudes of the Zionists to education changed considerably; since they no longer needed to fear the loss of their children if they sent them to mission or older church schools, they began using the public institutions, and five years later there were almost as many children from Zionist as from Ethiopian parents in one group of 186 schools, even though their later start meant they were congregated at the lower levels.[9]

Other prophet-healing churches were prepared to use the schools of the older churches at the more elementary levels, but to discontinue attendance after a few years. Thus in Rhodesia among the Ndaza Zionists one of the bishops stopped his child at Standard 3 in the Dutch Reformed Church school, for after that point there is a tendency to identify more with the school and the sponsoring church than with the family and its religion; this process was assisted by the growing sensitivity of the child to the opinions of other children about the 'crude' church of the Zionist family, and the increasing desire to conform.

The alternative to this truncated education was to develop schools in the western manner belonging to the prophet-healing church itself, and this has been done in many cases after the initial struggle to become established. The Christ Apostolic Church, the largest independent church in Nigeria, has an extensive education system with six grammar schools and a teacher-training college, and has graduates on its staff. Even the highly individualistic Holy Apostles' Community in its remote lagoon-bound city of Aiyetoro in Nigeria has its own school system, and has been willing to use the Methodist Church to supply the teaching staff that will secure government recognition; at the same time it remains suspicious of higher education that will take its children away from the community, perhaps never to return. Most of the new holy cities of the Aiyetoro kind have a school prominent in the complex of buildings, perhaps with houses for teachers attached. In Ghana the dynamic Eden Revival (later Feden) Church has its own secondary school, and even a small remote body such as the 'Kingdom', a communal, adventist and perfectionist group, about 1967-8 had a two-teacher school in its new village, purveying the three Rs and the Bible.

The West African prophet-healing Church of the Lord (Aladura) began in 1930. In the first 30 years it had no educational activities except very sketchy training for its ministers, carried on in three different countries and resembling a traditional African apprenticeship rather than a western type of education — and this in spite of its founder having been a teacher-catechist with some educational aspirations within the Nigerian Anglican Church where the emphasis on education was strong. In the 1960s it had begun a primary school in Monrovia, and was the recognised religion in one or two institutions in Ghana, such as in a private girls' boarding school in Kumasi where the principal and proprietress was a member of this Church. In the present decade, however, it has launched out into the educational field with a secondary boarding school and theological seminary near Lagos, and supports plans for a memorial grammar school in honour of its founder in his home town. This represents the way many of the prophet-healing churches are likely to move in the course of time.

It is possible for this development to produce a split in the church, as seems to have happened among the diffuse congeries of congregations in Zaïre which trace their ancestry historically or spiritually back to the prophet Simon Kimbangu in 1921. The division into the *Eglise de Jésus-Christ sur la terre par le prophète Simon Kimbangu* and a range of less organised movements coincides with the development of the former into a coherent body late in the 1950s, and the establishment of a school system in the next decade. As early as 1960 the prophetic Church of Mayumbe seceded from any association with such worldly activities as schools, dispensaries, agricultural schemes, printing, and other new features in the E.J.C.S.K. Its concern was 'purely religious', allegedly in the true tradition of Kimbangu himself, and not with the social order, reform, or development.[10]

This split represents a general divergence among churches of this origin and nature in Zaïre and the Republic of the Congo. Some are copying the missions and older churches as best they can with schools and social services, and were encouraged to do so by the Government after the 'second revolution' of 1965. The E.J.C.S.K., the Kitawala (an African offshoot from Jehovah's Witnesses), and the indigenous Salvation Army groups have chosen this way, even while they try to retain the prophetic vision and source of authority alongside the bureaucratic organization these developments require. Others, such as the Holy Spirit Churches in the Lower Congo and north of the river, and the Croix Koma movement within the Roman Catholic Church, have sensed the dangers to spirituality that arise when leaders become bureaucrats or professional clergy engaged in administration, and have rejected schools and social services, and the kind of church organisation necessary to manage these. Some educated Zaïrians predict that the future lies with this latter group, which is more likely to preserve the original dynamic of the Kimbanguist movement; for the others, the adoption of western forms, including the school, may prove to be the kiss of death. The prediction concerning the two groups in Zaïre and Congo may well be right; in areas where government social services are expanding, it would be inappropriate for the churches, whether older or independent, to move into the field of education.

It remains to note yet one further reaction of the prophet-healing type of church: to think in terms of a special kind of education of its own, distinct from the western model found elsewhere. This was early adumbrated in the Alice Lenshina movement in Zambia, where parents sometimes deliberately kept their children from attending even the lower levels of instruction in schools; Alice herself was known to speak of children 'being educated by God'. And yet at the same time her members were reported as early as 1956, within the first three years of the movement, as wanting 'a Lenshina school, not a European one'.[11]

In some cases this aspiration has been followed into action. The most remarkable must be that found in Eastern Nigeria in one section of the Spirit Movement from the late 1920s. In 1936 the Oberi Okaime Church was discovered to have opened a school of its own using the special language and script that it claimed had been revealed to it by the Holy Spirit. The script was revealed in dreams, and the language given by inspiration of the Spirit, and in this medium children were being taught to read, write, and calculate — a remarkable cultural creation on the part of peasants. Needless-to-say, the Government was less than sympathetic to this creativity, and closed the school down.[12]

From this survey of the prophet-healing forms of independent church we see a form of Christianity in Africa which has established itself widely and continues to spread without the benefit of schools, or at least without relying upon education as an instrument of evangelism. Since the school is almost always cast in the western model this represents a distinction between the Christian faith and western culture that is highly significant, both for the future of Christianity in Africa, and for the shape of the African culture of the future. At the same time if this distinction hardened into a complete rejection of western culture, and in effect of other major cultures, as channelled through the school, churches of this kind would appear as reactionary forces standing in the way of modernization. But we have seen that this is not so, for many of these churches are caught up in the general African demand for more and better education, and endeavour to satisfy this demand by moving into the educational field without losing the priority given to religion as their dynamic.

MIXED MOTIVES:
IMITATION AND REFORMATION

Any analysis of the reasons why a particular independent church, of whatever type, wanted its own schools would probably reveal the interplay of several of the following factors:

(1) The discrimination in education by the schools of missions and the older churches, both as regards admission and treatment.

(2) The fear that children might be won over to the faith of the Church managing the school, especially in the higher classes.

(3) The expectation of certain financial gains through school fees or government assistance, that could be applied to the work of the independent church itself.

(4) The attraction of the model of what a 'real' church must be like, established by missions.

(5) The general status in the community accorded to 'proper' churches on this model.

(6) An over-estimation of the value of education as the *open sesame* in all matters.

(7) A genuine concern for education, both secular and religious, and dissatisfaction with the quantity, the quality, or the type of education available in the existing provision by the government or by other bodies.

I shall examine this last factor more fully at a later point, but for the moment let us return to my earlier suggestion that the independents represent a dissatisfaction with the Christianity embodied in missions and the older churches. It is possible to detect here an intention at reform of western Christianity as it has been worked out in Africa, and this category of reforming agencies may be employed as a means of interpreting the independent churches in relation both to religion and to education. Scholars have been finding this a useful way of understanding these bodies, however unlikely such a category might have seemed a decade ago.

There is no doubt that many independents see themselves as applying the full powers of the Christian religion for the first time to their own people, and regard the older churches as weak, faithless, and worldly. The criticism may be muted, but it is there. In so far as these older churches have come to regard their schools not only as a service to the community, but as the main evangelizing instrument of the church, the independents have an important point. It does in fact appear that many older churches have settled down to 'grow' their own Christian members rather than to win them from the still unevangelized peoples around them. A recent book on a charismatic movement in Katanga describes how Fr Placide Tempels over 30 years ago came to the conclusion that his own Catholic missions in the then Congo had become nothing more than educational agencies for children, and had ceased to win adults;[13] hence his own fresh study of the African world view and its remarkable outcome in the Jamaa movement for adults.

The concentration on education imposed further disabilities upon the older churches in the eyes of some Africans, for it meant increasing co-operation with the government. As Sundkler has pointed out, there were areas where the vast majority of mission personnel were not only engaged as teachers rather than evangelists or pastoral workers, but were on the payroll of the state education department.[14] Even where the position was less extreme, it was easy for mission and government to be identified in African eyes, and where there were white settlers, as in Kenya, Rhodesia, and elsewhere, for missionaries to be identified with these also. It mattered little that the priests were probably being criticized by the government and the settlers for disturbing Africans with political notions, or for retarding educational advance by stubbornly fighting to retain control over their schools when they could no longer supply the increasing resources that education demanded. It mattered little also that the independents themselves (usually, but not always) hankered after government assistance when they came to establish their own schools, and were even less able to supply the necessary educational resources. The feeling remained that the older churches and missions failed to concentrate on the things of the spirit, and that 'the power' had departed from them.

The independents therefore, especially the prophet-healers, were in the position of religious reformers calling the older churches back to preaching, to itinerating, to evangelism, and to the mediation of divine power for African needs. In their own unschooled ways, these are the things upon which they have concentrated with such extensive results across sub-Saharan Africa.

There was one particular area where the promises of the Bible and the dynamic of the Gospel were not being adequately applied to urgent African requirements, and that was the growing problem of sickness —

growing under the stresses of social change, and the new diseases introduced from the outside world that sometimes assumed epidemic proportions. It is not surprising, therefore, that the independents have tried to fill this gap with their own healing activities in the power of the Holy Spirit. The Church Missionary Society in Yorubaland had to be prodded into starting its first hospital at Ado Ekiti in 1936 by Archdeacon Dallimore, who insisted that it was essential to counteract the activities and appeal of the *aladura* prophet-healing movement that had spread like wildfire in his area from 1930 onwards. So to some extent it is possible to regard the independents as reforming mission Christianity, both through their own new and more spiritually powerful appeals, and through their reverse influence by way of challenge to the older bodies.

Nor was mission education itself immune, and this has been documented in two areas where the criticisms came early and in strength, in Nyasaland and in Kenya, and in both countries it was intimately involved with the development of independent Christian movements, although of an Ethiopian rather than a prophet-healing type.

HUNGER FOR EDUCATION IN NYASALAND

In Nyasaland we have the studies of George Shepperson and Thomas Price,[15] and later of R. J. Macdonald,[16] and from these a fascinating story emerges of the connection between religious independency and the hunger for more and better education. As early as 1899 that many-hued missionary, Joseph Booth, who spoke for Africans as much as for himself, organized a petition to the Queen seeking education for Africans equal to that received by the British. The Government, however, was conspicuously slow in this field; it relied upon the missions to provide schools, and in the decade before 1918 gave them only a thousand pounds a year for this purpose. Indeed, its own education department was not created until 1926. Nor was there help from the large private employers, as sometimes occurs, for the Bruce Estates banned both schools and churches from its land. African interests and desires were consequently focused on the education the missions provided. For its day this was both comparatively extensive and enlightened, and at the higher levels included the Overtoun Institution at the famous Livingstonia Mission of the Scottish Presbyterians.

It must have been particularly galling, therefore, for missionaries who were so educationally minded and active to watch the succession of teachers and ministers whom they had trained seceding to found their own churches and schools, starting with Elliott Kamwana and Charles Domingo in the first decade of the century, and continuing right up to World War II. This of course was a backhanded tribute to the success of missions both in religion and in education, and an indication that Africans wanted more education, and quickly, and more freely accessible — the introduction of school fees was one of the sources of complaint. Almost all those who seceded in these 40 years had educational plans, usually over-elaborate for their resources, and most began with a school; in later years some were sufficiently organized to secure small government grants.

Perhaps the most successful system was that introduced by John Chilembwe in his Providence Industrial Mission, dating back to 1901–2. By 1912 he could report 906 pupils in seven schools, based on the British seven-standard system, and including both agriculture and scripture, like the best mission schools. In one respect he went beyond the latter, and that was in the emphasis he laid on the education of women; in this his wife assisted him both in school and extra-murally in the community.

One can only admire the courage and tenacity of these founders of churches and schools who had a vision of what education could do in Africa, based on what it had done for them, and who persisted in spite of the woeful failures of so many of their schemes. They understood that education must be both widely available and free, and not only practical in terms of the needs of rural Africa, but also of high literary and academic quality in terms of western culture. Something of all these themes can be detected through the only too pathetic history of their efforts, and amid the political overtones that were also frequently present.

DEMAND FOR LITERARY EDUCATION IN KENYA

It was the political concern that was perhaps still more prominent in the similar story of independent churches and schools in Kenya.[17] Here also the Government had left African education to the missions, with small grants-in-aid, and indeed there were no state-provided facilities till the 1930s. Here also mission schools made sincere attempts to provide a relevant rural education, backed by the famous Phelps-Stokes Reports during the early 1920s. This American-orientated Commission saw the local inhabitants too much in terms of the poor rural Negroes of the southern United States, and not in terms of Africans even then awakening to the possibilities of nationhood in the modern manner. Both missionaries and educational experts did their best according to their lights, but their best was still 'rural science' and this led back to the hoe, and not onwards to a desk in a government office and a share in the kind of life displayed by Europeans in Kenya. African reaction to this type of education was first dramatised by the boys at the C.M.S. School at Maseno who went on strike in 1908; they refused to take part in any manual work and demanded more reading and writing.

Attention has frequently been focused upon the two independent educational associations and their churches that emerged among the Kikuyu after their clash with the Church of Scotland on the issue of female circumcision in 1928–9. The pattern of combined independent church and school was, however, established before this period, and in other areas. Back in 1910 a former C.M.S. teacher, John Owalo, formed his Nomiya Luo Mission and built his own churches and primary schools, which continued until taken over by new public authorities in 1958. And in the early 1920s there was Johan Okwala's church and schools formed upon his departure from the Independent Nilotic Mission, a Western missionary body.

There were also precedents among the Kikuyu themselves, for there was an independent school used also as a church by its sponsors at Gakarara by 1927, and at Githunguri a completely independent school had been opened in 1925 by a group that emerged from the Gospel Missionary Society. This school charged no fees, although like all other such independent institutions it must have needed them badly.

There is no room here to explore the complex history of the Kikuyu Independent Schools Association and the Karing'a Educational Association, both founded in the early 1930s, or their relationship with the African Independent Pentecost Church and the African Orthodox Church associated with the black South African, Archbishop Alexander. This history has been surveyed tendentiously by the official government reporter, F. D. Corfield, in 1960,[18] and more satisfactorily by John Anderson in 1970;[19] the former was dominated by the recently suppressed Mau Mau, but the latter manages to discuss the subject without so much as mentioning that movement. This enables the educational and religious concerns of this complex of schools and churches to stand out more clearly. It then becomes plainer that whatever the truth may be about Mau Mau and the rôle of Kenyatta, here was another example of an independent religious movement reforming, or attempting to reform, on a large scale, the education provided by the missions. And the general drift of the criticisms is much the same as in Nyasaland: not enough education, and not freely accessible, and not designed to lead Africans to equality with the whites and to share their kind of life.

In a sense the issue raised by earlier independent churches as between practical and more literary forms of education has now been transcended. Equality with the whites is seen to depend on acquiring the obvious technical and professional European skills at all levels, and this ambition governs both individual students and state educational philosophies. In the terminology of Paulo Freire, education 'domesticates' and 'socialises', as it always did in its traditional tribal forms, rather than 'liberates'.[20]

Even most of the new affluent élites are still very much part of the system that supports their privileges, although there are individual independent voices.

As our final question, therefore, we may ask where the independent churches stand as between these two philosophies. Their own pragmatic concerns with healing and success would seem to bind them to the more utilitarian view of education, and no doubt where they have schools this is reflected in their curricula, as much as in any others. On the other hand, their very existence has often represented a struggle for spiritual independence and responsibility, for being themselves as Africans in their own way, rather than conforming to the more powerful public models of what churches ought to be and do. This integrity, authenticity, and confidence, as well as the determination to be distinct both from the Western types of church and from the contemporary political authorities, suggest that they may possess hidden resources to encourage the more liberating — and liberal — kinds of education that are important for the future of Africa. Whatever the outcome, their concern for education will certainly increase, and they must be reckoned with in this as in so many other spheres.

Notes

1. J. V. Taylor in *C.M.S. News Letter* (London), 355, December 1971, p. 2.
2. T. O. Ranger, 'Nationality and Nationalism: the case of Barotseland', in *Journal of the Historical Society of Nigeria* (Ibadan), 1, 2, June 1968, p. 228.
3. M. L. Daneel, *Old and New in Southern Shona Independent Churches*, Vol. 11, *Church Growth: causative factors and recruitment techniques* (The Hague, 1974).
4. J. D. Y. Peel, *Aladura: a religious movement among the Yoruba* (London, 1968), pp. 196–7.
5. Mary Aquina, 'Zionists in Rhodesia', in *Africa* (London), xxxix, 2, April 1969, p. 114.
6. Daneel, *op. cit. passim*.
7. B. G. M. Sundkler, *Bantu Prophets in South Africa* (London, 1961), p. 123.
8. Mary Aquina, 'Christianity in a Rhodesian Tribal Trust Land', in *African Social Research* (Lusaka), 1, June 1966, p. 38 and *passim*.
9. Sundkler, *op. cit.*, pp. 121 ff.
10. A. Doutreloux, 'Prophetism and Development', in *Africa Quarterly* (New Delhi), vi, 4, 1967, p. 335. According to Cecilia Irvine in a seminar paper at Aberdeen in 1971, by the end of 1960 an estimated 15,000 children were in E.J.C.S.K. schools. Ten years later 100,000 were reported as under instruction in primary, secondary, and post-secondary schools, and in teacher-training and theological colleges. See G. Bernard, 'La Contestation et les églises nationales au Congo', in *Canadian Journal of African Studies* (Ottawa), v, 2, 1971, p. 149.

    The Ntwalanist Church, a split from E.J.C.S.K. in 1963, has an extended statement of its educational philosophy: see G. Mwene-Batende, 'Le

Phénomène de dissidence des sectes religieuses d'inspiration kimbanguiste' in *Cahiers du Cedaf* (Brussels), 6, 1971, Série 4: Religion, pp. 28–37.
11. A. D. Roberts, 'The Lumpa Church of Alice Lenshina', in Robert I. Rotberg and Ali A. Mazrui (eds.), *Protest and Power in Black Africa* (New York, 1970), p. 556; see also p. 519.
12. R. F. G. Adams, 'Oberi Okaime: a new African language and script', in *Africa*, xvii, 1, January 1947, pp. 24, 34, and *passim*.
13. Johannes Fabian, *Jamaa: a charismatic movement in Katanga* (Evanston, 1971).
14. B. G. M. Sundkler, *The Christian Ministry in Africa* (London, 1960), pp. 93–7.
15. George Shepperson and Thomas Price, *Independent African: John Chilembwe and the origins, setting and significance of the Nyasaland native rising of 1915* (Edinburgh, 1958).
16. R. J. Macdonald, 'Religious Independency as a Means of Social Advancement in Northern Nyasaland in the 1930s', in *Journal of Religion in Africa* (Leiden), 111, 2, 1970, pp. 106–29.
17. John Anderson, *The Struggle for the School: the interaction of missionary, colonial government and nationalist enterprise in the development of formal education in Kenya* (London and Nairobi, 1970).
18. F. D. Corfield, *Historical Survey of the Origins and Growth of Mau Mau* (Nairobi and London, 1960).
19. Anderson, *op. cit.*, especially ch. 8.
20. See Paulo Freire, *Pedagogy of the Oppressed* (New York, 1970), *passim*.

27
Study Centre for New Religious Movements: A Contribution to Inter-Cultural Understanding and Third World Development

> *This statement was drawn up in 1969 to outline the need for a special centre for the study of these religious movements, and to offer a plan for its work. The statement was geared to the strong interest of the 1960s in Third World development, rather than to Christian missions, to theology, or to the other academic interests that lie behind many of the other essays. Some aspects of this proposal have been implemented since 1973 when the Project for the Study of New Religious Movements in Primal Societies (PRONERM for short) was established in a modest way within the Department of Religious Studies in the University of Aberdeen.*

The Western World, increasingly uncertain in its aid to the Developing World with its "primitive" societies, needs deeper understanding of their nature.

Inner forces and motivations in these cultures are revealed nowhere more clearly than in the vast range of little-known new indigenous religious movements that have arisen from the impact of the West upon the peoples of the less developed world.

These grass-roots movements require thorough study by a multi-disciplinary approach that will uncover their influence for or against modernization in the Third World.

THE BACKGROUND SITUATION

Western culture, technology and religion have made increasing impact on the so-called "primitive" peoples of the world (here called the primal societies) especially in the last few decades. This encounter usually began in a colonial situation, and has now been replaced by the relation between the West and the independent Developing or Third World, where most of the primal societies are located.

The end of the 1960's, designated as "the Development Decade", saw a distinct pause on the part of the Western nations — as U Thant expressed it, a certain "fatigue and disenchantment". A more profound and sophisticated approach to the problems of modernizing the Third World is now being sought.

It is realized that the economic and technical approach alone is insufficient, even dangerous, that political and social factors must be reckoned with, and that behind these lie largely unknown cultural and religious dimensions. These too must be taken into account in our understanding of human development, where men's systems of values and corresponding incentives to action are of decisive importance.

This development pause is remarkably similar to the pause for self-examination and reorientation evident among Western Churches after a century and a half of missionary expansion. It seems, therefore, that neither economic, technical nor religious "aid" is proving as simple or as successful as had been assumed, and that the West needs a new depth in its approach to the developing peoples.

THE PRIMAL SOCIETIES' REACTIONS TO THE WEST

Among the less known reactions to encounter with the Western world there has been a vast range of new movements of a religious nature, entirely independent and indigenous in origin and leadership. These reflect the efforts of primal societies to readjust traditional life, either by repelling the invading culture through a revitalized traditional religion, or by adopting a new faith largely drawn from the West but recast in local patterns.

This astonishing world-ranging phenomenon is without previous parallel in human history. It deserves attention both in its own right, and as a major index of the reaction of the primal societies to modernizing encounters with the West. Here we see the Third World's own most intimate new developments, rather than those fostered and directed by others. These may hinder the newly developing nations, as when the Zambian Government was forced into military action against prophetess Lenshina's revolt in 1964. In other instances remarkable socio-economic development has been generated within new religious movements without any outside help, as in the prosperous Aiyetoro City in Nigeria, Prophet Wovenu's community in Ghana, and others in South Africa and elsewhere. Indeed, these might be regarded as spontaneous pilot-schemes which development agencies need to examine more closely, and in their full dimensions. Since ultimately "no country can be developed from the outside", these grass-roots indigenous movements have considerable significance for the future of their peoples.

A STUDY CENTRE FOR NEW RELIGIOUS MOVEMENTS

Many academic disciplines have been discovering the importance of these new movements from their own viewpoints: historians, as significant popular movements; sociologists and anthropologists, as examples of culture contact and social change; political scientists, as reactions against colonialism and associated with nationalisms; psychologists, as exemplifying stress and adjustive phenomena. Students of linguistics, medicine, missiology and theology have also found them of special interest.

As lying between local ethnic or traditional religions and the world faiths, these movements with their creative popular nature are of great interest to the phenomenology and history of religion, which can contribute an analysis and a perspective lacking when the study is confined to the social sciences alone. We have also been reminded that religious studies have "played almost no part in the burgeoning foreign area studies programs, which can stand a great deal of strengthening precisely from those disciplines that come closest to the spiritual engine of other . . . societies". (L. H. Legters, former Chief, Area Centers Office, National Defence Education Act, U.S.A.)

While the social and historical studies expound the contexts and forces which condition and foster these movements, and their social influence, systematic analysis and interpretation by the religious disciplines will open up their further dimensions. A study Centre for New Religious Movements would thus provide the instruments for their treatment as fully-dimensioned human developments. The work being done from limited viewpoints, with inadequate resources, especially for world comparative study, and scattered across many universities and organizations would then be brought together and lifted to a level where it can contribute the understanding needed in this field.

BUT WHY IN THE WESTERN WORLD?

On any realistic assessment no single Centre in any one of the Areas concerned could attract scholars from all the other continents, nor even perhaps from every part of its own Area. For instance, Southern African scholars would have great difficulty elsewhere in Africa, and vice versa; and African scholars in general are much less likely to go to a Centre in Latin America, etc., than to one in a Western country. Thus comparative study on a world scale, or even intra-Area study, would be much less feasible if attempted under present conditions from within any one of the areas concerned. At the same time it is not impossible that within a generation a world Centre could assist in laying the basis for Area centres, establish links and develop comparative studies to the point where decentralization could occur if other conditions were also suitable.

It must be remembered that substantial sections of these new movements exist among the indigenous peoples of advanced Westernized nations — in North America, South Africa, Australia and New Zealand. In these situations there may be special dimensions of the problem, such as internal race issues.

A Western venue can provide ready access to extensive academic and economic resources, political stability, an opportunity for nationals from the Third World to secure international perspective by meeting others, and above all to enjoy a period of relative detachment from local involvements; this last is especially important, for local attitudes to these new movements are often sharply divided.

Even if an adequate Centre were immediately possible in the Third World, the West would still need to fill this gap in its own studies, in order to understand what it has been instrumental in arousing among primal peoples. From all points of view one strong Centre in the West seems desirable at present. How it could also strengthen the developing areas is further examined below.

WHY IN THE UNITED KINGDOM?

Britain offers the most international language, and has had the widest connections with primal societies through her history as a colonial and commercial power and missionary base, and her Commonwealth associations. As a result, extensive experience, and colonial and missionary society archives and libraries are available. In lesser degree the same applies to the Western European nations whose corresponding resources are also within easy reach. In addition, some of these new movements are now operating in Britain through the influx of immigrants and students from the Third World, so that further study here can reveal how they adapt to this still closer encounter with the West.

WHY NOW?

These new movements are no merely historic or passing phenomenon, for further examples continue to appear. Thus, to take Africa alone, prophet-healing movements have arisen among the western Botswana peoples for the first time in the last few years, and it has been estimated that on average, seven additional tribes are involved annually in the African Continent, so that now over 300 tribal peoples have exhibited this development, with up to seven million adherents. Unknown numbers exist in Brazil and other less charted areas. Most primal societies are also sharing in the population explosion.

The desire for deeper understanding of what is happening in the less developed world is reflected in an increase of interest in these new movements on the part of administrators and those concerned with development, churches and educators, and scholars of many disciplines. One indication of this is the rapidly rising number of students choosing this field for postgraduate research.

The time is undoubtedly ripe for a full-scale planned approach with an international outreach that would produce a recognized world Centre in this field.

THE ACTIVITIES OF A CENTRE FOR NEW RELIGIOUS MOVEMENTS

1. *Bibliographical*: undertaking ongoing bibliographical research and publication, co-operating with wider projects, such as area bibliographies, UNESCO's "International Bibliography of the History of Religions", etc.

2. *Documentation*:
a) Assembly of all major published materials (microfilm, photocopy, etc., where necessary).
b) Collection of primary source materials — movements' own documents, papers of founders, ephemeral publications and manuscript materials (by field work, and close relations with the movements themselves).
c) Assembly of basic information — cartographical, historical, statistical, etc. — about movements, their founders, developments and influence.

3. *Publication*: edited primary sources and texts: English translations of important materials from less familiar languages; occasional papers and monographs; bibliographies; a Centre bulletin.

4. *Teaching and Research*: An M.A. level course would introduce students with suitable first degrees to this field, and train those proceeding to advanced degrees and research. Occasionally a multi-disciplinary study, including field work, might be made of a major movement, with a team embracing members from both the Western and the Third Worlds.

5. *Clearing House, Information and Liaison Service*: Registers of recent developments, of research under way elsewhere, of scholars and dissertations in this field; periodic colloquia and inter-disciplinary seminars. Liaison and exchanges with interested bodies — with universities in developing areas, with government and mission agencies, and with individuals involved.

6. *Commitment to mutual development in the Western and the Third Worlds.*

To avoid the danger of so enriching the resources of the West in this field as to widen the gap with the rest of the world, the Centre's activities should be structured to encourage a matching development of resources and scholarship in other Areas. For example, there could be a plan for archiving original documents in their Areas of origin, and for duplicating documents deposited at the Centre with a copy at a suitable depository in the Area concerned. In particular good graduates from the Third World could be encouraged to come to the Centre for initial training, with an arrangement for their return to their own areas to study local movements from the world perspective acquired at the Centre. This would build up future strength in their own countries, and liaison with the Centre.

In these and all possible ways the Centre should aim to link its own development with the accumulation of resources and skills in the areas it would be serving outside the Western World.

ADDENDUM

Other Kindred Publications

An account of other publications not included in this collection but connected with this subject may be useful for some readers, and may avoid possible confusion between different items or as to the different locations of similar materials. The following list excludes reviews and forewords, but includes more popular articles.

I AFRICAN MATERIALS

A. Books:
   1. *Profile through Preaching.* London: Edinburgh House Press 1965, 88 p. See extracts in essay 20.
   2. *African Independent Church.* Oxford: Clarendon Press 1967.
      Vol. 1, *History of an African Independent Church: the Church of the Lord (Aladura)*, 232 p.
      Vol. 2, *African Independent Church: the life and faith of the Church of the Lord (Aladura)*, 400 p.
   3. With Robert C. Mitchell: *A Comprehensive Bibliography of Modern African Religious Movements.* Evanston: Northwestern University Press 1967, 132 p. Two supplements appeared as follows: Bibliography of modern African religious movements: Supplement I. *Journal of Religion in Africa* 1 (3), 1968, 173–210; Bibliography of new religious movements in Africa: Supplement II. *Idem* 3 (3), 1970, 161–208.
   4. *Bibliography of New Religious Movements in Primal Societies.* Vol. I: *Black Africa.* Boston: G. K. Hall & Co. 1977, 277 p.

B. Articles

5. Independent religious groups in eastern Nigeria. *West African Religion* 5, February 1966, 7–18; *idem*, 6. August 1966, 10–15.

6. *Modern African religious movements.* Nsukka: Department of Religion, University of Nigeria 1963. 10 p.

7. The Catechism of an independent West African Church. *Sierra Leone Bulletin of Religion* 2 (2), 1960, 45–57; reprinted in *Occasional Papers* 1 (9), International Missionary Council 1961; also in item 2 above, vol. 2, 169–181; German translation, Katechismen unabhängiger westafrikanischer Kirchen, in E. Benz (ed.), *Messianische Kirchen, Sekten und Bewegungen in Heutigen Afrika*. Leiden: E. J. Brill 1965, 72–88.

8. The Church of the Lord: the expansion of a Nigerian independent church in Sierra Leone and Ghana. *Journal of African History* 3 (1), 1962, 92–110. Most of this material also appeared in item 2 above, vol. 1, chs. 6, 8 and 9.

9. Back to paganism, or . . . . *The Outlook* (Christchurch, New Zealand) 71 (17), September 19, 1964, 5–7.

10. 6,000 movements like Ringatu among African people. *Idem* 76 (18), September 27, 1969, 5, 32.

11. Don't condemn the power of the Spiritual churches. *Presbyterian Messenger* (Accra, Ghana) 10 (12), November 1970, 10. (Erroneously published as by Jesse Jones)

12. Praying People. *Now* (London, Methodist Missionary Society) May 1977, 4–5.

13. L'églises indépendentes d'origine et de formes africaines. *Concilium: Revue Internationale de Théologie* 126, juin 1977, 133–140; also in Dutch, German, Italian, Portuguese and Spanish editions.

II NEW RELIGIOUS MOVEMENTS IN GENERAL

A. World Surveys

14. Tribal religious movements – new. *Encyclopaedia Britannica* (1974 edition), vol. 18, 697–705; also 24 briefer articles on individual movements in the Micropaedia section.

15. New religious movements in the primal societies. *World Faiths* (London) 95, 1975, 5–10.

16. New religious movements among primal peoples: repercussions

of the Christian contact. *Milligan Missiogram* (Milligan College, Tennessee) 2 (1), 1974, 13–16.

17. New religious movements in primal societies, in V. C. Hayes (ed.), *Australian Essays in World Religions*. Adelaide: Australian Association for the Study of Religions 1977, 38–48.

B. Area Surveys

18. Old and new religions among North American Indians. *Missiology* (Pasadena) 1 (2), 1973, 47–66.

19. *Bibliography of New Religious Movements in Primal Societies*. Vol. 2: *North America*. Boston: G. K. Hall & Co. 1978, 286 p.

20. Old and new religions in Melanesia. *Catalyst* (Goroka, Papua New Guinea)

21. New religious movements in the Caribbean, in B. E. Gates (ed.), *Afro-Caribbean Religions*. London: Ward Lock Educational 1979 (expected 1979).

C. Bibliographical Surveys

22. New religious movements in primal societies, in W. O. Cole (ed.), *World Religions: a Handbook for Teachers*. London: Community Relations Commission 1976, 185.

23. Understanding the new world of religious movements in primal societies. *Expository Times* 89 (6), 1978, 167–172.

D. Primal Religions

24. Tribal ('Primal') religions, in W. O. Cole, *op. cit.*, 183–184. (A bibliographical survey for school teachers)

25. *Living Tribal Religions*. London: Ward Lock Educational 1971, 40 p. (A systematic phenomenological analysis as first introduction)

26. Primal religions and their study, in V. C. Hayes, *op. cit.*, 27–37.

INDICES

General Index

Note: Authors of books and articles are indexed by name only. People who are not authors but who, though not indigenes, are involved in movements, are indexed with the country concerned shown in parentheses, e.g., Booth, J. (Malawi), 118, 326.

Acquah, I., 95
adjustment cults, 54
African Inland Mission (in Kenya), 320
Afro-American cults (Caribbean and South America), 22, 61, 260
Aladura (as term), 99–100, 124, 130, 226
alcohol, 13, 27, 98, 122, 123, 160, 197, 222, 261, 311
ancestors, 259, 306
ancillary cult, 59
Anderson, J., 328
Andersson, E., 71
angels, 170
anthropological study, 80–81
Aquina, M., 318, 319
Acquarian Gospel of Jesus the Christ, 279, 283
asceticism, 192, 197–8
Assemblies of God mission (in Nigeria), 127
Australian aborigines, 4, 7

Baëta, C. G., 90, 93–94, 100, 102, 222–3
Baha'i, 259
Balandier, G., 17, 64
baptism, 71, 97, 99, 122, 123, 124, 126, 168–9, 282
Barrett, D. B., 22, 109, 110, 112, 117, 150
Barrington-Ward, S., 195
Bastide, R., 44–45, 312, 313

Becken, H.-J., 118, 149, 176
Beckmann, D. M., 115
Beecher, L. J., 84, 95, 100
Beyerhaus, P., 73
Bible, Scriptures, 8, 10, 27, 28, 86, 96, 155, 160, 166, 186, 194, 206–7, 210, 216, 222, ch. 20, 259, 265, ch. 23, 292
Binney, J., 275
Black Christ or Messiah, 52–53, 67, 85, 264
Booth, J. (Malawi), 118, 326
Brazil, cults in, 67, *and see* Afro-American cults
British Apostolic Church, 126, 127, 131
Buddhism, Buddhist movements, 4, 26, 27
Burke, F. H. (South Africa), 266

causes, 11; religious, 11, 19, 69, 70, 112; situational, 11, 24, 25; contributory, 17; precipitative, 11; enablng, 11, 12; sociological, 19, 67, 68, 70; economic, 17, 19, 68, 76; political, 17, 18, 19, 51, 67, 68; psychological, 67, 68, 80; *see also* colonialism
charisma, charismatic leaders, 183–185, 305, 320
Chomé, J., 137
Christian Institute for Southern Africa, 177, 188, 320
Christianity (as specially relevant), 12,

16, 19, 20, 26, 27, 35–36, 42, 61, 65, 72–75, 92–94, 182, 256–9, 290–1
Christology, 127, 212, 228
Church Missionary Society (in Nigeria), 129, 138, 326
Church of Christ mission (in Thailand), 265
Church of God mission (in Nigeria), 127
classification, *see* typology
clientele, 58–59, 103, 104, 168
Coleman, J. S., 64, 67, 149
colonialism, colonial governments, 17, 27, 45, 67, 68, ch. 11, ch. 15, 196, 226–7, 312, 314
comparative study, 60–61, 66
Corfield, F. D., 328
councils of churches, x, 7, 10, 57, 60, 174–5, 215, 222, 264, 310; *see also* Associations of New Movements
crisis cults, 54, 110

Dallimore (Archdeacon, Nigeria), 326
dancing, 41, 196, 197, 200
Daneel, M. L., 50, 117, 177, 180, 188, 266, 318
Dayrell, E. (Nigeria), 138–9
Debrunner, H., 97
definitions and characteristics, 22, 23, 50–51, 52, 332; new religious movements, 58, 83; neo-primal, 56; syncretist, 56; Hebraist, 56; independent church, 57, 58, 72, 86–103, 301; Ethiopian movement, 57, 95–96, 101, 105, 181, 320; Zionist, 57, 97, 105; prophet-healing, 10, 57, 90, 97–101, 105, 133, 181, 320–3; older churches, 92–94
Deschamps, H., 95
Desroche, H., 53
development, *see* modernization
Dirven, P. J., 179
Doutreloux, A., 312
dreams, 38, 98, 122, 124, 169, 206–7, 281

Earhart, H. B., 23
Eastern Orthodoxy, 28
Eberhardt, J., 45, 96, 97, 104
ecumenics, 263–4; *and see* councils of churches
education, 124, 175, 180, 182, 187–9, 272, 277, 310, ch. 26
Eliade, M., 69
eschatology, 5, 11, 28, 250
Ethiopianism, 10, 65, 139, 301
Ethiopian movements, *see* definitions
eucharist, *see* Lord's Supper
Evans-Pritchard, E. E., 69
exorcism, 195

Faith and Truth Temple mission (in Nigeria), 125
fasting, 124, 125, 127, 167, 171, 193, 195, 198, 281
features, characteristic, *see* definitions
Fernandez, J. W., 115, 116
Friedman, R., 235–6

Global Frontier mission (in Nigeria), 127
glossolalia, *see* Pentecostalism and possession
Good News Training Institute (Ghana), 176
Gospel Missionary Society (Kenya), 328
Guariglia, G., 21, 148

Haliburton, G. M., 115, 118
healing, spiritual, 4, 97, 98, 100, 102, ch. 9, 130, 161, 166–7, 182, 195, 218, 228–9, 310
healing, Western medical, 97, 180, 259
Hebraist movements, 8, 56, 73, 84–86, 103, 208, 264
Hinduism, Hindu movements, 4, 26
historical study, 71, 114, 207–9, chs. 9–12
history of religious study, 39, 212–3
holy cities, 28, 58, 61, 99, 104, 181, 183, 194, 208, 311, 322, 333; *and see* sociological forms
Holy Spirit, 100, 122, ch. 9, 169–70, 193, 208, 212, 233, 241, 282, 284, 323, 326; *and see* Pentecostalism
Horton, R., 37
hymns, 197, 226

independent churches, *see* definitions
Independent Nilotic Mission (in Kenya), 328
influenza epidemic (of 1918), 4, 5, 11, 125, 229
Islam, Islamic movements, x, 4, 6, 26–27, 71, 83, 114–5, 132, 161

Janzen, J., 182, 184
Johnson, J. (bishop, Nigeria), 139

Kemmer, M. A. (Nigeria), 141
knowledge, as power, *see* power
Köbben, R. J. F., 96
Kopytoff, I., 151

LaBarre, W., 54, 55, 110
language, 37
language, revealed, 37, 124, 130–1, 170, 213, 284
Lanternari, V., 21, 110, 148, 149

Latter Rain mission (in Nigeria), 127
leadership: charismatic, 183, 185, 305, 320; organizational, 184, 185, 306–8, 320; education of, 187–8; succession in, 187, 194; *and see* charisma
legalism, 85–86, 99, 171, 197, 208, 241
Legion of Mary, 152
litany, ch. 21
literacy, 275, 277
literature, 125, 126–7, 130, 131, ch. 13, 283–4
Lord's Supper, 38, 43, 99, 167, 169, 219

Macarthy, S. S. (Nigeria), 130
magic and charms, 19, 40, 72, 85, 97, 98, 122, 123, 161, 163, 166–7, 172, 193, 208, 216, 232, 251, 259, 261, 279, 310, 313; *and see Sixth and Seventh Books of Moses*
Maoris (New Zealand), 4, 7, 10, 30, 61, 259–60, 273, 275
marriage, and polygamy, 16, 38, 96, 97, 99, 199–200, 210, 211–2, ch. 18, 281, 307, 310; *and see* matriliny
Martin, M.-L., 116, 266
matriliny, 310
membership, plural, 163, 175
Mennonite Mission Board, and individual missionaries, 110, 111, 175, 188, 264, 266, 275
messiah, messianism, 52, 102–3, 108, 110, 118, 304; *and see* Black Christs
methodology, ch. 4, 51, 55, ch. 6, 206; *see also* historical study, history of religions, phenomenology of religion, theological study
millennialism, 52–54, 57, 61, 62, 134, 236, 260, 313; *see also* messiah
ministry, ch. 15; *see also* prophets, women
missions, Christian, 3, 5, 13, 123, 125, 127, ch. 12, 151, 208, 209–10, 216–8, 277–8, 292–3; new dimensions for missions, ch. 22, 291; *see also* various missionary societies
Mitchell, R. C., 102, 115
mobility of movements, 60
modernization, 12–13, ch. 25, 331–3
Molland, E., 96, 97, 101, 235
monogamy, *see* marriage
Montanism, 28–29
Moody, C. N., 74
Moral Rearmament movement, 132
morality and ethics, 99, 196–8, 250, 261; *and see* legalism
Mormonism, 24
Mühlmann, W. E., 28

myth, mythologies, 308–9

nation, nationalism, 18, 67, 70, ch. 11, 178, 262, 298–9, 301–2
nativistic movements, 19, 260
negative instances, 19, 65, 68
neo-primal movements, 8, 10, 56, 73, 83–84, 103, 113, 313
Nida, E. A., 89

occult literature, occultism, 170, 172, 259, 313
older churches (as term), 92–94
Oosterwal, G., 110
Oostuizen, G. C., 118

Parrinder, E. G., 95, 100, 234
Parsonson, G. S., 275
pastoral care, 167–8
Pauw, B. A., 90, 91, 92–93, 95, 97, 101, 241
Peel, J. D. Y., 111, 112, 115, 185, 318
Pentecostalism, 19, 43, 82, 90, 97–98, 101, 102, 112, ch. 9, 191; *see also* Holy Spirit; possession
Perrin Jassy, M.-F., 185, 186
phenomenology of religion, 22, 23, 70–72, 113, 212–13
Platt, W. J., 266
politics, 302–8
polygamy, *see* marriage
possession, possession cults, 16, 41, 71, 114, 169
power, 5, 6, 198, 210, 227, 250–1, ch. 23, 325
prayer, 195, 196, ch. 21, 278, 307; *and see* healing, spiritual
preaching, and sermon texts, 74, 207, ch. 20
pre-contact movements, 25
primal religions and societies, 5, 25, 256–9, 341
Primitive Methodist mission (in Nigeria), 123
prophet-healing movements, *see* definitions
prophets, prophetesses, 71, 172, 210, 225–30, 300
Protestantism, 28, 43
Psalms, use of, 239, 280, 284

Qua Iboe Mission (in Nigeria), 123

Ranger, T. O., 114, 117
reductionist theories, 69
ritual, 184–5, 193, 278
Roman Catholic studies, 111–2

Roman Catholicism, 28, 29, 43, 65, 111, ch. 12, 160, 162, 282

sacrifice, 43
salvation, 98, 212
Schlosser, K., 21, 26, 64, 70, 96
sect (as term), 73, 81–82, 87–88, 182
sermon-texts, *see* preaching
Shepperson, G., 64, 67, 326
Sixth and Seventh Books of Moses, 170, 279, 283
Smalley, W. A., 89
sociological forms, 36, 58–60, 103, 104, 182; *see also* holy cities, ancillary cults, clientele
sociological study, 19, 58–60, 67, 68, 70, 74–75, 80, 81, 83, 206
spirituality, ch. 16
statistics, 16, 64, 177, 193, 199, 289, 292, 298, 329, 335
succession, *see* leadership
Sudan Interior Mission, 86
Sundkler, B. G. M., 17, 52–53, 79, 91–92, 95, 96, 97, 99, 101, 104, 109, 118, 186, 306, 319, 321, 325
Swiderski, S., 116
syncretism, 89–90, 260
syncretist movements, 8, 56, 103, 151, ch. 13, 171–2, 313

Talbot, P. A. (Nigeria), 130, 138–43
Taylor, J. V., 65, 217
Tempels, P., 153, 325
terminology, 5, 16, 49–50; *and see* definitions, millennialism, sects

theological method, and study, 46, 72–76, 211–12, chs. 18–20, 228–9, 248–50
tobacco, 123, 171, 197, 222, 261, 311
tongues, speaking in, *see* glossolalia
tribalism, 177–8, 186, 262, 300–2
typology, 7–10, 52, ch. 7; *and see* definitions, terminology

United Christian Missionary Society (in Thailand), 265
United Free Church of Scotland mission (in Nigeria), 123

water, 71, 98, 122, 125, 127, 140, 151, 161, 162, 167, 171, 195, 232; theology of water, 228–9
Webster, J. B., 101
Welbourn, F. B., 82–83, 91, 100
Wesleyan Methodist Missionary Society, 265–6
Wilson, B. R., 110
wisdom literature, 239–40
women, 88, 107, 181, 186, 199–200, 310; as founders or leaders, 261; *see also* marriage
World Council of Churches, 87, 88, 100, 111, 175, 176, 188, 211, 216, 235
World Wide Missions Incorporated (in Nigeria), 127
Worldwide Evangelization Crusade, 86
worship, 41, 99, 167, 198, 200, ch. 21
Worsley, P. M., 70

Zionist movements, 10, 45, 51, 97, 99–100, 105, 117, 118, 311, 321

Movements: Their Own Associations and Centres

Aaronista (Peru), 264
Absolute Established Maori Church (New Zealand), 10
Adulawo Movement (Nigeria), 84
African Apostolic Church (Rhodesia), 57, 284
African Brotherhood Church, 16, 175, 177, 183, 185, 186
African Catholic Legio (Tanzania), 152
African Christian Churches and Schools (Kenya), 176, 188, 320
African Congregational Church (South Africa), 311
African Greek Orthodox Church (East Africa), 56, 91, 154, 298–9, 320, 328
African Independent Churches Association (South Africa), 176, 177, 188, 194
African Independent Pentecost Church (Kenya), 320, 328
African Israel Church Nineveh (Kenya), 57, 300
African Methodist Episcopal Church, 92, 179, 181, 187
African Universal Church (Ghana), 65
Aiyetoro (Nigeria), 58, 104, 115, 183, 194, 305, 311, 322, 333
Aladura Apostolic Church (Nigeria), 226
Amicale Movement (Congo), 134
Ancestors, Cult of (Kenya), 56, 84
Anglican Church of Nauru, 10
Antonians (Congo), 56; *and see* Beatrice
Apostolic Church (Nigeria), 126, 131
Apostolic Church of Jesus Christ (in U.K.), 290
Apostolic Revelation Society (Ghana), 102, 115, 184, 320
Arathi (Kenya), 135
Aruosa Cult (Nigeria), 56, 84; *and see* Godianism

Assembly of Zionist Apostolic Churches (South Africa), 177
Associations of New Movements, 84, 151, 176–7, 194, 301, 310

Bagatla Free Church (Botswana), 57
Balokole (East Africa), 199; *and see* East African Revival
Bamalaki (Uganda), 86, 135, 154
Bamidele Movement (Nigeria), 26
Bayudaya (Uganda), 56, 117, 208, 264
Bethesda Communities (South Africa), 104
Bible Success Society (Ghana), 195
Big Candle Movement (Russia), 6, 260
Bisoki Movement (Zaïre), 194
Bituma Cult (Zambia), 284
Botswana Association of Inter-Spiritual Churches, 177
Brazil Indian "Church" (1583), 6, 284
Brotherhood of the Cross and Star (Nigeria), 198
Burkhan Movement (Russian Asia), 260
Bush Negro Movements (Surinam), 260
Bwiti Cult (Gabon), 5, 6, 84, 111, 116, 283, 300, 303

Cargo Cults, 7, 193, 267, 276, 279, 283
Celestial Church of Christ (Benin and Nigeria), 180, 198
Cherubim and Seraphim (West Africa), 16, 53, 57, 102, 115, 153, 179, 184, 289–90, 292
Children of the Sacred Heart (Zambia), 151; *and see* Church of the Sacred Heart
Christ Apostolic Church (West Africa), 16, 102, 115, 125, 126, 127, 131, 175, 179, 183, 185, 321

349

Christ Army Church (Nigeria), 123, 138
Christian Catholic Apostolic Church in Zion (Rhodesia), 135, 311
Christian Fellowship Church (Solomon Is.), 7, 8, 282
Church of Christ (South Africa), 86, 299
Church of Christ in Africa (Kenya), 184, 219, 300
Church of God of Prophecy (in U.K.), 290
Church of Orunmila (Nigeria), 84
Church of the Ancestors (Malawi), 84, 281
Church of the Blacks (Congo), 135
Church of the Lord (Aladura) (West Africa), x, 19, 130, 135, 154, 159, 175, 178–9, 181, 184, 187, 188, 226, ch. 20, 282, 290, 300, 307–8, 322
Church of the Sacred Heart (Zambia), 56, 104
Church of the Twelve Apostles (Ghana), 102
Church of the White Bird (Rhodesia), 135
Churches of the Holy Spirit (Zaïre), 182, 185, 186, 199, 323
Colombia Movement (1546), 6
Comité Mixte Gabonais (Gabon), 303
Confrérie D'Ait-Atelli (North Africa), 26
Congregation of the Poor (Fiji), 10
Croix-Koma or Crucifixion Movement (Congo), 153, 323

Daku Community (Fiji), 10
Déima Cult (Ivory Coast), 18, 56, 84, 115
Delaware Prophets (U.S.A.), 284
Dieudonné Movement (Angola), 136
Dini ya Jehovah na Michael (Tanzania), 302
Dini ya Misambwa (Kenya), 56, 117, 298, 300
Divine Church of the Lord (Ghana), 192

East African Revival, 186, 199
Eden Revival (later Feden) Church (Ghana), 57, 115, 176, 184, 322
Église Chrétienne Évangelique d'Afrique (Zaïre), 175
Église de la Foi (Zaïre), 193, 278
Église Reformée Indépendante de Madagascar, 175
Elcho Island Movement (Australia), 7
Epikilipikili Movement (Congo), 134, 298
Eskimo Movements, 22
Ethiopian Church in South Africa, 57
Ethiopian Community Church (Nigeria), 234

Eto Church, see Christian Fellowship Church
Etodome Prayer-Healing Group or White Cross Society (Ghana), 102, 192, 198

Faith Tabernacle Church (Nigeria), 92, 125–6, 130, 180, 226
Fiji Movements, 7, 8, 10
First Century Gospel Church (Nigeria), 125
First Ethiopian Church (Rhodesia), 57

Ghana Evangelical Fellowship, 177
Ghost Dances (U.S.A.), 6, 25, 260
God Is Our Light Church (Sierra Leone), 19, 68
God's Kingdom Society (Nigeria), 57, 85–86, 87, 135, 187
Godianism (Nigeria), 56, 61, 292
Good Samaritan International Movement (Nigeria), 196
Guatemala Messianism (1530), 6
Guta ra Jehovah (Rhodesia), 58

Hallelujah Religion (Guyana), 260, 267, 284
Handsome Lake Religion (U.S.A.), 6, 260, 292
Harris Churches and Harris, W. W. (Liberia, Ivory Coast), 18, 53, 57, 75, 85, 95, 100, 102, 111, 115, 134, 136, 139, 148, 154, 174, 208, 265–6, 299, 304, 309, 310
Hau Hau Cult (New Zealand), 8
Herero "Church" (Namibia), 40, 56, 84
Holy Apostles Community, see Aiyetoro
Holy Ethiopian Community Church (Nigeria), 234
Holy Face Society (Nigeria), 150
Holy Spirit Church (Kenya), 188
Holy Water Movement (Congo), 151

Ibandla Lika-Kresto (South Africa), 106
Iglesia Sagrada ng Lahi (Philippines), 283
I-Kuan-Tao Cult (China), 26
Independent Baptist Churches (Ghana), 320
Independent Church Associations, see Association of new movements
Indian "Church" (Brazil), 6, 284
Indian Independent Churches (North America), 6, 260
Indian Shaker Church (U.S.A.), 6, 260, 263, 267
Israel Movement (Kenya), 86
Israelites (Polynesia), 8

Israelites (South Africa), 56, 134, 208, 264

Jamaa Movement (Zaïre), 29, 117, 153, 325

Karing'a Educational Association (Kenya), 328
Kausapala (Angola), 148
Kikuyu Independent Schools Association (Kenya), 320, 328
Kimbanguist Church (Central Africa), 4–5, 10, 16, 53, 60, 95, 135, 153, 154, 175, 179, 182, 185, 188, 196, 198, 208, 211, 263–4, 266, 281, 299, 300, 301, 304, 305, 312, 322
King Movement (New Zealand), 8
Kingdom Movement (Ghana), 183, 194, 322
Kitawala Movement (Central Africa), 53, 56, 117, 135, 154, 298, 299, 305, 311, 323
Kokamba Movement (Ivory Coast), 312
Kokeri Movements (Papua), 25
Kukuaik Movement (New Guinea), 10
Kurrangara Movement (Australia), 7, 285

Legio Maria, see Maria Legio
Letub Movement (New Guinea), 280
Living Faith Apostolic Church (Nigeria), 226
Lou Prophet Movement (Holland), 24
Lumpa Church (Zambia), 57, 64, 95, 111, 117, 136, 150, 154, 196, 300, 302

Maji Maji (Tanzania), 117
Malagasy Movements, 16, 114, 175
Mama Chi Movement (Panama), 6, 260, 267
Maori Evangelical Fellowship (New Zealand), 10
Maria Legio (Kenya), 11, 57, 112, 152, 154, 177, 179, 183, 184
Mayumbe Kimbanguists (Zaïre), 199, 305, 322
Mazano and New Mazano (Ghana), 58, 104; and see Musama Disco Christo
Messifident Holy Spiritual Church (Nigeria), 124
Movement for the Social Development of Black Africa (Central African Republic), 154
Mumbo, Cult of (Kenya), 56, 113
Murids (Senegal), 26
Musama Disco Christo (Ghana), 57, 102, 187

Mwana Lesa Movement (Central Africa), 114, 135
Mwari Cult (Rhodesia), 50

Narragansett Indian Church (U.S.A.), 6
National Church of Africa (South Africa), 319
National Church of Nigeria, 56, 84, 87, 299, 301, 303
Native American Church (U.S.A.), 6, 260, 263, 267, 285
Native Baptist Church (Cameroon), 135
Nazarite (= Amanazaretha) Church (South Africa), 52, 53, 57, 196, 300, 311; and see Shembe, I.
Ndaza Zionists (Rhodesia), 321
New Tadzewu (Apostolic Revelation Society, Ghana), 58
New Testament Church of God (in U.K.), 290
Nkamba (Kimbanguist centre, Zaïre), 58
Nomia Movement (Kenya), 86
Nomiya Luo Mission (Kenya), 153, 328
Ntwalanist Church (Zaïre), 329
Nyabingi Cult (Uganda), 113

Obere Okaime Church (Nigeria), 124, 284, 323
Order of Ethiopia (South Africa), 118
Oruuano Movement (Namibia), 118

Pai Marire Cult (New Zealand), 8
Paliau Movement (Admiralty Is.), 10, 281
Pau Cin Hau (Burma), 284
Pentecost Movement (Irian Jaya), 10
People of God (Kenya), 84
Peyote Cult, see Native American Church
Practical Church of John 14:6 (Ghana), 195
Precious Stone Church (Nigeria), 130
Providence Industrial Mission (Malawi), 327

Ras Tafarians (Jamaica), 6, 267, 285
Ratana Church (New Zealand), 4, 7, 10, 30, 264
Red Star Church (Angola), 118, 136
Reformed Ogboni Fraternity (Nigeria), 56, 61
Religion of Jehovah and Michael (Tanzania), 136
Religion of Mary (Kenya), 151
Religion of the Ancestral Spirits (Kenya), 298
Remnant, The (Solomon Is.), 8
Resurrection, The (East Africa), 199

Revival, The, *see* East African Revival, 197, 199
Ringatu Cult (New Zealand), 8, 30, 264, 267

Salem (Nigeria), 58; *and see* God's Kingdom Society
Saviour Church (Ghana), 102
Second Adam, Sect of (Ghana), 65
Secret Prayer Groups (Soweto, South Africa), 279
Seven Wells of Jehovah (New Zealand), 8
Society of the One Almighty God (Uganda), 135; *see* Bamalaki
Society of the Secret Power of Jesus (Ghana), 279
Spirit Churches (Kikuyu, Kenya), 117
Spirit Movement (Nigeria), 123, 135, 282, 323
Spiritual Healing Church (Botswana), 57

Tadzewu, *see* New Tadzewu
Taiping Movement (China), 25
Telakhon Cult (Burma), 265, 274
Toko (or Red Star) Church (Angola), 118, 278, 299, 305, 311
Tonsism (Angola), 136
True Apostolic Faith (West Africa), 192
Tuka (Fiji), 280
Tupi-Guarani (South America), 25

Turban People (Kenya), 85
Umbanda (Brazil), 267
United Independent Churches Fellowship (Nigeria), 151
United Native African Church (Nigeria), 57

"Vailala Madness" (Papua), 279
Vapostori (Central Africa), 179, 186, 187, 284; *and see* African Apostolic Church
Voodoo (Haïti), 267

Wata Wa Mngo (Kenya), 135
Watchtower (Central Africa), 134, 135, 196; *and see* Kitawala
West African Methodist Church (Sierra Leone), 89
West Indian Independent Churches (in U.K.), 290
White Cross Society (Ghana), *see* Etodome
Worgaia Movement (Australia), 285

Xhosa Cattle Killing (South Africa), 53, 56

Yakan Water Cult (Uganda), 56, 141
Yaqui Churches (North America), 6, 263

Zion Christian Church (South Africa), 187
Zion City Moriah (South Africa), 58

Individuals in New Movements

Abimbolu, D. O. (Nigeria), 228
Adejobi, E. O. A. (Nigeria), 184, 187, 308
Agbebi, Mojola (Nigeria), 116
Ahui, J. (Ivory Coast), 310
Aina, J. A. (Nigeria), 130, 225
Ajuoga (Bishop) (Kenya), 184, 319
Ake, Bodjo (Ivory Coast), 56
Akinsowon, Christianah Abiodun (Nigeria), 124, 153, 184
Akinyele, Isaac B. (Nigeria), 126, ch. 10, 192, 226
Alexander (Archbishop, South and East Africa), 328
Arianhdit (Dinka), 135

Babalola, Joseph (Nigeria), 89, 126, 130, 131, 135, 208, 226
Bakwafula (Zaïre), 278
Beatrice, 116, 134, 150, 260; *and see* Antonians
Bichywung (Guyana Indian), 284
Birinda (Gabonese), 283
Boganda (Central African Republic), 153
Braid, G. (Nigeria), 95, 122–3, 130, 134, 138–43, 208
Bullamatare (Congo), 56

Chilembwe, J. (Malawi), 117, 134, 148, 261, 298, 300, 301, 303, 319, 327

Diangienda, J. (Kimbanguist), 184, 187, 281
Dingiswayo (Rhodesia), 135
Doh (Ghana prophet), 192, 198
Domingo, C. (Malawi), 117, 319, 326

Edjro, J. (Ivory Coast), 184
Emmanuel, N. (Congo), 153
Eto, S. (Solomon Islands), 282

Harris, W. W. (West Africa), *see* Harris Churches
Hayford, M. K. (Ghana), 320

Jehu-Appiah (Ghana), 187
Johannes (South Africa), 134

Kamwana, E. (Central Africa), 53, 134, 326
Khambule (South Africa), 53
Kimbangu, Simon (Zaïre), 18, 116, 134, 148, 187, 192, 298, 304, 322
Kivuli (Kenya), 300

Lalou, Marie, *see* Déima Cult
Lassy, S. Z. (Cabinda), 153, 305
Lekganyane, E. (South Africa), 53, 187, 311
Lenshina, Alice (Zambia), 57, 136, 184, 274, 285, 318, 323, 333
Limba, J. (South Africa), 86, 299
Luntadila, L. (Kimbanguist), 153

Makanna (Xhosa), 56, 134
Malaki (Uganda), 135, 148; *and see* Bamalaki
Malanda, V. (Congo), 153
Maranke, Johane (Rhodesia), 186, 284
Matswa, A. (Congo), 134, 153, 299, 302, 312
Mba, L. (Gabon), 303
Mgijima, E. (South Africa), 56, 134, 208, 298
Mpadi, S. (Congo), 135
Mugema (Kenya), 135
Mulele, P., and Mulélisme (Zaïre), 153
Mulolani, Emilio (Zambia), 151
Mumbo, Cardinal (Kenya), 184

Neolin (American Indian), 284
Ntsikana (Xhosa), 56
Nyengwa, T. (Central Africa), 135

Ofa Mele Longosai (Tonga), 8
Okwala, J. (Kenya), 328
Ondeto, Simeon (Kenya), 152, 183, 184
Oppong, S. (Ghana), 53, 89, 137
Oshitelu, J. O. (Nigeria), 124, 126, 130–1, 135, 137, 144, 187, 226, 232
Owalo, J. (Kenya), 153, 328

Papahurihia (New Zealand), 8
Paraguayan Prophet (1558), 6

Ragot, Mariam (Kenya), 152
Rua (New Zealand), *see* Seven Wells of Jehovah

Shadare, J. B. (Nigeria), 130
Shembe, Isaiah (Natal), 187, 285, 318; *and see* Nazarite Church
Simbinga (Zambia), 284

Smohalla (American Indian), 284
Spartas, Reuben (Uganda), 184, 298, 303, 320
Sturmann (Namibia), 298

Te Whiti (New Zealand), 8
Toko, S. (Angola), 136, 299
Tunolase, Moses Orimolade (Nigeria), 124, 318

Umhlakaza (Xhosa prophet), 53
Urhobo, Gideon (Nigeria), 135, 153, 187
Uzoechi, Monday (Nigeria), 195

Veronica (Nigerian prophetess), 152

Witbooi (Namibia), 298
Wovenu (Ghana), 102, 184, 311, 320, 333

Yaliwan (New Guinea), 283
Yeboa-Kurie (Ghana), 176, 184

Zwimba, M. (Rhodesia), 135